Pious Warriors

Thucydides' Account of the Spartans

Travis S. Hadley

political animal
PRESS
TORONTO · CHICAGO

Political Animal Press
www.politicalanimalpress.com

Distributed by the University of Toronto Press
www.utpdistribution.com

Cataloguing data available from Library and Archives Canada
ISBN 9781895131703

Typeset in Adobe Garamond Pro, designed by Robert Slimbach.

Cover design and illustration by TintoDeVerano. Illustration based on the painting *A Spartan Woman Giving a Shield to Her Son*, by Jean Jacques François Lebarbier, 1805

Printed and bound in Canada.

For my parents.

Contents

Introduction

This book seeks to provide a detailed account of Sparta, Athens' antagonist, in Thucydides' *War of the Peloponnesians and the Athenians*.[1] Currently, there is no book length treatment of Thucydides' presentation and analysis of Sparta. Athens, imperialism, democracy, and Pericles have traditionally received the bulk of attention from those looking to Thucydides for guidance on their own contemporary political situation. Yet focusing on Sparta offers, I believe, key insights into the war, into Thucydides' fundamental themes, and thus into his account of political and human life. Isolationist Sparta decries imperialist Athens as unjust, and while the Athenians imply this is merely "hypocrisy," I will contend that the Spartans' moral objections to empire and the impending war reveals their genuine understanding of politics, rooted as it is in their traditional laws and law-abidingness, religious convictions, and strong sense of moral propriety and citizenship. The Athenian accusation of hypocrisy implies all politics is animated by self-interest and any claim to the contrary is mere pretext. But this Athenian view of "power politics" (despite endorsement by most scholars) is neither stated nor supported by Sparta and its allies. The story of Sparta can only be glossed or ignored at a reader's peril.

Sparta's declaration to liberate Athens' subject cities is the foundation of their war effort, and rather than being a hypocritical veil, Thucydides himself presents this declaration, as well as moral expectations of human beings in general, as genuine, even if, and sometimes precisely when, they are neither acknowledged nor noticed. Apparent hypocrisy for Thucydides, I argue, has deeper roots in what he calls "the human condition" (*to anthrōpinon* – 1.22.4) and studying the Spartan view of, and approach to, the war offers clarity on this key element of his political psychology.

1 The title used here is derived from the first line of Thucydides' text. As I argue below (and in the Appendix), Thucydides' presentation of the war is not a "history" in our contemporary use of the term, and thus I avoid it.

Political rhetoric and justifications of policy cannot simply be viewed with skepticism; rather, such claims must be understood through the psychology of the actors, with the regime (*politeia*) of the city (notably, its domestic politics) guiding and differentiating the moral judgments human beings make. As I will present it, Sparta is *the* moral city. Spartan *nomoi*, the peculiar and notable laws and customs, form their citizens' character in ways the Athenians fail to comprehend. While the Athenians thus repeatedly declare what they take to be the truths of human nature (*anthrōpeia physis*), particularly the exculpatory nature of necessity (*anankē*) and therefore a rejection of justice (*dikaion*), genuine belief in justice, its demands and significance, weighs heavily on the Spartans, affecting both their strategic decisions and handling, and thus the trajectory, of the Peloponnesian War.

In turbulent times such as ours, when citizens declare fellow citizens as enemies (and worse) and when hypocrisy is a daily accusation found in political discourse, studying morality (and often its source, piety) and political knowledge, the effects of the former and what we may expect from the latter, is especially needed. Thucydides' Sparta and the Spartans are remarkably un-Athenian, and I would argue, therefore, un-modern as well. In declaring his work a possession for all time, Thucydides offers compelling insights into the deeper psychology of morality and the hold it has over political decision-making, policies, and actions especially during the necessities of war, when we would most likely expect morality to be abandoned for calculated self-interest. This book, therefore, clarifies Sparta's understanding, conduct, and view of the war, as well as non-Spartans also betraying a "Spartan" moral psychology. Comparing Sparta's prosecution of the war and its regime, as a foil to the hard-nosed and brash Athenians, sheds important light on perplexities arising during the war that "realist" accounts are unable to solve.

My study aims, specifically, at detailing Thucydides' presentation of Sparta, both the city and its citizens. This includes their most novel characteristics – their customs and laws, their piety, their regime; Spartan actions during the war – giving rise to accusations of Spartan duplicity, hypocrisy, and even brutality; and Spartan domestic politics as it bears on foreign policy. This will challenge scholarly interpretations that, I believe, misunderstand each of these by reducing Spartan psychology to the views stated by Thucydides' most prominent Athenian speakers as if they are simply Thucydides' own.

To achieve our aim of understanding Sparta, I will treat Thucydides' presentation as a single study, rather than one part of a larger theme. Rather than encomium to Athens, Thucydides' praises of Sparta and critiques of Athens warrant closer scrutiny and can only be appreciated by treating events in the text often overlooked (including Thucydides' own commentary) and by understanding his presentation of Sparta as it unfolds over the course of the war. Narrative details (and even speeches) have been ignored or inadequately weighed due in part to the long-held scholarly view that Thucydides' text is not a unified whole. Despite the literary turn in Thucydidean scholarship, which began to view the work as unified and containing a coherent political teaching (as discussed further below), many parts of the text remain underappreciated, treated as second-rate compared with Thucydides' most famous passages (notably, Pericles' Funeral Oration, the civil war at Corcyra, and the Melian Dialogue). Studying Sparta is inextricably linked to this literary question given Thucydides, as an Athenian, is often accused of bias. Thucydides' account is charged with shortchanging its readers on explication and details of Sparta. Both of these issues will be discussed in their proper place.

Finally, applying the literary turn requires a revisiting, and re-emphasis, on Thucydides' text as a work of literature (in the broadest sense of the term), a work of imagination and intention, meant to educate future readers about their own times through a meticulously crafted presentation of the greatest war of Thucydides' own.

Thucydides' Political Teaching

Interest in Thucydides' account by scholars, statesmen, and citizens, has always been with a view to discerning the causes of the Peloponnesian War, of political strife, and of war simply. Why we engage in violence and sacrifice, rather than discovering other means to resolve grievances, is a permanent problem in politics and thus a permanent problem for political science. Both political actors and political scientists seek solutions to the origins and duration of war and thereby attempt to eliminate its causes and conditions. Thucydides' account of what he regarded as the greatest war among the Greeks has therefore remained of interest for scholars investigating the history of Greece, but more critically, its period of turmoil.

Thucydides depicts the precise moment when an isolationist regime was compelled to confront an imperial one; therefore, international relations theory in particular looks to Thucydides as the first writer to lay bare some of the fundamental aspects of war between states.[2] Something about Thucydides' account endures. Scholars today perhaps recognize what Thucydides himself strove for – that his work would be a possession for all times and that his pursuit of the truth would reveal political lessons "useful" (*ōpelimos*) not just for his own time, but for the future as well (1.22.4).[3]

2 We should bear in mind that Thucydides was not translated into English until Thomas Hobbes' 1629 translation. There have been waves of interest in Thucydides – in the ancient world; after the dissemination of Hobbes' translation; during the World Wars of the 20th century; and during and after the Cold War. In each case, scholars, statesmen, and journalists have looked to Thucydides to help explain times of rising political tensions and war. The scholarship on Thucydides is vast, in part because he is studied by classicists, historians, and political scientists. These disciplines all have competing, if also overlapping, interests. While impossible to cover all scholarship, I will treat classicists and historians, along with political theory, as applicable to Sparta in particular. In my view, the best works on Thucydides tend not to fall neatly into one category and offer insights on why Thucydides is of permanent importance. Marinatos (1981) shows how scholarly theories changed throughout the 19th and early 20th centuries and were responsible for a number of shifts in the interpretation of Thucydides' intention and views. There have also recently been numerous compilations of essays on Thucydides' reception, as well as influence more broadly, including Brill's *Companion to Thucydides* (2006), *Thucydides and the Modern World: Reception, Reinterpretation and Influence from the Renaissance to the Present* (2012), *A Handbook to Reception of Thucydides* (2015), *Thucydides and Political Order: Concepts of Order and the History of the Peloponnesian War* (2016), and *The Oxford Handbook of Thucydides* (2017).

3 Citations of Thucydides refer to book, chapter, and sentence. In instances when the same book is cited in short succession, I have dropped the book number and referred only to paragraph and sentence. While the widely used *Landmark Thucydides* edition (edited by Strassler [1996]) is stylistically most enjoyable, the Crawley translation is, in my view, too loose with Thucydides' Greek; therefore, translations have been either modified to render them into English closer to the original Greek or borrowed from other translations. I have benefited from those of Jowett (1881), Hobbes (1989), Woodruff (1993), Lattimore (1998), and Mynott (2013). (As this book was being prepared for publication, I became aware of Woodruff's expanded second edition, a translation of select passages entitled: *The Essential Thucydides* [2021].) Hornblower's three volume *A Commentary on Thucydides* has also been indispensable in offering various readings of important, and difficult, passages (along with corrections of the Jowett [1881] translation, which Hornblower uses as a guide). I have also consulted *A Historical Commentary on Thucydides* by Gomme, Andrewes, and Dover. For both commentaries, I have used Roman numerals to indicate volume and dropped year of publication. For the latter, I use "Gomme" throughout, parenthetically noting volumes completed later by Andrewes and Dover, after Gomme's death. Hornblower's *Commentary* can be consulted for those interested in differences among

While few would therefore deny that Thucydides has value, the character of these political lessons is still debated. Numerous scholars have interpreted Thucydides through different lenses and drawn competing conclusions as to his views on perennial political questions: empire and freedom, justice and necessity, religion and its absence, democracy and tyranny, and of course most immediately, Sparta and Athens.[4] Much of the scholarship on Thucydides within political science has focused on what is now called power politics or "realism" – the compelling interests political communities attempt to secure through an exercise of their power or strength.[5] Justice or

---

the three authors' interpretations. The Greek text of Thucydides, against which translations have been checked, is Powell and Jones (1942). It is used by the Perseus Digital Library, which has been a most useful resource (http://www.perseus.tufts.edu/hopper/). Other primary sources are referenced by their standard pagination when available (e.g., Stephanus pages in Plato) or author's divisions (e.g., book and paragraph number in Machiavelli's *Discourses on Livy*). See the Bibliography for primary and secondary sources.

4 The history of Thucydides scholarship involves key phases and shifts within the various disciplines. Allow me to note the following brief observations, by way of an overview, with additional scholarship to be discussed throughout the Introduction. Historians and classicists are interested in what Thucydides teaches us about the ancient world; but their treatments debate Thucydides' accuracy, methods of composition of his "history," and therefore the reliability of his account. Cornford (1907) and Kagan (1969), for example, are deeply skeptical and even challenge Thucydides' presentation of the Peloponnesian War. Ste. Croix (1972), however, defends it. Part of the debate here revolves around the apparently incomplete character of the text itself, or as Romilly calls it, the "Separatist thesis." This next shift, initiated by Romilly (1963), argued that Thucydides' text should be read as a coherent whole and not understood as a patchwork without rhyme or reason. Connor (1984) continued the "Unitarian" argument in his commentary on the whole of the war. Strauss (1964) also questions the Separatists, but as one part of his larger interest in comparing Thucydides to Plato and Aristotle, wondering in what sense Thucydides can, or cannot, be called a "historian," and further, the relationship between history, poetry, and philosophy (see especially pp. 141-44). Scholarship on Thucydides then turned to thematic treatments, including book-length studies on: the role of chance versus human agency (Edmunds 1975), human nature (Cogan 1981), necessity (Ostwald 1988), tragedy (Lebow 2003), religion (Marinatos 1981), and ambition (Forde 1989, Palmer 1992), to name a few. Others have focused (again) on Pericles, but casting a more critical eye, including Foster (2010). More recently, there have been studies on kinship (Fragoulaki 2013), freedom (Nichols 2015), and Book One (Jaffe 2017).

5 Notably influential, of course, was Romilly's (1963) study of Athenian imperialism (consider pp. 98-104, 291-93, 306-7). Thucydides as a realist has a long tradition, including Waltz (1959) and (1979), Keohane and Nye (1977), Walzer (1977), Gilpin (1984), among others. Qualified or modified realism includes Garst (1989), Doyle (1997), Forde (1992), Johnson Bagby (1994), Rahe (1995), and Gustafson's compilation (2000).

morality is not a consideration in sober calculations of how to act in order to guard against the encroachment of others. More recent scholarship, though, (within political theory in particular) has noted that Thucydides pays careful attention and is sympathetic to those cities that eventually take a stand against the continued expansion and encroachment of Athens. Despite the prominence of Athenian imperialism (and the Athenians' arguments for it), he does not neglect those cities who protest the injustice of Athens. For far from being a realist in the generally accepted sense, it is argued, Thucydides does not dismiss such claims as mere pretexts or naivety but places before his readers the challenge of discerning the proper weight to be given to these claims. Just as in political life itself, so in Thucydides' account, the reader is compelled to face the competing claims of the war's participants, particularly claims about justice.[6]

The moral compass of contemporary readers, however, has been influenced both by certain interpretations of Thucydides and also by Thucydides' students, Niccolò Machiavelli and Thomas Hobbes, the true originators of so-called power politics. "Thucydides the realist," as well as his modern heirs, obscures to these readers the manner and degree to which Thucydides presents Sparta, and not Athens, as the city to be admired and emulated. Taking the weakness of justice for granted without locating the source of that weakness is thus to conceal Thucydides' most fundamental insights. Sparta therefore appears to exist in a deeper stratum of Thucydides' thought precisely because we contemporary readers are tempted to side with Athens and believe their view is Thucydides' own. Acceptance of the Athenian point of view is not clearly identical, however, with Thucydides' own understanding of politics and war.

From the beginning, as I will argue, Thucydides presents Sparta in a

6 The shift in Thucydides scholarship within political science broadly, and political theory in particular, can be seen in one instance by the titles of two competing compilations of essays on his teaching: Morgenthau's (1978) *Politics Among Nations* has received scholarly response from Pangle and Ahrensdorf's (1999) *Justice Among Nations*. Scholarship in political theory emphasizing Thucydides' attention to the issue of justice (and piety) began with Strauss (1964). On my debt to Strauss' Thucydides, see Appendix note 10. His influence then found its way into numerous studies concerned with these themes, including: Bruell (1974), Forde (1986, 1992), Palmer (1992), Ahrensdorf (1999), Bartlett (2001), Burns (2010), Nichols (2015), Jaffe (2017). Orwin (1994) should receive special note since he engages classics and history scholarship (including French, German, and Italian works) the most and has received, it seems to me, the widest readership outside of political theory of this group.

favorable light. The growth of Greece is one of peoples beginning to settle, acquiring laws, and founding stable political communities protected from the flux of former times, ruled as they had been by piracy, tyranny, conquest, and re-conquest (1.2-5). Only with a reprieve from this flux (or "motion" – *kinēsis*) were cities established (12.1). And it is Sparta, not Athens, that Thucydides first mentions as a people who founded a city with good laws while repelling the longstanding tyrannies across Greece (18.1). Additionally, it was Sparta's fear of Athens' continually expanding empire, Thucydides contends, that led ultimately to the outbreak of the war (23.5-6). Perceived injustice of Athens' encroaching empire leads Sparta and its allies to urge action against this encroachment (71.1, 86.1-4). When Thucydides details the fifty-year growth of Athens, between the Persian Wars and the Peloponnesian War (479-430), from a voluntary hegemony to an involuntary subjugation of these and other cities, this is not obviously a favorable portrait of Athens. After all, Thucydides restates the cause of the Peloponnesian War, with notable rhetorical effect, immediately after detailing the rise of Athens' empire (1.118). Is there nothing then to support the accusation of injustice by Sparta and its allies other than a lack of strength to stop Athens? Should the other cities not expect to enjoy autonomy from an empire that, while beginning as a bulwark against Persian encroachment, is now itself an encroachment which can no longer be justified as defending against that threat?

Issues of justice present questions and problems that Athenian imperialism in particular (and imperialism in general) should ignite in a reader of Thucydides. Very naturally, the question arises whether imperialism is a necessity for political survival and flourishing, or if its costs can be avoided. Thucydides' first set of speeches, in an initial dispute between the cities of Corcyra and Corinth, clearly signal justice (*dikaion*) and necessity (*anankē*) as fundamental themes. But it is here specifically where we contemporary readers face a problem. Most approach Thucydides' text already sympathetic to the Athenian point of view and the general tenor of their arguments: the strong rule the weak by necessity, everywhere and always; to expect states not to rule when they can is to expect human nature to be other than it is; even gods would excuse human beings for acting as necessity dictates and therefore one may dispense with the restraints of morality and religion. Readers today have already been influenced, albeit indirectly, by this strand within Thucydides' political thought. Many of us first encounter Thucydides while already holding assumptions about his "realism." And today, realism fills our political and cultural climate. Guided as our contemporary politics has been by the Enlightenment philosophy of Thomas Hobbes and John Locke, to say nothing of the inestimable influence of modern science and technology, we contemporary people are clear-sighted, informed, rational, aware but not cynical, realists.[7] And this realism predisposes us to Athens rather than Sparta.[8] In other words, we are liable to brush off or even laugh at Sparta's protests against power politics as hopelessly naïve and politically obtuse, to ignore the psychological manifestations of justice, and to accuse the Spartans (as the Athenians do) of transparent hypocrisy.

Acceptance of the Athenian view as the truth about war and politics does not, however, dispense with our other, perhaps increasingly dominant, reaction. Passionate objections to war, revolution, and civil conflict as immoral, repugnant, anger provoking, and thus worthy of our indignation because an offense to the human desire for liberty, comprises this other reaction. We may not experience it immediately. We may even be realists one moment, and then moralize the next. But in tackling Thucydides' account, once the violence and oppression of the Peloponnesian War begins, we will find ourselves pausing to confront it, a reminder to be wary of the temptation to accept casually the Athenian view of human affairs.[9]

In confronting this reaction, a reaction that reveals our abiding concern with justice, our demand for justice, we may become aware both that our own views regarding justice color our interpretations of political events and that we have found ourselves on the side of Sparta. Once we have arrived here, we must necessarily contend with Thucydides' Spartan narrative. If we do so, we will notice that Thucydides presents Sparta more approvingly than is often assumed. For with Sparta, we first encounter moral

7 Bartlett (2001) makes a similar comparison in his suggestively titled book *The Idea of Enlightenment: A Post-Mortem Study*. In a chapter on Thucydides, he argues that enlightened self-interest is not the only human motivation Thucydides presents. Bartlett's study touches on Sparta, with some useful observations on Archidamus and Plataea (pp. 75-84).

8 On the relationship between our contemporary realism and what has been called "classical realism," see Johnson Bagby (1994), Forde (1992, 1995), Rahe (1995), Pangle and Ahrensdorf (1999).

9 This is not to suggest that all readers come to this recognition at the same time or even on a first reading of the text, if at all. It is to suggest that one cannot ignore our emotional reaction to such events as the plague at Athens, the civil war at Corcyra, and the attack on Mycalessus late in the war, among many others.

indignation at the injustice of Athenian imperialism as an encroachment on the autonomy of Sparta and Greece as a whole, the Spartans declaring war in the name of liberating Greece from Athenian tyranny. When we begin to question the basis and justification for Athenian imperialism, we do so by confronting Spartan objections, as well as *their* basis, a clear departure from the Athenian view.

To throw aside Sparta's claims as simply arguments of the weak is to deny without consideration the possibility, and I think most of us would say, the hope, for peaceful relations existing between political communities; and further, it is to deny without consideration the grounds of those claims by the peoples making them (and thus to impose a denial of justice onto the divergent views of others). Today, we need only consider the charges of illegitimate preemptive attacks, border encroachments, and human rights abuses as violations of human dignity, as well as the excessive use of force (including war crimes, a disregard for the manner in which war is conducted) to notice that a serious and abiding concern with morality animates *our* view of contemporary international affairs. And even if one insists on denying that justice has any place in sober conduct of foreign politics, this requires a penetrating portrait of what morality is, why it has no such place, but nonetheless why human beings everywhere, at some time or other, make such appeals. A thorough portrait of human life without morality must then at least confront, in Thucydides' terms, the relationship between justice and necessity. For foreign policy, this means whether states are compelled to pursue their interests or whether they can be reasonably expected to refrain from these interests in cases when such pursuit will encroach on others. For domestic policy, this means a thoroughgoing consideration of the costs of foreign entanglements, whether compelled or not. As we will come to see, Sparta and its view of the war is the lens through which Thucydides presents a challenge to Athens and its view, not merely as the city Sparta is at war with, but most exemplifying an opposing understanding of politics, and human psychology, itself.

Pious Spartans, Rational Athenians

Of particular interest for assessing the Spartans is the Athenian accusation that the Spartans simply call "justice" what is advantageous for their city (5.105.4). This remark (and its tone) implies both that this is an inadequate view of justice and also one the Athenians themselves do not share. This claim is what we may call (and has been called by scholars) Spartan "hypocrisy." Contrary to Spartan appeals to justice, the Athenians accuse them of merely acting as all cities act – pursuing their interests while masking these interests behind a moral facade. As Gregory Crane observes of the most infamous case of apparent Spartan hypocrisy, "their actions at Plataia have drawn almost universal disdain from historians."[10] Yet this episode is not merely of historical interest. The accusation of Spartan hypocrisy is directly relevant to the question of whether any political community (or individuals) who raise moral objections are doing so from a genuine belief in justice, the expectation that it guides political action, or merely to excuse pursuit of their own interests or mask their own weaknesses. To conclude without due consideration of Sparta's view of the war, as well as possible reasons for initiating the war, that Sparta's professed concern with justice, notably divine justice, is hypocrisy is to reduce the seriousness with which we approach the issue of justice. As I will argue, Thucydides does not take the Spartan view for granted, does not condemn the Spartans as most scholars do, instead portraying the lens through which they view the war with more sympathy and complexity than is appreciated.

That Thucydides is not a realist in the sense he is often taken to be is, nevertheless, not to deny that he presents a strong case for the motive of self-interest in the relations between states. But the compelling character of necessity (along with what we mean by "necessity") is most clearly a problem when considering the Spartans, particularly in explaining strategies and policies they adopt throughout the war that hinder securing a victory over Athens or even minimizing the present threat of Athens' unchecked growth. To reduce these actions to their interests, hypocritically pursued, is to neglect the strength justice has over the beliefs of the Spartans themselves. And it surely leaves much of Spartan foreign policy shrouded in mystery, not to say leaving one shaking their head at the old Spartans.

But once we notice certain details, a clearer picture emerges. Throughout the war the Spartans repeatedly appeal to oaths (both amongst themselves and with others), to the proper pious customs before engaging on foreign campaigns, and to obligations imposed by treaties, all of which are guided by an abiding concern with their traditional religious practices

10 Crane (1998) p. 195. See for example: Romilly (1963), Finley (1967), Pouncey (1980), Cogan (1981), Macleod (1983) and Connor (1984). The invasion of Plataea by Thebes, and Sparta's subsequent involvement, along with how hypocrisy is understood by various commentators, will be discussed in detail in Chapter Two.

and beliefs. I will argue not only that Thucydides pays attention to these acts of piety, but that they figure prominently and are fundamental to his account; not in way that is immediately obvious, but in his presentation of events, concerns expressed by certain speakers, and in the life of both cities. As is clear by this book's title, I take piety to be both of central importance for understanding the Spartans and something Thucydides treats with the utmost care.[11]

Educated as we have been in realist interpretations of Thucydides, it perhaps appears foolish to admit that religion and its appeals to morality, its moral demands, are truly politically operative. Yet today the language of statesmen continually makes such claims, even while admitting the needs of a state to secure its interests against foreign influence. And is not the open admission that a state is in fact pursuing its interests viewed as legitimate only when its interests are not morally inferior to the interests of other states, states that lack the moral superiority that would sanction the legitimacy of the very same interests? Nuclear states today (especially liberal democracies) would not admit any hypocrisy in continuing to possess nuclear weapons while denying this very right to other states. That those states denied such a right charge liberal democracies with hypocrisy does not lead to an admission by liberal democracies that their principles are less just; it receives as a response a justification of such a right, over and

11 Crane (1998) p. 5 summarizes the orthodox view when he states: "Thucydides is notorious for the degree to which he minimizes the role of religion." Crane goes on to argue, however, and I believe correctly, that Thucydides' apparent bias may be more the part of "modern scholars" than of Thucydides himself. Hornblower (1992), for example, accuses Thucydides of a lack of religious detail; but his examples of Thucydidean omissions – the 432 Olympics, the contest and torch race portion of the funeral (of which Pericles' Oration is a part), and the Plataeans' religious custom of only wearing one sandal – seem insufficient evidence to draw the broad conclusion of "Thucydides' neglect of the religious factor in his narrative" (169). Gomme III (1974) p. 569 famously remarks on the dispute between the Boeotians and Athenians regarding the former's refusal to allow the Athenians to collect the bodies of their dead, a grave impiety, that "Thucydides is curiously interested in this sophistical stuff." Gomme thereby accidentally reveals that Thucydides *does* recount a debate over sacred (i.e., religious) matters, despite his failure to notice *why* this might be significant. Within political science, realists have also implicitly or explicitly, rejected religion in an "anarchic" international system: see, for example, Waltz (1979) and Gilpin (1984). For a challenge to this view, cf. Ahrensdorf (1997) pp. 231-41. Orwin (2000) argues that attention to piety would strengthen Cawkwell (1998), Crane (1998), and Rood (1999) in their book-length interpretations of Thucydides. For those who notice Thucydides' attention to religion or dedicate studies to it, see Marinatos (1981), Jordan (1986), Orwin (1994), Parker (1998), Furley (2006), Dolgert (2012), Kallet (2013), Balot (2015), Bruzzone (2016), Flower (2009, 2017), and Rahe (2017).

against that of others. During the Peloponnesian War, the Athenian claim regarding the Spartans implies (besides what we have mentioned) that one should not mask one's intentions behind such pretexts, but rather frankly state one's aims, even though there would seem to be manifest benefit in masking what could be perceived by others as injustice. And only Athens is notable for precisely this frankness in stating that the relations between cities are dictated only by necessity – all cities will pursue their interests and to expect otherwise is naïve and foolish. This view, however, is neither that stated nor supported by those opposed to Athens, as evidenced by the accusations preceding the outbreak of the war – Athens is a tyrant city holding an empire unjustly. Sparta's declaration to be liberating Athens' subject cities gains the support of both their own allies and those cities seeking to live autonomous of the Athenian empire (2.8.4-5). And interestingly enough, the Athenians themselves claim not simply to be securing their interests abroad, but to be *worthy* of their empire because they act with more justice or restraint in the exercise of their superior strength (1.76.2-3). Even the Athenians look to give themselves a moral pat on the back.

What Sparta and Athens claim in speech may, however, be opposed by what they do in deed and thus the Athenian view of the true motivations behind political actions would still be sound. Understanding political actors requires, therefore, listening to what they say together with observing what they do.[12] But that the Spartans were able to gain support does

12 The relationship between the speeches (*logoi*) and the deeds (*erga*) has long been one of the most contested issues among Thucydides scholars. It is in fact synonymous with interpreting Thucydides' text as a whole, and thus I do not view it as one theme that can be treated simply in isolation. I must note a few key points for my interpretation here. First, no single speech is the voice of Thucydides himself, but rather of a particular character in a specific political situation in which that speech occurs. Any attribution of ideas to Thucydides must include consideration of the work as a whole. As Hobbes (1989) argues, Thucydides "...setteth his reader in the assemblies of the people and in their senate, at their debating; in the streets, at their seditions; and in the field, at their battles" (p. xxii). Rood (1998) helps to revive this approach, although others have also done so. Cf. Strauss (1964) pp. 163-66 and Orwin (1994) Appendix I, pp. 207-12 who both discuss the purpose and place of speeches in Thucydides. Orwin, in particular, details the key clauses in 1.22 and the scholarly debate on this passage. Speeches contrast and must be compared with deeds, as they must be in political life itself. The issue of speeches and deeds is ultimately tied to how we understand the *purpose* of Thucydides' account. While many scholars claim Thucydides as the exemplar of objective history (Cochrane [1929]: consider pp. 8-9, 26, 31), this view eventually came under attack. Connor's widely cited 1977 article is an excellent discussion of the movements in Thucydides scholarship; it is, however, limited to classics scholarship and one wonders whether the influence of

not explain *why* cities appeal to justice and autonomy in legitimating their actions, especially in declaring war; they could, on the Athenian view, simply declare war in the name of their interests, with no justification or pretext being necessary. Indeed, why Sparta sought *any* justification at all complicates the Athenian view. And this view itself includes an appeal to justice by the Athenians. For if all cities rule when and where they can, the Athenian claim of being *worthy* of their empire (deserving more due to a moral superiority of the principles *they* adhere to as a city) raises the question of what hold justice has over, not simply the actions, but the expectations of all cities.

The Spartan Regime

Given this difference, part of a consideration of the charge of hypocrisy against the Spartans is what might be its cause and source – why Sparta

other disciplines, such as political theory, played a role in coming to see "Thucydides the Artist" (291), in particular because this shift also led to scholarship highlighting the moral components of Thucydides' presentation. In my view, it is best to take to heart Thucydides' statement that his work is a "possession for all time" (*ktema es aiei*), its purpose being to educate his future readers. Further, he states: "What I have set down is how I think each of them would have expressed what was most appropriate (*ta deonta*) in the particular circumstances, while staying as close as possible to the overall intention of what was actually said" (1.22.1 – Mynott [2013] translation). Hornblower I pp. 59-60 believes these two claims cannot be squared. Macleod (1983) pp. 69-70, however, correctly notes that Thucydides "refashions his subject in order to draw out its significance." In my view, Thucydides presumes, or rather has located, permanent and universal lessons contained within the particularities of the Peloponnesian War. Speeches, therefore, reveal how a particular character views an issue; but since Thucydides admits to modifying the speeches, he may use such occasions to point the reader to the flaws in the character's assessment of a given situation. The first set of speeches in the text provide a clear clue: the Corcyraeans' speech begins with the word "justice" (*dikaion* – 1.32.1), while the Corinthians' response begins with "necessity" (*anankē* – 1.37.1). Given these become obvious themes running through the text, this part of the speeches cannot possibly be accidental. Like a good screenwriter, Thucydides' "dialogue" makes sense within the narrative context, while providing material for a reflective reader to consider how it contributes to our understanding of his key themes: land versus sea; hoplites versus navy; moderation versus daring; justice versus necessity; Sparta versus Athens, etc. While these themes occur, as it were, in the nature of things, it is Thucydides' writing that frames how we first encounter them and how our understanding evolves as we work through his account. Ultimately, Thucydides writes in such a way to lead us to what *he* believes is of essence in the Peloponnesian War.

does not state or agree to this view, what has come to be called the "Athenian thesis."[13] Surprisingly, Thucydides' account is notable for the detail it offers on domestic politics generally, including for our purposes those of Sparta, largely ignored by scholars due in part to a neglect of Book Five.[14]

13 The first use of this term is in Strauss (1964) p. 183. Orwin's *The Humanity of Thucydides* (1994) popularized its use and he is commonly cited as its originator. It is now the accepted way of referring to the Athenians' first justification for empire at 1.72-78 (along with later, but differing, articulations of the thesis by Diodotus, Hermocrates, the ambassadors on Melos, and Euphemus, although this depends on interpretations of those passages). Cf. Johnson Bagby (1994) p. 136.

14 Book Five, for a long while, received little or no commentary from most scholars. What commentary it did receive was negative. Romilly (1963) and Westlake (1971), as two examples among many, point to the absence of speeches in Book Five and its apparently disorderly character as an indication of its lack of "polish" and evidence of its incompleteness; however, they both note its kinship to Book Eight and, I believe, point us in a better interpretative direction. Westlake, for example, does admit that the narrative in Book Five offers more detail and subtlety than appears at first sight (p. 318), although he ultimately agrees with the Separatist thesis that Thucydides' "style" is evidence of incompleteness. By "style," Westlake and others mean in particular the lack of speeches as well as Thucydides' attention to treaties, alliances, and the other (lesser) cities involved in the war. Further, Westlake argues that in Book Five Thucydides does not "shed much light upon the aims of Athenian diplomacy" and "to a greater extent than in his treatment of other states he seems content with a bare factual record" (p. 321). Yet as I will argue, if one compares Books Five and Eight, the lack of focus on Athens in Book Five is paralleled in Book Eight by the lack of focus on Sparta. These books are therefore more similar than different – both draw our attention to the relation between the domestic politics of each city and how this affects their prosecution of the war: Thucydides presents each city's internal dynamics, its regime, dealing with war's pressing necessities (see next note). One means Thucydides uses to achieve this is to focus our attention on the action, on the deeds (*erga*), by limiting the speeches. In contrast to this neglect of Book Five, Strauss (1983) p. 101 responds to the orthodox view that both Books are incomplete by instead emphasizing their similarities, and thus suggests Thucydides intended a relationship between the two. This is, according to Strauss, at least a "plausible hypothesis," as an alternative to the accepted view which rejects much of what we find in Books Five and Eight. Rood (1998) defends the integrity of the text as a whole, including Book Five, and has helped to revive a reconsideration of the long-held scholarly views. Forde (1989) dedicates an entire chapter to Book Eight, with the aim of showing both its coherence, and its contribution to Thucydides' account of political ambition, his own book's theme. Hornblower III pp. 1-4 defends a unitary approach, arguing that Andrewes' *A Historical Commentary on Thucydides* (Volume V of the work begun by A.W. Gomme, which Hornblower distinguishes by author) goes much too far in criticizing Books Five and Eight because of anomalies in Thucydides' presentation and style, anomalies Hornblower believes can be explained. Hornblower's own *Commentary* as a whole trends in this general, unitary direction; however, he still falls into lengthy digressions, some seemingly out of the necessity to deal with long fraught passages in Thucydides' text, others where he speculates

Although traditionally viewed as focusing on the war underway and, therefore, foreign policy (resulting in Thucydides' influence on 20th century international relations theory) observations on domestic politics and the characteristics of differing cities are not at all absent from his account. From the founding and growth of cities in the "Archaeology" of Book One to the decay of Athens in Book Eight, we must observe how domestic affairs in each city are intimately related to their conduct in the war. Indeed, the debates, tensions, and power struggles within prove to be as important, if not determinative, for understanding the overall war as any policy or strategy decisions are. And it becomes plain that Sparta is a radically different city from Athens. Guided by rigid laws and customs (*nomoi*), the strong adherence of each Spartan citizen to the regime (*politeia*), as even the Athenians admit, made them the most virtuous city, where the citizen acts most with a view to the (common) good of Sparta (5.105.4).[15] Thucydides himself praises Sparta for the measured relations among their citizens and a moderation even in prosperity (1.6.4, 8.24.4). Sparta is the only city during the war which does not experience profound domestic strife or civil war; and Sparta was not the imperialistic city Athens was, but wholly dedicated to domestic stability and security rather than with continued imperial expansion. Yet Thucydides' praise of Sparta, a praise of moderation, must also be

---

on compositional questions of when a passage was written (early or late in the war), possible sentences or passages added later (where Thucydides corrects himself), etc. His *Commentary* is invaluable and has tremendous virtues, although it still voices many Separatist objections scholars such as Romilly, Connor, Orwin, and Rood (to name a few) have compellingly refuted.

15 "Regime" (*politeia*) is distinct from "city" (*polis*) for Thucydides, as it is for Plato and Aristotle. The regime is the form given to the city. In contemporary terms, it makes a great difference if Germany is a democratic republic or ruled by a dictator. City is the political unit of the ancient world; it is not to be understood in the contemporary sense, but very generally speaking, as we would use the term "state" today (cf., however, Fustel De Coulanges' *The Ancient City* [1864] particularly Book Three.) Difference of regime is one not only of governmental structure or constitution; it alters the lives of the citizens themselves. As Rahe (1984) p. 269 observes: "The *polis* was not a conspiracy of self-seeking individuals joined for mutual profit and protection in a temporary legal partnership that would be dissolved when it ceased to suit their interests. It was a moral community of men permanently united by a common way of life." And as Thucydides presents it, the Spartan regime must also be contrasted with democratic Athens. It is no accident (and quite striking) that Thucydides presents the Athenians' praise of the Spartans' civic virtue in the same part of their dialogue with the Melians where they boldly state their view of the divine, contradicting as it does that of the pious Spartans. Cf., by way of introduction, Aristotle's *Politics*, Book Three and Plato's *Republic*, Book Eight for alternative presentations of this key issue.

weighed against a brutal fact: the Spartans (and Chians), he notes in this very context, possessed the greatest number of slaves (8.40.2). The Spartans thereby needed to be always watchful, guarding against a possible revolt of this slave-farming population: the Helots (4.80).

Thucydides distinguishing the two cities raises questions as to the inevitability and desirability of Athenian imperialism, and therefore the view that his account is a vindication of Athens begins to appear problematic.[16] In fact, Sparta wins the war not so much on its own as by Athens' failures, failures due precisely to civil strife at home (2.65.10-13). But Spartan moderation, Spartan justice, will have to be considered in light of what all is required to avoid this civil strife. Sparta is of interest to us then, not merely as foil to Athens in the Peloponnesian War, but as embodying a form of political health this imperial power lacked.

Admiration of the historical Sparta, as a stable, long-lasting ancient regime, is found in ancient writers, but also a notable feature of modern political thought, particularly in the writings of Machiavelli and Jean-Jacques Rousseau. For both, Sparta stands as the exemplar of the ancient community and offers itself as a possible model for the new and modern world each of these thinkers had a hand in shaping. While Machiavelli's judgment decides against Sparta (because it could not expand beyond a modest size and scale),[17] Rousseau offers the strongest praise of Sparta among modern political philosophers. Contrasting the ascendancy of liberalism and its emphasis on the individual as the basis of modern natural right (particularly in the thought of Hobbes and Locke), Rousseau looked to Sparta as *the* regime where the citizen is wholly dedicated to the common good of the political community and possessed the civic virtues required for sound political life. For the Spartans, the very notion of an "individual" would be all but incomprehensible. So striking were the laws and institutions of Sparta precisely because they appeared contrary to human nature.[18] While the Athenians in Thucydides' account present politics as a game of self-interest openly pursued (thus sharing this characteristic with modern politics and the thought that formed it) the Spartans offer the example of, and possibility for, a moral and communal civic life at odds with the

16 Cf. Romilly (1963) pp. 252-55, 257, 292.

17 Machiavelli, *Discourses on Livy* 1.6.2-3. See Proietti (1981) pp. xi-xii.

18 *Emile*, Book One (p. 40 of Bloom translation). Cf. Plato, *Republic* 419a1-420c4.

movement of Hobbesian and Lockean liberalism.[19] Fearing the weaknesses of modern citizens (raised on excessive liberty) and the consequences for civic virtue, Rousseau finds in Sparta the exemplar of morality rooted in law-abidingness and uncorrupted by the influence (as he viewed it) of philosophy and science. Dedicated rather to cultivating the robust virtues cities require, Spartan citizens were most beneficial to their regime.[20] Rousseau's praise also hints at an awareness of Thucydides' view that domestic strife at Athens was behind certain decisions made during the war that weakened their ability to succeed in Sicily and thus the larger war; these are the "secret causes" Thucydides does not allow us to notice easily which led to Athens' defeat, causes all the more notable for directing our attention away from the seemingly obvious one (i.e. an outright attack on their city by the Peloponnesians) and towards the question of the regime.[21]

Thucydides' Spartan Narrative

As the foregoing remarks imply, Thucydides' *War of the Peloponnesians and the Athenians* raises questions and confronts problems we may not have expected and not in the straightforward manner characteristic of a historical account. Any beginning point for a study of Thucydides must therefore contend with the continued debates over the status of his work as belonging to the genre or discipline we call "history," along with the various interpretive approaches. How I approach the text must be briefly noted to explain how this book will proceed; for to neglect the strange character of Thucydides' account is to fail to appreciate the subtlety with which he presents his Sparta. This study aims to explicate Thucydides' Sparta because such a

19 *Letter to M. D'Alembert on the Theatre* (p. 32 of Bloom translation). This of course situates Rousseau as a partial critic of the thought of Hobbes and Locke, despite numerous similarities.

20 Rousseau, *Discourse on the Arts and Sciences* para. 24-25 (following Gourevitch's numbering of original paragraphs). One need not agree with Rousseau's understanding of Sparta to notice that his appeal presumes a familiarity among his readers with Sparta such that it could serve as an example. On the issue of Sparta's reception in the West, see especially Tigerstedt (1965) and Rawson (1969). Cf. Cartledge (2004).

21 Rousseau, *Discourse on the Arts and Sciences: Replies* para. 41-46 (with Rousseau's footnote). It is worth noting that Rousseau, as with Hobbes, alludes to Thucydides' artful (and deceptive) writing.

focus can contribute to his political thought as a whole. Other archaeological and textual fragments of Sparta's history are not the subject here.[22]

In a recent (and rare) study focused exclusively on Thucydides' presentation of Sparta, "Sparta and the Spartans in Thucydides," Paul Cartledge and Paula Debnar argue for a reconsideration of city and citizen in light of this shift in Thucydides scholarship from the Separatist (or compositionalist) view to the Unitarian (or literary) Thucydides.[23] But despite announcing

22 For a fuller discussion of my interpretative methodology, see the Appendix. Francois Ollier's *Le mirage spartiate* (1933-43) began what has come to be called (in studies of historical Sparta and after his study's title) the "Spartan mirage." Ollier argues Sparta was idealized in the 4th century B.C. and thus we cannot be sure of much of the praise we find of Spartan (or Spartan-like) institutions. Sparta is a topic of fascination generally in Plato, Aristotle, and Xenophon, Ollier's conclusion being these authors praise Sparta (incorrectly) as an idealized polis. Ollier's thesis has been (and still is) both very influential and widely challenged in classics and history scholarship. Ollier's argument rests on the presupposition that ancient authors had motives to dissemble about Sparta, particularly its flaws. But most striking is that all the philosophers mentioned, while praising some elements of Sparta, were also highly *critical* of certain Spartan institutions, laws, and practices. E.N. Tigerstedt's *The Legend of Sparta in Classical Antiquity* (1965) followed, a massive two-volume study of all classical sources on Sparta, from ancient Greece to the Renaissance. As his title implies, he also notices this fascination with Sparta; but his interpretation of the evidence is more balanced than Ollier. With Thucydides' presentation, he identifies both praises and critiques (see especially, pp. 127-48). More recently, Hodkinson (2013) p. 18 argues that "... what most scholars have missed is the imbalance between the pro- and anti-Spartan viewpoints." Rather "...among the surviving sources there is *no substantial account* which indulges in unalloyed idealization of Sparta" (emphasis added). As I will contend, Thucydides himself recognizes both Sparta's best qualities and its shortcomings; but I disagree with Hodkinson's conclusion that Thucydides can be counted as one of the "negative portrayals" (p. 19). For further refutation of Ollier's thesis, see Hodkinson (2005) pp. 222-25 and Hammond's early book review (1947). See Rahe (2016) pp. 1-6 with 147n23 for an overview of "The Spartan Enigma" particularly scholarship treating Plato and Aristotle on Sparta. On the relationship between the "mirage" and archaeological evidence, see Cartledge (2001) pp. 169-84. In discussing knowledge of the origins of Sparta, Rahe (2016) pp. 64-65 notes: "For what we know of traditions in other places and times suggests that most of the time only a part of what is contained therein is pure invention...What survives from the past even in modern times is never more than part of the story...But they are most unlikely to be wholly and simply false."

23 Cartledge and Debnar (2006) pp. 559-87. Cartledge, of course, has numerous other works on Sparta, drawing on historical and archaeological evidence. I will treat those in the appropriate place. This article, though, is important for Cartledge and Debnar's view on *Thucydides'* Sparta, as well as their approach, to offer contrast with my own.

their departure from the Separatist thesis, which furnishes scholars with a framework to reconsider neglected portions of Thucydides' text, Cartledge and Debnar still focus on central Separatist *questions*: Thucydides' objectivity, terminology, sources and reports that may have provided him information, before then turning to the narrative and speeches, and to his account of individuals. With each of these themes (contrary to the literary approach), emphasis is placed on *what* Thucydides presents regarding Sparta rather than the *manner* in which he presents it. Cartledge and Debnar's approach and interpretation is, therefore, informative for showing how Separatist questions still find their way into purportedly literary interpretations of Thucydides, betray an entrenched view of what qualifies as "history," and will allow us to see other questions related to Thucydides' Sparta that such an approach fails to give due weight or consideration.

The authors begin by noting the significant shift in Thucydides scholarship after the "literary turn," which they define as the thesis that "*how* a historian says what he says can now seem to matter quite as much as *what* he says" (560 – emphasis in original). Their own study, however, quickly turns largely to questions of Thucydides' "objectivity" and his possible sources for information on Sparta. Only in the section of their study dealing with the Spartan narrative and Thucydides' imputation of motives do they implicitly respond to the literary turn thesis, suggesting Thucydides did not invent narrative events and would refrain from drawing conclusions (about Sparta or the Spartans) when he lacked reliable source information (568). If this view is correct, we may be forced to conclude that the amount of space Thucydides dedicated to an event or character is dictated simply by the information at his disposal. Lack of discussion or explication of an event or character might lead us to conclude Thucydides was compelled by his resources to leave out what might be a notable facet of the war.

Two objections must be raised here, and they return us again to noticing Thucydides' literary art: First, Thucydides could have had other information he chose not to include in his account because it did not serve his (literary) purpose – the existence of information or sources for his claims cannot therefore be a measure of what he chose to discuss. Second, Thucydides could have written his account in such a manner to make clear precisely what his sources were, or the lack thereof, when they were completely absent; he could have *stated* that an important matter is said to have taken place but that he could not ascertain the truth of the rumor. In the very example Cartledge and Debnar use in this context (Sparta's secrecy regarding its battle formation, which Thucydides discusses in Book Five), Thucydides *does* admit that it was difficult to know precisely the number of men who died in the battle (5.74.3). But he offers a calculation of the number of troops engaged in the battle because of the precise formation the Spartans employed (68.1-3).

Thucydides openly states in this instance what he did not know with absolute certainty. This highlights a key interpretative lesson – in any other part of his account of the war, Thucydides could have made known a similar difficulty. As for the possible imputation of motives as it relates to Thucydides' "source information," we must ask: Could Thucydides have known the motives from firsthand information regarding *any* of his characters? Did he not have to interpret motives from an individual's speech (when they gave them) and from their actions? Does any speech not also hide while it reveals? No one would claim (and Thucydides does not) that he interviewed every individual in the war, particularly those whom he presents as having distinctly *private* motives; yet he makes claims about such motives and desires and ambitions of his characters throughout.[24]

Cartledge and Debnar also argue that Thucydides' reticence on certain topics may be due to editorial choice or lack of interest in modern questions (568). These are obviously competing claims, but in enumerating some of the questions *they* are concerned with, perhaps an answer emerges to how best to read Thucydides. Cartledge and Debnar express disappointment, for example, that we do not have information about numerous aspects of Sparta, such as their connections abroad, certain individuals known from other writers or only briefly mentioned (such as Meleas at Mytilene), and economic considerations, such as Spartan financing for the war. Further, when Thucydides does present, for example, an account of Pylos (where a Spartan contingent became surrounded by the Athenians on the island of Sphacteria, just off the coast from the city of Pylos), Cartledge and Debnar argue he does not "explain fully" how policy choices were made, especially why the Spartan authorities decided the situation at Pylos was hopeless (569). Thus they conclude not only that we lack information from Thucydides about the Spartan regime, but also about Spartan political and military events as well.

What does it mean, though, that Thucydides did not "explain fully"

24 Chapter Four will discuss, in particular, the Melians, Nicias, and Brasidas.

Spartan motives and actions at Pylos? Let's note a few elements of this particular incident which Thucydides does highlight, as demonstrative of how I believe he expects to be read. Believing the situation hopeless and that the war was going poorly for them, the return of their men trapped on the island took on such importance that the Spartans ultimately surrendered to the Athenians and sued for a more general peace. In this instance, Thucydides does not openly pass judgment on the Spartans' decision (as he might have done and will do on other occasions). Certainly, their decision stands out by contrast to their heroic reputation, forged as it was with their self-sacrificial actions at Thermopylae during the Persian War. In fact, Thucydides alludes to Thermopylae in this very context (4.36.3), while also repeating his statement that the Spartans' abiding concern was the return of their men trapped on the island, shocking as their capture was for the city (4.40.1-4, 5.14.3). The reader is thus compelled to ask why *this* was their abiding concern (as opposed to fighting to the death, as they had done at Thermopylae), as Thucydides' repetitions urge us to do (4.41.3, 108.7, 117.1, 5.15.1). We cannot imagine the Athenians suing for peace after losing such a relatively small number of men, even of their first or best men, in a battle the scale of which Thucydides himself remarks was rather small. And while Cartledge and Debnar may be correct to note that we do not garner an *abundance* of information on Sparta's domestic situation from Thucydides' account (as it informed their handling of Pylos), I will argue there is more than first appears.[25]

For such an understanding of Sparta (and therefore a resolution to the incident at Pylos and other complexities in the Spartans' prosecution of the war), one would have to consider Thucydides' portrait, not focusing only

25 One could also make this claim about Athens. We have to figure out, for example, precisely why Pericles is trusted by the demos, for Thucydides' explanation that he could quiet them and even use confounding contradictions, is not an obvious explanation (2.65.8). And besides Pericles, it is in the preparations for the Sicilian expedition, including the motives for its undertaking, that Athens' domestic situation receives additional, and novel, scrutiny. This scrutiny in Book Seven and Eight is explained by the fact that Thucydides openly states domestic discord in Athens was the cause of their losing the war. But this too requires understanding and bringing together numerous considerations, including: the significance of the loss in Sicily, the occupation of Decelea by the Spartans, the charges against Alcibiades, and the shifting regimes within Athens near the end of the war. The Athenians would not have failed in Sicily had Alcibiades been in charge; and the Spartans would not have sent Gylippus to Sicily nor Agis to Decelea had it not been for Alcibiades. On the importance of Alcibiades to Athens and the events late in the war, see Forde (1989).

on isolated incidents, but as a whole. This includes Pausanias, Archidamus, Alcidas, Brasidas, the revealing but neglected Book Five, as well as Agis and Gylippus late in the war. I will discuss all these facets of the Spartan narrative, arguing that once we become alert to what Thucydides does present, he leaves clues to explain what kind of city Sparta was, what kind of citizens their domestic life cultivated and fostered, and therefore leads readers to a fuller explanation of such perplexities as the incident at Pylos, as well as their overall prosecution of the war.

This, indeed, is Thucydides' art of writing "history." His history, as I will argue and show, is an artfully arranged narrative, with character and psychology driving his analysis, intertwining foreign and domestic politics. With a view to our focus on psychology, regime, and strategy, we can observe the following: We are allowed to hear the traditional Spartan king, Archidamus, appeal to Spartan education and the virtues it inculcates; we are allowed to see the Spartans' appreciation for their commander, Brasidas, followed not long after by the envy his successes aroused, fueling Spartan indifference to his objectives when the authorities at home wanted peace (alleviating the city from necessities of war and securing the return of Spartan prisoners from Sphacteria); we are allowed to notice a host of new problems for Sparta first introduced in Book Five, including the surprising restrictions religious customs placed on their foreign policy, the failures of their king, Agis (Archidamus' son), in successfully prosecuting the war, and how this laid bare the tension existing between the king's hereditary position and the ephors' authority over him; we are allowed to see the laws that formed Spartan character (the source of the education Archidamus praises) were the same laws governing their conduct in battles, governance Thucydides quietly notes Brasidas, in his victories, did not employ (to say nothing of the absence of legal governance of Athenian strategy).

This is not to argue Thucydides replaces what we gain from a treatise such as Xenophon's *Regime of the Lacedaemonians* (assuming one understands that difficult text); but it is to suggest that for Thucydides' purposes, and the education of his readers, we learn *much* about Sparta and the Spartans and are able to draw a marked contrast to Athens and the Athenians. External or archaeological evidence has shed light on the historical city of Sparta; yet since Thucydides is well aware that cities decay (and that Sparta in particular would not leave much behind to recommend it for future study and consideration – 1.10), I do not assume he expected us to have even the amount of evidence we do possess. Is Thucydides himself not preserving what *he* believes makes Sparta, Sparta, and thereby fundamental for teaching us, his future readers, how a war between the pillars of the Greeks, Sparta and Athens, pillars of civilization, can be instructive for *us*?

With incidents such as the one at Pylos, and other points in his narrative, I will argue that Thucydides presents his account from a Spartan point of view, in a (so to speak) Spartan voice; it is left to the reader to disentangle Spartan motivations and puzzle through Spartan strategy. Why? Because such reading, Thucydides' literary art and the attention it demands, imitates a *key* difficulty we all face in understanding politics itself – distinguishing truth from falsehood, knowledge from opinions, prudential courses of action from foolish hopes. It is this activity, weighing the deeds and speeches of his Spartans (along with their enemies and allies), for his purpose of educating us, that Thucydides compels us to engage in.[26]

Thucydides' study of Spartan individuals, and what we learn from the presentation itself, also cannot be neglected. Praise of characters such as Demosthenes or Alcibiades is striking when comparing their qualities with those of prominent Spartans, including Archidamus or Alcidas, Agis or Gylippus; or when we observe the shortcomings of Sparta's prosecution of the war when compared even with their own commander, Brasidas,

26 The issue of motive, and notably, Thucydides' attribution of it to various individuals and the cities themselves, is a focal point for Hornblower throughout his *Commentary*; it has also figured into a longstanding debate on Thucydides' "sources" (see Hornblower I p. 23 for his first mention of this issue, as well as other scholarship). Hornblower questions Thucydides' ability to attribute motive to individuals he surely did not consult with (the preeminent example being Cleon). But is discerning motive not a key part of what *we* are supposed to learn, as Thucydides' readers? Does political analysis, not of the data variety but of the statesmen variety, not rely on the ability to know the motives (and thus strategy) of one's opponent? And relatedly, when scholars question Thucydides' sources they point to the question of what Thucydides could, or could not, have known, this itself depending on what we mean by knowledge. But even more, possessing the best sources still assumes human beings have perfect self-knowledge and thus what *they* claim as their motive is in fact true. Some concede this point: human beings lie, and thus Thucydides' attribution of motive is problematic, with or without sources. Yet the world of politics, a world of gossip, is the art of discerning motives when we cannot know them with complete certainty – predicting the plans of an enemy at war. Thucydides, I believe, would be the first to agree that he does not know with unfailing certainty. But I also believe he would press us, his interlocutor, to demonstrate why *we* believe his analysis of an individual's or city's motive to be flawed, and he would defend the attempt to know the motives of other human beings as part and parcel of the path to political wisdom.

and his successes. Thus, while Cartledge and Debnar (and others) argue Brasidas is one of the most enigmatic characters in Thucydides, we must hesitate at their conclusion that we do not know what his political goals might have been and that his apparent desire for personal glory "does not preclude more ambitious aims" (aims which they do not attempt to name or elucidate – 573). In another case, they continue this line of critique, arguing the Spartan king, Agis, "remains remote" as to his place in the war and in Sparta. But we must protest at their insufficient treatment in both cases of what Thucydides *does* relate. Agis' policies before and during the battle of Mantinea, his hesitation to enter battle due to the customary pious sacrifices holding Sparta back, his post at Decelea late in the war (and his striking employment of it), and how his hatred for Alcibiades might have figured into his strategy and policy decisions, are all quite revealing, both of Spartan piety and of a Spartan king leading a contingent abroad. Without investigating what Thucydides does offer, they are led to the assumption that Lysander would have been included in Thucydides' account of the Spartans if he had completed his work (584), that this addition would provide insight into Spartan character his existing account lacks.

I will begin instead by noting what we do learn from Thucydides' depiction of Spartan individuals. Agis, for example, fails, learns, adapts, and ultimately, leads Sparta more decisively late in the war, as Sparta's internal regime dynamics bend under the pressures of the Peloponnesian War. In the case of Brasidas, he is praised for his virtue and intelligence, as well as his gentleness and daring, in one of (if not *the*) most open praises Thucydides offers on any individual in the war (4.81.2, 108.3). Thucydides presents Brasidas' daring, in his advances during battle, as most surprising to the Athenians, this quality being wholly unexpected from a Spartan. And this exceptional quality is in keeping with the early remarks of the Corinthians, along with Thucydides' explicit judgment late in his account, that the two cities' characteristics were most different, and it is the daring and inventiveness of the Syracusans that allowed them to defeat the Athenians at Sicily (1.70.1, 8.96.5). By comparison, one could consider Xenophon's presentation of Lysander, a commander also at odds with his competing Spartan authorities, but similarly successful like Brasidas in prosecuting the war. Yet such a portrait is not required, I believe, to raise fundamental questions we will explore in the relationship between outstanding Spartans and their city – Brasidas provides this portrait.[27] Thucydides' Brasidas, as we will see, bids the reader to ask how and why the most effective Spartan commander is in a continual fight with his city both regarding policy initiatives and aims, as well as the desire for war.

In focusing on issues external to Thucydides' text, scholars lose sight of the significance of Sparta for us and, in my view, the reasons why Thucydides presents it in the manner *he* does. Rather than reading the text from what is contained within, as a literary approach bids us to do, one approaches it with questions of their own, not allowing themes, problems, and judgments of Thucydides to reveal themselves and direct our reading, however laconic he may first appear to be. In other words, despite recognition of the literary turn in Thucydidean scholarship, we still encounter the common error of failing to allow Thucydides' novel presentation of the war to guide our study. Only by understanding the nuances of this presentation may we begin to observe how a "history" such as his can be informative and provide guidance for us today.

For our study of Sparta, I will focus on evidence internal to the text and begin with a linear presentation. This beginning imitates how the combatants themselves would experience it, how Thucydides experienced it, and compels us to consider what the cities and individuals face as the war proceeds, and why. The "why" for Thucydides is grounded in human nature (*anthrōpeia physis*), particularly our political "psychology." I employ this term not in conventional scientific usage; rather, etymologically, psychology is "*logos* about the *psychē*" or a rational account of the soul.[28] Certainly,

27 Similarly, Wasserman (1964) p. 294 looks to Xenophon's Lysander in an attempt to explain Thucydides' Brasidas, thereby not fully exhausting Thucydides' account. Cf. Palmer (2015) p. 80 who rejects a Brasidas-Lysander parallel.

28 As Cornford (1907) p. 64 observes "[i]t appears to be characteristic of the ancient historians in general, that in so far as they look for causes of human events, they look, apart from supernatural agencies, solely to *psychological* causes – the motives and characters of individuals and cities" (emphasis in original). I disagree, however, when Cornford goes on to argue that "...Archidamus and Brasidas are the only two individuals on the Peloponnesian side whose motives are even dimly apprehended." The Spartan king, Agis, figures prominently in Book Five (discussed in Chapter Three) and the Spartan commander, Gylippus, proves crucial during the Athenians' Sicilian expedition, and thus is an important figure in the narrative of Nicias (discussed in Chapter Four). See, as well, Ste. Croix (1972) pp. 29-33 on Thucydides' mentions of human nature and its cognates. Cogan (1981) pp. 185-96 distinguishes "human thing" and "human nature," as I will discuss in Chapter One. Jaffe (2017) pp. 6-9 also quotes Cornford's observation and similarly emphasizes the Greek root of the term.

the soul does not feature in Thucydides' text as it does in Plato or Aristotle.[29] Understanding politics for Thucydides, however, is understanding, not human nature alone, but how its various manifestations (to the degree available to human thought) reveal the power of both nature (*physis*) and customs or laws (*nomoi*) in molding our psychology, what Thucydides calls "the human condition" (*to anthrōpinon* – 1.22.4).[30]

Human psychology has political, and crucially, moral origins and manifestations; it is, therefore, intimately attached to the character of the city itself, its laws, constitution, and way of life. For our study of Sparta and the Spartans, Chapter One will introduce key Thucydidean themes, detailing the direction Thucydides' Spartan narrative will take: the founding of the Spartan regime (as a regime distinct from Athens), the Spartans' pious invocations and preoccupation, and their contention that the Peloponnesian War originates in Athenian injustice. This, coupled with Athenian arguments grounded in human nature, proves to be a disagreement of the utmost significance.

With Chapter Two we will consider the early stages of the war, comparing Sparta's treatment of allies and enemies with that of Athens. Culminating in their defeat and surrender on the island of Sphacteria, the first ten years of the war lead to the Spartans suing for peace, resulting in a seven-year official armistice very much at odds with their stated goal of declaring war for sake of Greek liberation from Athenian imperialism.

---

29 The term "soul" (*psychē*) is largely absent (cf. 1.136, 2.40, 3.39, 8.50: all are speeches, three quoted and one reported. All but 2.40 seem to use *psyche* to refer more broadly to "life"). If Thucydides was interested in or had articulated a version of the "soul" similar to the manner in which Plato treats it, it does not follow that this would properly fit into, and therefore be included, in his account.

30 For other discussions focusing on these terms, consider Strauss (1964), Saxonhouse (1978), and Lebow (2001). Both *physis* and *nomos* will figure prominently in my analysis, as it does in Thucydides' own. These terms are central to Greek political thought: Plato, Aristotle, Xenophon, even Aristophanes. It is beyond the scope of our analysis here, however, to include the arguments of all these authors. As for *to anthrōpinon*: this is difficult to translate and occurs in this form only here (Young-Breuhl [1986] p. 4; however, cf. 3.40.1, 6.78.2). "Human nature" will not do, since *physis* is absent in this formulation, while Thucydides does use it elsewhere (for example, 1.76, 2.50, 3.45, 82.2). Most translate it "the human condition" including Hornblower I p. 61: "the human condition or situation." Cogan (1981) pp. 185-96 argues for "the human thing." Thucydides will offer us reflections on two key elements of *to anthrōpinon* (1.22.4), both *physis* and *nomos*, but within the context of the city at war. See Plato, *Timaeus* 19c1-d1 with Strauss (1964) pp. 140-41. See also Chapter One, note 37 below.

To understand why the Spartans take this step, Chapter Three will detail Thucydides' presentation of the Spartan regime: First, through examining this period of official peace (unfolding in Book Five), marked as it was by continued hostilities and military campaigns. Tension within Sparta between the hereditary kings and the elected ephors over the handling of strategy and warfare point to the broader issue of who Sparta's most prominent citizens are and how the city functions. Second, in pursuing the importance of the regime for Thucydides, we will distinguish Sparta from the regime change and decline occurring in Athens, along with the civil war (*stasis*) at Corcyra. And finally, canvassing evidence across the text, we consider seemingly passing details of Sparta's domestic situation that may be overlooked: internal discord arising from the Helots (Sparta's slave-farming population); their hegemony over the Peloponnesus; a Spartan foreign policy prioritizing their Dorian kin; and distinguished Spartan citizens, their kings and commanders, directing the city throughout the war. Bringing together Thucydides' praises and critiques, readers are offered a clear assessment of the Spartan regime, its domestic power and foreign weaknesses.

With Chapter Four we will broaden our study of "Spartan," following Thucydides' initial characterization set up in the Corinthians' speech in Book One (1.70). Spartan characters under consideration – the Melians, Nicias, and Brasidas – are different degrees or types, admixtures, of Spartan psychology. The Melian Dialogue, and Thucydides' Sicilian narrative (with its focus on Nicias), reveal more deeply than anywhere else the power of divine justice and kinship in guiding political calculations. Nicias, while an Athenian general, is the "Spartan" among them and Thucydides' portrait of him, I will argue, augments his overall Spartan narrative. Brasidas, as noted above, occupies a unique position both within the city and within Thucydides' account. Sparta's early success in the war relies on Brasidas, a Spartan by birth and education, but also decidedly un-Spartan, even "Athenian," who finds himself, as it were, estranged from his own city. Thucydides' praise of Sparta, the power of its regime (1.10.2, 18.1), finds its most notable limitation in the tension between their leading commander, Brasidas, and the city he could not wholly serve (despite his death being instrumental in Athens accepting Sparta's peace overtures).

Demonstrating the Spartan understanding of war reveals important details both about the Peloponnesian War, but as per Thucydides' greater aim, about politics generally, and about "the human condition" that we overlook by focusing exclusively, not only on Athenian politics, but also the Athenian view of human life itself.[31]

31 Bradford (1994) makes a nice observation, as a corrective to a merely factual Thucydides: "Thucydides, however, was Thucydides because of his interest in the psychology of the people involved, as individuals and as groups. His psychological analysis was his genius" (68). Unfortunately, for our consideration of Spartan psychology, Bradford errs by going on to claim that Thucydides, as an Athenian, "was exposed to, if not wholly convinced by, the Athenian understanding of Spartan character" and thus ultimately "Thucydides' portrait of the Spartans is the Athenian portrait" (70). Bradford appears to reach this conclusion by missing key pieces of the puzzle. In his list of the "three significant episodes" in Book One offering Thucydides' view of Spartan psychology, he fails to include the most important: Archidamus' speech on the wisdom and propriety of going to war (73). Since Bradford's theme is "Spartan duplicity" this omission is especially problematic. To state it succinctly here – Archidamus' speech is the very opposite of duplicity. It is in the subtlety and detail of Thucydides' portrait of Spartan psychology (in speech and action), I will argue, that he shows being very much aware of the shortcomings of the Athenians and their thesis, elevating himself above reductionist equations of his understanding to that of his contemporaries.

Chapter One

Sparta and the Outbreak of the Peloponnesian War

Book One deals, expectedly, with the causes of the war and how each city faces the prospects of a coming war. The Spartans charge the Athenians with breaching a treaty intended to ensure thirty years of peace between the two major powers in Greece. The war's outbreak does not occur without this Spartan accusation of injustice. The Spartans and their allies will charge the Athenians with the treaty's breach, but even more so with injustice against so to speak everyone, a subjugation of all the other cities – Athens has become the tyrant city of Greece. These are not obviously the same accusation; nor are they necessarily unrelated. Those who began as Athens' allies during the Persian War, to fight off the Persian attempts to expand their empire, have now become subject cities of the Athenian empire. Spartan fear of the growing Athenian empire, however, is the "truest pretext" leading to war according to Thucydides – a wrought phrase I will unpack shortly.

Fundamental to Thucydides' account through Book One, then, is Greece's beginnings – not only the actions leading up to the war with Athens, but also, in his so-called Archaeology, the origins of each city, their differing characters (or "cultures") and regimes, as well as the manner in which each city responded to the decades of hostilities culminating in the Peloponnesian War. Sparta, we note, does not debate the war on the same terms as Athens. Each city differs in their motives (actions) and justifications (speeches) for post-Persian War foreign policy. And this is not all – each city's understanding of itself and of what makes it superior *as a city* is expressed by two of the main speeches in Book One: Athenian envoys present in Sparta when the Spartans and their allies are debating war; and Archidamus, the Spartan king, in his response to their ally city, Corinth, who was pushing for war and blaming the Spartans for their past, and current, hesitation in confronting the Athenian empire. These speeches, along with the narrative's unfolding in Book One, establish Thucydidean themes and for our purposes, highlight what makes Sparta distinct and their role in the outbreak of the war.

All these factors introduced in Book One must be weighed with a view to the most pressing question for any war: "What happened?" by which the questioner means "What caused the war?" In answering this question, I will argue that Thucydides sets before the reader the following puzzle: How are we understand the competing views of the war's cause – the apparent but unstated Spartan fear, identified by Thucydides and inextricably linked to the growth of the Athenian empire; but also the stated but imprecise accusation of Athenian injustice, identified by the Spartans and supported by their allies? Is the answer to the question of the war's cause merely in the eye of the city proclaiming it, be they strong or weak? Or can we arrive at a clearer answer? After all, Thucydides, often proclaimed to be a "scientific historian," seems clear in his determination of cause: Sparta was afraid of Athens. Yet the Spartans were not simply unwilling to state this fear; they were unaware of it. Or more precisely, the Spartan accusation of Athenian injustice overshadows any acknowledgement of their fear of Athenian growth. Book One is Thucydides' demonstration of the Spartans casting not only the war, but their movement from alliance to suspicion to antagonism with Athens, in moral terms.

Understanding Book One is difficult, however, due to its structure. Thucydides does not proceed linearly, at least not entirely. The structure is, rather, as follows: Chapters 1-19 are the Archaeology proper (literally "account of the beginnings"). Chapters 20-23 shift abruptly to discussing the nature of Thucydides' inquiry, including his purpose for writing, use of speeches, and evidence collected. Chapters 24-88 then trace the beginning (or beginnings, when we consider all the evidence) of the Peloponnesian War, with speeches by the major cities involved. Chapters 89-118, rather than presenting Athens' response to Sparta's declaration of war, instead present the rise of Athens (referred to as the Pentecontaetia or "Account of the Fifty Years"), from a hegemony to empire over the Greeks. These latter chapters, which focus in detail on the slow, growing tension between Sparta and Athens, amount to a fifty-year "digression" in Thucydides' account, but prove as integral to understanding the outbreak of the Peloponnesian War as the more immediate actions, complaints, justifications, and votes of the cities involved. Chapters 119-146 then close Book One with Athens' official response to Sparta, found in Pericles' first speech.[1]

On the one hand, we would expect a linear account and therefore this use of a digression is an interruption in the narrative; but on the other hand, this presentation achieves other ends – it imitates the act of discovery Thucydides himself would have undergone, moving from present events and working backwards to understand their possible sources and causes, before then returning to the present. And given that we will have just heard a wide array of claims by all actors involved or about to be involved in the conflict, Chapters 24-88, covering the more immediate events and causes, leave us with questions the digression (if it can truly be characterized as such) may be able to answer.[2]

The structure of Book One as a whole therefore places the reader in a unique position – Thucydides states what he believes to be the war's cause, Spartan fear of Athenian growth (1.23.5-6), before detailing *either* the allegations or the observable events leading to its outbreak. While Thucydides himself thus appears to provide a singular cause for the war, his reader cannot even begin to fully appreciate the import of this statement without unfolding the complex structure of Book One. The Peloponnesian War is the manifestation not only of numerous, proximate events, but of the

1 Compare Connor (1984) pp. 20-51. As he, in my view correctly, states "...Thucydides' narrative often performs many tasks simultaneously. The Pentecontaetia, like the Archaeology, is not a simple story of events in a given time period. It is again highly selective and focused on themes and ideas rather than on comprehensive coverage" (42). For other discussions of Book One, see Adcock (1951), Orwin (1994) pp. 30-63, Rood (1998) pp. 205-24. Jaffe (2017) is a book-length treatment focusing exclusively on Book One. Allison (2013) summarizes the current state of the scholarship: "The debate about the compositional integrity of Book 1 is less noisy today in part because questions about historical accuracy and omissions especially in the Pentecontaetia seem to be talked out. In general, modern scholars prefer to look for plan and unity in the entire *History*, and a coherent purpose in the Pentecontaetia, while still admitting layers of composition" (258). It must be immediately added that not all modern scholars engage in speculation on composition.

2 For similar observations, see Strauss (1964) pp. 180-82 and Connor (1984) pp. 32-34, respectively. Both interpret the text having noticed that Thucydides is interested in educating his reader, is a philosophic historian, and therefore expectations for a linear account of "just what happened" are far from his overall purpose. Hobbes' biographical essay "Of the Life and History of Thucydides" (accompanying his translation: *The Peloponnesian War*) is the first account outside of antiquity to focus on how Thucydides writes and the character of his text. See the Introduction note 30 and context above.

interpretation of, and response to, those events by the cities and individuals themselves. While the Corinthians will complain of Spartan inaction, and the Athenians justify their imperial expansion, for the pious Spartans who declare the war, their view can only be fully understood once we notice another variable introduced in Book One: Thucydides uniting natural disasters with pretexts and causes of war, the Spartans weighing the possible religious implications of both. Given Athens is a tyranny and tyranny rings as an injustice for the pious Spartans, the cause of the war cannot be divorced from Spartan fear of not only Athens, but of the gods. The gods may be on their side in combatting an unjust enemy; but they may also be against them should they initiate an unjust war.

The Origin of Two Cities: Thucydides' Archaeology

By way of the Archaeology, Thucydides poses a core problem: With the outbreak of the Peloponnesian War, all establishments are threatened – the city of Sparta, the Athenian empire, all alliances and allied relationships (those formed as Sparta and Athens became individually more powerful), and the very existence of Greece itself, signaled by the return of Persia in Book Eight.[3] Part of the Spartan story is what is lost when rest is disturbed and the greatest motion initiated. Sparta is, in one sense, the embodiment of rest (1.12.1), or peace.[4] As Thucydides observes, despite the magnificence, the visible beauty of Athens' greatness, manifested in the city, in its philosophic and scientific achievements and in its expanding empire, Sparta possesses significant "power" (*dynamis* – 10.2-3).[5] How that power will

3 Finley (1942) pp. 87-93 notices that the Archaeology introduces ideas key to understanding the rest of Thucydides' account. See also Hornblower I pp. 7-8.

4 Strauss (1964), for example, treats the terms motion and rest in detail, suggestive of the broader philosophic meaning each could have. There are two words Thucydides uses: "peace" (*eirēnē*) and "rest" (*hēsuchazō*, most often the verbal form "to be at rest"). The latter is broader and its opposite is "motion" (*kinēsis*). The former derives from the name of the goddess, Eirene, daughter of Zeus and Themis. It is used, in a more political sense, first appealed to by the Corinthians in direct contrast with "war" (*polemos* – 1.40.2).

5 Connor (1984) notes that: "...the modern reader will not miss the thrust of Thucydides' argument: the early history of Greece shows the importance of naval and financial power. It points to Athens, not to Sparta" (33-34). Yet, as Hornblower I p. 8 observes, Sparta is mentioned five times in the Archaeology. This reinforces the

manifest itself is not yet clear; but with the account in the Archaeology, Spartan rest first appears as a domestic form of political power, issuing from the Spartan regime (*politeia*), and not insignificant even in light of Athenian greatness. Knowing of Athens' loss in the war, Thucydides' oftentimes overlooked praise of Sparta in Book One sets the stage for weighing the precise challenge Sparta presents to the greatness of Athenian imperialism. Imperialism's costs are necessarily to be weighed against a stability provided by Spartan restraint.

Thucydides' purpose in the Archaeology (Chapters 1-19) is therefore three-fold: to show the establishment of the city as a distinct political entity, along with the various kinds of cities; to distinguish Sparta and Athens in particular; and to argue for the weakness of ancient times compared to the present (and thus the gravity of a full-scale war now).[6] Thucydides calls

---

difficulty I noted in the Introduction: We must be especially attentive to Sparta given the obvious impressiveness of Athens early on; we have to discover Sparta.

6 Thucydides' Archaeology is one of the most disputed parts of his work. See Ellis (1991) for a good overview of this debate which, not surprisingly, has its origins in the Separatist versus Unitarian divide. Ellis is a Unitarian, arguing that "the first book is painstakingly ordered, its components from largest to smallest arranged and interrelated to an awesome degree, the formal framework facilitating and articulating its two great arguments on the significance and the cause of the Peloponnesian War" (345). Orwin (1989) places Thucydides' statement of his method within the context and purpose of the Archaeology as a whole, thereby revealing key hints for understanding Thucydides' "contest" with Homer. Connor (1984) pp. 19-32 details the many objectives he believes Thucydides is pursuing in the Archaeology; see especially p. 30n29 for his demonstration of Thucydides' use of a ring composition from 1.1.1-1.23. Connor's book also has nine appendices treating other ring compositions and general structural details explaining the significance of the stages of Thucydides' argument. By contrast is Luraghi (2000) pp. 227-28: "Although writing for eternity, Thucydides, as every author in every time, could not escape conceiving of his implied audience as very similar to his real audience, thus presupposing in his readers a large contextual competence we fatally lack" and "[t]he implicit communication between Thucydides and his audience does not facilitate comprehension of the Archaeology to modern readers." Thucydides makes statements, however, precisely at odds with Luraghi's argument – he expected his account to be permanent and therefore the "allusive" (231) character of the Archaeology must be accessible and appreciated by later audiences. Luraghi continues: "Our knowledge of fifth-century literature is clearly insufficient to allow speculation about the other sources Thucydides is alluding to besides Herodotus, not to mention the knowledge he could suppose his audience to possess without the mediation of a written source. Nevertheless, there is no *a priori* reason to doubt that the familiarity with the past required from Thucydides' implied audience in the Archaeology is not limited to Herodotus and the epos" (235). But could Thucydides not have informed us of his references, if he

the war itself the greatest "motion" (*kinēsis*). To understand this motion, we need to understand its origin and cause; we also presumably care about it being a greater war than previous wars in the past. Something about this war matters more than others. As the Archaeology portrays it, there is a movement from motion to rest to motion: Thucydides depicts widespread piracy and violence, the establishment of Sparta and Athens, including the Athenian empire, and finally the Peloponnesian War. The weakness of ancient times is the lack of rest required for growth, a growth that issues in the flourishing of cities and political life (1.2.2, 12.1). This lack of rest, or peacetime, means the origins of Greece were chaotic. For Thucydides, political life establishes order, an order through which human life changes and progresses, moving beyond necessity, i.e., beyond mere self-preservation and survival. When this order breaks down, therefore, it results in a motion greater than that of ancient times. Or we might say, the consequences of the Peloponnesian War are greater since what is lost is greater than with the wars of the past.

It is Sparta that is representative of order, as we trace out the subtle movements of Thucydides' Archaeology. His first mention of Sparta, as well as his observation near the end of his account, associate the city with order and stability. The Spartans are the first to adopt a "measured" (*metrion*) way of life, not only in their dress, but more importantly in the relation, in the degree of equality (*isodiaitos*), between the rich and poor within the city (1.6.4). Sparta lacks the adornments of Athens, and Thucydides argues that little to no relics or monuments of Sparta would be left behind to suggest their power as a city (10.2). Indeed, Sparta is closer to ancient times than Athens, their city still being comprised of villages. Sparta is characterized more by an approximation to these times than Athens; they did not lack the wealth that Athens first enjoyed, but as Sparta became Sparta, the wealthy

---

saw fit? After all, we learn of the Peisistratus story because Thucydides tells us what most Athenians believed, how they were wrong, and why they were wrong; similarly with the Cylon incident. Rather than attempting to dissect the possibility Thucydides left something essential out of the Archaeology (which seems absurd considering it is a highly selective and time-compressed account), I will seek to draw out the lessons on Sparta, Athens, and the war in general from what he does provide us. Whatever one's view, it is generally accepted that the Archaeology is as Ellis describes it – highly organized and with a clear purpose. Similarly, Romilly (2012) pp. 144-79. Other studies include Fragoulaki (2013) pp. 59-64 on the importance of kinship (*xyngeneia*), first introduced in Archaeology. See Rood (2015) on the reception of the Archaeology, including important comments on the 19th century origins of the term.

assimilated themselves to the way of life of the many. They moderated themselves to reduce or eliminate the distinction between rich and poor. While Athens became a naval people, the Spartans dealt with factions owing to the virtue of the soil in the Peloponnesus and the resulting fights over the land. Sparta was the first city to "have good laws" (or "be well-ordered" – *eunomeomai*) and maintained the same regime (*politeia*) for four hundred years leading up to the Persian invasion of Greece (18.1).[7] Thus the city was "moderate" (*sōphrosynēn*) in prosperity as a whole (8.24.4). In introducing both cities, Thucydides is cautioning the reader, through Sparta, against being enamored with the magnificence, the beauty, of Athens. This, despite the fact that Sparta is closer to ancient times, while Athens will become thoroughly modern.[8]

While many coastal cities at this time battled piracy as the dominant, yet destabilizing, political and economic means of power, Sparta's founding resulted in a stable regime. Thucydides notes that piracy was not initially considered "shameful" (*aischros*) but understood simply as a means of survival (1.5.1-2). It is only after the colonization of island populations (those particularly susceptible to piracy) by Minos that Thucydides speaks of those involved with piracy as "wrongdoers" (*kakoyrgoi*) threatening these coastal populations. In other words, piratical activity is judged to be morally reprehensible as walled cities were being founded and peoples attempted to live

7 Andrewes (1938) argues *eunomia* means obedience by the citizens to a constitution, rather than laws necessarily being good ("good order or government"). He and Erasmus (1960) trace the term's origins and usage, beginning with Homer. See also Rahe (2016) p. xv with n19. Hornblower I pp. 51-54 notes this definition. But the greater scholarly debate deals with the age of Sparta's regime. After much wrangling, the best evidence falls, not surprisingly, on the side of Herodotus' and Thucydides' testimonies. Compare Aristotle, *Politics* 1270a1-10; Machiavelli, *Discourses on Livy*, 1.2.1, 2.6. Particularly important is that Sparta's regime, its constitution, is *old* and this antiquity is the source of its power. In bringing both these issues together, we will notice the following: While the Spartan constitution demands obedience, the content of their laws is also not unimportant for understanding both their successes and failures.

8 As Allison (2013) correctly observes: "Part of why we are so affected by this Athenocentric view is that the History stops before the final events of the war, where Lysander's activities and Sparta's victory would have been recorded. But there are places in the Archaeology where the historian qualifies the necessity of the two components of power so long associated with Athens by insisting on societal development and governmental integrity as equally important...The components of power that supported Athenian superiority, revenue and sea power, are reevaluated against governmental stability and strong allies, things Sparta could boast had brought her victory" (259).

a settled way of life. The first glimpse of notions of justice appear to arise once cities begin to form, both the basic necessities and interests supplied, and luxury also possible (8.2-3). It is in seeking to protect the interests of a founded and settled way of life that these new cities, or their founders, view piracy as unjust. In other words, the rise of the appellation "wrongdoers" originates during settlement, as a way of distinguishing those individuals or groups refusing to recognize laws, nor worthy of political trust. This appellation demarcates those harming the budding city's interests: justice arises in the city but is also inseparable from the interests of the city, the lives of its inhabitants. Yet those interests are not merely viewed as interests; the city as city becomes morally superior to the interests of others – the citizens of the cities no longer recognize certain pursuits, such as piracy, as a justifiable means of self-preservation, as they had been before, even if the act itself allows for some degree of protection or even profit. No longer is piracy prestigious, but now carries a negative moral evaluation. The life of the city takes over, not merely as the best means to secure one's interests (in cases when it does or did when it was founded), but as the morally superior way to do so.

In fact, this introduces a complication in Thucydides' portrait: Piracy was considered "prestigious" (or "worthy" – *doxē*) even *before* cities were settled (5.2). Human beings praise and blame certain practices, bestowing moral value even on self-preservation itself. Morality shifts, though, from according moral worth to the pirate for his successes, to political justice where goods are secured not only for one individual but for all: The city is the rise of the notion of the common good, even if by "common good" we mean simply mutual defense against piracy and accumulation of wealth, a good striven for by both the strong and the weak (5.1-2, .7, 8.1-3).

Thucydides' origin account is a progress through time, but not simply a progress in conditions, be they geographic, commercial, or political. It is all of these, but more notably, a *moral* progress. Thucydides presents ancient times as somehow worse, i.e., not a golden age worthy of veneration. This would seem to explain a complexity with the issue of piracy – despite Thucydides' claim piracy was not shameful but even honorable, his evidence for this evaluation is Homer (5.2). But Homer presents piracy as just the opposite: pirates *do* bring "evil" (*kakos*) to those who have begun living a settled way of life.[9] When piracy was supreme, it was a practice

9 See *Odyssey* III 70-82 and IX 251-55 and context.

praised as "noble" (5.2 – *kalōs*). Shame, which comes later with pirates now labeled as "wrongdoers," is only the reverse of this (8.2). A clear dichotomy, therefore, between nature (most especially human nature) and convention (the justice established by a city's laws) becomes murky.[10]

This is not to deny changes the founding of cities bring: Even with a distinction between good and evil in the earliest times, human life is not wholly recognizable to us, since in Thucydidean terms, there is no "greatness" (*megethos* – 1.2.2). Life according to necessities is only mere survival. To recognize and act according to necessity is, in these early times, to secure oneself through acquisition of wealth. Peoples lived nomadically, and therefore being unsettled and without fortification, the best locations were taken and re-taken. No regard existed for right of first occupant, since fertile soil conferred so much power on individuals. Conventions such as borders, rights, and property did not exist; without laws, human beings appear to live according to nature, i.e., recognizing as constraining on them only the necessities required to survive. And this means, especially, laws and the rule of law did not exist, including notions of equality, notions that will later come to play in the relations between cities. The convention of establishing cities, rest from the motion and faction (*stasis*) of the early times, allows for growth otherwise not possible. And with this growth comes all that Thucydides catalogues as absent before cities: commerce, communication, cultivation beyond necessity, agriculture, and the building of cities as a precondition of greatness (2.2).

Once cities are established, with their diverse customs and practices, each living according to a particular notion of justice only masks what is

10 Scholars focus, not incorrectly, on the absence of justice before the founding of cities (see, for example, Jaffe [2017] pp. 147-48). But we must also recognize the moral roots of human decision-making even before the regimes and laws of the various cities are fixed in place. Jaffe notes, for example, the absence of speeches in the Archaeology, drawing a connection between speech and the establishment of justice. Certainly, laws must be articulated and debates about justice presuppose language (cf. Aristotle, *Politics* 1253a1-20); but we notice that Spartan laws, while not adumbrated here, are referred to by Thucydides in the Archaeology (1.18). Additionally, noting the broader meaning of *nomos* ("law") as inclusive of conventions and customs (also noted by Thucydides in this context – 1.6.1-6), the roots of morality are not simply discovered or set down with the establishments of cities. Thucydides' Archaeology is not Hobbes' State of Nature, where justice arises only with the legal establishment of the social contract (consider Chapter 13 of *Leviathan*). What I want to emphasize here, by contrast, is the origin of morality in a pre-political beginning, even before the settling into cities.

common to all human beings – we are moral and social or political beings. Yet Sparta and Athens each adopted a particular way of life differing from the other, including especially their regimes. What is common to all human beings as moral beings cannot lead us to overlook their foundational differences. The way of life of each city and the power of each differs, as the necessities they face differ.

As for the cities individually, both Sparta and Athens ceased the practices of the barbarians, including the carrying of arms as a means of protection within the city itself, a practice originally necessitated by piracy. Life in a city changes how peoples secure their survival and flourishing, and it presupposes at least two things: First, in the case of Sparta, recognition of the need or advantage of living together, such that citizens share in the political community. Inequalities exist, as Thucydides presents it, before the founding of cities and thus those inequalities may become incorporated into its founding.[11] Sparta sought to avoid these inequalities and the faction accompanying them, in reducing the division between rich and poor by bringing the rich in line with the "commons" (*isodiaitoi*).[12] In the case of Athens, a laying down of one's arms in a large city means that one is able to trust one's fellow citizens, along with the laws set down to punish offenders should that trust be broken.

As Thucydides notes, it was Sparta's regime which became the source of their power (18.1); they avoided the tyrannies that characterized much of the rest of Greece; they were the supreme power at the outbreak of the Persian War due to their regime. Athens, on the other hand, relied on its wealth and naval abilities to leave their limited geographic area, and sail out to subject other cities throughout Greece. The Athenians were compelled to leave Athens and become a naval people during the Persian invasion. Piracy brought instability to those cities easily accessible by sea, while the Spartans' position on land allowed them to avoid what Thucydides argues was the most problematic feature of antiquity – its constant war and faction, stifling growth and therefore greatness. Sparta was one of the first cities to civilize and find peace from these smaller wars that characterized ancient times. The Persians initiated the war after their name, yet Sparta's power on

11 Compare the beginning of Part Two of Rousseau's *Discourse on the Origin and Foundations of Inequality*.

12 Sparta discovers or creates, and later takes to the extreme, the notion of the common good. Cf. Strauss (1964) pp. 145-46, Orwin (1994) p. 84 and context.

land allowed them to take the lead in pushing back the Persian invasion. At first allied with Athens, the alliance during this period was short lived, as each city had additional allies that went over to what became competing sides – a once united Greece began to quarrel amongst themselves following the Persian defeat (18.2-3). Sparta set up oligarchic regimes friendly to their interests; Athens exacted tribute from their allies in the form of money, while also reducing competing navies that could rival and threaten their own. Thucydides notes that the dissolution of the Persian War alliance increased the strength of each to such a degree that each city (with its allies) was alone greater than the alliance they had established together for the sake of defeating Persia (19), foreshadowing the threat of each to the other.

Pretexts and Causes for War

Thucydides' narrative now shifts contrary to our expectations. We do not hear of the continued growth of each city, nor an obvious explanation of how this account of ancient times relates to the present war. Here, Thucydides turns instead to considerations one would have expected as a sort of preface: Chapters 20-23 are a discussion of his manner of writing and then, before describing Athens' imperial growth, he states his own opinion on the cause of the war. Upon closer consideration, this is not a relic of his compositional order or a late insertion but presents the war to the reader with a particular purpose, and significant puzzles. After all, Thucydides begins these chapters by stating that most people accept what is first presented to them as "truth" (*alētheia*).[13] Is this not an invitation to recognizing how *Thucydides* is presenting what he understands as the truth, to us, his readers? And, moreover, that neither our initial impressions nor Thucydides' initial observations will allow us to sufficiently grasp the truth as he understands it?

Let us look at his steps after concluding the Archaeology: Thucydides first notes the policy of Sparta and Athens with regard to their allies (and how the regime of each city affected their alliances – 1.19). He then turns to

13 "So little trouble do people take to search out the truth, and so readily do they accept what first comes to hand" (1.20.3 – Mynott [2013] translation). Hornblower I p. 58 notes that Thucydides mentions "truth" (*alētheia*) four times in short succession (1.20.3, 21.1, 22.1, 23.6).

a story about an Athenian tyrant as proof of his contention that most traditions passed down are simply believed by those who hear them, rather than being carefully considered – most do not attempt to investigate the truth of such traditions (20.1-3). Following this claim, he questions the accuracy of the poets (the source of those traditional stories alluded to) and adds to this a description of his own procedure in writing the speeches in his account of the war (21-22). From here he moves to the differences between the Persian War and the Peloponnesian War, including not only the vastly greater sufferings of the latter, but the sufferings that befell both sides as the result of earthquakes, famines, the plague, and the like (23.1-3). And we then discover his own opinion on the cause of the war after the dissolution of the Thirty Years' Peace treaty between Athens and Sparta, a treaty which he mentions here for the first time (23.4). This treaty was broken by Sparta due to the growth of Athenian power which, instilling fear in the Spartans, made war inevitable (23.5-6).

How are we to account for this sequence of events, which not only lacks the chronology one would expect from an account of a growing, encroaching empire and resulting war, but also the seemingly irrelevant details regarding natural disasters that Thucydides places in this very context, to say nothing of the other non-narrative elements?

These catastrophes are followed by Thucydides' statement on what he understands as the "pretext" for the Peloponnesian War, but then followed by a long discussion of the outbreak of the war, including its lead-up, accusations cast on either side, and a digression on the growth of Athenian imperialism (24-88). Thucydides' judgment on the "necessity" (*anankē*) of the war, Spartan fear of Athenian imperialism, thus appears more as a puzzle than a solution to our questions about the war, particularly in light of Sparta's later profession to be liberating Greece from Athenian imperialism (a claim we are only allowed to hear much later, at the beginning of Book Two).[14] It is a puzzle because Thucydides thereby complicates what seems a very straightforward statement. After all, scholars have beat their heads against the wall despite this statement. Let's consider this famous and much discussed passage and then return to the issue of tyranny, past wars, and his catalogue of natural disasters.

---

14 Connor (1984) p. 32 supports the view that *anankē* should not be understood as philosophic or scientific determinism (citing Ste. Croix [1972] among others). See also Hornblower I p. 66, Macleod (1983) p. 88.

Thucydides argues that the "truest pretext" (or truest "allegation/justification" – *alēthestatēn prophasin*), Spartan fear of the growth of the Athenian empire, was not openly avowed (23.5-6); further, there were also "causes" (*aitiai*) alleged by either side. The causes that were openly avowed are the accusations or blame each city directs against the other, *aitia* translating either "blame" or "cause." This passage is notoriously difficult, as it is not clear why Thucydides employs the terms "pretext" and "cause" in this way – one's expectation would be that pretexts are those reasons which are openly avowed on either side as a *justification* for waging war; and on the other hand, that there is presumably only one *true* cause of the war, avowed or not. To suggest that there is a hidden pretext that is in fact the cause of the war would seem to imply that pretexts, whatever they may be, could be true, i.e., motivating, for those who claim them, although this may not always be the case.[15] The issue of fear in particular looms large: Fear, as we

15 Consider 5.53 where Thucydides uses *prophasis* in the sense of an openly avowed reason for going to war, thus reinforcing that *aitia* and *prophasis* are not simply opposites. These two terms are, not surprisingly, widely debated. Ostwald (1988) pp. 1-5 provides a brief overview, one which touches on the predominant scholarly views of 1.23.5-6. Adcock (1951) pp. 2-12 offers a fairly balanced analysis of the passage, rejecting the often-made assertion Thucydides inserted the passage due to his changing view of the war's causes. (Adcock does, however, support some speculation of compositional phases in Book One). Andrewes (1959) pp. 224-25 suggests Thucydides is not assigning blame but explaining action. Perhaps he does not blame, but the question of blame cannot be divorced from 1.23.5-6 since the other cities will, so to speak, do nothing but blame each other and respond, in turn, with justifications meant to deflect that blame. And action will not proceed without the moral justification for it. Even the stark "power politics" expressed by the Athenians in the Melian Dialogue deflects blame for wrongdoing. In this vein, Badian (1993) pp. 125-62 argues that "…it is Thucydides' main aim, in his account of the origin and outbreak of the war, to show that it was started by Sparta in a spirit of ruthless *Realpolitik*." Much of this interpretation relies on Badian repeatedly referring to Thucydides' presentation as "disinformation," since it is at odds with Thucydides' own statement at 1.23.5-6 that Sparta was compelled into war due to fear, a fear resulting from Athenian, not Spartan, aggression. Badian, as he admits, seeks to revive the approach of Schwartz (1919), one of the originators of the Separatist thesis (pp. 125-29). This leads to Badian doubting much of Thucydides' account, comparing him to a dishonest journalist. On 1.23.5-6 generally, see also Hornblower I pp. 64-66, though I would note that his scholarly selections do not highlight the best treatments of the passage. Cf. Orwin (1994) Appendix 2 pp. 213-14 and Burns (2010) p. 50 n21 for similar discussions to my own. Strauss (1964) pp. 174-82 details 1.23 and *aitia*, and importantly, does so within a broader treatment of Thucydides' presentation of justice. With a view to Sparta in particular, we should note Kagan's position: He blames Corinth for the war, not Sparta, by minimizing both Thucydides' claim that fear necessitated it, as

have noted, is not openly avowed by the Spartans and certainly not as a necessity exculpating their actions, notably in their key decision officially to declare war – the Spartans never appeal to necessity in doing so. But neither is fear invisible in Thucydides' narrative, in either Book One or throughout. Fear of the Athenians is manifest in Thucydides' remark; other fears will become apparent in his narrative of the cautious and apprehensive Spartans.

The distinction between a true and professed cause is key in understanding the Spartans' role in the outbreak of the war since their eventual decision to wage war is apparently decided based on the arguments of the Spartan ephor, Sthenelaidas, who does not mention fear, but accuses the Athenians of "doing injustice" (86.4 – *adikeō*).[16] The professed causes, then, become as true as the true causes, since without these professed causes or "pretexts" the actions of cities may not be possible. Do the professed causes of war by any city or state, their public statements, not *always* appeal to the (perceived) justice of their cause?[17] There is no doubt that the Spartans blame the Athenians for starting the war, accusing them of breaching the treaty, of an injustice. These considerations clarify the puzzle created by 1.23.6. For Thucydides, the professed cause, that which is made public, appeals to justice and seems to be required for a city to initiate open war

well as the growth of the Athenian empire ([1969] pp. 306-16, 345-46). Kagan reaches this conclusion, in part, by maintaining a false distinction between the "first" and "second" Peloponnesian wars, a distinction Thucydides rejects (5.26). In Kagan's estimation of the war's cause and Sparta, we must also note the following: He fails to appreciate the distinction between Archidamus and Sthenelaidas, and therefore fails to see Archidamus as the outlier in advising against war; treats the Athenian empire as fair and mild, despite Thucydides' evidence to the contrary (e.g., 1.98.4, 99.1-3, along with the objections of the Peloponnesians); maintains that the Spartan vote for Athens' treaty violation is not the same as the vote for war, despite Sthenelaidas clearly advocating for war. Most importantly, Kagan leans on evidence of Spartan slowness to maintain the view that they hesitated to go to war (and thus were not the cause of it), contrary to Thucydides' assertion that war was inevitable. Spartan slowness is not something new, as becomes clear throughout Thucydides' account. This slowness does not mitigate or contradict their fear, but rather is reinforced by it, as we will see Archidamus' speech make evident.

16 This is not to deny, as we will see below, that his speech also appeals, though not as loudly, to the interests of Sparta, particularly their allies. Cf. Orwin (1994) p. 58 with n55. In Sparta, an ephor is an elected official who watches over the laws and the hereditary king. See note 43 below.

17 As Hobbes' "Of the Life and History of Thucydides" in *The Peloponnesian War* p. 582 succinctly states: "For without a pretext, no war follows."

against another. In the first instance, justice means adherence to treaties and agreements between the various cities. Breaching a treaty is an injustice, treaties being legal or quasi-legal agreements binding the participating cities. But here we are also reminded of a broader definition that works for, and against, the Spartans throughout the war: injustice as wrongdoing, as immoral actions, those beyond simply human laws or agreements.

Returning to where the chronology of his account breaks off and considering Thucydides' order of presentation, we notice the following sequence: tyranny, poetic accounts of the past, use of speeches, greatness of Peloponnesian War, catastrophes and other phenomena. This particular order is telling. Immediately after discussing inaccurate knowledge of the past and claiming his work will be a possession for all time, i.e., not simply a chronological account of this war but somehow revealing the truth about human affairs everywhere and always, Thucydides argues for the greatness of the Peloponnesian War and includes a catalogue of earthquakes, eclipses, droughts, famines, and especially the plague (23.3). Notable (and we note) frightening natural disasters are presented by Thucydides together with the causes of the war itself. In this same context, Thucydides discusses the past and, by implication, the wars of the past – his writing of the Peloponnesian War bears comparison; it bears comparison to Homer. But unlike Homer, Thucydides' account does not detail gods intervening in human affairs. Or so it seems anyway. Despite this apparent omission, for Sparta in particular we will notice that the gods are far from absent. Spartan belief in the gods is bound up with decisions they make and plays a decisive role in how they view the war and their participation in it. Thus we can begin to make sense of Thucydides bringing together natural disasters, causes of war, and religion – all could be explained by one cause for the pious Spartans: divine justice.[18] When we consider that Sparta's accusation against Athens occurs

18 I use the term "religion" because it is so pervasive in scholarly and popular discourse today (hence its appearance in the Introduction). My hesitancy in using it, however, is its implications. It is, one may say, a "sociological" or "anthropological" term – studying something from a distance, a bird's eye view, as it were. But for Thucydides, I will argue, human beings' pious beliefs and customs cannot simply be understood from the outside. These beliefs are a key part of human nature and our condition, our psychology; they share or are inextricably bound up with other affections of the human condition, such as chance, hope, desire, fear, and guilt, to name only a few. One example Thucydides presents must suffice here: the pious overtones he associates with the Athenians' Sicilian expedition. Psychological causes of, or motives for, actions, whether recognized or not by oneself or others as "religious," may reveal their

within that context, the suggestion seems to be that we do not know for certain whether these catastrophes are natural, i.e., follow natural, knowable necessity, or whether they are instead sufferings caused by the gods as punishments for acts of injustice.[19]

The question of the cause of the war seemingly cannot be fully answered unless we know whether just gods intervene in human affairs, and thus will punish either Athens or Sparta for starting the war. This suggestion is strengthened if we consider Thucydides' later account of Corcyra's civil war. There, civil war is not only materially and psychically destructive; it is presented as undermining piety and divine law, human nature rebelling against all laws (3.82.5-83.3). In the Archaeology, it is Sparta that was said to have good laws, and later, a prosperous and moderate regime.[20] But if Sparta was compelled by Athens to start the war, then Athens would be the one responsible and thus incur blame, and possibly punishment by the gods, gods that support the oaths of solemnly sworn treaties and punish their breach.[21] Piety looms large in Thucydides' account because it looms

pious character, taking the term pious in a broad sense. This line of inquiry with be pursued in detail as it unfolds as a theme in the text itself.

19 Furley (2006) p. 422-23 argues that Thucydides "emphasizes the great disasters that happened with unprecedented frequency and intensity during the war, but their relevance in context is more to the increased suffering they caused to the affected populations than their significance as tokens of 'cosmic' disorder." This interpretation does not address the fact (and deeper significance) that Thucydides places these occurrences immediately before stating in his own name the cause of the war. Gomme (1945) Vol. I p. 151 argues that Thucydides (presumably as a follower of Anaxagoras) could not believe these phenomena portended anything disastrous; however, he does note Thucydides "may therefore mean here only that popular opinion put all these things together as inevitable accompaniments of a human disaster." Cf. Strauss (1964) p. 151 who argues that eclipses are not disasters but may seem to signal a disaster. Strauss' remark occurs in the context of his discussion of Sparta, in particular Spartan piety and divine law. In this, Strauss follows Thucydides. In other words, Thucydides is less certain than modern scholars that suffering and one's view of the cosmos (and its possible intentions) are unrelated. Even for the Athenians, such disasters are psychologically relevant (2.54.1-5). Relatedly, see Kallet (2013).

20 Allison (1989) pp. 11-27 views the Archaeology through Thucydides' use of the terms "power" (*paraskeue*) and "preparedness" (*paraskeuazein*). And while the Archaeology presents naval power and capital as key elements of this preparedness, Allison argues it is an error to underestimate the importance Thucydides places on Sparta's political stability.

21 Orwin (1994) p. 58 notes: "Like all treaties, this one rested on the most solemn oaths: the very word for treaty (*spondai*) refers to these oaths." So too Hornblower I p. 195.

large for the Spartans, even if we do not hear the gods speak or see them personified as they are in Homer.[22]

Finally, in detailing Thucydides' order of presentation in the first portion of Book One, we need to ask: What are we to make of his claim that most do not accurately understand the past, along with his use of an Athenian tyrant to illustrate this misunderstanding? What is the significance of this tyranny, particularly as it pertains to stories of the past? Thucydides in fact offers two versions of this story. In the second, as a correction or supplement to the story we are considering here, he argues the tyranny (led by Hippias, not his brother Hipparchus – 1.20.2) was in fact not harsh, but moderate and gentle, protecting Athens' existing laws and practicing the traditional religious customs (6.54.5-7). This second version is told in the midst of Thucydides' narrative of the Sicilian expedition in Book Six, an expedition that was morally questionable from the point of view of the

22 Hornblower I pp. 62-63 objects to 1.23.2-3 because Thucydides mentions natural disasters but then (save for the plague) does not make them a centerpiece of his narrative; instead they occur "rarely, sporadically, and [are] very briefly recorded." Hornblower continues: "One might be tempted to insist that the present passage is not overtly irrational or superstitious, because Th.[ucydides] alleges no explicit causal connection (he does not say, like [Herodotus]...'this showed that the gods were angry'), but merely records, as a matter of fact, even of coincidence...that the 27 years of his narrative were unusually rich in such calamities. Certainly, we are expected to remember that in the austerely human pages which follow. But this will not quite do. The better view is that [Thucydides'] attitude is not wholly consistent." By "irrational" Hornblower seems to mean Thucydides is bringing together events in his narrative that, apparently, warrant no connection (be they earthquakes and plagues or such events as they relate to the war). The issue here is whether Thucydides is "rhetorical rather than 'scientific,'" Hornblower critiquing Woodman (1998) who argues he is the former. Yet Hornblower in a sense seeks an uninhabitable middle ground: He feels the need to place quotation marks around the term scientific and yet agrees with Woodman, in so far as Thucydides is a writer who can provide readers with moving descriptions and flourishes, including what we find at 1.23. It seems rather clear that Thucydides intends his narrative to make certain impressions on his reader at certain times, emotional impressions, and has manipulated his narrative to this end, both in Book One, and throughout. No one argues, however, that Thucydides wholly invented the events nor even the speeches he presents. Can a writer not present a historical event with the intention of drawing out what he believes is of lasting relevance to future generations from that very event? This, it seems to me, is what Thucydides, in very forthcoming fashion, has told us is his approach and its aim (1.22).

pious Athenian general, Nicias (among others).[23] This expedition sought to expand the Athenian empire all the way to Sicily, at a time when domestic issues (and the Peloponnesian War) were much more pressing concerns. In other words, the question of the possibility of an Athenian empire that rules Greece moderately is implicitly raised, for Pericles himself later admits that the Athenian empire is "so to speak" a tyranny (2.63.2). While the juxtaposition is not precise since the moderate tyranny of Hippias was "domestic" and that of Athens "foreign," I believe Thucydides intends for the reader to wonder whether the Athenians could rule their empire moderately, and even more striking, if this empire does not violate piety as practiced by the Athenians themselves. And further, whether Athens' imperial expansion did not cause severe harm to their own domestic situation, to maintaining a peaceful, law-abiding city. After all, as we learn at the beginning of the Archaeology, the Spartans were only able to live peacefully after suppressing various tyrannies across Greece (1.18.1). By contrast, the Athenian empire will quickly come under attack by Sparta and its allies as a form of tyranny, imposing itself on other cities wishing to live free. In other words, why do the pious Spartans and the enterprising Athenians differ in their customs, characteristics, and civic life? And who is in fact to blame for the war? Thucydides' statement at 1.23 appears as a statement of fact; but understanding the causes of the "truest pretext" and attending implications means understanding more about the nature of fear and power, justice and blame.

Understanding the past, good government, war, "natural phenomena," and most importantly, what human beings believe about these matters (expressed in their speeches) are bound up in understanding the totality of "the human condition" (22.4). Yet since we human beings misunderstand even the facts about the past, to say nothing of what the past means for us, Thucydides knows he will need to be our guide. And revealing to us the truths of the Peloponnesian War requires going beyond the shortcomings of his predecessors, both "the poets" (*poiētai*) and "the chroniclers" (*logographoi* – 21.1). It requires understanding not simply the obvious growth of Athens, but Sparta's moral response, their blame of Athenian imperialism as a presumably unnecessary interruption of Greek peace. Suffice it to say that the cause of the war appears both obvious, Spartan fear resulting

23 The bearing of this story on Thucydides' understanding of domestic politics will be discussed further in Chapter Three.

from Athenian imperialism, and mired in confusion arising from numerous complications we must consider: third party pressures, alliances made, hatreds renewed, treaties violated, and skirmishes among the several other cities.

Justice and Necessity: Dual Motives Leading to War

Growth of the Athenian empire culminates in precisely such skirmishes: the episodes at Epidamnus and Potidaea place Athens in direct conflict with Corinth, and eventually, Sparta. While Epidamnus was a colony of Corcyra, Corinth was its mother country. When factions arose within Epidamnus and barbarians took advantage of these factions by siding with the people and expelling the rulers, the latter sent for aid from Corcyra. With Corcyra refusing to intervene, they appealed now to the god at Delphi about whether they should involve the Corinthians, the god advising them to do so. The Corinthians agree to offer assistance out of duty *and* hatred for Corcyra, as they believed the Corcyraeans had not honored them as a colony should. In repeating Corinth's reasons for assistance, however, Thucydides drops any mention of a sense of duty on the Corinthians' part (1.26.1; cf. 25.3). The Corcyraeans realize the Corinthians have increased their navy and added allies to their side, while the Corinthians fear the Athenians will ally themselves with the Corcyraeans, bringing together the two largest navies in Greece against them. Following an attempt to place Epidamnus' rulers back at the head of the city, the Corcyraeans offer the Corinthians the chance to leave or to send the dispute to arbitration, including referring the matter to the god at Delphi. As neither side is willing to withdraw, arbitration is not accepted, and Thucydides seems to attribute the aggression to the Corinthians (29.1).

After the skirmishes between Corcyra and Corinth, each send envoys to argue before the Athenians, the Corcyraeans seeking an alliance and the Corinthians trying to prevent it (31.1-3). Being the first in Thucydides, these speeches are particularly significant; we now observe the need to incorporate speeches into actions, and overall narrative. Indeed, the two speeches allow us further insight into Thucydides' art of writing – they require evaluation not only as to their content, but also what Thucydides himself may be intimating through the manner in which they are crafted. We recall both his adherence to accuracy, along with the license he allowed himself (22.1).

The Corcyraean speech begins with the word "justice" (*dikaion* – 32.1). Our expectation would be that this opening term is Thucydides' signal regarding its theme; yet this is only true in a qualified sense. The Corcyraeans appeal to justice in addressing the Athenians because they have not been involved in any of the Hellenic alliances, Spartan or Athenian, and thus they must now present (as they admit) a case for Athens' support when they have offered no previous service which could expect to be reciprocated. But as their speech unfolds, they speak less of justice, with advantage or interest instead becoming more prevalent (33.2-3, 35.5-36.2). This is particularly noteworthy in light of their accurate assessment of the Spartans and the relation between Sparta and Athens – they echo Thucydides' statement that the war between Athens and Sparta is inevitable, and this is due to Spartan fear of the Athenians (23.6, 33.3); they have their finger on the pulse of where each city finds itself and what each wants. They still assure the Athenians granting them an alliance is not in breach of the treaty; the Athenians are not committing any injustice. But Corcyra, they remind the Athenians, is also conveniently located on the passageway to Sicily and Italy. Although beginning their speech appealing to possible blame for their past actions (or inactions) involving any alliance, and thus to the Athenians' sense of justice, their concluding summary fails to mention justice at all (36.3). And when we contrast their remarks to Thucydides' own comments on the Athenians' decision, the Corcyraeans demonstrate an understanding of the Athenians' true motives – they did not want to risk breaching the terms of their treaty in allying themselves with other cities, although they were aware of the inevitability of the war with Sparta *and*, apparently even at this early stage, thoughts of Sicily and Italy were guiding their strategic decisions (44.3).[24]

24 Connor (1984) p. 35 provides archaeological evidence, as well as analysis of the phraseology used here, to argue that westward expansion by Athens was in fact in the cards. Hornblower I p. 88 complains that Thucydides' imputations of motives "goes a long way beyond what Th.[ucydides] could have known." Bruell (1974) p. 12, on the other hand, implies that given the expansion of the Athenian empire over the previous fifty years, those who were enemies of Athens may have had their opinions on designs for Sicily even before the war broke out. I would add that it may have been the worst kept secret in Greece. After all, Pericles' warning not to expand their empire further during the war, as reported by Thucydides (2.65.7), makes little sense were Sicily (or other possible conquests) not a temptation he was aware of and hoped

Similar to the Corcyraean speech, Thucydides signals his overarching themes: the Corinthian speech begins with the word "necessity" (*anankē*). But the Corinthians' argument relies on moral language – it abounds with references to justice and injustice, honor and nobility, implying or believing these considerations should guide the Athenians' decision. The Corinthians argue, in particular, that the Corcyraeans are unjustly involved at Epidamnus. Besides, Corinth served Athens as an ally during the Persian invasion, and therefore deserves Athenian repayment now for aiding Athens in the past. Most importantly, though, is their claim (one counter to their own understanding of Athenian character stated later in Book One) that the Athenians will be sacrificing "secure power" only for an uncertain and temporary advantage if they should ally themselves with Corcyra (42.3), implying the Athenians are both currently inactive and seeking quiet or peace. They also imply that the war is not inevitable, with the exception, of course, that they bid Athens to ally with them, and failing this, Athens will become Corinth's enemy (40.3). And once the conference of Spartan allies comes together at Sparta to urge them into action, of all the accusers of Athens, the Corinthians are the ones Thucydides allows us to hear – they become the main accusers, not surprisingly in part due to these early skirmishes over Epidamnus and the Athenian defensive alliance with Corcyra.

The Athenians ultimately side with the Corcyraeans, but only after two assemblies were held. Initially disposed to Corinth, they changed their decision only upon reconsideration. Their initial disposition was thus on the side of justice, the thrust of the Corinthians' argument; but after the second assembly, their decision shifted to one based on interest or advantage. While they were concerned with a breach of the treaty (45.3), they decided this alliance would not be a breach, so long, it seems, as they acted within certain conditions. It was to be a defensive alliance only, to which Athens was not bound. Besides, Corinth and Corcyra were two powerful navies in Greece, and with Athens' naval supremacy, the Athenians were not unaware of the advantage of allowing these two cities to fight amongst one another, if a war that involved all of them was possible (44.2).

This defensive alliance, we note, will not avoid the charge of injustice even if it avoids a breach of the treaty. Legality and justice (or morality) are not simply synonymous. Even if we, as hardened realists, agree treaties are

the Athenians would avoid. Thucydides understood Athenian (and human) motives, whether he had the "evidence" required by modern scholars or not.

nothing but conventions, and justice therefore is not operative between cities, political actors act as though it is. And do we not expect, somehow, some way, that justice or something akin to it *should* be operative for political actors, as individuals of course, but even as cities, or for us, as states?

Returning to the narrative: Each city appeals to justice or necessity in their speeches to the Athenians, and while the Athenians weigh Corinth's moral claims, Thucydides in his own voice indicates the reason for their decision, including reference to Sicily and Italy (44.1-3). This reference is obvious when one places it alongside the later Sicilian expedition; but even upon an initial reading one notes Thucydides' narrative confirming Sparta's fears of further Athenian expansion. Corcyra with Athenian assistance will stave off the Corinthians' attack, and Thucydides concludes this dispute noting it would be the "first cause" (*aitia*) Corinth had against Athens – during the time of the treaty, the Athenians fought against them (55.2).[25] It is nevertheless unclear whether Athens sided with Corcyra strictly or even primarily for reasons of interest. After all, they were concerned *both* with avoiding a breach of the treaty and with Sicily. In fact, even the Sicilian expedition will be an Athenian action questionable in serving the purpose of preserving their empire and winning the war. It may, however, be in keeping with their desire for honor and nobility (cf. 6.24.3, 31.6).

Athens' defensive alliance appears, then, as an example of the compromise states often seek; it is the compromise we human beings often seek – what is better than believing you are doing the right thing *and* being benefited? This is one of many cases where Thucydides presents what I will call "dual motives," instances where cities are torn even when advantageous policy seems to present an obvious choice. The Athenians try to find not a middle ground or compromise between interest and justice, but a perfect *union* of the two. Thucydides foreshadows the difficult balance cities seek to strike between justice and necessity, a concern even for the Athenians, even for those who claim to be hard-nosed "realists" and are labeled by scholars as such.[26]

---

25 Scholars have noticed Corinth plays a vital role in the outbreak of the war, even if it takes Sparta to declare it. See Allison (2013) pp. 261-64 for this observation and further details.

26 Gomme I p. 177 on 1.44.1: "The Athenians were at least anxious not to be technically the aggressors in a general war, even if their conduct as a whole was provocative." Finley (1942) p. 115 ignores the Athenians' change of heart after their initial siding with the treaty obligations.

Notable in spurring the Spartans to action, doing nothing to alleviate, and much to heighten Spartan fear, it is worth noting in this dispute the character of the Corinthians themselves. Corinth is the city Thucydides most clearly presents acting for their own private interests, despite repeatedly lodging grievances against other cities cast in the language of justice. Interestingly, though, the Corinthian complaint of Athens' possible alliance with Corcyra (in disregard for Corinth's support of Athens during the Persian War) is a particular accusation of injustice, i.e., an expression of ingratitude. This ingratitude, rather than a legal breach of the treaty, seems to be the true but hidden cause behind Corinth's supposed concern with the treaty. After all, they declare war even after offers of an armistice from Corcyra (29.1); thus, while Thucydides never allows us to believe Corinth is genuinely concerned with justice,[27] their offense at Athenian ingratitude is nevertheless moral in a deeper way – while at first blush self-serving, the Corinthians still cannot help taking offense; they betray their moral impulses. Animated by hatred, their actions against Athens are rooted in private interests, yet fueled by this passion, rather than furthering interests shared by Sparta and their own Peloponnesian allies. Attempting to be shrewd calculators, they play other cities off one another based on their insight into the characters of each city, most notably in their manipulation of the Spartans through an appeal to oaths, and thus Spartan piety. Corinth also continually gives advice to other cities on what should be done (to Sparta in particular) and then itself does nothing (5.25). A nasty incident of this involves (again) playing off Spartan piety (5.30).[28] Indeed, Corinth is always stirring the pot among the Peloponnesian allies, but then leaves the leader of that alliance, Sparta, to respond.

From the early actions and the first speeches, Thucydides signals to the reader themes animating his account of the war. But for Thucydides, these are not simply leitmotifs of his tale; rather, it represents how to articulate and understand the political options available, given pressures acting upon us. Thucydides is interested in both the push of moral exhortations and the pull of self-interest; it is in this that he begins with the Sparta-Athens, justice-interest dichotomies.

27 Consider 1.66, 103.4, 119, 5.25.1, 27.2, 30.1-4, 115.3.

28 This will be discussed in detail in Chapter Three, where I focus on Book Five.

The Athenian Empire: Complaints and A Justification

The Athenians were aware of the hatred they had incurred from Corinth as the result of aiding the Corcyraeans. This conflict over, its repercussions only continue. The city of Potidaea was a Corinthian colony but paying tribute to, and thus being allies of, Athens. The Athenians now make demands that the city sever all relations with Corinth, worried the Corinthians would attempt a revolt there as revenge for the skirmishes at Corcyra (which indeed they did – 1.56.1-6). Yet the Athenians knew that the actions in Potidaea would renew Sparta's involvement in Athenian movements. Sure enough, Potidaean and Corinthian envoys arrive in Sparta to seek their assistance and Sparta promises to invade Attica if Athens attacks Potidaea (58.1). While the Spartans are allied with the Potidaeans, Corinthians, as well as Perdiccas of Macedonia, Thucydides alludes to the possibility that they did not *directly* involve themselves in any actions (65.1). The Peloponnesian War is still at arm's length. Nevertheless, this episode leads to the conference at Sparta and to "causes" or "accusations" (*aitiai*) by both sides – each believed they had a right to Potidaea, Corinth as their colony, and Athens since the Corinthians had initiated a revolt of a tribute paying ally.

Despite these accusations, and the movements of the cities involved, Thucydides refrains from calling this the outbreak of the war; the action of Corinth was a "private" one (*idios* – 66). This claim immediately precedes the four speeches that take place at Sparta, speeches which result in a vote for war on the part of Sparta and its allies. In other words, these hostilities must be weighed against Thucydides' statement on the cause of war and the distinction between pretexts and causes. For while the narrative presents the involvement of Corinth and Athens at Corcyra and Potidaea, respectively, as candidates for the war's causes, this is clearly at odds with Thucydides claiming Spartan fear is the truest pretext. The most obvious question, therefore, is whether the Corinthians were correct in claiming Athens breached the treaty with their involvement in Corcyra, and later, in Potidaea. The truth of the Corinthian claim is obviously a partial one and we need to hear the speeches of each side on their understanding of the treaty and what precisely constitutes its breach. And even if the treaty had not been breached by Athens, as their envoys at Sparta will contend, this does not stop Corinth from *claiming* as much; and later, the Spartan ephor, Sthenelaidas, securing the Spartan vote for war also by claiming the

Athenians *in fact* did.[29] Before we hear any defense of their empire, Thucydides indicates that the Athenians were anxious not to breach the treaty and this explains their willingness to enter only a defensive alliance with the Corcyraeans (1.44.1).

Clearly, Thucydides presents motives, and thus political psychology, as difficult to untangle. In the speeches of the Corcyraeans and Corinthians, justice and necessity are first presented at odds with one another, as competing motivations or justifications for action, and, we must add, as motives the cities themselves introduce, abandon, and return to, sometimes intentionally and sometimes not.[30] The truest pretext for the war was Spartan fear of the growth of the Athenian empire, which necessitated (*anankē*) the war. The war was the result of a necessity; it was inevitable. Since the Athenian empire grew and was still growing, the Spartans at some point had to engage it to preserve their city. Yet the speeches at Sparta will hide this from our view – Corinth and its allies, Sparta included, will argue Athens has committed an injustice by holding an empire, while the Athenians will counter these claims by arguing they were compelled to found an empire and hold it (nor should their empire, which they present as moderate, even just, be an offense). It is through this debate at Sparta that competing explanations of the war are further defined.

The Corinthians summon their Peloponnesian allies to Sparta to put forward two accusations against Athens: Athens was in breach of the treaty and was committing "injustice against the Peloponnesus" (*adikoiev tēn Peloponnēson* – 67.1).[31] Before we even hear the Corinthians speak, the truest pretext for the war as Thucydides understands it appears to differ from the claims of those seeking to stop Athenian actions. These immediate complaints, however, only mask the Corinthians' overarching one – their speech, despite its accusations aimed at the Athenians, is in fact directed

29 Thus Romilly (1963) p. 21 is incorrect in downplaying the incident at Potidaea as "little more than a pretext for action" since even if Corinth does not truly believe Athens breached the treaty, there is no vote for war without this or a similar incident. Sparta will refuse to go to war without a pretext. Cf. Cogan (1981) pp. 137-38, Ostwald (1988) pp. 27, 35, Orwin (1994) p. 36, Jaffe (2017) pp. 56-58.

30 This is not to deny that those cities that appeal to interest, particularly Athens, may still display a concern with justice, whether they are aware of it or not.

31 Hornblower I pp. 107-8 remarks on the uniqueness of this debate since four speeches are presented, rather than one or two: Corinth, Athens, Sparta (Archidamus), and, again, Sparta (Sthenelaidas).

primarily against *the Spartans*. It is the former's inaction to halt the Athenian empire's march that is to "blame" (*aitia*) for this imperial growth. And the Corinthians again, apt to stir things up, go further. This inaction is due to a larger problem, the "character" (*tropos*) of the Spartans themselves – they keep what they have, lack innovation, do not use their power, are unwilling to leave home due to fear, distrust their own judgment, believe they are always in danger, and are slow to act, while the Athenians are very much the opposite of these (70.1-9). The Athenian empire has grown precisely as a result of these clashing characters. Thucydides' account of the Spartans after the defeat of Persia confirms this, Sparta allowing Athens to carry on the Persian War while they themselves withdrew (95.7). This withdrawal was motivated by Spartan disinterest in continuing the war; but it was also due to the actions of Pausanias, a commander who finds himself at odds with his city as a result of his un-Spartan actions, as well as causing the increasingly tense relations between Sparta and Athens. Yet the Corinthians, despite this history, will attempt to convince the Spartans to act contrary to what they themselves identify as their character.

The Corinthians' speech alludes to a particular attribute of the Spartan character – its first word is "trust" (*pistos*). The Spartans trust in their regime (*politeia*) yet are distrustful of others. The Corinthians contend that this trust in their regime is the source of their "moderation" (*sōphrosynē*). The character of the Spartans from the Archaeology also suggests this – Sparta was moderate due to its good laws and gained its supremacy from its regime. Spartans stayed at home, as it were, and controlled the Peloponnesus, while Athens patrolled the sea. But the Corinthians argue this moderation, presented by Thucydides as a quality of their city foundational to its stability, is also a source of Spartan ignorance and weakness in dealing with others. The Athenians, by contrast, have minds that are their own, but used on behalf of the city (68.1, 70.6). It is necessary, the Corinthians contend, for the Spartans to improve and innovate; but the Corinthians seem unaware that a Spartan regime which cultivates moderation is unable to innovate. Guided instead by adherence to "custom" (*nomos* – 71.3), an adherence the Athenians lack, Spartan ways or manners, their character, are determined by the laws of their city.[32] Thus, the Corinthians blame not

32 Note especially the Melian Dialogue and the Athenian assessment of the Spartans (5.105.4): "They hold" (*nomizō*) is a verb related to *nomos*, i.e., what they hold or believe is according to law or custom (Liddell- Scott [1889] p. 534), while a short

simply the actions of the Spartans, but Spartan character as it pertains to their being good allies in guarding against Athenian encroachments (71.5-6); they must become more "Athenian" for the sake of being good allies and becoming the liberators of Greece from the Athenian empire.[33]

The Athenian envoys, though, will respond by urging the Spartans to remain as they are in every way. Thucydides' introductory remark to the envoys' speech indicates they wanted to show the Spartans that the question of waging war should not be decided quickly, and the Spartans should prefer peace to war, this latter objective being achieved, they hope, through an account of the power (*dynamis*) of their city (72.1). Their intention is only to keep Sparta at rest, by making the prospect of war frightening. Yet they cannot avoid, or seem unable to resist, answering the accusations against them, i.e., the question of justice. And the envoys do in fact offer a justification of empire; this justification frames their speech.[34] Perhaps feeling the sting of the accusation that their empire is harsh and unjustified, they end up going beyond the original intention for their speech.[35]

---

while later the Athenians accuse the Melians of "showing much irrational thought" (*pollen te alogian tēs dianoias parekhete* – 5.111.2) – the Athenian understanding of what is honorable and just originates not with their laws or customs, but with their free thought. This agrees with the Corinthians' claim that the Athenians' bodies belong to the city, but their minds are most their own (1.70.6). This is borne out in the speech by the Athenian envoys immediately following it – they come forward on their own accord and offer an account of the Athenian empire. That Thucydides leaves these speakers anonymous only reinforces the impressiveness of their defense of Athens. Whether the Athenian assessment of the Spartans (and the Melians) is correct will be considered in our analysis of the Melian Dialogue in Chapter Four.

33 It should also be noted that the Corinthians were perhaps secretly hoping for the defeat of Athens and the hegemony of Greece being overtaken by their ally, Sparta. The Corinthians could not openly state this is what they hoped for, while liberation of Greece is a publicly defensible claim for siding with Sparta.

34 Raubitschek (1973) p. 36: "The first and main theme of the speech of the Athenians is the Justification of Empire: 'we do not hold what we possess unreasonably (*apeikotôs*)' they say at the beginning (1.73.1) and 'we are worthy (*axioi*) of the empire we hold' they say at the conclusion of their account of their achievements during the Persian Wars (1.75.1)." Stahl (2003) pp. 42-49 rejects the view that the Athenians are offering a justification of empire; he does so to counter the view that Thucydides himself is using the speech to justify Athenian imperialism. As we have noted previously, Thucydides' speakers, individually, do not represent his own views. Nevertheless, Stahl downplays both the Athenians' critique of Sparta post-Persian War, along with their claim to rule justly, key points in excusing their empire.

35 Ste. Croix (1954) p. 3 believes the Athenian empire was not harsh, despite Thucydides portraying it (in speech and narrative) as such and that Thucydides' "own detailed

In addressing their empire directly, the envoys offer an account of Athens' past, culminating in their claim that Sparta's failure to aid in finishing the war against Persia led Athens' current allies to voluntarily join them. And as we have seen, Thucydides' account in the fifty years leading up to the Peloponnesian War agrees with this. The Athenians argue, therefore, that "not unfairly" do they hold their empire; in fact, they placed themselves in danger. The Athenians were both daring and vigorous, despite acting alone, in their war with the Persians. Owning to such risks, along with Sparta's withdrawal and the voluntary alliance of Greek cities, the Athenians ask how it is that they deserve the hatred their empire has now brought upon them. For it was from this episode of the Persian War, and under these circumstances, that the Athenian empire was formed (75.1-2). The Athenian envoys argue they were *compelled* to acquire their empire "first by fear, and then by honor and interest" (75.3). What began as fear of the Persians initiated the Athenian empire; but as they ascended to hegemon, they were further compelled by fear once they began to realize the suspicion and hatred resulting from their imperial actions. Now, according to the Athenians, to act out of fear including securing one's interests, is unobjectionable. And the compelling motive of fear did not end with their ascent to holding an empire as opposed to mere supremacy among the cities – in Thucydides' account of the fifty years leading up to the Peloponnesian War, the Athenians are still engaged with the Persians *after* Thucydides allows us to observe the shift from supremacy to empire (100).

Yet it is apparent that the motivations for Athenian imperialism do not end here and, despite the Persian threat, their compulsion to pursue empire is not apparent. While fear (*deos*) was their *initial* motive in acquiring empire, they admit honor (*timē*) and interest (*ōpheleia*) were not absent (75.3). This admission hints at the Athenians' mixed motives. It was the shift from an accepted supremacy to the founding of an empire which led their allies (as allies) to begin to fear and hate them, realizing alliance had become subjugation. In fact, it is in the beginning of the Pentecontaetia that Thucydides relates the Athenian response to the revolt of the small

narrative proves that it is certainly false." The difference between Thucydides' initial summary of the speech, and what the Athenians actually say, has caused much consternation among scholars, especially the Separatists (see Raubitschek [1973] and Stahl [2003] for these discussions). Cf. Palmer (1992) p. 53: "The disparity is, in fact, only an apparent one." Justification of their empire is bound up with the power required for them to attain it.

island of Naxos: "This was the first allied city to be enslaved, in contravention of established practice" (98.4).[36] And therefore we must consider what it means, for their understanding and justification of empire, that *other* motives contribute to this shift from alliance to subjugation. When the envoys repeat the three motivations for empire, they (which is to say Thucydides) do not present them in the same order – "fear, honor, and interest" is replaced by "honor, fear, and interest" (75.3, 76.2). While fear led Athens to ascend to the position of hegemon of allied Greek cities, honor and interest motivated them in holding an empire over these cities and continuing to expand it. That fear became less compelling or less their true motivation is further revealed when the Athenians also claim their empire could be crueler and harsher on its subject cities than it is. Even interest takes second place to honor: On their own view, the Athenian empire does not simply serve Athenian interests because it practices a gentleness that refrains from exercising its true strength. All cities are compelled to expand; only one "superior to human nature" could refuse an empire (76.3), or more generally, no city allows justice to restrict their rule. This, taken together with the motives for empire, is what we have referred to as the "Athenian thesis."[37]

36 While there is scholarly debate over the meaning of Thucydides' language here, all of whom soften this remark (see Gomme I p. 282, Hornblower I pp. 150-52, along with Mynott's [2013] notes to 1.98.4, whose translation is used here), it seems clear that the Athenian empire's rise and expansion was not simply business as usual for the rest of the Greeks. Not surprisingly, then, Thucydides does not minimize the reaction of those cities subject to it.

37 On the Athenian thesis, see the Introduction note 13. The Athenians are the first to use the term "human nature" (*anthrōpeia physis*); this is immediately preceded by their mention of "the way of human beings" (76.2 – *tou anthropeiou tropou*). The movement seems to be from the particular to the universal, from observing regularity in human actions to seeking to understand what this indicates about our "nature." By contrast, it was the Corinthians' speech that first identified what we today would call "culture" – Spartans and Athenians are different cities, different peoples who are animated by different characters and ways of life. But the Athenians take this further, finding their basis for justice, not in laws (as the Spartans do), but through an account of human nature. Thucydides is interested in "the human thing" (or "condition" – *to anthrōpinon*). See Cogan (1981) pp. 185-96 for these terms, along with Hornblower I pp. 61 and 121 (discussed in the next note). I disagree, though, with Cogan's assertion that Hobbes and Thucydides "...share an almost identical view of the nature of mankind, of its motives, of the origin of those motives and of the usual result when this nature is allowed a free rein to operate." Cogan takes "this nature" to be one of selfishness and cruelty "attributable to appetite" (186). In the famous civil war at Corcyra (which is the context for Cogan's remark) we find instead, as I will discuss in Chapter Three, the *moral* nature of human beings. In other words, the

The Athenian empire, far from deserving of blame, is "worthy" (*axios*) of praise, worthy because, while clearly holding an empire, it is more "just" (*dikē*) than it has to be and "measured" (*metrion*) in its conduct (76.2-4). Is Athenian restraint in administering their empire not synonymous with justice? Is their measured conduct what Thucydides means when identifying Sparta as moderate?[38]

The Athenian envoys claim *both* that the empire does not simply serve their interests, since to act justly or honorably is a restraint on these interests, *and* that it is impossible for any city *not* to serve its interests. The Athenian envoys are attempting to preserve the possibility that they deserve honor for their empire given its noble or just character, while also openly stating that Athens cannot be accused of injustice since it simply acts as all cities act (given the requisite power). For if their admission is correct, that all cities are compelled to act in accordance with what is beneficial to them, rather than the Spartan compulsion of fear, "what under certain circumstances might be allowed to fear, could not without the gravest consequences be granted to the desire for honor and profit."[39] If honor and interest are

motives located by Hobbes and Thucydides differ, and thus their views of politics and government which follows also differ. Compare Forde (1992) and Johnson Bagby (1993) for further elaboration of these differences. For our purposes, there are many instances beyond simply Corcyra, notably those involving Sparta, that are instructive for dismantling this Hobbesian view of human nature.

38 Hornblower I p. 121 cautions, correctly I believe, against assuming Thucydides establishes a "law" of the stronger here (and contra Gomme [Andrewes] IV pp. 174-75). The term *nomos* is absent, and while it does appear at 5.105, it is not "law" in a strict sense – Hornblower goes on to note that *nomos* can be taken as either "law" or "convention/custom." Gomme I p. 236 calls this statement at 1.76 the "first frank expression of selfish imperialism." The term "selfish," I believe, is especially problematic in characterizing what I take to be the envoys' justification. Selfish has the moral overtone implying one can, and should, act selflessly. Gomme, in other words, opens up a can of worms with his remark, but does not provide further articulation of the very complex issue it raises: justice versus interest, but also moral imperatives (or lack thereof). For the Athenian envoys, to act "selfishly" is at the heart of what it means to be political and human, what is to be both expected and excused in human actions. Cf. Orwin (1986) p. 81 who speaks instead of "the selfish strong to the selfish weak" reminding us that all cities seek their own self-interest.

39 Bruell (1974) p. 13. Orwin (1986) p. 78 discusses the three "compulsions" noting: "[The Athenians] seek to narrow the realm within which it is proper to hold them to account for justice. To be praised are those who exercise their unjust rule as justly as possible; to refrain from exercising it is not possible." Cf. Romilly (1963) p. 251-54 who, despite the claim of the Athenians, argues that honor is a more exculpatory motive than fear.

regarded as exculpatory, then all actions cities take against one other would be as equally justifiable as fear. Self-aggrandizement and self-defense would be indistinguishable. Yet the Athenians imply that honor is not a compulsion; they admit they *could* have been harsher than they have been (as were the Persians, for example – 77.5). In fact, their subjects should be "grateful" (*charis*) toward them for this mild, uncompelled, treatment (77.3).[40] The Athenians were compelled by fear initially, but it was especially the honor attending empire that they sought; they *chose* to pursue honor, where a city merely acting to secure its safety would not. Athens' willingness to engage in such risks is indicative of the character of the city Sparta and its allies will face should they vote for war (73.3). Recognizing the risks involved and subjecting themselves to these risks, they are thus worthy of the empire they have attained (75.5, 76.2). For the Athenians could not expect to receive this praise if they were simply compelled to act as all cities do; all cities merely set aside justice to pursue their interests when their strength allows them to do so. The Athenians, however, strive beyond this. To strive for honor is to act beyond the necessities cities must face merely to preserve themselves.

The Athenian envoys, without being aware of it, hold *both* that cities are compelled by interests that can never be set aside for the sake of justice, and that they themselves freely chose to pursue empire for the honor that attends it. What is more, if all cities act based on fear, honor, and interest, then all of these motives would be excusable, even when issuing in imperialism; at various times, a city would act, or believe it was acting, on these bases. But the Athenian position is, for them, a comfortable bringing together of justice and necessity. Recognizing political necessity, they do what they need to do to thrive amongst other cities doing what they need to do; yet the Athenians do not quite do what all cities do, that is rule others harshly (as they will accuse the Spartans of), instead restraining themselves in the exercise of their dominion. Why human beings find it honorable to apparently abandon necessity for the sake of considering the interests of others is something of a mystery. It is not, as we will see, a justification acceptable to the other cities, something the Athenians fail to appreciate.

40 Romilly (1963) p. 249 argues that the Athenians are worthy of hegemony due to a consensus that they should rule (after the Persian War). Romilly does not add, however, that this consensus was short-lived, and most cities found the empire harsh once the Athenians forced them to comply with their conditions. See 1.98.4-99.1-2 where Thucydides makes clear the *shift* in acceptance of Athenian hegemony, along with its harsh character. See Hornblower I p. 118 who highlights the reference to Persia.

Indeed, in light of the Athenians' claims, this first iteration of their thesis, the hatred and blame being directed against them (of which they themselves are keenly aware) is not sufficiently accounted for in their justification for empire. The envoys' tone is one of frustration or almost disbelief at this hatred; instead, they betray a belief in their worthiness to rule, an expectation of honor for ruling. But one's worth could only be determined by past actions and the rewards or punishments that attend such actions. The Athenians thereby betray moral motivations, a concern with justice, fairness, what is due to them, despite their claim no city restrains pursuing their interests from justice. The honor and nobility they seek from foregoing simple considerations of fear or profit is precisely why fear or profit are not honorable. Fear is not blamed since it is a compulsion; advantage is blamed because it is a harm to others (even though all cities seek their advantage, however understood). But seeking the glory of empire (2.64.6) is not this kind of compulsion. When considered from the point of view of Athens' subjects, we are thus no longer surprised at the hatred. For since the Athenians admit to freely choosing to pursue empire, encroachment on the autonomy of the other cities will undoubtedly be viewed as unjust. Could the Athenians not have been even gentler? Do their subject cities view their conduct as just or measured *at all*? Are other cities to simply accept that *their* interests are the cost of Athens' desire for glory?

Accusations of injustice by Corinth and the other Spartan allies rest on the assumption Athens could have acted otherwise. The argument for justice, considered broadly, presupposes that the motivations put forward by the envoys are not compelling in all cases or simply not at all. To act according to justice, according to specific laws or conditions limiting or restricting one's self-interest (in this case the treaty), presumes that one is not compelled to act in *any* particular manner – compulsion or necessity is in tension with justice. The tension between the Corinthians' complaint, and the Athenians' justification, disagrees as to what manner the desire for honor is compelling for human beings, and if in fact it is a compulsion at all. And in the case of justice, the envoys claimed it never limits those who have the strength to pursue their advantage, and in particular, pursuing it at the expense or harming of the weak. For the envoys do not argue that the Athenian empire *benefits* those who are its subjects; they do not argue that their empire serves a common good for all of Greece; they adhere to justice in the qualified sense that they do not harm their subjects to the degree to which their strength would allow them. But this justification does not fully answer charges of injustice – the Corinthians and their allies can still claim the Athenians do not have to hold an empire now; for even if they conceded that fear of the Persian threat is a compulsion, that self-defense is a compulsion, that threat (they could argue) has been put down.

The Athenian response, their thesis, thus appeals to "human nature" (*anthrōpeia physis* – 76.3); human nature itself restricts them from giving up their empire; to do so would only leave them exposed to another city, possibly Sparta, who would simply replace them as the strong and compel them as the one who is weak, as Athens does now.[41] But recalling the stated purpose of their speech was to keep the Spartans from declaring war, and thus presumably to allow the Athenians to continue their imperial expansion, we wonder whether their defense does not have the opposite effect. While the Athenians state what they believe to be the motivations of all cities, apparently from a desire to be open about these motivations (for the purpose of self-congratulations?), it is notable that this view is not recognized by others. The Athenians' failure to state a justification for their empire *recognizable* to the other cities actually hinders their ability to secure their empire against the charge of injustice. And have they not instead struck fear in the Spartans? The Athenians underestimate the attachment other cities have to just causes, i.e., justifications to action; they believe the other cities will recognize the same principles that they (and all cities) apparently adhere to. Indeed, Thucydides' Pentecontaetia detailing Athens' expansion confirms their subjects' disinterest in contributing to the Athenians' warlike practices; they wanted to remain peacefully at home (1.99.3).

Whether this is politically possible may be to ignore necessities imposing themselves on these cities. Nevertheless, it reveals a key disagreement on the limits of necessity and thus the compelling character of action, including the corresponding justification of self-interest and self-preservation, in contrast to the scope justice may have. It is shortly after this remark on the

41 And as Orwin (1986) p. 83 observes, there is a tension in their claim: "For a city to rule as justly as possible therefore means for it to refrain as much as possible from ruling." Forde (1986) focuses on Athenian daring as a cause of imperialism, the immoral character of daring: "The speech of the anonymous Athenians at Sparta is a good index of this [amorality]. What those Athenians say shows that they have liberated themselves in thought as well as in action from the restraints that the Greeks and others thought applied to cities in their relations among themselves" (437).

reception of continuing Athenian imperialism that Thucydides notes what the Spartans thought of Athenian character – the Athenians are different than others (102.3). Most obviously, this refers to their daring and innovating character. But let us weigh this against the Athenians' defense. That defense presented Athenian imperialism as limited, even moderate; the Athenians are more moderate than they need to be and expect honorable recognition for this very fact. Yet honor, one of the Athenians' stated motives, figures precisely into Spartan distrust. For what is honor for the Spartan? Archidamus, the Spartan king, will defend honor not as empire, but rather as the education and reverence for the laws (which includes not only honor, but its opposite, shame) of which the Spartan is most proud. There is certainly no Sicilian expedition for the Spartans. Nor in either Spartan speech, Archidamus' or Sthenelaidas', will the language of justice be abandoned. This characteristic striving of the Athenians, and thus of their imperial rule, is most at odds with Sparta. We might say that the Athenians' love of honor is merely the reverse side of their daring and enterprising character. Or stated another way, only daring action is deserving of honor. And as the anonymous Athenians also reveal, daring speech – without pretext, falsehood, or excuse – characterizes this pursuit.

Sparta's Debate For and Against War

The Spartans privately discuss the arguments of the Corinthians and Athenians. The Corinthians had not claimed that the Athenians should cease from their ambitions; they know better than to expect this. Instead, it is the Spartans who are to blame for failing to counter these ambitions. And as the admission of the envoys makes clear, Athens will not relinquish its empire. The Spartans vote, therefore, that the Athenians "committed injustice" (*adikeō*) and that war should be declared (79.2).[42] But Archidamus, the Spartan king reputed to be "intelligent" (*sunetos*) and "moderate" (*sōphrōn*),

42 While the Athenians have been unjust according to the Spartans, it does not clearly follow that war against Athens should be declared, especially if Sparta is not prepared to do so, as Archidamus will argue. Yet it is in keeping with the Spartan understanding of the war that this charge against Athens and the declaration of war belong together.

comes forward to speak despite this vote and resolution.[43] Thucydides does not explicitly remark in advance the purpose of his speech, its goals, as he did with the Athenian envoys. The lack of an introduction to Archidamus' speech might be taken to indicate that its goals are not as clearly defined, although we note that the envoys also departed from their original purpose. Archidamus' speech should either reinforce the resolution for war or object to it. In either case, we will be offered a glimpse into how the Spartan king understands his city and its relation to Athens.

Reminding his fellow Spartans of his age, experience, and thus knowledge of matters pertaining to war, Archidamus argues it is mistaken to expect that war is good or safe. Instead, he quickly turns to enumerating Sparta's many disadvantages from which Athens is immune. Athens, not Sparta, has the advantage in almost every respect regarding the resources and arts of war; therefore, he cautions against haste and questions the Spartans' source of assuredness when confronting such a formidable enemy. Even in those arts of war where Sparta has the upper hand, their hoplites and abilities to fight on land, he doubts how advantageous these are against an enemy such as Athens; a drawn-out war could even continue into the next generation (81.6). Despite these surprising admissions of a king regarding the weakness of his city, Archidamus concedes that if war is going to come to pass the Spartans must delay, to prepare themselves to face an enemy such as the Athenians. Their city must acquire money, allies, and in general, undertake the preparations to defeat a city different from their own, especially given Athens' ability at sea. Archidamus urges Sparta to proceed cautiously, both in deciding to go to war and in prosecuting the war should they still be in favor of it. Archidamus, in other words, implies Corinth is correct: Sparta is not prepared now, and this means they have not been actively working to contain the Athenian empire. Yet how do we square this with the Athenian envoys' claim that all cities expand?

In the context of arguing for slowness and delay, Archidamus suggests further talks with Athens, neither threatening nor submissive, to negotiate and make demands with regard to the present situation; he favors

---

43 For an overview of the king and his relationship to other Spartan offices, see Rahe (2016) pp. 41-49. As Rahe notes, the Spartan king was not all powerful (there were, after all, two kings); also, as we will observe here, Thucydides presents Sthenelaidas the ephor challenging Archidamus' advice. Ste. Croix (1972) pp. 138-51 discusses Spartan kingship, along with the ephors. He also discusses Archidamus and Sthenelaidas, albeit in general, historical terms (141-43).

a diplomatic solution to Athens' imperial activities. This exhortation to caution is an echo of the end of his speech which warns against proceeding with war without arbitration – the Athenian envoys openly referred to sending the matter, the differences (*diaphora*) between the cities, to arbitration (78.4). Archidamus also questions Sparta's allies' motives in voting for war, suggesting their appeals to Spartan aid are for "private" interests (82.6). Thucydides' remarks immediately preceding Corinth's speech reveals that this is in fact the case, all grievances of the allies being based upon to their own interests (67.1-4).[44] That Corinth was angry over the siege of Potidaea, due to having men there (67.1), casts light on Thucydides' previous remark that war did not begin with the Potidaea incident, since this was a "private" action of the Corinthians (66). Countering these exhortations to war by Sparta's allies, Archidamus instead reminds his fellow Spartans that "responsibility" (*aitias*) will fall on them for instigating war (83.3). Archidamus quietly reminds the Spartans that justice, as responsibility for action and blame for consequences, must be a part of their war calculations. This is a warning he has already mentioned (81.5).

On the surface, the second half of Archidamus' speech (84.1-4) shifts from these strategic considerations to defending the Spartan way of life, thereby directly addressing the Corinthians' blame and slander of their character. According to Archidamus, the Spartans should "not be ashamed" (*mē aischunesthe*) of their characteristic slowness but consider it evidence of their "sensible moderation" (*sōphrosynē emphrōn*). This allows the Spartans to avoid being hubristic in their successes and give in less when misfortunes befall them. They are apt at war and "of good counsel" (*euboulos*) because they are "well-ordered" (*eukosmon*). Their moderation's greatest part is "reverent shame" (*aidōs*), and "courage" (literally "goodness of soul" – *eupsychia*), "shame" (*aischunē*). Educated in a lack of learning, Spartans are of good counsel because they do not look down on the laws and are too moderate through harshness to disobey them. In a word, while Archidamus contends that there is little difference among human beings, "he is strongest who is reared in the most necessary things" (*kratiston de einai hostis en*

44 The Aeginetans lacked the independence the treaty presumably guaranteed them, while the Megarians were excluded from the ports of the empire and market of Athens as established by the Megarian Decree. For further discussion of the treaty, see note 54 below.

tois anankaiotatois paideuetai – 84.4). Spartan education is the laws passed down by their ancestors and the source of their strength.[45]

Archidamus' praise of Sparta is a praise of antiquity, of tradition, and very much at odds with the Corinthians' demand that Sparta innovate and change their character (85.1). Adherence to law that instills moderation is the source of their slowness and delay, in contrast to the rashness and daring of the Athenians. The wisdom of their laws guides them, while the Athenians' freedom of mind, a freedom the Corinthians had praised, and which Thucydides allows us to observe in the speech of the envoys (among other instances) guides them. The Spartans, by contrast, look down on "useless intelligence" (*achreia xynetoi* – 84.3). Being moderate means, in part or principally, not questioning the laws. To breach Sparta's laws is to be immoderate because it is to act above the city. To innovate with regard to their regime, as one who innovates in the arts of war, would be an act of immoderation.[46] Sparta's obedience to the laws is borne out of their fear of acting shamefully, of being dishonored by the city. So while the envoys highlight (and demonstrate) the desire for honor, Archidamus reminds

45 Hussey (1985) pp. 123-28 has a very different view of Spartan education when he first argues that "[Spartan] discipline works by crushing and chilling the natural appetites making for private enjoyment, including those that foster imagination and intellectual curiosity" but then goes on to state that "[i]t is the limited Spartan imagination that makes the Spartans reject Archidamus' policy immediately after his speech, and causes them, in the war named after Archidamus, to be surprised and outmaneuvered by Athenian resourcefulness." Hussey fails to wholly distinguish between Spartan and Athenian education (despite alluding to such differences). And while he is correct to distinguish Archidamus from those that vote for war, he overlooks that Spartan education in their *nomoi* (laws/customs) is what they view as a corrective to the liberty (and its attending consequences) allowed to the Athenians. Finley (1942) p. 132 argues Archidamus scorns reason, seemingly due to precisely his defense of the Spartan way of life. But what might seem irrational to an outsider, may not seem so to a Spartan even if it appears contrary to calculated self-interest. For the Spartan, it is very much reasonable, that is, virtuous, to be dedicated to their city, as the source of their strength and what has placed them beside Athens as the leaders of Greece. This is not to deny the moral basis of Spartan education. Notable here are Archidamus' mentions of "shame," particularly the term *aidōs*. It is used by Thucydides, if I am correct, only in this instance. It is related to other words of similar root (*aisch-*), but seems to allude to one's sense of reverence or respect. Thucydides, in using both *aidōs* and *aischunē* together in the same sentence, distinguishes them. The latter is much more common across the text; it occurs, for example, throughout the Melian Dialogue. See Chapter Four note 20. For further background on Spartan education, their *agōge*, see Cartledge (2001) pp. 79-90 and Rahe (2016) pp. 10-35, 145-47, 153-57.

46 Aristotle, *Politics* 1268b23-1269a27.

us of its converse: shame restricts. The Athenians must use their minds because, to speak anachronistically, Athens promotes a certain "individuality." But Spartan laws inculcating shame direct the individual back to the collective, back to obedience to laws that have as their end adherence of the citizen to the good of the city, to the common good, including or especially courageous acts in war. The Athenians, far from submitting to the laws, offer their own views on human nature itself. Their "guide" is the world as it appears to them, as they come to have knowledge of it, presented through the actions of men at war and peace. For the Spartan, there is much to be feared and only the laws provide moral, and we might even say, cosmic, guidance.

We cannot fail to note that Thucydides' introduction of Archidamus states that he was *reputed* (or "held" – *dokeō*) to be intelligent and moderate.[47] Archidamus' praise of the laws and exhortation to their wisdom is in keeping with his reputation as moderate; in stunning contrast, it is Pericles in his Funeral Oration, a speech prescribed by law, that questions that very law. Spartan moderation, however, including their tendency to delay, has not been unquestionably good – it is this caution and slowness that has allowed Athens to ascend to its current position. And despite Archidamus admitting that the Spartans are not strongly positioned against Athens to carry on a large-scale war, he defends as a "necessity" (*anankē*) the Spartan education (84.4) even though it has hindered their ability and willingness to anticipate, if possible, or prosecute, if necessary, such a war to their advantage. Even once prepared (assuming the Spartans would not continue to delay), Archidamus' hope is that the Athenians will submit and keep what they have (82.3). After all, he seems to believe the Athenians are the same type of men as they are (84.4). The limit of Archidamus' intelligence is thus revealed in his flawed comprehension of Athenian character: He attributes similar motives to all human beings, assuming the enemy thinks as the Spartan thinks. This will prove to be an error. Intelligence perhaps means Archidamus is knowledgeable of Spartan laws and most closely a manifestation of the regime. After all, the king's position was hereditary. Or perhaps more than this: Archidamus' views and predictions must be

47 Hornblower I p. 124-25 remarks on the qualifications here (as does Tigerstedt [1965] p. 128). But it is also the case, as Hornblower further observes, that Archidamus is the only individual in Thucydides who is said to be "moderate" (*sōphrōn*), as opposed to the city itself (1.18.1 and 8.24.4).

compared both with those of his counterpart, Pericles, as well as to other Spartan actions throughout the war.

Despite Corinth's complaints that Athens has been unjust, Archidamus only mentions "injustice" once, at the end of his speech; but there the context is the injustices Sparta's allies accused Athens of, not Archidamus treating the issue of justice in his own name. In other words, he is reluctant to cast the same accusation as everyone else. Yet the surface level shift I have alluded to, from the first part of his speech (treating strategic issues such as preparations and supplies) to the second part of his speech (defending Spartan character), only masks his greater, overriding fear. Archidamus mentions or alludes in numerous instances throughout his entire exhortation to the potential "blame" Sparta could incur for starting the war. In the last instance, he states directly that "it is not lawful" (*nomimos*) to proceed against those who offer arbitration, capping off repeated references to this very issue (81.5, 82.1, 82.6, 83.3, 85.2). So far from agreeing with his fellow Spartans' subsequent decision to go to war, he warns that they *themselves* could be guilty of injustice in declaring war against Athens.[48] Arguing that

48 Blame (*aitia*) and its cognates are specifically mentioned at 1.82.1 and 83.3. Hornblower I pp. 126-29 refers multiple times to Archidamus' numerous allusions to the arbitration clause in the treaty, but misses the point when, in citing Dover, he affirms the interpretation that the Spartans later, in complaining to Athens (1.126.1), do not truly have arbitration in mind. Kagan (1969) p. 308-9 ignores this fact, instead arguing that Archidamus must have believed the Athenian empire was becoming gentler. I find no evidence in Archidamus' speech that this is the case, particularly in light of his exhortation to Sparta to prepare for war while also (hopefully) delaying it. In fact, according to Archidamus, in preparing for war and with words following deeds, the Athenians may be willing to back down and keep what they have (82.3). Cogan (1981) pp. 31-33 emphasizes that Archidamus' purpose is to delay Spartan action. Yet Cogan misses the theme of arbitration and injustice, suggesting instead that Archidamus is confident and little worried since Sparta can make war when they choose. This too overlooks numerous elements of his speech. To mention only two: Archidamus' opening on the gravity of the decision about to be undertaken (80.1-2) and his prediction that this war is not "the same as all other wars," as Cogan attributes to him, because it may last into the next generation (81.6). Orwin (1994) pp. 57-58 argues that the case of Spartan injustice in breaking the treaty would be clear, and thus needs less discussion than the strategic considerations. Orwin does note, though, the rhetorical effectiveness of placing the arbitration issue at the end of the speech, yet seems to thereby minimize the other allusions to it. Badian (1993) pp. 142-43 argues that the Spartans are unaware of the arbitration clause since: 1) Sthenelaidas does not mention it; and 2) Archidamus is not clear about the Spartans' obligation to its terms, only instead stating that "it would not be in accordance with customary Greek rules of behavior to treat one who has offered arbitration as manifestly guilty"

caution and slowness are not hindrances appears, therefore, not simply or only as a prudential strategy; it is rather a fear of committing injustice – he is not sure on which side the blame may fall should war occur and thus advises against it. And perhaps most telling is what he does not say – Archidamus' speech is the only one of the four at Sparta (Corinthians, Athenians, Archidamus, and Sthenelaidas) that refrains from any reference to oaths and the gods.[49] Even the Athenian envoys appeal to the oaths undergirding treaties (78.4). And in addition to the harsh education in Spartan laws that molds the Spartan soul, the divine source of those laws cannot be overlooked.[50]

Regardless of Archidamus' appeal to antiquity and Spartan education, including his appeal to the potential unlawfulness should a declaration of war be a breach of the treaty, the Spartan ephor, Sthenelaidas, succeeds in procuring the vote for war.[51] While Archidamus' speech attempted to avoid the grave question of the justice in going to war, Sthenelaidas' speech seems to succeed almost solely due to its appeal to injustice – "to do injustice" (*adikeō*) and its cognates are mentioned five times in his laconic speech (86.1-5). He is not convinced that the Athenians answered the charge of committing injustice against Sparta and its allies. This is not to deny his appeal to interest as well: Sparta cannot afford, now or in the future, to lose its allies (86.2-3). But for the Spartan, this does not present the dichotomous

---

(85.2). But is Archidamus not anticipating exactly what will happen, that the Spartans are going to treat the Athenians as guilty *despite* the treaty? Badian's argument ignores the number of times Archidamus alludes to precisely the treaty issue and, as we will notice, presages the outcome of Sthenelaidas' speech. Debnar (2001) p. 69 mentions Archidamus' treaty concern, but only in passing. Connor (1984) pp. 38-39 sees wisdom in Archidamus' speech without suggesting any possible shortcomings. Jaffe (2017) p. 112 offers a proper corrective to Strasburger (2009), who views Archidamus as simply reducing justice to advantage. Archidamus is, in fact, *more* concerned than other Spartans that the treaty may compromise their case for going to war. But most Spartans are convinced by Sthenelaidas, not their king.

49 Cf. 71.5, 78.4, 86.5. See Bartlett (2001) p. 79.

50 Xenophon, *Regime of the Lacedaemonians* VIII.1-5.

51 Hornblower I p. 130 notes that nothing else is known of Sthenelaidas besides his brief speech in Thucydides. On the selection of the ephors, see Rahe (1980), who details evidence from Plato, Aristotle, Xenophon, and Plutarch. Rahe concludes that "unless additional evidence turns up, certainty [on the selection process] will remain beyond our grasp" (401). On the power of the ephors, generally, see Rahe (2016) pp. 48-53, who notes that "[t]he importance of the ephors is perhaps most obvious from their relationship with the two kings" (50). Cf. Cartledge (2001) pp. 55-67.

choice it might appear – Athens need not have harmed Spartan interests. After all, Sthenelaidas could have appealed to the necessity now presenting itself to the Spartans, drawing on the Athenians' own defense. But this is not the Spartan view.[52]

Most important in his speech is an ambiguity, which Thucydides himself pointed to in his introduction to the Corinthians' speech – the accusation against Athens was breach of the treaty *and* injustice against the Peloponnesus (67.1). For while oaths are sworn on each side to protect the sanctity of the treaty (and remind everyone that the gods serve as its guarantor) the Athenian envoys do not truly answer the accusation of injustice, the broader question of what allows them, Athens, to rule over the other Greek cities. The envoys' justification loosely rests on necessity, thereby calling into doubt even such agreements as treaties (and therefore, in this way, divine justice) – they present a case for breaching justice when necessity requires it. *This* is the issue for the Spartans.

And certain it is that Archidamus reminds Sparta and its allies,

52 Allison (1984) p. 12 observes: "The repetition of so many words in so short a span is peculiar to this speech...the injustice of the Athenians and the allies' suffering are precisely what Sthenelaidas wants to stress." Gomme I p. 251 argues that Sthenelaidas' speech is "excellently in character" since it is only concerned with Spartan interests, as opposed to "the wrongs of Athens' subject allies." If Sthenelaidas is only concerned with interest, his speech is able to hide this. But does he hide this merely from others, or does he hide it from himself? After all, the Athenian envoys speak at length about necessity and self-interest, and while Sthenelaidas refers directly to their speech in his own, he highlights the problem of their injustices, aside from their (or any other) possible justification. Orwin (1994) pp. 57-58 argues that Sthenelaidas uses the concern with allies to secure the vote; but Orwin also highlights the Spartan conflation of justice and necessity, as does Jaffe (2017) pp. 114-15. Burns (2010) pp. 41-43 alludes to Sthenelaidas not ignoring interests, despite his repeated accusations of injustice. Debnar (2001) p. 71 notices that Sthenelaidas "implies that the Athenians have used words merely to obfuscate their deeds...effectively dismiss[ing] the Athenians' explanation of the purpose of their speech as well as their insistence that the current assembly is not the proper venue in which to respond to the allies' complaints." While Sthenelaidas certainly believes the Athenians are dancing around the issue, he may also have noticed how they do in fact attempt to justify their empire (on his view, their wrongdoing), a justification which rests on dubious grounds for a Spartan. His silence, in other words, speaks volumes about his view of Athenian imperialism and perhaps even hints at how absurd he, and the Peloponnesians, view the Athenian justification. Connor (1984) pp. 38-39 sees the speech merely as "specious sloganeering" and its "shallowness is evident in the jingles and equivocations of the language." Nonetheless, he notes the Spartans siding with Sthenelaidas, without weighing the basis for their decision.

repeatedly, of the treaty. But this is only a partial understanding of justice, for Sthenelaidas and for the allies. Noticeable, then, is the fact that the Athenian justification means nothing to the Spartan case of injustice. And, I believe, Archidamus is aware of this: His silence on the issue of justice is a silence avoiding the deeper problem. By emphasizing the treaty obligations specifically, he casts the issue in a strictly legal light (as Pericles will also do). He hopes, in other words, to avoid precisely what happens – that the Spartans take a broad view of the "differences" between the two cities. After all, how does the treaty expect the broad issue of *these* differences to be treated? While the various Peloponnesian allies have particular grievances, those add up (in their eyes) to the very problem of Athens' imperial expansion, well beyond Athenian claims they are protecting against Persia. Besides, on the envoys' own arguments (were the Peloponnesians to appeal to them), the treaty would no longer be binding if necessity forced Sparta to defend itself out of (at the very least) fear. And Thucydides' own statement is that fear compelled the Spartans to act.[53]

The question of imperialism remains open. We have yet to determine whether the Athenian thesis is sufficient justification for encroaching on the other cities. Are cities compelled to expand, as the Athenians claim? Or does justice demand restrictions on a city's pursuits beyond even the measured conduct the Athenians boast of? And whatever this boast, it did little to impress the other cities, nor does Thucydides present it as mere rhetorical rejection by the Peloponnesians. So while the tone and rhetoric of Archidamus and Sthenelaidas differ, as many scholars have pointed out, it is the issue of justice, approached quietly and loudly, respectively, to which Thucydides draws our attention when we turn to considering the war "through Spartan eyes."[54]

---

53 Scholars marvel at "[t]he astonishing fact that [Archidamus' speech] was totally ineffectual" (Bloedow [1981] p. 131). Bloedow attempts to understand how Sthenelaidas' speech could possibly be more convincing to its audience. Yet even while pointing to a possible reason, contending that Sthenelaidas' speech was "pure emotion" (142), he never remarks on the issue of justice (including, that is, the anger at injustice, an emotion), nor on Archidamus' repeated mentions of the treaty. Connor (1984) pp. 38-39 emphasizes the wisdom of Archidamus (in contrast to his critique of Sthenelaidas) without noting Thucydides' qualifying "reputed."

54 The phrase is Orwin's (1994 p. 56). Hornblower I pp. 124 mentions the treaty, but does not draw out the issue of justice, only noting that arbitration was a clause in the Thirty Years' Peace of 446. Details of the clause, however, are unknown to us. Badian's (1993) pp. 137-45 discussion of the outbreak of the war focuses on trying to

And we might wonder, in this instance and others to come, whether all Spartans understand justice in quite the same way. Archidamus warns against injustice, perhaps because he is a more thoughtful (and moderate) Spartan, more thoughtful about justice. But the Spartans side with Sthenelaidas. Does this not detract from the notion of virtue emerging from Archidamus' canvassing, and praising, of Spartan life, especially his repeated warning about violating the treaty? Sthenelaidas' appeals are more direct, but cannot be treated as a rejection of Archidamus simply. But this is the first crack in Sparta's armor – two key figures do not see eye to eye on the coming war, on the justice, the propriety, of being the instigator in declaring war. Sthenelaidas' emphasis on Athenian injustice overshadows Archidamus' warning of Spartan injustice. There are at least two understandings of justice for the Spartans, the latter version a more careful attention to justice as obedience, not to Spartan interests, but to justice as treaty obligation, oaths, expectations of the gods; the former, justice as revenge and punishment, especially for "doubly bad" men such as the Athenians (1.86.1-2). While many scholars who focus on Thucydides' account of justice highlight Sparta's conflation of justice and self-interest, and thus their hypocrisy in expecting others to abandon their interests for Sparta's, we must notice this cannot be the whole story. For this is not how the Spartans understand themselves.[55]

piece together what might have been included in the treaty. Yet we must wonder how Thucydides could be so sloppy as to leave out key elements of it, were they integral to comprehending the war. Badian, for example, objects to the lack of detail Thucydides provides on the autonomy clause of the treaty (mentioned at 1.67.2) thereby suggesting we cannot properly judge the overall causes of the war. But what is ambiguous about Athens' subject cities lacking autonomy due to the Athenian empire? Part of the issue here is Badian's treatment of the Pentecontaetia: it is Thucydides' "apologia" for the Athenian empire and "sets out to show [99] that the conversion from league to tightly controlled empire was essentially the allies' own fault" (132). This interpretation is highly problematic, and it is only by contending that Thucydides sought to justify Athenian hegemony that Badian can object to the lack of treaty detail, along with objecting to the structure, narrative, and presentation of Book One as a whole. As Stadter (1994) p. 338 argues in his book review: "B[adian]'s prosecutorial rhetoric creates a Thucydides who is in the end a very simple writer, deceptive and artistic (a negative word), but easily caught out by the perceptive reader. Not everyone has or will find him so transparent."

55 Jaffe (2012) p. 116: "Hypocrisy, then, is the manner by which the Spartans combine the rival necessities of Archidamus and Sthenelaidas. Hypocrisy is the manner that the Spartans harmonize justice with advantage, when the two seem to diverge, all the while denying the tension between them." Jaffe does go on, though, to note that

The difficulty here is understanding Spartan psychology. Do the Spartans see and feel necessity as such, as the Athenians do? Or, since the Spartans pride themselves on being better men, and their allies are good allies (perhaps even in the moral sense, as Sparta's own), are they justified in breaching one form of justice (the legality of the treaty) for another deeper, or more fundamental, justice — the injustice of the Athenian empire expanding *unnecessarily*, an encroachment on Sparta, on what is theirs?[56]

Imperialism and Revolution: Thucydides' Pentecontaetia

By placing his presentation of the Athenian empire later in Book One, out of order in time and as a digression, Thucydides compels us to consider imperialism from within the debate of necessity and justice, compulsion and morality. On the one hand, we might have formed the impression that Athenian imperialism is justified, since we have already heard, and perhaps accepted, the notion that necessity compels, that the Athenians were acting as all cities would act, both generally and given their particular circumstances after the Persian War and their split with Sparta. But if we have been paying attention, we are also cognizant of the reaction of so speak everyone else, most notably, of course, Sparta: Athens is an unjust imperial power which forces all other cities to either join with, or battle against, their strength and designs. This reaction is led by the Corinthians. And while it is Sparta that first votes that Athens has violated the treaty (1.88), we recall that Chapters 89-118 detail the rise of the Athenian empire, before we hear the vote of Sparta's allies (119). Thucydides is certainly allowing us to test this Athenian justification.[57]

"harm and injustice are indistinguishable for the majority of Spartans." If this is the case, then we need to detail what is meant by Spartan "hypocrisy" and distinguish it from other forms (as I will proceed to do). For the Spartans will prove to be very much unaware of the distinction others (Athenians [see 5.105.4] and scholars) apply to their decisions, since their conflation of justice and advantage is precisely what most Spartans fail to see. Understanding this conflation is where some of Thucydides' key psychological insights lie.

56 On the moral superiority of the Spartans, consider 1.84, 1.102.3, 3.92, 4.17, 5.105.2, 7.18.2.

57 This structure is clearly for the sake of a literary (and I would add, philosophic) purpose. Allison (2013) p. 265: "The *Pentecontaetia* has the dramatic effect of intensifying the suspense between the vote the Spartans at 88 held among themselves

While Sparta began this period (approximately 479-430) as the supreme power in Greece, their leading commander, Pausanias, drove away their allies due to his "violent" (*biaios*) actions (95.1). This allowed Athens to gain supremacy; those who grew to hate Pausanias voluntarily allied themselves instead with Athens (96.1). From this time until the Peloponnesian War (the fifty-year period of the growth of the Athenian empire, the "Pentecontaetia"), the "alliance" of Athens with various cities across Greece developed. Athens engaged in attacks against the barbarians, against their own allies who revolted, as well against enemies from the Peloponnesus.[58] We note the quick shift in Thucydides' account – the supremacy of Athens began as voluntary, but Thucydides' list of Athenian activities also points to allies now in revolt. Thucydides calls his discussion here a "digression" (97.2), required it seems by the inaccuracy of previous accounts of the past that have not made this growth clear. This digression is a preface to a new stage or development: Whereas Thucydides first speaks of Athenian leadership or hegemony (97.1), he quickly turns to the origins of the Athenian "empire" (*archē* – 97.2). The shift from hegemony, the leading of allied cities (*hēgeomai*), to empire is due to the subjugation of those cities, suppressing the previous autonomy they enjoyed (97.1, 98.4). Allied cities revolted to avoid paying tribute to Athens. Yet given wealth was the source of Athenian power, they did not easily let their subjects go but rather subjected them to "necessity" (*anankē*). Athenian imperialism compelled many cities to submit to its demands. It was the Athenian *empire*, rather than simply being the supreme city in Greece, that was the cause of the war because it was the cause of the Spartan fear.[59] But the Spartans, after

and the subsequent league vote at 119 and framed by the activities of the Corinthians, as Stadter and Rood observe, its significance for the narrative of the *aitiai* must be intentional" (citing Stadter [1993] p. 61 and Rood [1998] pp. 216-21). Strauss (1964) pp. 180-82 goes even further, placing all of Book One, after 1.23.5-6, within the context of the issue of cause.

58 See Hornblower I p. 133 for the scholarly controversy on these dates. Thucydides' presentation in the Pentecontaetia covers somewhat less than fifty years.

59 Strauss (1964) p. 18 and Bruell (1974) p. 14 both remark on this shift. Ste. Croix (1972) pp. 34-43 suggests Thucydides may have exaggerated this hatred. Gomme II pp. 9-10 remarks on Athens being both imperial and aggressive, but is hesitant to agree with Thucydides' comment on the other cities supporting Sparta's professed cause of liberation. Hornblower I pp. 246-47 also sees this support as an exaggeration "...perhaps the most extravagant in all Th.[ucydides]." Yet considering Thucydides' accusation against the exaggerations of the poets, we wonder why he would find it

Pausanias had been recalled for his actions abroad, were no longer willing to send out other commanders, fearing they too would be corrupted and resort to the actions of Pausanias (95.7). Athens expanded its empire largely unimpeded.[60]

At this time the Spartans were involved in a war with rebels from Ithome in the Peloponnesus; but unable to subdue them, they requested aid from the Athenians. While Athens had taken over as supreme city in Greece, hostilities had not yet developed between the two. Athens agreed, therefore, to aid the Spartans, but the "daring" (*tolmēros*) and "revolutionary" (*neōteropoiia*) character of the Athenians was of concern to them, for they feared the Athenians might attempt something within the Peloponnesus (102.3).[61] Sparta did not advance this as the reason for dismissing the Athenians, however, but claimed rather that they were no longer in need of aid to deal with the rebels.

The Athenians, though, being aware of this, left offended and broke off the alliance, an alliance still in place at this time from when the two cities fought together against Persia. Thucydides notes that this was the first open quarrel between Athens and Sparta (102.3) and led to the Athenians developing a "hatred" (*echthos*) for the Spartans (103.3). While the offense the Athenians felt at the Spartans' actions is perhaps not surprising, generally, it does raise questions about the Athenian thesis. Their reaction, as Thucydides presents it, implies they felt slighted – they offered their services to Sparta in suppressing the revolt at Ithome and were summarily dismissed. The Spartans seemed to lack consideration for the Athenians' willingness to offer assistance; they did not recognize Athens was acting not in their own interests, but for the sake of Sparta. Athenian hatred results from being offended, expecting a reward for their apparently selfless actions. The Athenian envoys admitted, after all, they were not without concern for honor;

necessary to exaggerate the sentiment of most Greek cities in getting behind Sparta's liberation claim. After all, Corinth charges Athens with being a "tyrant city" (1.122.3), a charge neither Pericles, nor Cleon, can deny (2.63.2, 3.37.2). Hornblower himself, in this context, remarks on this tyranny issue for Athens. And while some cities certainly recognized the benefit to Athenian imperialism (see, for example, the Plataeans' admission at 3.55.3), this does not stop them from voicing objections at those times when being a subject weighs on them.

60 Pausanias and his relation to Sparta will be discussed in Chapter Three.

61 For a discussion of the significance of *tolma* in Thucydides' account, see Forde (1986) pp. 434, 436-38 and (1989) pp. 17-19. Hornblower I pp. 114-15, 159 translates *tolma* as "boldness." See also note 67 below.

it was one of the motivations for maintaining and expanding their empire (75.3). Spartan fear of the Athenians is also evident in this episode. But this fear was not necessarily or primarily a rational calculation of Athenian power. It was a recognition of the Athenians as different men, as "others." Hatred animates this period, cities reacting not solely based on calculations of interests and advantage. Past history with a city and its people cannot help but play a role.

As a result of Spartan dismissal from the Peloponnesus, the Athenians occupied Megara, the Megarians being displeased with the Corinthians, Sparta's allies. And thus the Corinthians now grew to hate the Athenians for this action, a hatred that will manifest itself in the main actions before the outbreak of the war. [62] Back in Sparta, the rebels at Ithome eventually surrender. The Spartans were gentle and allowed them to leave the Peloponnesus, complying with an old oracle from Delphi (1.103.1-2). And while the Athenians continued their expansion after this incident, the Spartans were characterized by inaction or failure (108.1-3, 109.2-3, 112.5, 114.2). More precisely, while the Athenians are campaigning in faraway Egypt, the Spartans are securing Delphi in what Thucydides calls a "sacred" (or holy – *hieros*) war.[63] For the Spartans, securing a sacred site takes priority over the predictable, continued expansion of the Athenian empire, despite the truce signed at this time; for the Athenians, a campaign in a distant land catches their eye, now that said truce frees them from dealing with the Spartans. Perceptions of interests differ – Athenian reasons are not Spartan reasons. Of all the actions Sparta could have taken at this time, this was the one. In fact, Spartan piety will guide their forthcoming complaints against the Athenians. Before detailing these complaints, which take us, I will argue, into the heart of the Spartan view of the war, into Spartan psychology, we will turn to the end of Book One: Pericles' first speech.

62 Hornblower I p. 162 notes that Thucydides' Greek emphasizes this event as the *origin* of hatred between these two cities.

63 Hornblower I pp. 182-83 (on 1.112.5) complains of how little Thucydides relates of this event, contrasting his treatment of the Delphic oracle (and the political issues surrounding it) with Herodotus. Elsewhere (Hornblower [1992]) he critiques Thucydides for neglecting religion generally. Yet as he admits (pp. 194-97) Thucydides does refer, repeatedly, to religious matters; it is Hornblower's conclusion, instead, that he does not "connect" or "explain" events. Sparta's pious observances will become a key interpretative point we will return to throughout.

Pericles' Response to Sparta's Vote For War

While the Athenian envoys offer something of an unofficial response to the charges of Sparta and its allies, Pericles offers the first official response to the impeding war, as well as a justification of imperialism from Athens' "first man" (1.139.4).[64] In this way, Pericles' statement on Athens bears comparison to Archidamus' praises of Sparta. Each present not simply strategic matters pertinent to the impending war, but the character of their city and way of life that will define its trajectory.

Pericles' first speech addresses the question of how Athens is to proceed with the war (140-144). He warns that should the Spartans be victorious, the Athenians will be enslaved to them as well as losing their allies through revolution. Since Sparta has rejected the possibility of arbitration as stipulated by the treaty between the two cities, Athens must not acquiesce to any demands or threats lest they set a precedent of appearing weak. Since Athens' superiority rests with its monetary resources and navy, in contrast to the numerical superiority of Sparta and its allies, Athens must rely on their sea power against Spartan skill on land. Pericles therefore recommends the Athenians treat themselves as islanders, rather than attempting to defend both the city and their ports, as well as the surrounding countryside of

---

64 The scholarship on Thucydides' Pericles is vast. Fortunately, it can be broadly categorized based on support for one of the following views: 1) Thucydides admires Pericles, making him his hero or spokesman (for example, Cornford [1907], Kagan [1991], Farrar [1998]). 2) Thucydides presents Pericles' war policy as best and the Athenians suffer by departing from it, i.e., by extending their previously restrained empire into Sicily; Pericles himself was not imperial (for example, Romilly [1963]). 3) Thucydides is critical of Pericles because, while Pericles was able to restrain the demos, Pericles' vision of Athens is not in fact at odds with later imperial overexpansion. After all, Thucydides states that the best Athenian regime of his lifetime was the regime of 411, i.e., not Periclean Athens (for example, Forde [1986], Palmer [1992], Monoson and Loraux [1998], Foster [2010]). This has been a relatively recent development in assessing Pericles, distinguishing Thucydides' views from the Periclean speeches and from Athenian imperialism generally. My view (see Diduch and Hadley [2016]) is a version of #3 – Thucydides is indeed critical of Periclean Athens, critical especially, I argue, of the shift away from traditional laws, homegrown piety, and rural customs foundational to pre-Periclean Athens. To this end, Athens' domestic changes and troubles throughout the war, and what they teach us about Sparta, will be discussed in detail in Chapter Three.

Attica. His argument is that the homes and land of the Athenians are not fundamental, but rather the "bodies" of men (*sōmatōn* – 143.5).

Broadly speaking, Pericles has hope for the outcome of the war to fall in Athens' favor provided they refrain from any new conquests or enterprises. His fear is less of the enemy than of errors the Athenians commit themselves (a prescient remark, as we will later see). The prize for victory in war is the greatest "honor" (*timē*) and, although war is a "necessity," willingness to engage in it will show the Spartans and their allies Athens' strength, particularly the "daring" (*tolma*) and "judgment" (literally: "mind" – *gnōmē*) which characterizes the Athenians (144.4). Pericles refrains, however, from speaking about how Athens acquired its empire; he only later alludes, in a different speech and context, to the Athenians defending themselves (2.36.2-4).

Thucydides himself did not refrain, though, from speaking about this acquisition. The digression we have observed in Book One details the growth of the Athenian empire during the fifty-year period leading up to the outbreak of the Peloponnesian War, noting the shift from Athens' alliance with other Greek cities to subjugation of those cities and their severe treatment of them (1.97.1, 98.3, 99.1). While Pericles fails to discuss this growth, and therefore avoids the question of the justification for empire, Thucydides implicitly raises it. We are reminded of it in his first speech, as Pericles "blames" (*aitia*) the Spartans for breaching the treaty by not submitting to arbitration (140.2); while the Spartans may indeed be legally responsible for the war, we must recall that Thucydides compels us to weigh the matter of blame more broadly, since the Spartans acted out of fear and fear for one's own safety is exculpatory (1.75.3, 6.83.2). Pericles' legal blame of the Spartans, therefore, does not clearly establish the justice of the Athenian empire, an empire that *led* to what he claims is a breach of the treaty by the Spartans.[65] But here, in his staunch defense against Sparta's declaration, Pericles both deflects the injustice charge and avoids any mention of empire.

While Pericles' first speech leaves the question of justice unanswered, we may draw briefly on remarks in his Funeral Oration, which does offer

65 Bruell (1981) p. 25: "According to Thucydides, then, the Spartans cannot be blamed for starting the war because the Athenians compelled them to start it. Perikles' treatment of the issue was too narrow, too legalistic: the Spartans acted out of legitimate self-defense."

a moral justification of Athens and Athenian imperialism. As Archidamus had done at Sparta, Pericles speaks at length about the character of Athens and especially the Athenian citizen, culminating in his declarations that the Athenians "love the noble with thrift and philosophize without softness," "combine in the same persons both daring and calculation," making Athens the "school of Greece" (2.40.1, 40.3, 41.1). The virtue of the individual for Pericles is this combination of "daring" (*tolma*) and "calculation" (*logismos*). The reward for empire is honor or nobility, both for the city and for the individual (43.1-2, 44.4, 46.1) and this requires a daring to sacrifice one's body for the sake of the city.[66] Further, the Athenian citizen's "courage" (*andreia*) is "not so much instilled by laws as arising from our ways" (*tropōn* – 39.4). Previously, Pericles had spoken about the difficulty in giving his speech in part due to the "envy" (*phthoneō*) that might affect some should he hear anything surpassing his own "nature" (*physis* – 35.2). With these remarks, we begin to understand Pericles' view of Athens and Athenian character – Athenians are *by nature* superior to others because they are able to act on behalf of the city, not due to strict, shame-induced obedience to law as the Spartans do (and as Archidamus praised), but by freely becoming "lovers" (*erastai*) of the city (43.1, 43.4).

Pericles also speaks, however, of "daring" together with "eternal memorials of deeds evil and good" (41.4). His conflation of daring and courage (speaking repeatedly of the former where one would expect the latter) is an admission and new rhetoric casting clear doubt on Athens' justice.[67] Archidamus praises his Spartans for their moderation issuing from law-abidingness, not for daring. Pericles continues: "Our city alone...gives no grounds...for her subjects to complain that they are being ruled by those who are unworthy" (41.3) and later admits that Athens' empire is "so to speak a tyranny" that "to take it *perhaps* was wrong [*adikon*], but to let it

66 Pericles mentions "body" (*soma*) three times in the Funeral Oration (2.41.1, 42.4, 43.2). Cf. 1.143.6.

67 Pericles refers to "daring" (*tolma*) at 1.144.4, 2.39.4, 40.3, 41.4, 43.1, and 62.5; courage (*andreia*) is only mentioned once at 2.39.4. That he extols *tolma* as Athenian virtue signals his departure from traditional Athenian morality. Forde (1986) identifies *tolma* as one of the main forces behind Athenian imperialism and notes its ambiguous, if not immoral, status, which I would add also hints at its recklessness and impiety. Hornblower I does not discuss *tolma* in any of the above passages, and thus overlooks it as a quiet yet important theme running through Pericles' speeches.

go is unsafe" (63.2 – emphasis added). In the Funeral Oration dedicated to praising the men of Athens who died on behalf of the city (a speech which Pericles began by questioning the very law that demands it, in striking contrast to Archidamus' praise of Sparta's laws), he in fact praises the city of Athens or its power (despite the fact that he claims it needs no such praise – 41.4, 42.2). Pericles asks citizens to sacrifice their own self-interest for the sake of the city's because it is noble to do so; Pericles himself had offered to relinquish his private property to the city (2.13.1). Nobility implies a relinquishing of one's own good; to act merely out of one's own interest or good is not noble. Only self-sacrificial action can be deemed noble.

Pericles' speeches offer extensions or supplements to the Athenian thesis and do in fact offer a justification for Athenian imperialism. The Athenian empire was perhaps wrong, i.e., unjust, in its establishment, but now it must be held. Could it have been avoided initially? Would the Persians still threaten Greece if Athens had not expanded? What about Sparta's role in defending Greek autonomy? In any event, it is precisely the daring and innovating character of the Athenians detailed by Pericles the Spartans feared the most. Pericles confirms this in presenting Athenian character as the cause of their imperialism. The Athenian thesis is thus *the* Athenian innovation. It is part of a new "philosophizing without softness" characterizing leading Athenians. The Spartans and their allies are not impressed by Athenian justifications, however, nor by the new necessities their empire imposes on others – they reject this innovation in action, and even more so in speech. Whether Athenian imposition was truly necessary for the self-preservation of the Greeks to counter the Persians is in this sense irrelevant for the outbreak of the Peloponnesian War – the other cities did not recognize that it was. The Athenian thesis faces obstacles to its acceptance. It is only on a superficial reading of Pericles' first speech that we can easily accept Athenian imperialism.

As for the Funeral Oration, Pericles still does not answer the Spartan (and allies') charge of Athenian injustice. His justification of Athenian imperialism is only legal, not trans-legal – Sparta has breached the treaty. The Athenian envoys at Sparta appealed to justice as a restraint only after one is secured against, or has confronted, necessity. Pericles' view of justice similarly does not answer the question of blame for the war outside the letter of the treaty; rather, the reader is now compelled to confront two conflicting views: Thucydides argues fear of Athenian imperialism led to war, while the Athenian envoys, Archidamus, and Pericles focus strictly on the treaty's breach. The precise relation between necessity and justice is still unclear, for the Athenians introduce other apparent compulsions Thucydides has yet to pass judgment on. And more immediately, the Spartans admit to none of these compulsions as exculpating; in fact, their leading men make no comment at all on Athenian appeals to necessity.

Sparta's Pious "Pretexts"

Understanding the outbreak of the war is further complicated by a flurry of pious requests arising just before Pericles' first speech, near the end of Book One. In fact, nearing its conclusion, we are once again reminded of the striking structure of the Book. Thucydides moves from the four speeches debating the Athenian empire and war (1.73-87) to the Pentecontaetia detailing Athens' rise (88-117). He now summarizes the latter (118.1-2); but he also adds that the Spartans, still apparently unsure of their decision to go to war, seek divine guidance at Delphi (118.3). But this is not all. Book One concludes with another Corinthian speech promoting war (120-24), the Cylon incident involving past impieties and curses (126-27), the "biographies" of Pausanias the Spartan and Themistocles the Athenian (128-38), and finally, the first speech of Thucydides' Pericles we have just considered (140-44). Nor can it be forgotten that all this occurs in the context of the decision to go to war, of which we are reminded by Thucydides' short insertions of Spartan deliberation (125), negotiation (139), and a signaling of the war's imminent outbreak (146). It is a dizzying sequence, moving forward and backwards in time in relation to the Pentecontaetia and the current debate for or against war.[68]

Taken together, we notice Thucydides already highlighting a theme which finds its most forthcoming expression in the civil war at Corcyra – the destruction of the city from within: *stasis*. Given Athens' loss in the war is attributable to internal faction (2.65.7-12), it becomes incumbent upon us to notice Thucydides prioritizing domestic political health. It frames his

68 Cf. Hornblower I p. 203. Foster (2010) pp. 119-27 discusses the lead-up to Pericles' first speech, including some scholarly objection to Pericles' place in the narrative. Her emphasis is on what she calls the "Athenian acme" traced through Book One, although as she correctly notes: "...Thucydides' presentation of the Athenian acme is just one narrative strand in book one" (122).

account, from the founding and development of cities in the Archaeology to their decay as the war drags on, highlighted by the fall of Athens in Book Eight. And in the vivid description of Corcyra, it is the loss of piety that I will argue takes center stage, binding together the many mutations within the city Thucydides' descriptive analysis presents there.

Spartan adherence to pious practices and the need for divine reassurance, preceding the beginning of the war and near the conclusion of Book One, thus sets up and reinforces Spartan justice. When the Spartans inquire to the god at Delphi on the propriety of going to war, the god communicates to them that they will be victorious if they put forward all of their strength and that he himself will be with them, called or uncalled. It does not seem the Spartans asked whether the war was a breach of the treaty or whether the Athenians had in fact been unjust in their actions (1.118.3).[69] Thucydides presents their decision to go to war alongside their submitting the question to Delphi whether it would be "better" (*ameinōn*) for them to make war.[70] In this context, Thucydides notes that the Spartans were attempting to attain a "pretext" (*prophasis*) for war; the Spartans burden themselves with at least appearing just in declaring war. On the other hand, Thucydides never states in Book One that the treaty was clearly breached by the Athenians.[71] Does the god even demand the Spartans be just in initiating or prosecuting the war? The Spartans seem to believe so.

When we consider Thucydides' own remark after the conference at Sparta, we are struck by his reiteration that the cause of the war was not *any* of the accusations Sparta's allies levelled against Athens, but Spartan *fear* of the growth of Athenian power (1.88). Necessity, rather than justice, is the cause of Sparta declaring war against Athens. When Thucydides returns from the Pentecontaetia, however, he claims *both* that Sparta was typically slow to go to war unless due to necessity *and* that they themselves were convinced of a breach of the treaty and injustice by the Athenians (118.3). Yet regardless of Athens' growth, if the argument of their envoys is correct,

69 Gomme I p. 413: "this is the Spartan war party's version," implying Thucydides only included this observation because it was provided by a Spartan source. But Hornblower I p. 195 notes that the "religious association between this part of the sentence and the first part is more obvious in the Greek." The term for "treaty" is etymologically related to the term for pouring libations, a pious practice.

70 This word is related to *agathos* (good). It is perhaps noteworthy that the Spartans do not ask if making war is just (*dikē*) or holy (*hieros*).

71 Strauss (1964) pp. 175-76.

then Sparta was compelled to go to war due to fear – and as we have seen, fear is the least questionable of compulsions. No one would argue against allowing one, city or man, to defend itself. Rather, the complication arises when we observe that the Athenians at Sparta argued not only that fear compelled them to empire, but their desire for honor and interest did as well. And these motives, as forms of "compulsion," are open to serious doubts as being truly compulsory, as exculpating one from blame. While the Spartans were compelled out of fear for their city given the growth of the Athenian empire, this does not allow us, therefore, to draw the conclusion that the Spartans did not truly believe the Athenians were unjust.[72]

Yet the Spartans are clearly not as convinced as their vote for war suggests: The last actions we observe in Book One are their attempts to secure a "justification" (or pretext – *prophasis*) for war. Apparently, breaching the treaty was insufficient. With the Cylon incident (which we will detail further below), they send envoys to Athens to demand the Athenians cleanse themselves of an ancient curse that occurred due men being slain who had taken refuge at the Acropolis as suppliants, sheltering themselves within the altar of the goddess (127.1-3). To kill men in such circumstances was to commit a crime against the goddess herself, an impious act. But this Spartan demand is odd. As Thucydides details it, we learn first that it is an old curse; and second, that the Athenians are able to respond with two more recent curses committed by the Spartans themselves. Thucydides introduces this Spartan attempt as a "pretext" and claims they did not expect the Athenians to comply, only wanting to create slander against Pericles (who was their most vehement opponent, with his own family tied to this incident). This appears, then, as a calculated (not to say hypocritical) attempt on the Spartans' part to disguise their otherwise self-interested decision to declare war in the clothing of moral propriety.

But we wonder why they sought any pretext at all. According to their own accusations (emphatically expressed by Sthenelaidas), the Athenians were guilty of injustice, to which their allies concurred, voting for war (87.4-88). Thucydides does not comment on whether they in fact believed in this new accusation, i.e., that a curse may have been involved, only that the Spartans believed an impiety would create slander against Pericles because the Athenian demos would fear a curse hanging over their "first man." Yet the Athenians can, and do, respond with counteraccusations, rendering the

72 For similar points, see Orwin (1994) p. 59 (who also cites Heath [1986] on 1.23.5-6).

Spartan attempt rather futile. The Spartans assume the Athenian people are genuinely pious; but they also assume the moral propriety of going to war is relevant at all. Was the pretext, the justification, then for the sake of the Spartans themselves, placing them on the just side of a coming war? This is the only way the Spartan accusation, viewed from the outside, makes sense.

Despite the Athenians announcing their novel thesis, the Spartans do not believe, nor have they grasped, that appealing to necessity as a compulsion would alleviate any blame on their part for starting the war (at least based on the Athenians' own claims). In other words, Athens compelling Sparta to go to war out of fear does not solve the issue of the Spartans' own beliefs. Nor does it seem, on Thucydides' presentation, to be an explanation for the cause of war simply. This is confirmed by our interpretation of *aitia* and *prophasis* noted above – while initially appearing as opposites, Thucydides leads us to noticing causes, justifications, and pretexts often overlap in how the cities and individuals understand their own decisions and actions. Thucydides uses the terms psychologically, not scientifically. Or more cautiously, the psychological muddling of *aitia* and *prophasis* is equally as important for understanding war as the underlying and hidden causes, only perceptible to those able to disentangle what the cities may not be able to see themselves.[73] The Cylon incident stands as evidence of the Spartan need to believe they were in fact on the side of justice in the war – one can defend oneself out of fear *and* believe one's cause is in fact just. If Thucydides believed the Cylon demand was merely pretext for a war the Spartans believed was justified on the basis of necessity, and a war that was to commence anyway, he would have dismissed, not detailed, this complaint.

Spartan reluctance to excuse their declaration of war due to the compelling nature of fear is the result of their unawareness, their inability, to see that fear, rather than Athenian injustice, is behind their resolve to stop Athenian imperialism. For it was the Athenians who made that argument, and it is Athens, based on the actions and speeches of Book One, that appear to have no regard for justice, thereby strengthening Sthenelaidas' convincing blame of Athenian injustice. Given the Athenians did not appear to advance pretexts during the growth of their empire in the fifty years leading up to war and only appeal to justice at Sparta, we might wonder if this is properly called "justice" at all. Yet it is also notable that

73 See note 15 above and context.

the Athenians nevertheless offer what *they* believe to be justifications for their empire – their measured conduct in ruling means they relinquished their own interests or good for the sake of something higher, for honor. They want to be viewed as deserving or worthy of their empire *because* their empire is not as harsh as it could be. Thus, even though Athens' conduct is unjust, according to Sparta, we cannot neglect to notice Thucydides' Athenians betray a concern with something beyond their mere interests, while proclaiming those interests to be their (and all cities') only truly compelling motive now. And relatedly, we must ask whether the Spartan appeal to justice is merely a hypocritical appeal to a standard that they themselves will never meet. Or is it that their attempt to secure a pretext, despite its obvious problems in light of Pericles' response, is evidence of the Spartans' longing to protect themselves against a possible further impiety, another pollution, by committing an unjust act in declaring war, an act that may doom any attempt to protect their city while at war?

The details of the Cylon incident, and the broader context in which it occurs, is notable for the difficulty it causes Thucydides scholars.[74] But it is more than this: Thucydides' account, as scholars and commentators

74 Hornblower I p. 202 views the Cylon digression as having two functions: 1) to correct Herodotus; 2) "…simply to provide a bridge the more substantial excurses on Pausanias and Themistokles." Yet as Hornblower later notes, there are a number of puzzling attributes in this portion of the text, and he is forced, it seems, as was Dover, to take Thucydides' relation of religious events or discussions seriously (as evidenced by his almost ten pages of commentary on 1.126-127). This includes Hornblower's remark on 126.6: "Why Th.[ucydides] introduced this detail about the sacrifices is beyond me…" (p. 208). Details about piety of various peoples is set forth by Thucydides as the result of his narrating the pious Spartans' demand. And the Cylon pretext, whatever one thinks about its strength or validity, is nevertheless such a demand Thucydides chooses to relate. But it is also a reminder that, despite differences Book One brings out between Spartans and Athenians (notable of course in the Corinthians' comments at 1.70), piety matters to varying degrees and at varying times for *all* peoples, including the Athenians (126.5). In this instance, it is a further explication of the main thrust of Book One: the cause of the war expressed at 1.23.5-6. Gomme I p. 425 errs, therefore, when arguing that "Thucydides, when he does digress (and this whole digression is irrelevant to his main narrative), allows himself to mention matters which he felt were of interest for their own sake." And this error is especially fatal for comprehending the Spartan view of the war. Cf. Palmer (1982) pp. 116-18 who sees Thucydides using this "digression" to illuminate some of his key themes (including tyranny and Alcibiades' role in Athens). Rood (2013) discusses the (distant) origin of the Cylon incident and its "Herodotean" character in narrative and style.

have only recently come to notice, contains far more details of the pious, the sacred, the holy than appears, or at least, has been previously admitted and discussed. Our canvas of Book One reveals this: Delos, Delphi, earthquakes, oracles, pious tyrants, oaths, sacrifices, are hardly the product of an author's "neglect of the religious factor in his narrative," nor does it allow one to conclude "that Thucydides seriously understated the religious aspect of the war he himself set out to describe."[75] With the Cylon story, Thucydides tells of a former Olympic victor and prominent Athenian who sought to become a tyrant. Unfortunately for Cylon, he misinterpreted an oracle and thus chose the wrong time to seek to take over Athens for himself. With Sparta, the support of the Delphic Oracle, if it truly is support (as opposed to perhaps a cautious prediction), does not protect them against their guilt later in the war for having initiated it (7.18.2). In other words, Cylon and the Spartans are both perhaps too certain of their interpretation of an oracular pronouncement.[76]

---

75 Hornblower (1992) pp. 169-70. Recently, Dolgert (2012) has sought to revive the view that Thucydides neglects religion, its role in the outbreak of the Peloponnesian War, and the Spartan narrative more broadly. Dolgert's interpretation, though, is plagued by an impossible hermeneutic position: He wants to contend both that Thucydides does not provide sufficient religious detail and explanation for the cause of the war; but also, that what Thucydides *does* present of religious matters must be treated with skepticism since Thucydides' text is "a highly partisan defence of Pericles' leadership" and (apparently) "Thucydides does not even bother to hide his partisanship" (663). Dolgert admits, citing a phrase of Hornblower's, that he is "correcting Thucydides out of Thucydides." What he does not quote is Hornblower noting that: "Our justification for doing this, a perilously arrogant justification, consists in the little we know of Greek religion." In practice, this often means scholars ignore what we do know, and Dolgert fails to cite Marinatos' (1981) important study (among others), thus treating Jordan's (1986) study as a lone voice supporting Thucydides' treatment of religion (p. 671n57). But more importantly, when Dolgert does finally turn to discussing what *he* views as the religious causes of the Peloponnesian War (pp. 672-76), he provides details (drawn from Thucydides) of both Spartan and Athenian piety, showing convincingly that this piety *did* affect decisions during the war. What Dolgert highlights, unbeknownst to himself, is that scholars, influenced by International Relations theory and by Hornblower (as Dolgert himself is), claim Thucydidean neglect when the neglect is on the part of those misreading him. (It should be noted, in Hornblower's defense, that the third volume of his *Commentary* is much more receptive to Thucydides' presentation of piety.)

76 Marinatos (1981b) p. 139 sees the Cylon narrative as evidence "that Thucydides is defending the oracle here" contra a broad portion of the scholarship who argues Thucydides views oracles as superstition. It appears to me she is defending two things at once: accepting oracles is different from "consistent interest in oracular puzzles and

But the thrust of Thucydides' narrative, along with the preoccupations of his speakers is clearer – piety motivates action. It motivates as part of the pretext, part of the cause, of the war. And relatedly, the impieties arising from the Cylon incident lead Thucydides to close Book One with a nod to what we would label "domestic politics." Pausanias and Themistocles are both instances of individuals at odds with their city, suspect due to their motives and the abilities that set them apart. Foreign dealings undertaken by each draw domestic scrutiny. The transition to Pericles thus becomes apparent: Athens' first man defends his city's empire and directs it largely unimpeded (2.65.9). But the appearance of Pericles at the end of Book One, taken together with the narrative dominating the first half of Book Two, offers pointed remarks on the cause of Athens' defeat – *stasis*. I intentionally leave the term untranslated here: lack of social cohesion, civil strife, or all-out civil war (as at Corcyra) all draw Athens into numerous (and fatal) mistakes and miscalculations which will open the door for newly able Spartans, and later, the Persians, to take advantage, both being aided by an ostracized Alcibiades, ostracized as a result of his trumped up, but believable, impieties.[77]

Thucydides' Spartan narrative, artfully presented and invaluable to comprehending Book One, draws attention away from any simple allegiance to the bold and thus highly noticeable principles expressed by the Athenian envoys, and instead aids in pointing in that very speech to the Athenians' own hidden moral motive: the motive for duly recognized honor. Taken together with the closing of the Book, animated by Sparta's pious demands and seeking of divine approval for going to war, Thucydides reminds us of the common root of both cities' actions: the moral side of human nature.

---

their correct interpretation." Were Dover (1973) right that Thucydides believes oracles are superstition, we will see that he nonetheless understands their importance *for the cities*: at the war's outbreak, during the plague, preceding the Sicilian expedition, on the length of the war; these cannot be ignored. Dover concedes as much, but is too quick to define historiography as "the exclusion of the divine" (44). Piety thus becomes merely the beliefs of this or that people, studied as it were, from above. On the difficulty in distinguishing superstition and religion (a distinction casually made by many scholars), see Strauss (1964) p. 180.

77 Debate surrounding the term *stasis* will be discussed further in Chapter Three, along with Athens' domestic problems.

Chapter Two

Spartan "Hypocrisy" versus the Athenian Thesis

With Thucydides' Book Two, the war is underway.[1] Moving into Books Three and Four, Thucydides continues his direct juxtaposition of Sparta and Athens, both in thought and action. Sparta's prosecution of the war, in particular, raises questions about the precise aim of their war effort, its claim to be liberating Greek cities from the Athenian empire as well as the justice of their cause; it also leaves us puzzling over their rather timid and uninspiring strategy. Three episodes we will focus on in this chapter illuminate Spartan thinking: their infamous intervention in the fighting between Plataea and Thebes; their disaster at Pylos when Spartan soldiers find themselves surrounded on an island by the Athenians; and finally, the culmination of their losses during the war's first ten years, resulting in the establishment of a treaty and official alliance with Athens. With these developments, Spartan justice, Spartan strategy, and Spartan resolve in fighting a war of liberation, all come to light largely as failures. Thucydides' narrative makes clear why.[2]

Skirmishes begin in Book Two with the Spartans attacking the Athenian countryside, a conservative approach advocated and led by Archidamus and anticipated by Pericles. The Spartans are, as it were, firing warning shots without notable effect. The Athenians, many of whom are rural people living in the countryside surrounding Athens, will be brought into the city by Pericles' policy of abandoning what he considers old Athens (the rural), protecting them partially, for now, against Archidamus' strategy. Pericles' new, wartime Athens will be an entirely seafaring city, a people designed to resist Sparta's superior land force.

The principal combatants of the war, however, are not those Thucydides

1 As Hornblower I p. 236 observes, the first word of Book Two is "begins" (*archō*).

2 For discussions that seek to piece together, from Thucydides, Sparta's strategy in the war, see Brunt (1965), Kelly (1982), and especially, Rahe (2015, 2019, 2020), who draws on all available ancient sources.

first draws our attention to with the war's opening hostilities. Instead, it is the invasion of Plataea, an Athenian ally, by a force from Thebes. Plataea and Thebes have been enemies "always" and thus the Thebans, foreseeing the Peloponnesian War on the horizon, attacked Plataea before an official declaration (2.2.3). This attack leads both Athens and Sparta, along with the allies of each, to begin preparations and launch their own first assaults. What Thebes seemed to view as a necessary preemptive attack against a city they were sure to fight in the larger war was in fact an attack that led to war. This action was a cause of war in the immediate and legal sense – Thebes' attack on Plataea breached the treaty. Curiously, Thucydides does not say Thebes *itself* breached the treaty; rather, only that the "affair" (*ergon*) at Plataea was a breach, leaving open the possibility the breach was not the action of Thebes simply (7.1 – my emphasis).[3] After all, Sparta is drawn into the Plataea-Thebes incident, leading to a debate between Sparta and Plataea on how Thebes' aggression will be handled. After witnessing the invasion and defeat of Plataea, we hear Spartan speeches, and most telling, witness the Spartans as judges of the fate of a vanquished city. Thucydides scholars point to this incident in their near-equivocal blame of Spartan "foreign policy" or conduct, but the details of this episode are more nuanced than is often noticed.

Thebes' attack on Plataea, and Sparta's involvement, leads to a three-city debate, the first major exchange of speeches since those at Sparta resulted in the decision to go to war. And there is a striking contrast, something surprising we must immediately notice: The debate following the hostilities between Plataea and Thebes revolves around both justice and piety. None of the cities expresses anything like the Athenian thesis; instead, all three justify their actions in moral terms. Thucydides has placed before the reader a new piece of the puzzle in understanding the moral claims voiced by the Spartans, the dictates of necessity (expressed in the Athenian thesis), now

3 This helps explain the problem of the two beginnings of the war: 1) Thebes' attack on Plataea, and 2) Sparta's invasion of Attica (2.10.1, 19.1-2). Hornblower I pp. 236-37 entertains various possible interpretations of this double beginning. Ultimately, he correctly alludes to 7.18.2 and argues that "...it was perhaps for literary reasons that Th.[ucydides] represents the attack on her [Plataea] as a turning of the page." In my view, 7.18.2, which reveals the Spartans' guilt for starting the war (as they viewed it then, in the war's 18th year) signals that it is the entire *incident* at Plataea, not simply the actions of the Thebans alone, that Thucydides wants us to understand as the beginning of the war. It is Sparta and Athens that are the key belligerents, the cities bringing so to speak the whole Greek world into the conflict.

placing this puzzle within the context of hostile actions and foreign policy precipitating the Peloponnesian War.

Sparta at Plataea: The "Hypocritical" Spartans

The invasion of Plataea by Thebes is complicated by the manner in which it begins. The Thebans are invited into the city by a faction within Plataea itself. Certain Plataeans wished to shift the regime away from the democracy to an oligarchy, the former in place as a result of Plataea's alliance with Athens. While the Thebans hoped to gain the city to themselves through the invasion, it is questionable whether such an opportunity would have arisen if not for faction within Plataea. This interpretation is further strengthened by the manner in which the Thebans carry out their assault. The Plataean faction demanded the Thebans immediately kill their own enemies after entering the city, an act the latter refused to do. Instead, the Thebans hoped to arrive at a "friendly" (*philios*) agreement with the Plataeans, appealing to the previously existing Boeotian alliance (2.2.4). Further, the Thebans, as the Plataeans themselves observed, had not engaged in any violence upon entering the city. They of course agree to the alliance immediately, due to it being dark and therefore unaware of the number of Thebans within their gates. This misperception on the part of the Plataeans once realized, they attack the Thebans and are able to subdue or kill many of them. The "greater number" (*plēthos*) of Plataeans were not in favor of revolting from Athens, confirming the pro-Theban faction inviting outsiders into the city was oligarchic (3.2).

Worried about Theban reinforcements arriving to support the initial assault, the Plataeans sent word to the Thebans that they had taken prisoners; if the Thebans did not leave their countryside without further harm, the prisoners will be killed. However, the prisoners will be handed over should the Thebans leave at once. The Thebans agree to these terms and oaths are exchanged between the two to protect this arrangement (5.5-7). When the Thebans leave the Plataean countryside, however, the Theban prisoners are killed.

Now this account is the Theban one. The Plataeans present a different story: They argue no oath was given and the return of the prisoners was contingent upon further negotiations (5.6). Here, Thucydides offers his own remarks: the Thebans complied by not harming Plataean land, yet the Plataeans still killed the Theban prisoners. While the Plataean account of the arrangement may be correct on the issue of whether an oath was in fact exchanged, they did not allow for any further negotiations. Therefore, even according to the Plataeans' own account, they reneged on the conditions of the discussion, sealed with an oath or not – they killed the Theban prisoners "immediately" (*euthus* – 5.7).

This dispute is relevant not only to the Spartan invasion of Plataea on their way to Attica, an attack which seems to follow from both Athens and Sparta hearing of the events at Plataea (7.1), but to understanding the causes of the war. Not Sparta and Athens themselves, but cities tied to each again bring the two major powers into conflict (similar to the Corinth-Corcyra dispute). On seeing the Spartans' intention to attack the countryside in response, the Plataeans urge them to refrain. They appeal to the promise that Plataea live "independent" (*autonomos*) after they helped the Greeks defeat the Persians in the Persian War; this was guaranteed both by the Greek allies and the fathers of Sparta, and in particular through Pausanias' assurance to them. Not surprisingly then, the Plataeans appeal here to the oaths and gods of each city, as well as the gods of Sparta's forefathers. They acted with "virtue" (*aretē*) and thus ask the Spartans to recognize past service rendered as well as past oaths sworn (71.3). This is an appeal the Spartans themselves will later make (4.20). The Plataean appeal is to justice traditionally understood, expecting their virtue be rewarded; they apparently do not pursue virtue as its own reward, but rather virtue serves their interests, precisely when it is a sacrifice of their immediate interests. Virtue then, at least for the Plataeans, appears to be a long-term calculation of interests and thus in keeping with what the Athenians claim about the compelling nature of such interests.

Yet is this how the Plataeans understand their own appeal to the Spartans? Is this not reading their arguments from the Athenian point of view, based on the Athenian thesis? It might appear that virtue is pursued in a mercenary way, i.e., based on long-term calculation. But how can the Plataeans be sure of reciprocity, that the Spartans (or any peoples) will recognize their past good deeds when the time comes to "collect" their rewards? It seems they cannot; or more precisely, they must rely on the will of the gods to support the oaths and agreements between the two cities, even agreements that occurred a generation ago. From the point of view of the

Athenian thesis, this is quite stunning. For even if the Plataeans were acting out of a mercenary view of self-interest, they now expect the Spartans to possibly forgo theirs to side with the Plataeans in a dispute unlikely to sway an ally of Thebes. We can never imagine the envoys at Athens, nor Pericles, making such recommendations or appealing to such demands. In Plataea's appeal to Sparta, along with the moral language of other cities, the reader is led to consider such moral aspects of the war more closely. The Plataea-Thebes-Sparta debate also sets the stage for comparing the manner in which moral language finds its way even into Athens, their treatment of Mytilene being an incident Thucydides presents immediately after (and thus by way of comparison with) the Plataea affair (narratives of both intertwined in the first half of Book Three).

Archidamus' reply to the Plataeans' demand begins with the word "justice" (*dikaion* – 2.72.1). He does not deny the Plataeans' claims simply, for example as arguments of the weak. Rather, the Plataeans must abide by what they themselves appealed to and be independent, if they cannot join the Spartans in the war. Remaining subject to Athens (as Archidamus views all of Greece) and friends of Sparta is not acceptable. The Plataeans confer, but cannot agree to such terms. They fear for their city, that the Athenians may take it from them or that the Thebans would attempt a second invasion. Even if Thebes were also to exchange oaths with Sparta to leave Plataea to its independence, the Plataeans are fearful (72.2). This mention of oaths in reference only to the Thebans may hint that the Plataeans had in fact made an oath with the Thebans previously, but breached it when they killed the prisoners and expect the Thebans to repay them in kind. Or they may surmise that their long-standing enmity with Thebes will continue regardless of any oaths. Appeal to oaths and the past cooperation between themselves and the Spartans indicates that the Plataeans expect this to be convincing – they do not appeal here to Sparta's interest or advantage (71.4). And they seem to assume the Athenians will retake their city after Sparta leaves, a strategy or action that recurs repeatedly throughout the war when Sparta fails to fully conquer Athens' allied or subject cities.

Archidamus, though, assures them they will be restored to their city after the war, but must leave now. He grants a truce for the Plataeans to consult with the Athenians on the Spartan proposal; he refrains from taking any action against the city. But the Athenians promise they will not abandon Plataea to the Spartans and will protect the city; the Plataeans are told to maintain their alliance with Athens and to stand by the solemnly sworn oaths made by the Plataeans' fathers. And they do so (73.3).

On receiving this response, Archidamus delivers a speech addressed directly to the gods (74.2).[4] He contends that the Spartans have not been aggressors in the past, nor will they be now with an invasion of Plataea; it was the Plataeans who departed from their oaths. He appeals to the gods to see to it that "vengeance" (*timōria*) be received by the Plataeans for their breach of these oaths. Being an ally of Athens, their "alliance" makes them an enemy of Sparta in the war now. After offering them a chance to leave the Athenian empire and given their failure to do so, the Plataeans are violating their solemnly sworn past agreement with Sparta. Archidamus does not raise any other considerations; nor does he address the potentially mitigating circumstance that the Plataeans may be compelled to remain tied to Athens. After all, compulsion borne out of fear would be in keeping with the Spartan claim to be liberating those cities held involuntarily as part of the Athenian empire (2.8.4). A war of liberation presupposes those under the Athenian empire as subjects are not voluntarily remaining in subjugation. Archidamus assumes, instead, that Plataea can act freely, if not to be allies of Sparta, at least not be subjects of Athens; he therefore believes his proposals to be "reasonable" (*eikos*). Given his silence on these considerations, he seems to implicitly disregard the Plataeans' appeal to their past alliance with Sparta and their service in the Persian War where they fought alongside other Greek cities.

But in fact, Archidamus agrees with the appeals made by the Plataeans themselves, arguing past oaths protected them as an independent city. As Archidamus understands it, however, they have not maintained their independence; their alliance seems to be freely joined. Yet even if Plataea did not join in alliance with Athens, this does not negate their claim that it would be dangerous to leave Athens now. To switch sides with the war underway

4 This is the only speech in Thucydides where a speaker directly addresses the gods. Badian (1989) p. 98 characterizes the speech as "all rhetorical display." Wassermann (1953) takes a notably different view: "Even after the negotiations have broken down owing to the insistence of the Plataeans on staying by their alliance with Athens, Archidamus does not start the fighting without, in a solemn invocation to the local gods, stressing the righteousness of his cause (2.74.3). These are the last words he speaks in the *History*, ending with a reference to *nomos*, as he began with the concept of *dike*, both keys to his conservative creed" (198). Debnar (2001) p. 100 notes Herodotus 6.56: the king is a priest. See Rahe (2016) pp. 41-48 on the king as priest, especially on campaigns.

would be considered a breach of their new oaths, now to Athens, as well as risking that Athens would reestablish a democracy friendly to their alliance. And while their appeal to justice may be due to a genuine belief they should be recompensated for past service to their fellow Greeks, we must also weigh the fact that they cannot appeal to Spartan interests, the Thebans standing by the Spartans as their allies. The Plataeans realize Spartan interests lie with Thebes, their old enemy. For Archidamus, the reason behind Plataea's current alliance with Athens has not been sufficiently addressed. Sparta thus invades and subdues the city, eventually leading to surrender. Upon Plataea's surrender the Spartans send to Sparta for "judges" (*dikastais*) to discern who the guilty party is in this dispute (3.52.2).

The Spartan judges do not charge the Plataeans with a specific crime, but only ask what "good service" they have done for Sparta in the war (52.4). In response, the Plataeans ask to speak at length, and this is granted. In fact, the Thebans themselves only come forward to speak in response to the Plataean speech – on hearing it, they were afraid it may have been persuasive to the Spartans (60, 61.1). The Spartans do not simply follow through with their apparent pre-arrangement with the Thebans, which Thucydides only allows us to notice after the Plataeans' speech. That the Spartans drop their agreement with the Thebans signals they were not simply puppets of their allies.[5]

Aware they have not benefited Sparta in the present war, the Plataeans as Athenian allies must appeal to past service as a means to receiving

5 According to Romilly (1963) p. 40, the Theban speech had no effect. Crane (1998) p. 193 argues the Plataeans and Thebans "might as well have said nothing." Mara (2009) p. 121 marks this as a telling instance of Sparta's relationship to *logos*: "The extended speeches of the Plataean and Theban representatives (covering more chapters than the Mytilene debate) are pointless exercises in the shadow of a sentence already passed." Hornblower (1987) p. 68 concurs: "the arguments of both the Plataeans and the Thebans are ignored at the end by the Spartans." Macleod (1983) pp. 105, 119 takes the proceedings too literally, claiming "this trial is a travesty of legal forms" and "since the legal form is a sham, still less can any moral considerations weigh." Hornblower I p. 446 cites Macleod approvingly and adds that, at 3.68 "…the Spartans simply repeat their original question *as if the speeches had never been delivered at all*" (emphasis in original). Hornblower ultimately concludes that "[t]he message of the Plataian Debate is that it would have made no difference if there had been no debate at all" (462). These views disregard both the fact that the Thebans did not want the Plataeans to speak, that the Spartans allowed them to nonetheless, as well as Thucydides' narrative remark on the Spartans' motives: they reconsidered their own question after the fact (3.68.1).

preferential treatment now. They ask Sparta not to act on behalf of their enemies, the Thebans; they do little, however, to appeal to Sparta's current needs in the war or to recent just actions. Even admitting they had become "enemies" (*polemioi* – 55.1) of the Spartans currently, they excuse this by arguing they were "compelled" to do so (*anankē* – 58.2). Compulsion has acted upon them, and this is not an alliance at all – it was Sparta that refused an alliance with them. And as we know, Athens was able to compel its allies in a manner that rendered them subjects (1.99.1).[6] The Plataeans were not in a voluntary alliance but were forced (at least eventually) to contribute to the Athenian empire; they were forced to submit to what was in the interest of Athens, to sacrifice their interests for Athens' own. This compulsion to submit instead of fighting was brought on by Athens' strength and also by their small size.

This latter consideration is not stated directly. However, Thucydides later allows us to see the fate of Mytilene in their attempt to rebel, as well as the fate of Melos, even in their neutrality.[7] The small Plataea would have no choice but to accept Athenian terms of alliance or potentially accept the fate of Melos. Importantly, they do not argue this point at length because their speech is concerned with demonstrating their justice, not that they submitted to Athens out of necessity; therefore, they only briefly mention (in one sentence) being "enemies" of Sparta and "compelled" to be at war (3.55.1, 58.2). Since they were compelled, they are "friendly" (*eunous*) to Sparta. Compulsion, though, is never mentioned again. Rather, the Plataeans appeal to justice, as the Melians will later in the war, because they hope for a just judgment from Sparta because the Spartans were held to be just (53.1); the Plataeans do not mention that the Athenians were held to be just. Dropping the discussion of compulsion, they appeal to their past service to Sparta in the Persian War and refer to themselves as "benefactors" of Sparta then because they are not benefactors of Sparta now. And they have already admitted that Sparta should consider its own interests (56.7).

---

6 Forde (1989) p. 5: "The new and openly immoral doctrine of power and justice proclaimed and acted upon by the Athenians exerts a similar compulsion on those who are forced to confront the Athenians at war."

7 The island of Melos will be confronted by the numerically and strategically superior Athens in Book Five, leading to Thucydides' infamous "Melian Dialogue," a debate between the two cities. The situation ends violently, with the Athenians attacking and slaughtering the island's people, despite the Melians' insistence on their insignificance and offering to remain neutral in the Peloponnesian War.

The Spartan question implies, however, that the Plataeans had free choice to act contrary to the manner in which they did. All blame for actions taken or not taken presupposes the ability to have acted otherwise; to deem actions just or unjust presupposes they are possible. But this does not mean either city understands the full import of their own arguments – when the Plataeans appeal to their alliance again, the terms are those of justice. They had a duty not to leave their alliance with Athens. While they were compelled to serve Athens' interest, they were also just men in acting as Athens wanted. Yet oddly, they also admit to having their own interests served – they "receive[ed] benefits at [the Athenians'] hands" (55.3); they even requested to obtain Athenian citizenship for themselves. The Plataeans are able to state these facts, which would hardly seem to aid their case, due to the fact that Sparta had set the stage for Plataea to ally with Athens. The Spartans allowed the Athenians to take over the alliance of Greek cities that fought off the Persians; the Plataeans imply they did nothing more than follow the leader (55.4). However, a difficulty exists since the Spartans, though glad they did not have to further lead the war against Persia, were also constrained by Pausanias and his corruption – his conduct was "like that of a tyrant" and "[t]he Athenians...succeeded to the supremacy by the voluntary act of the allies through their hatred of Pausanias" (1.95.2, 96.1).[8] The Spartan commander could no longer lead the Spartans in the war; the Spartans were handicapped by their own man. Yet whatever Sparta's reasons for leaving Athens in sole control of the allies fighting against Persia, the Plataeans' arguments prove problematic. Appealing first to compulsion, then to duty, and then to their own interests, they attempt to find an acceptable justification for being Athens' ally. The Plataeans are trying to offer the Spartans all possible explanations for this alliance. Do these various appeals clarify, or confuse, their current alliance?

As for their relation to Thebes: The Plataeans argue the Thebans initially invaded their territory, thereby suggesting they had a right to kill the Theban prisoners – the punishment for invasion is "taking vengeance" (*timōreō*). In killing the Thebans, the Plataeans were acting according to the

8 Cf. Machiavelli, *Prince* Ch. 19 "Of Avoiding Contempt and Hatred" with *Discourses on Livy* III.6 "Of Conspiracies." In Thucydides' account of Pausanias, hatred towards him results from his violent disposition. The Spartans ultimately plot against him, as he was conspiring both with the Helots and Persians, neither of whom were particularly friendly with the Spartans.

"law" (*nomos*) of resisting an invader (3.56.2).[9] However, from the Spartan point of view, as allies of Thebes, this argument is also problematic. The Plataeans had promised the Thebans a negotiation for the return of the prisoners, contingent on the Thebans leaving Plataean land without further harm. And the Thebans *did* comply with this demand. The Plataeans reneged on their own conditions in failing to offer this negotiation and instead putting their old enemy to death. Appealing to the Spartans not to act vengefully towards them now, they appeal to a sentiment that they themselves, in a similar situation, did not act upon. They plead for Sparta not to kill them for the sake of their Theban alliance, despite the fact they killed Theban prisoners themselves. The Plataeans urge the Spartans to grant gentle treatment of an enemy they themselves did not grant. It seems they believe these more recent actions (alliance with Athens and the killing of the Thebans) are ultimately more of a concern for the Spartans than their past good service; for otherwise raising these considerations, which thereby serve as a reminder, would only seem to harm their attempt to be granted Spartan clemency (56.1-2).

Arguing the Spartans' "reputation" (*doxa*) will suffer if they are put to death, the Plataeans end their speech by appealing (again) to the Spartans not to breach the "common custom of the Greeks" by killing men who have surrendered (59.1).[10] It is not clear precisely what *nomos* the Plataeans are

9 This is commonly translated as "universal law" (for example, Strassler [1996], Jowett [1881]). The Greek phrase is *kata pasi nomon*, literally "according to the law of all." Thus, Lattimore (1998): "the rule observed by all." Mynott (2013), similarly, translates *nomos* here as "convention," which reminds us that "law" in English is not wholly sufficient to capture the range of meanings *nomos* has. Macleod (1983) pp. 108-109 believes this is a law of nature. Hornblower I p. 451, though, disagrees, arguing that the language throughout points to impieties (both *spondais* and *hieromania*) which in Jowett is rendered "…in time of peace and at a sacred time of month." Thus the Plataeans' argument here, Hornblower notes, "contains a double charge of impiety." And I would add: Is the issue not that all three cities here are confronted with lack of knowledge of what the gods expect and thus are forced to justify their actions based on what they perceive the gods to forbid or allow?

10 See Fustel de Coulanges (1980) p. 199; Burckhardt (2002) pp. 107, 109-10. Both authors argue that the general action taken among Greek cities was to execute prisoners captured in times of war. This is perhaps rendered problematic by the fact that both use Thucydides as one source of confirmation of this. We can at least observe within Thucydides' account that even among the Athenians, who claim to act out of calculated self-interest, killing prisoners is the rule (3.36.1, 5.32.1, 116.3-4. Cf. 3.49.1). See also note 27 below. The term used here is *nomimos*: "conformable to custom, usage, or law" (Liddell-Scott [1889] p. 534).

appealing to, other than reciprocity for past service to Greece. The granting and guarantee of independence by the Spartan commander, Pausanias (referred to by the Plataeans in this context) is not without difficulties as well, however, given his cooperation with the Persians. And Pausanias was eventually killed by the Spartan ephors as punishment for his corruption while fighting during that war. Are Pausanias' decisions and agreements binding on the Spartans now? Even if such a law or custom existed between Greek cities to spare those who surrender, the Plataeans themselves breached it with the killing of the Theban prisoners. Fearing the complications of the case, their alliance with Athens, and knowing the Spartans were disposed toward the Thebans, their speech ends with an additional ground of appeal, most notably a flurry of pious invocations: Greek customs, ancestors and the long history the cities had with one another, the justice of the case, and the gods are all mentioned in quick succession, ending with a final plea to the Spartans to be their liberators and "saviors" (59.4 – *sōtēras*).[11]

The Theban speech, a response to Plataeans' lengthy appeal to Spartan justice, argues they were not guilty of allying with the Persians because, first, the Thebans were under a tyrannical regime (62.3 – *dunasteia*); and second, the Plataeans chose an alliance with Athens when they could have sided with Sparta. While the Plataean speech could only focus on the past, the Theban speech focuses on the present.

In keeping with this focus, the Thebans detail the matters surrounding their unannounced invasion of Plataea. They were invited in by Plataeans, a faction of the leading men of "wealth" and "birth." However they are wrong to assert further that they were brought in as friends serving all of Plataea; the Thebans had to reject the request of the Plataean faction to kill all of their enemies immediately.[12] Besides, the openly avowed cause of the war is the liberation of Greece from Athens and the Thebans have no claim to hold Plataea for themselves; they claim the men who called

11 This term appears to be used in only one other instance in Thucydides: Brasidas as savior of Amphipolis (5.11). (Cf., however, *sōtēria*, "safety" used throughout the text, but in particular, during the Melian Dialogue – 5.87). If this is correct, the irony of Sparta as savior of Plataea (which they will not be) is in keeping with also not being the liberator of Greece as a whole, that is, without the actions of Brasidas. Surprisingly, neither Gomme nor Hornblower mention the term, despite Hornblower emphasizing the pious language in the Plataeans' speech (see note 9 above). Cf. Herodotus 7.139.

12 Cf. 5.17.2 where the Athenians seem to accept this claim since Plataea is not returned to them in their treaty with Sparta.

them in intended to moderate the regime, presenting their decision to invade Plataea as rooted in the claims of a faction supposedly instituting a better regime (65.1-2). But Thucydides has already presented the true reason as being the old enmity between the two cities – since the war between Athens and Sparta would draw, so to speak, all of the cities of Greece into it, the Thebans expected war to break out between themselves and Plataea as well – they preemptively struck the Plataeans, therefore, without any open declaration of war (2.2.3). Thucydides is silent on their justification. And even on the Thebans' own terms, the problem now arises that they exculpate themselves (and blame Plataea) because they were invited in by a faction within the city; yet in having to deal with an issue in their own past, they argue they were not to blame for previously supporting the Persians because in that case support was due to the power of a few in the city at that time. According to the Thebans, factions within a city both do, and do not, exculpate the city itself.

Despite the difficulties with these arguments, they deflect attention away from these issues in their past by returning to the present considerations at hand. The Plataeans, they argue, have committed three injustices: the violation of an agreement of neutrality with Sparta, the killing of Theban prisoners, and deceiving the Thebans by promising the return of their men should they leave the Plataean countryside unharmed (3.66.3).

After hearing both speeches, the Spartan judges decide their question was a "correct" one (*orthos*) because they had offered the Plataeans the opportunity to remain independent, as their agreement with Pausanias had stipulated, or to leave Athens now and remain neutral in the war. Both ancient treaty and the current offer now being rejected, the Spartan believe "by their just intentions" (*tē heautōn dikaia boulēsei*) to be released from the prior conditions connected with the promises of Pausanias. And further, the Plataeans have done "evil" (*kakōs*) to the Spartans now (68.1). The Plataeans' arguments regarding their past service are not recognized by the Spartans as exculpatory for their current alliance with Athens, an alliance the Thebans focused on. The view that the Athenians are unjust and have harmed Greece, and thus led Sparta to wage a war of liberation, is in keeping with the Spartan decision. The Plataeans' claim to be "friends" of Greece is problematic considering the war now underway; they speak as though the war were still one of a united Greece fighting a foreign invader. The Thebans' claim it was not themselves but a quasi-tyrannical regime that led their city to ally with the Persians may have persuaded the Spartans, considering their own difficulties with Pausanias himself – but the "Medism" of Pausanias and the Thebans is less decisive than the "Atticism" of the Plataeans (62.1).[13]

The error of the Spartan decision lies in their blame of Plataea for its lack of good service to Sparta. The Spartans could not expect that the Plataeans, as Athenian allies or subjects, to have served Sparta's interests. The only point, it seems, upon which the Plataeans may be blamed is for their execution, without the promised negotiations, of 180 Theban prisoners. Yet the Spartans focus in their decision on neutrality – *this* is the point on which the Plataeans are blamed by the Spartans themselves. Plataea has not harmed Sparta directly except through their alliance with Athens. What is most striking to note about this incident as a whole and the speeches of all three cities, though, is that they argue almost exclusively in terms of justice. Even with their lives on the line, the Plataeans argue they were justified in killing the Thebans that had invaded their city, affirming vengeance as the proper response to injustice. No city argues in terms approaching the arguments of the Athenian envoys at Sparta, the Athenian thesis. The Plataeans, in failing to avail themselves of such terms, may be aware that an appeal to necessity or advantage would have no effect on the Spartans. Problematic, though, is their appeal to punishment, which establishes a precedent for Sparta – they unwittingly appear to help the Spartans view the issue as the Plataeans themselves fear, i.e., that Sparta will mask a decision serving their own interests behind an apparent concern with justice (56.3-4).

Concluding this episode, Thucydides states: "In practically every respect [*schedon*] the Spartans turned against the Plataeans for the sake of the Thebans, believing the latter would be helpful in the war that had then

13 Cogan (1981) pp. 66-73 focuses on the term "Atticism" and argues that this episode represents an "ideological" shift in the war, Athenian imperialism being viewed in a new light. But while alluding to the difficulties discussed (see note 5 above and context), Cogan does not investigate them further. Whatever the epithet Athens' subject cities gave to their empire does not appear to affect their view of the conditions of subjection nor its injustice. The Plataeans even note the benefits of alliance with Athens, which presumably would have been partially responsible for Athens' subjects not revolting in the past. Cf. 1.99 where Thucydides observes Greece's increasing awareness of the compelling character of the empire and the shift from allies to subjects. For the ambiguous nature of Plataean independence and neutrality and their relationship to Athens, see Hornblower I pp. 358-59, 449-50.

just started." Most commentators interpret Thucydides' remarks at 3.68 as a clear indication of Sparta's so-called hypocrisy. But these remarks are not as clear as they appear.[14] Arguing here (and throughout Thucydides' account) in terms of justice, yet seemingly acting in accordance with their own advantage, the Spartans are accused of blatant hypocrisy. Knowingly using pretexts of justice to advance their own cause, they are fully aware they are merely employing such arguments as a ruse. Thucydides certainly lends evidence to this interpretation given his claim that the Spartans *did* consider their advantage when killing the Plataeans. However, the issue of the fate of the Theban prisoners, the restatement of the Spartan judges that their question was a correct one (implying a reconsideration of what had been argued by the Plataeans), and Thucydides' own remark that they acted "mainly" (*schedon*) for the usefulness of the Thebans in the war all complicate this view. These details lead us to raise the question of how the Spartans understand the relation of justice and expediency or advantage, for Athenians' later statement at Melos implies they knowingly, and hypocritically, conflate the two (5.105.4).

Orwin, for example, argues: "Long habituated to act as their interests seem to require, [the Spartans] do so as *smugly* as if meting out impeccable justice" (emphasis added).[15] Orwin's claim of smugness seems to imply that the Spartans are *aware* of their own conflation of interest and justice and thus are only concerned with the *appearance* of being just. Now, smugness may not imply hypocritical pride and instead point to actual pride

14 Finley (1967) p. 19: the Spartans are "supremely guided by self-interest" and (1942) p. 180: "every action" is for the Thebans; Cogan (1981) p. 66: the Spartans killed the Plataeans because the Thebans wanted them to; Romilly (1963) p. 40: the Spartans acted only out of self-interest; Pouncey (1980) p. 19: "…self-interest as the [Spartans'] only legitimate concern"; Connor (1984) p. 93: for the Spartans "advantage decides." Mara (2009) p. 121: "The extended speeches of the Plataean and Theban representatives (covering more chapters than the Mytilene debate) are pointless exercises in the shadow of a sentence already passed." Hornblower (1987) p. 163 believes this comment is sufficient to establish Thucydides' opinion on Spartan motive. Romilly pp. 279-81: "egoism and hypocrisy" of the Spartans is shown by Thucydides at 3.56.3. Romilly takes the Plataeans' assessment of the Spartans as decisive and apparently Thucydides' own view. Cf. Crane (1998) p. 193 who parenthetically alludes to one of the complications of the case, i.e., the Plataeans killing the Theban prisoners and the offer of neutrality by Archidamus. Debnar (2011) pp. 145-46 similarly observes that the Spartans' view their question as fair. However, she makes a distinction between pious actions and amoral ones, a distinction foreign to the Spartans themselves.

15 Orwin (1994) p. 78 and context.

– they believe they are truly just men. Orwin notes we need not doubt the Spartans' sincerity in believing they are just. Smugness can be taken, then, in two ways: as believing oneself morally superior or as pretending to be morally superior and knowing this posture has benefits. The Spartans are of course roundly accused of the latter. Nevertheless, however we classify the motive for their smugness, it is hard to see the Spartan as proud; their actions throughout the war betray the very opposite of hubris. In this incident, as well as many others, they instead reveal a fear of their own (possible) injustice, including being punished by the gods, not an assuredness in their doing the right thing. This explains why they are so cautious and hesitant to get involved abroad, preferring to stay at home. Men who believe the gods watch their every move are very doubtful of making any moves, especially given the unsure character of actions during war. As Orwin himself goes on to note, the Spartans' motives in the Plataea episode are not exclusively to aid the Thebans.[16]

Macleod, on the other hand, is one of the strongest critics of the Spartans' actions and does not mince words. He accuses the Spartans of "indolent egoism," "an exclusive concern with her own interests," and thereby concludes that "in the war one big power displays its reputed virtue no more than the other – whatever they say about themselves and others may believe about them."[17] Beginning from Thucydides' statement at 3.68, he then reads this observation back into the entire incident. And since Macleod's concern is also with assessing the legal language of the debate, he appears to force the expectation onto the terms used by each city that they will be strictly legal in nature.

Now, the Spartans do call in special judges. But Macleod applies Thucydides' other remarks on *stasis* (civil war) and *nomos* (law) directly to this debate, as though those remarks, which relate to domestic politics, epitomize a procedural standard upon which to judge the Spartans' "trial" of the Plataeans, a debate between three cities. Yet, as noted above, what *nomos* is at play here? The debate is grounded in justice (including divine justice) more broadly understood – expectation for reward, obligations, moral propriety versus previous ill treatment, the right to punish breaches of oaths – matters the Spartans very much have in mind. And in these

16 Orwin (1994) p. 78: "…we need not doubt the sincerity of the 'judges'' conclusion that the question put to the Plataeans was just."

17 Macleod (1983) p. 105.

considerations, the Spartans weigh this incident seriously. In other words, the Spartans are believers in their own procedure and in the outcome. While Thucydides does lend the impression the Spartans are merely self-interested calculators, this is part of the process of discovery, the discovery of morality's hold, that requires we readers dig deeper. Nor is Thucydides' statement at 3.68 as unequivocal as it first appears, as we will discuss below. It makes all the difference in our understanding of human nature if we reduce actions to calculated self-interest versus untangling how a pious and moral people justify their wartime decisions.

Thucydides' language here allows us to see, as I argue, the Spartans' dual motives. The Spartans genuinely believed Plataea was at least partially at fault for the dispute with Thebes. But that their decision rested also on service to Sparta, and did not draw out the merits of the Plataean case, suggests they lacked in the case itself the clear justification for their final decision. Perhaps somewhat or at times aware of its tentative character, the Spartans dispensed their "justice" cautiously. That they were aware of their blindness to these dual motives, however, is far from clear.[18]

We must distinguish, in other words, between conscious and unconscious hypocrisy. The phenomenon we most often identify as hypocrisy is the conscious manipulation of others, especially in politics, to disguise our self-interested ends behind moral pretexts that protect those ends from being discovered. It lends moral propriety, which we notice human beings trouble themselves with, to actions which otherwise would be resisted by others.

---

18 For other mentions of the hypocrisy issue, cf. Strauss (1964) pp. 216-17; Burns (2010) pp. 40, 42 speaks of Spartan "hypocrisy *or* self-delusion" (emphasis added); Forde (1989) pp. 45-47, 151-55; especially p. 153 where he argues that Spartan hypocrisy is "all the more effective for being invisible to the Spartans themselves." Jaffe (2017) p. 180 suggests that the "adorned or magnified justification for war is the Spartan *prophasis*." Following Strauss (1983), Jaffe points here to the Spartan view that causes in human life are connected to the gods. Surprisingly, Jaffe previously spoke of Spartan hypocrisy (116). Yet if the Spartans believe their own *prophasis*, and if other cities in the future will also do so, then we misunderstand belligerents by labeling them "hypocrites." Magnifying the cause of the war by tracing or relating human events to the gods may disguise from a city their interests, i.e., necessity; but if Thucydidean necessity is not causally deterministic (as Jaffe argues) then does not the claim of adornment and magnification presuppose the gods, or our belief in them, are *not* a cause? I do not believe Thucydides goes this far. All cities, even Athens, justify their actions (at some time or other, before or after the action) in the language of divine justice.

Despite these considerations, the Plataeans' accusation (along with the Athenian statement at Melos) are taken to be decisive, to be Thucydides' own understanding of Spartan character (3.56.3, 5.105.4). Yet the complications mentioned above are only a few in the Plataean case – the Thebans were also allies of Sparta; the Plataeans, despite their independence, had allied themselves with Athens; and the Plataeans failed to avail themselves of yet another offer to leave Athens and remain neutral in the war. This expectation of neutrality is perhaps unreasonable on the part of the Spartans. However, we cannot fail to note that the interests of the Thebans and Plataeans are never raised in the debate – both argue in terms of justice or right. The Thebans especially could have argued that it was in their interest to kill the Plataeans and threaten to revoke any alliance should Sparta not comply. But Thebes feared Sparta would be swayed to clemency by a Plataean speech animated by appeals to justice and even to the gods. And the Plataeans as well argue that any Spartan decision would be unjust if it did not give serious, or all, consideration to the fact that they had been allies of Sparta during the Persian War. Both cities set aside arguments of mere self-interest, seeking rather to be on the "right" side (Sparta's side) in their appeals to their judges (the Spartans).

The comparison between Thucydides' remarks here (3.68) and the Athenians' claim of Spartan hypocrisy at Melos (5.105) is key to understanding the Spartan view. The Athenians at Melos accuse the Spartans, in particular, of holding what is expedient as just. Here, Thucydides merely says that the Spartans acted "mainly" (*schedon*) to please the Thebans. In other words, we are left to wonder what else motivated them, whether in the case of Plataea the Spartans also held that their interests and justice coincided. Thucydides' use of *schedon* cannot be ignored.[19] It suggests the Spartans did not act toward the Plataeans *entirely* out of a concern with the usefulness of the Thebans in the war. Nor is it clear the Spartans themselves

19 *Schedon* is an adverb that when used in the sense of degree means "nearly, all but, almost" (Liddell-Scott [1889] p. 786). The following are found in English translations of Thucydides: Hobbes (1989): "especially or rather altogether"; Jowett (1881): "mainly"; Lattimore (1998): "practically" and Mynott (2013): "in practically every respect." In other words, it has been translated in various ways, some of which depart from Liddell-Scott, who points to its function as an adverb, i.e., it modifies Thucydides' attribution of Spartan motive. Gomme II pp. 355-56 highlights how *schedon* qualifies the Spartans' motives, but also notes the Spartans are characterized by "unscrupulous *dishonesty*" (emphasis in original). Hornblower I on 3.68 does not remark on the term. See also 5.66 and 7.33 for Thucydides' only other uses of *schedon*.

were fully conscious of their own motives. Furthermore, while the Plataeans' assessment of the motives of the Spartans agrees with Thucydides (apart from the qualification just mentioned), Thucydides also notes, without an additional remark and in his own name, that the Spartans thought their question to the Plataeans to be "right" (*orthos*). The Spartans do in fact weigh the question they posed *after* the speeches of both the Plataeans and Thebans. And this reconsideration is presented by Thucydides as a private, closed-door debate amongst the judges, who then proceeded to ask their question again to the Plataeans, calling them in one by one to stand judgment (68.1). In other words, that they mainly consider the usefulness of the Thebans to their cause does not sufficiently establish that they believed their actions to be unjust and inconsistent with the dictates of justice as they understand them.[20]

Yet even if we want to ignore this qualifying term, we still have to wonder two things: First, why Thucydides adds *schedon* (a term he rarely uses). And second, whether the Spartans themselves would agree with his attribution. Did the Spartans only view their own motives as self-interested? This is our initial impression and the scholarly consensus. But then how does this square with the Spartans' claim to be judging justly? What exactly is the trial-like performance intended to achieve? It makes all the difference whether human beings are consciously or unconsciously hypocritical if we are to understand human, and therefore, political motives.

While their suitability as "judges" is questionable, since we expect justice not be colored by the interests of any one party, Sparta's uniting justice and expediency does not mean they did so *knowingly*, nor that they even believed these at odds with one another. Did the Spartans not believe they were justified in killing the Plataeans because the Plataeans were Athenian allies and failed to remain neutral? Is Sparta's concern with their own good and their concern with acting justly not the same because Sparta's cause, their cause in the war, is *the* just cause? After all, Athens (and by association, Athenian allies) is the tyrannical and imperialistic city. We are reminded of Cylon, Delphi, and the priority justice takes for the Spartans. In this case, which is far from the last, the justice of this situation is paramount for the Spartans. And while they do ignore the Plataeans' claims of

20 This is a reminder of the Plataeans' own argument that they were compelled to be Athens' allies, were just by keeping this alliance, but *also* were merely acting as their interests dictated.

past justice and this is a problem, a problem *for us*, they are able to assuage themselves by placing weight on the current situation, thus allowing points made by the Thebans (since the Plataeans are *not* on the right side of this debate, at least not entirely) to be persuasive.

Thucydides could have argued the actions of Sparta were a *mere* pretext, as he does elsewhere. Later in the war, Thucydides narrates the incident of Alcibiades and the Argives wanting to gain the city of Epidaurus (5.53). They initiated a war under the "pretext" (*prophasis*) that the Epidaurians had not sent an appropriate offering to Apollo, the Argives justifying the invasion as a means to enforcing the demanded offering the Epidaurians had not given. The reason for invasion, however, was to aid Athens strategically in the war (a policy pursued by Alcibiades). The openly stated reason for the invasion, which Thucydides first calls a "pretext," is *known* to be false by those demanding it. Yet it becomes a "cause" (*aitia*) since Argos will in fact invade Epidaurus, for the true reason of strategically benefiting Athens. In this case, Alcibiades and the Argives are acting in a manner we normally call hypocritical, conscious hypocrisy, for they are aware their pious complaints are utterly false; they in no way believe the Epidaurians are guilty of an injustice or impiety.[21]

The use of a pretext serves a purpose when the one utilizing it is aware of the pretext's true intention. For they expect the pretext will give less cause for the other side to protest they are being attacked unjustly. An unjust attack would possibly secure other allies to aid them, while if they were in the wrong, they may fail to win this support. Sparta acts in many, if not all, instances only when they believe a just cause is being served (e.g., 5.31.4). It is surprising that those advocating the literary nature of Thucydides' writing, and who pay careful attention to his other subtle remarks and turns of phrase, seem to ignore the one at 3.68. It makes a decisive difference whether the Spartans act merely from their self-interest, rather than mixed motives or a conflation of motives that may be at odds. This is to say nothing of their entire procedure during the Plataea-Thebes incident. Part of the difficulty with the Athenian thesis is its implication that human beings always act clear-sightedly and with an easy conscience. It is not clear that cities always, or even often, act with clear consciences and the Athenian thesis as presented by the envoys thus cannot be Thucydides' final word on human motives.

21 Cf. the dispute between the Spartans and Eleans at 5.49-50.2.

Athens at Mytilene: The "Rational" Athenians

Thucydides' order of presentation interweaves Mytilene and Plataea in such a manner that these incidents call for comparison – each city's treatment of enemy cities early in the war is on display. Both incidents are also accompanied by speeches, deepening our understanding of both the Spartans' claim to just treatment of their enemies and the Athenians' justification for their treatment of subject cities revolting. The Athenians' Mytilenian debate is also notable for its controversial characters: Cleon and Diodotus.[22] Both

---

22 Ste. Croix (1972) pp. 13-19 discusses Diodotus and Cleon in terms of *ta deonta* (1.22.1), i.e., as a speech some scholars see as problematic due to its content. Diodotus seems to be an invention of Thucydides. See Ostwald (1979) for possible individuals who could be Thucydides' Diodotus. The flaw in Ostwald's procedure, though, is his assumption that this individual must be someone who actually existed: "If we can rely on his narrative, Diodotus enjoyed but one very brief moment of glory in the history of the Peloponnesian War. He won no major battles, led no important missions, and was not even colorful enough to rate a mention in the surviving comedies of Aristophanes. He had an outstanding intellect, and he managed at one critical juncture to stem the tide of Cleon's successes in the Assembly by proposing a new policy…Had it not been for Thucydides' view of the importance of what he had to say on one occasion and on that occasion only, he would have been consigned to complete oblivion." Indeed. Hornblower I p. 432 also assumes Diodotus must have existed. Others who defend the "historicity" of these speeches (i.e., that they were actually spoken) include Cogan (1981) pp. x-xvi who cites Kagan (1975) approvingly when the latter argues that we cannot question the historicity of the speeches. This simply does not square with what we have seen of the problem presented by *ta deonta*. Nor does Thucydides guarantee the historical accuracy of any single speech. Would it ruin all speeches if *one* was an invention, an invention intended to reveal something about his theme of justice versus advantage, and thus, about the Peloponnesian War? Barring these concerns, others notice instead that the elevated and philosophical tone of Diodotus' speech may recommend him as being closest to articulating Thucydides' own views, of the speech of Thucydides. Diodotus, at the least, explicates key Thucydidean themes: justice versus necessity; hope versus knowledge; praise versus blame; gentleness versus punishment. More cautiously, we can simply recognize that Thucydides' Diodotus clearly contributes to key philosophic issues, especially observations on human nature. As for Cleon, the scholarly consensus centers on Thucydides' apparent bias towards him due to their possible personal connection (Thucydides was exiled, possibly at the behest of Cleon, as Plutarch presents it). See Westlake (1968) pp. 60-61 on Thucydides' "indisputable" bias, the "emotion arising from a conviction that he himself had suffered an injustice may have been too strong to be controlled." But accounts such as this one (see note 44 below) of Thucydides' Cleon fail to consider Thucydides' critique as a critique of what Cleon does to the city, as we would say, domestically. Cleon presents a danger to democracy, a danger Thucydides highlights in his striking remarks on Athens' decline (2.65). Gomme II p. 298 and later, Kagan

speakers offer striking remarks on the broadest Thucydidean themes. In one sense, the speeches appear to dive too deeply into matters; scholars have had difficulty with the elevated tone (especially of Diodotus) along with the lengthy discussions by both of speech itself. But since Thucydides wants us to compare the actions of each city in handling enemies (despite differences we will note below), along with how each justifies these actions, the nature of speech and deliberation is in fact germane. After all, the Spartans are judged harshly by commentators for their seemingly biased and predetermined judgment of the Plataeans. And this judgment is mirrored in the Athenians' original decision to execute the entire city of Mytilene.

Yet that decision is fairly quickly regretted and thus ensues a debate unlike anything we will see among the Spartans. The terms of the debate, and thus the nature of deliberation, bear comparison to those employed by Sparta, Plataea, and Thebes.[23] For our purposes, this debate offers psychological insights important for placing those terms, notably justice and piety, into relief. Diodotus also offers a corrective to the Athenian thesis, one which points beyond the blind spots of the Athenians themselves. His remarks offer some of the deepest views on human nature in Thucydides' text, as we will detail below. And these remarks are certainly not the Spartan view of the war. Instead, he compels us to consider both city's characters while battling against the harsh, vindicative justice of Cleon. And despite Cleon sharing something of a Spartan turn of mind, his justice is not simply synonymous with the Spartan variety.

The city of Mytilene, believing the Athenians were weak and would be weaker still if the Spartans would agree to an attack of their own on Attica, initiate a revolt they had long desired to undertake. But matters do not proceed as planned. Realizing Mytilene's revolt was due to their own perceived weakness, the Athenians not only resisted it and the attack on

---

(1974) p. 156, both remark on Thucydides' introduction of Cleon as the most violent citizen (3.36.6) and of his speeches (which they take to be accurate representations of Cleon) betraying this penchant. Aristophanes' portrait also agrees with Thucydides' own, casting doubt on the view expressed by Westlake. For a comparison of Cleon in Aristophanes and Thucydides, see Burns (2014).

23 Any disconnect between the parts of the speeches is thus only apparent, or represents a tension in the speakers' own understanding, not Thucydides'. Andrewes (1962) p. 74, for example, questions the coherence of Diodotus' extended discussion of the problems of public deliberation (3.43), which is a response to Cleon's accusation that the Athenians are swayed by specious arguments and too hasty in reconsidering their previous decision (37.4-5).

Attica, but "displayed their power and made descents upon the Peloponnesus wherever they pleased" (3.16.1). With this the Spartans became very disheartened and delayed support to Mytilene. This delay of the bulk of the Spartan fleet led the Spartan commander, Salaethus (being the only Spartan present at Mytilene) to make the grave error of arming the Mytilenian people in hopes of defending the island against Athens. But the people, once armed, immediately refused to support the oligarchic, pro-Sparta faction in the city who had initiated the revolt. The city was therefore compelled to surrender to the Athenians; the oligarchs, unable to meet the people's demands, hoped for a better outcome from surrendering rather than from any alliance between the people and the Athenians.

The Athenians thus decided (on the day before Cleon and Diodotus speak) that all men in the city should be put to death for their betrayal. But the following day, the Athenian demos had a "change of heart" (or "mind" – *metanoia*) regarding their decision, now viewing the previous day's resolution as "savage and excessive" (*ōmos…kai mega* – 36.4). This sets the stage for the general tenor of the two speeches: Cleon berates the Athenians for retracting their original decision since that decision was based on "anger" (*orgē*) and thus was the best response to ensure justice would be done (38.1); to that end, he exhorts the Athenians to return to their former state of anger and put the whole city to death. On the other hand, Diodotus recommends any decision be based on "good counsel" (*euboulia*), on what seems best to further Athens' interests in the given situation and with a view to what future use the city of Mytilene may have (42.1). The tension between justice and interest reappears. Yet policy gives way, perhaps not surprisingly, to the heart of key Thucydidean themes, his political psychology, as it explicitly presents two competing views of motives, actions, justifications, blame, punishment, and thus, of human nature itself.

For Cleon the proper way to deal with Mytilene, or any revolting city, is to act quickly, proceeding with all the anger felt from the injury. In this manner, justice is best served. Diodotus, on the other hand, opens his speech, by denying that those who seek to reconsider the case should be blamed. *He* does not "blame" (*aitia*) the Athenian people for changing their opinion on the punishment suitable for the Mytilenians' revolt. Unlike Cleon, who had wondered at the need to reconsider the matter, Diodotus objects to acting from haste and anger (Thucydides himself made this judgment in describing the Athenians' initial response [36.1-2]): these two things are "most opposed to good counsel" (42.1). And contrary to Cleon's emphasis on justice as revenge for the injury Mytilene has caused Athens, for Diodotus the focus of the debate, even on reconsideration, should be the benefit of Mytilene to the Athenian empire.

What justice demands and self-interest requires, therefore, animates this debate. Yet each speaker's position does not simply appeal to one "side." Cleon does not neglect advantage, arguing the revolt was not good for Athens' interests. Punishment, according to Cleon, serves Athens by acting as a deterrent for future cities that may contemplate revolt from their empire (39.2-3, 40.4). Diodotus responds by reversing Cleon's claim – not that the Mytilenian revolt harmed Athens, but rather how the Mytilenians can be made of use to Athens *now*. Since an act of revenge will not fulfill this end, as they can no longer supply it with anything it needs, the city should be allowed to continue to exist. And Diodotus focuses especially on the possibility of precedent: surrender for future revolting cities. If cities know they have no possibility for surrender because they will be put to death for the revolt, regardless of when they surrender, they will fight harder and to the death, given such a punishment already assuredly awaits them. However, if death is not the assured penalty, those revolting may surrender early on and become useful to Athens. Besides, Diodotus will leave open the possibility that deterrence does have *some* effect. So although Diodotus argues in terms of Mytilene's use to Athens, he acknowledges the attraction of justice to the people, particularly the desire for revenge at those one perceives to have done one harm. But Diodotus does not believe Cleon's appeal is the sensible way to proceed; he does not believe the death penalty is an ultimate deterrent for those driven to revolt. While Diodotus does admit Cleon's speech may seem more just, the considerations being undertaken are not those of justice, but those of the possible usefulness to Athens of the Mytilenians – they should act out of usefulness only, i.e., out of their own self-interest aside from *any* consideration of justice.[24]

24 Wasserman (1956) pp. 35-38 seeks to separate politics and ethics, arguing that "the concept of punishment (one may also say: war guilt), as analyzed in [Diodotus'] discourse, does not fall within the sphere of politics, but belongs to an entirely different category." While I am sympathetic to Wassermann emphasizing in this context the sophistic enlightenment, notably the newfound importance for the sophists of the distinction between nature (*physis*) and law (*nomos*), I believe his ethics/politics distinction goes too far and is a distinction foreign to Thucydides' (and Diodotus') thought. Punishment and guilt are paramount in the Mytilenian debate, and also are a key theme in the Spartan narrative as a whole. For Thucydides, "ethical" issues

Yet given Diodotus' acknowledgement of the attraction of justice, of the moral side of human nature, we must wonder, given his opening comments on public deliberation itself (i.e., the difficulty for advisers of the city – 42.1-6), how he expects his appeal to Athenian self-interest to be persuasive to the Athenian demos. In fact, his presentation does not wholly abandon justice – Diodotus alludes both to Athens "being wronged" (*adikeō*) by the Mytilenians and to the possibility of punishment or leniency, depending on which is beneficial (44.1-2). We cannot, in other words, fail to notice his *own* appeal to justice. Diodotus smuggles in moral language, appealing to the Athenians' sense of justice, while at the same moment arguing the Athenians are only to consider what is advantageous for the city in this, and subsequent, decisions.

Additionally, following on his exhortation to Athenian interests, we would expect Diodotus to argue for the ways in which Mytilene will be useful in the future (44.4). Could such punishment of revolting subject cities, for example, ever be good for Athens? Or do Athens' interests always mean recognizing the tendency of subject cities to rebellion? Surprisingly, Diodotus fails to discuss the practical benefits of punishing or pardoning the Mytilenians; he does not indicate here or anywhere in the remainder of his speech for what *precisely* Mytilene may be of use. Instead, turning to a consideration of "human nature" (*anthrōpeia physis* – 45.7), he attempts to explain to the Athenians what animates cities and men in their pursuit of various ends. For now, we may be able to say that Diodotus, in recognizing the concern for justice of the Athenian demos, does his best to defuse manifestations of that moral impulse: the demos' blame and anger, their righteous indignation, towards the Mytilenians. After all, Cleon's original recommendation of punishment the day before *was* successful (36.6). Diodotus, however, argues against execution based on his extended (and striking) detailing of human nature and its varying motives (45-46).

All cities, all men, strive for that which they hope to achieve, and it is human nature to do so. Cleon's argument, that justice as revenge is a deterrent, is rebutted through Diodotus' alternative depiction of what is human, denying the possibility of controlling certain actions via fear of

---

are intimately related to *nomoi*, the laws and customs of a particular city, as well as customs shared among the Greeks. And as Diodotus presents it here, human nature, the "human condition" Thucydides seeks to describe (1.22), cannot be understood apart from moral or ethical affections fueling political decision-making.

punishment. Human nature strives toward ends which it cannot attain. Since human beings are "prone to err" (*hamartanō*) regarding what is good for them, death not only will not serve as deterrence, but it does not seem appropriate punishment (45.3). Errors are ultimately an insufficient awareness of one's own good. Diodotus makes this apparent when he speaks of both hope and the ability for one, city or individual, to change its mind regarding what is possible or what is good (46.6). If all human actions proceed from what is believed to be best, then any injustice committed would be based on a lack of *knowledge*. No one does anything, voluntarily, that they *believe* is truly bad for them. To blame anyone for pursuing their own good is to blame human beings for striving after a mistaken understanding of what is in truth good for them. It is to blame them for being human.

If this is the case, Diodotus' argument undercuts the basis of Cleon's, and of the Spartans' punishment of the Plataeans. The distinctions Cleon maintains between just and unjust, ally and enemy, compulsion and free choice, break down. Cleon himself, in fact, seems to be confused about what justice is: He refers to Athenian rule as a tyranny (37.2). But his own criteria for injustice – that they "prefer might to right" (39.3), a criterion he uses against the Mytilenians – implies the Athenians are as guilty as the Mytilenians. Cleon's only defense of Athenian rule is the one he makes: Mytilene benefited under Athenian rule and should not have rebelled; the Athenian empire is not as oppressive as it could be, a claim we heard previously from the Athenian envoys at Sparta.[25] Yet is not the empire a tyranny,

25 This has, of course, led to comparisons between Cleon and Pericles (see Andrewes [1962], Westlake [1968], Cogan [1981]). Whereas Cleon boldly states Athens *is* a tyranny, Pericles hesitates to draw this conclusion in his much-discussed statement that Athens is "so to speak" (or "like") a tyranny (2.65.2), keeping, as it were, at arm's length from the type of admission Cleon makes. Both admissions are important. Nevertheless, they are not the same: The changes to Athens' empire are domestic. Popular with the demos (Cleon) is distinct from able to confound and restraint them (Pericles). Cleon is not as trusted as Pericles was. Thus, despite their identical views of the Athenian empire, their ability to defend it, and how they defend it, differ in tone and articulation, and thus, fundamentally, its moral justification. As Strauss (1964) p. 213 argues: "[Cleon's] version of imperialism is not ennobled by any thought of everlasting glory." Connor (1992) pp. 134, 194-98 also compares Cleon and Pericles, distinguishing Cleon's "style" which, as Connor suggests, pushes Athens toward revolution. Rahe (1995) p. 119 observes that: "[Cleon] denounces as a sign of softness (*malakía*) the Periclean notion that, by means of gracious acts (*charís*), an imperial power can somehow secure the good will (*eúnoia*) of its subjects."

one that can ill afford to show compassion and make concessions to allies? (37.2).

Cleon draws a further distinction exposing his view of justice, distinguishing it from the Spartan view. Cleon recognizes revolts borne out of necessity as exculpating; but he stops short of drawing out implications as per the Athenian thesis. Those who are compelled by an enemy should not be treated similarly to those who revolt of their own choosing; rather, Athens should have a different punishment for freely revolting cities compared to those compelled to do so. But even in this case, such a distinction rests on an error. Cleon argues the Mytilenians could have come over to the Athenians, but decided against this, and instead stayed with the few and revolted. But as we noted above, the Mytilenian people did not author the revolt from Athens; they rebelled, not from Athens, but from the oligarchs themselves as soon as they had the means to do so. By necessity, they were unable to act, unable to stay with Athens, since the well-armed few had initiated the revolution. The people themselves did not even have sufficient food (27-28).

Returning to Diodotus: His account of human nature continues, focusing now on "hope" (*elpis* – 45.1). Of particular note is his direct attack on Cleon's claim that men have free choice (39.7). Hope leads men to extend beyond their reach for that which they desire (e.g., liberty from an empire – 3.10.4); men and cities will act against what is more immediate for the sake of that which is not immediately before their view (e.g., revolution's benefits versus risks – 3.13.2); no law and thus no punishment will hinder action if the end set before them is strongly hoped for (e.g., threat from an imperial power – 3.2.3, 3.1, 4.2, 5.112.2-3); hope, together with *erōs*, directs human beings to undertake actions contrary to either their means or their good. *Erōs* drives men toward various ends and reason becomes subservient to *erōs* in conceiving of the hope and thus the possible means to such ends; these necessities of human nature drive action. To complicate matters further, however, Diodotus also speaks of the influence of "fortune" (*tychē*), sometimes seeming to favor particular ends of certain peoples, and thus it "helps the delusion" (3.45.6). The apparent coincidence of fortune with one's hoped-for ends leads to striving further, even with inferior means; therefore, it is "impossible" to stop human beings from striving after what they have determined to be their end; hope and *erōs* will not be bound by any law or "by any other terror whatsoever" (45.7). If this account of human nature is correct, then we understand why Diodotus stands in opposition to the punishment of death. With a view to its usefulness, nothing is to be expected from such a policy for the Mytilenians or any future allies of Athens.[26]

Diodotus' correction to Cleon's argument separates what Cleon (in his Spartan turn of mind) conflates: justice from interests or the good. But as noted, Diodotus only *appears* to argue in terms of usefulness, his speech containing within it an appeal to justice. Strangely, Diodotus argues that human beings are compelled by their nature, their natural tendency to hopes and passions and errors; yet he also claims the Athenians may freely choose punishment or salvation for the Mytilenians (free, presumably, of the righteous indignation at suffering what Cleon argued is an injustice). The Athenians should choose to save those who had the least to do with the revolt, only punishing those few who initiated it. In fact, Diodotus goes even further: Since the people surrendered the city to Athens, they have *aided* the Athenians in putting down the revolt and in now exposing the oligarchs who authored it. The Athenians will, therefore, betray their benefactors if they punish the people; they will commit an injustice (*adikeō*) against a benefactor (47.3). All of these appeals smuggle in moral concerns that need not weigh into self-interest, soberly assessed.[27]

In his appeal to the people of Athens, Diodotus apparently is himself compelled to appeal to justice. Even when concluding his speech with another appeal to Athens' interest in sparing Mytilene's demos, he argues one must put up with injustices, those that may justly deserve punishment,

26 Thucydides artfully interweaves these passions into the narrative of the Mytilenian revolt itself: The Athenians, for example, were unwilling to believe the Mytilenians were preparing to revolt because they "wished" (*boulomai*) it not to be true (3.3.1). Consider also 3.5.2, 6.1, 25.2, 36.1-2.

27 Hornblower I p. 438 notes that this is the only explicit invocation of justice by Diodotus. Heath (1990) p. 388 notes Diodotus' mention of unjust punishment, but ultimately sees Diodotus as recognizing the impossibility of justice and advantage being united (as Cleon had argued). Yet this does not allow us to overlook the fact that Diodotus aids the Athenians in believing justice and advantage can be united, and thus, contrary Heath's assertion, uses "moral argument" to convince the Athenians of advantageous policy. Cf. Debnar (2000) p. 178: "...Diodotus' *logos*, by admitting its deceit, works on the souls of the audience and reminds them of their ethical beliefs." Orwin (1994) details each step of Diodotus' speech to reveal his hidden appeal to justice. See especially pp. 151-54 with one of his concluding observations that "[i]n the case of the demos, to be sure, both justice and interest appear to be served by leniency" (156).

for the sake of furthering Athens' continued (imperial) interests (47.5). In other words, Diodotus conveniently allows his Athenian listeners to believe they are acting soberly and with a view toward Athens' interest, while also acknowledging the moral appeal of vengeance that characterized Cleon's speech, along with the doubt and guilt at their previous decision. Seeing as they had in fact reconsidered their judgment on Mytilene, precisely because of its harshness, its possible injustice, Diodotus allows the people to have it both ways – they can act justly in reversing their decision *and* clear-sightedly, with a view toward the interests of their city. Diodotus' speech reveals that for most human beings, appeals to self-interest cannot ignore or even divorce the pull that justice has for us. Apparently not noticing the tension between the two, most seek to be enlightened to their interests and not the dupes of those who would falsely advise them, while also not wanting to be merely petty calculators unconcerned with, or unable to forgo, their interests for a noble concern with justice.[28] The Spartan conflation of justice and interest can be seen even among Athenians.

Plataea and Mytilene Compared

Despite Thucydides linking the incidents at Plataea and Mytilene (including both being Athenian allies), the parallel is not without differences.[29] In Sparta's actions against Plataea, they are supporting their Theban allies. In punishing a faction in Mytilene for their revolt, the Athenians are controlling their empire and attempting to prevent future revolts in other cities. In the case of the Athenians' later attack on the island of Melos, however, the parallels are closer. The Melians plead to remain neutral, as the Plataeans had done; they appeal to justice and the gods, as the Plataeans had done; and the Melians are eventually killed by the Athenians, despite the glaring question of how it is advantageous for Athens to kill the citizens of a small island that bears little or no strategic significance on the course of the war. The Athenians kill the Melians because they claim others

28 See Orwin (1994) p. 154n18 and context, which includes a broad overview of additional scholarship on Diodotus.

29 Thucydides' order of presentation of his narrative is particularly striking in this case. He moves between the two incidents to heighten the effect on the reader when the Spartans sentence the Plataeans to death and the Athenians spare the Mytilenians.

will perceive them as weak if Melos is allowed to remain neutral; Melos is particularly an attestation of Athens' strength given its own weakness (5.97). Yet Athens is already feared by every city in Greece. Athenian imperialism is driven instead (as we have observed) by a concern with the nobility of the Athenian empire, despite claims of acting primarily according to their city's interests. And the slaughter of the Melians does not clearly alleviate the problem of cities revolting from Athens. That they kill the Melians and not the Mytilenians is telling – because Diodotus argued the treatment of subject cities must serve Athens' interests the Athenians refrained from punishing any but the conspiratorial faction within the city. It required a "Diodotus" to restrain, that is, to remind Athens of its true interests, to remind them to act moderately, while also conceding something to their need for punishment and revenge. Diodotus arguing in terms of interest is rare, even though the Athenian thesis claims to be doing precisely this because the argument from interest can, in fact, become an argument for moderation. Interest requires recognizing other cities are pursuing their own; simply punishing those interests working against one's own may not achieve a given end.

Just as we observe that the Athenians were never compelled to kill the Mytilenians, Thucydides does not say the Spartans were compelled to kill the Plataeans. But while Thucydides explicitly judges the Athenians' decision to kill the Mytilenians as "cruel," he does not render a similar judgment in his own name on Sparta's actions against the Plataeans (3.36.4), despite the clear comparison he has set up between the two. Why? The Spartans, after all, promised to judge the case of Plataea, presumably impartially or justly. But when the criterion of judgment is good service to Sparta, the Plataeans, as Athenian allies, cannot possibly fare well, even though they have not harmed Sparta directly (unless alliance with Athens constitutes clear harm). But does it not harm their interests? The Spartans' understanding of justice betrays a primary concern with their own regime, with Sparta, not with impartially judging merits of the case. To argue, as we have seen most commentators do, that the Spartans merely use justice as a pretext for their interests is an error; it is to expect from the Spartans what we hear from Diodotus (and even, to some extent, from Cleon). But the Plataeans are allowed to speak at length, despite the Spartans' long habituation to being distrustful of sophisticated speeches (1.84.3, 86.1, 4.17.2). And as we have observed, it is through both the complications of the case and the problematic admissions and claims of the Plataeans themselves that the Spartans ground their own actions as justified (along with the fact that the Thebans deliver a speech, so worried were they about the power of the Plataeans' appeals – 3.60).

Claiming and seeking to be just, the Spartans are unable to be the impartial judges they wish to be. That ultimately they act mainly to please the Thebans, their allies, reveals their error in connecting their own good or interests with their just intentions. It does not, however, allow us to ignore the gravity of their moral concerns, nor ignore their own understanding and justification of the situation. It does not allow us to ignore the fact that justifications for action can be justifications *for oneself* as much as they justify oneself to others. Thucydides is aware of the differences between Spartan and Athenian psychology.

Athens is, or becomes, then, the exception among cities. No other city so frankly states that they are compelled to rule; all other cities, to differing degrees, argue in terms of justice. The Plataeans, Thebans, and Spartans all present their views in moral language: wrongs have been committed, oaths broken, and each has a right to punish the other. Even when they act in their own interests, they always justify it to themselves in terms of justice. Now clearly some cities justify actions that are advantageous to themselves *knowing* these justifications are mere pretext; they know they are masking self-interest behind moral pretenses. The Corinthians are Thucydides' clearest exemplification (5.30). Yet even the Athenians are unable to act consistently in accordance with their own frank thesis, the compelling nature of self-interest. It is in this very context, between the Spartan invasion of Plataea and immediately preceding the Mytilenian revolt, that Thucydides shows the Athenians killing out of "anger" (or "wrath" – *orgē*). They kill the Spartan commander, Salaethus, who was hiding in Mytilene, despite his offer of securing the withdrawal of Peloponnesians from Plataea. They do not even consider his proposal's potential usefulness; he is killed "immediately" (*euthus* – 3.36.1).

Are the Athenians, therefore, also unable to avoid the pull of morally motivated actions? Or do we not begin to notice that the Athenian thesis does not represent the understanding of *all* Athenians? It is the Athenian demagogue, Cleon, who promotes vengeance on one's enemies as justice; Cleon's justice is an angry justice, while Thucydides does not present the Spartans at Plataea acting from anger. Part of Thucydides' critique of Cleon is a critique of violence as such, a critique that becomes all the clearer when we notice the contrast with other (more moderate) Athenians hoping to be rid of him altogether (4.28.5). After all, as we will observe, Nicias is the "Spartan" among Athenians. Nicias is trusted and popular with the Athenian moderates (and the Athenian demos), a trust reminding us of pre-Cleon Athens. Cleon proves to be at odds with Athens, with his city, creating enemies through personal enmities and his own actions (27.5), actions Thucydides later describes in his own name as "wickedness" (*kakourgōn*) and "slanders" (*diabalōn* – 5.16.1). Indeed, Cleon begins his Mytilenian speech by attacking his fellow Athenians whom he argues prefer rhetorical contests over the laws (3.37.4, 38.4-7).

Viewing these two incidents more broadly, we confirm through the narrative (and these speeches) what we have heard from each city earlier in the war: The Spartans, and others who expect justice to bind cities in their actions, presuppose these cities are able to do so. The Athenians treat their actions as due to compulsion, even if there are varying degrees or kinds of compulsion. Morality and self-interest, however, are often difficult to disentangle. It is not good for Sparta's interests to be infringed upon by Athens. This includes the wealth that attends empire, but also includes desires the Athenians seek to satisfy – the desire for nobility and honor. If human beings are compelled to pursue the good, however one understands it, then justice requires one to relinquish one's own good to some extent for the good of another. Justice proves to be a hindrance to that pursuit. It is not in the interest or good of the Athenians to allow the Melians to remain neutral in the war, just as it is not in the good of Sparta to allow the Plataeans, being enemies to their allies the Thebans, to remain a part of the Athenian empire. That free (moral) choice is possible is a key premise that began as a theme in Archidamus' response to the Plataean incident and continues through the speeches of the Plataeans and Thebans. This contrasts most notably with the argument put forward by Diodotus that nothing will hinder human nature from pursuing what it has set out for itself: compulsion includes self-interest along with apparent self-interest. But moral culpability presupposes free choice, while for Diodotus human nature is compelled by both hope and *erōs*, and thus the Mytilenians barely escape, for a second time, a judgment of death at the hands of the Athenian demos (49.1).

The Spartans' treatment of their enemies is perhaps clearest in another incident Thucydides relates in the context of Mytilene, one that initially appears to be of minor importance (3.32.1-3). Alcidas, a Spartan general, fails to arrive at Mytilene in time to aid the city and therefore leaves to return to the Peloponnesus. Before departing from the Ionia coast, however, he stops to slaughter allies of Athens. On noticing this, Sparta's own allies, the Samians, entreat him to stop, arguing these "allies" of Athens were so only by "necessity" (*anankē*) and that these men were not his "enemies" (*echthrōn*). They also add that the liberation of Greece from the Athenian empire would not be furthered by the killing of those very men one is supposedly freeing. Upon hearing these arguments, Alcidas ceases at once from his actions, realizing they serve no benefit and may even create additional enemies for Sparta. Failing to consider the benefits and harms to Sparta of killing, revenge for perceived injustice guided his actions. Most notably, he had no conception of necessity; he viewed all allies of Athens as unjust, and thus deserving of punishment, choosing as they had to be part of the Athenian empire.[30]

This Spartan treatment is in agreement with Cleon who had also argued punishment and revenge were the proper response to injustices committed voluntarily.[31] But we must immediately note that there is no mention of

30 See Orwin (1994) p. 76 for a similar observation. Roisman (1987) views Thucydides' portrait of Alcidas as unfairly drawn: "Unfortunately, Thucydides chose not to disclose his sources of information. In the case of Alkidas, however, the cumulative weight of the evidence indicates that Thucydides used a Brasidian source for his portrait of the Spartan admiral" and that "...Brasidas' slanderous remarks and Thucydides' inclination to generalize about Spartans at war, helped to turn the portrait of Alkidas from that of an individual into that of a type" (418-19). The difficulty of studies such as this one is that they use Thucydides' own text against him. This implies Thucydides blindly included information from his "informants" untested (which he explicitly denies – 1.22.1-4), and most importantly, information at odds with other evidence in *his own* account. Yet this mode of interpretation forces one to guess at Thucydides' possible sources of information (which can never be confirmed). Narrative contrasts such as Alcidas and Brasidas arise, according to Roisman, because "[t]he inspiration came from the sources: Brasidas and/or his Peloponnesian friends who recalled the events of the war both as they remembered them and as they wanted to remember them" (414). I can find no clear evidence for this claim, which runs counter to the other evidence we have seen of Thucydides' purposive presentation of his material. As for the supposed Brasidian bias of Thucydides' sources, Roisman himself is only able to call this a "premise" (414).

31 Cf. 2.67.4 – the Spartans butcher all at sea, Athenian ally or neutrals; they killed "as a matter of course" (Strauss [1964] p. 215). See also Hornblower I p. 418 on 3.36, confirming this practice among the Greeks.

anger with Alcidas, nor with the Spartans at Plataea. And unlike Cleon, who harangues the Athenians for reconsidering their decision, the Spartans allow the Plataeans to plead their case at length. Arguments from justice differ and Cleon's appeals are distinct from those of the Spartans. For example, we cannot help but look ahead to the Spartan general, Brasidas, who employs precisely the opposite strategy of Alcidas, yet still appeals to Sparta's proclamation of liberation. Even the allies of Sparta were nowhere near the moral blindness of the Spartans themselves. Athenian restraint (insofar as they employ it) is not the default position, however, despite the claims of the Athenian thesis. "Diodotuses" do not often come along, and quite troubling is the demos' attraction to the violent demagogue, Cleon. Suffice it to note that in politics, clear-sightedness of the kind demonstrated by Diodotus is exceedingly rare. And such instances do not promise that their example or teaching will be understood, nor that it may be applied.[32] The question becomes whether we can purge ourselves of the hopes and desires Diodotus argues cloud human judgment. Since hope presents *erōs* with possibilities, correcting such hopes through understanding the possible and impossible, necessity and its absence, would seem to be the means to overcoming apparent necessities of human nature. Cleon and the Corinthians (among others we will see) are prominent figures in Thucydides precisely because they embody passions affecting most human beings, most of the time: anger, revenge, belief, fear, trepidation, along with a sense of superiority and judgment of others for their moral flaws and misgivings. Yet neither

32 Diodotus gains the peoples' trust by pointing out that they fail to trust enough, notably those that seek to do good. This is what ties in the issue of deliberation to the content of the speech itself. But advising the good required Diodotus to deceive, since the demos is unaware of tensions or flaws in moral beliefs impeding their understanding of the political good of the city. They are unaware, that is, of how to separate justice from expediency or interest, the same problem we have observed for the Spartans. To appeal to Athenian interest, Diodotus must appeal to justice. Cleon's teaching of justice and revenge, of friends and enemies, of repaying harm, is so engrained that it is only through deception that Diodotus can move his audience (just barely) to a moderation borne out of expediency. To move them in this direction, he must bring them to a moral teaching that does not blame, as he proclaimed he does not in the opening of his speech. It is the hopes and longings that are part of human nature which exposes the demos (and all of us) to misunderstanding our own good and justice, to believing we are acting justly when it either is unjustified or when it conflicts with interests.

is the opposite absent. Diodotus belongs to Thucydides' cosmos, and his thought is thereby articulated, and understood, by Thucydides himself.

Sparta's Disaster at Sphacteria

With these observations on the early part of the war, in both actions and debates, deeds and speeches, the Spartan rejection of the Athenian thesis is apparent. The narrative reaches a turning point, a climax of the first ten years of the war, with the events at Pylos (a coastal city on the Peloponnesus) which significantly alters the war's course and not in Sparta's favor.[33] Sparta's best men will become trapped on the island of Sphacteria, just off the coast of Pylos, bringing their first serious adversity, and causing such distress that they will sue the Athenians for peace in an attempt to end the war entirely.

This incident and the Spartans' handling of it is relevant for several reasons. It is relevant for observing how the Spartans articulate themselves in suing for peace once their men are trapped; it is relevant the Spartans do not fight to the death; it is relevant that Sparta now seeks to end what was the war's clarion call: a war of liberation from Athenian imperialism. And finally, it is relevant because the outcome of these events will reverberate through the remainder of the war. It will scar the Spartan psyche in all future decisions of the city.

The Athenian general, Demosthenes, lands at Pylos while the Athenians are sailing to Sicily because he observed Pylos to be "naturally strong" (*physei karteron*) and possessing a harbor (4.2.2-3).[34] In anticipation of the Spartans' return from plundering Attica, the Athenians fortify it. While the Spartans become aware of this, they delay due to their ongoing invasion of Attica and their belief that they could engage the Athenians when they

33 See Cogan (1981) p. 74 and Hornblower II p. 149-50. The latter provides a brief overview of the scholarship. Much of this concerns topography (for example, Gomme [1937] 125-31).

34 The Athenians land at the harbor by chance, a storm blowing their ships into Pylos. Demosthenes, though, had designs on landing there from the beginning (4.31-3). As Hornblower II p. 149 observes: "Th.'s[ucydides] treatment of the Pylos/Sphakteria episode is...remarkable for its (undue) stress on the elements of chance." We will have to consider why Thucydides makes chance a feature of this section, in an episode clearly centered on the Spartans.

chose and defeat them with relative ease; they were also celebrating a festival (5.1). Perhaps the Spartans did not observe the distinct nature of Pylos as Demosthenes had done. But the Spartan king, Agis, and the Spartans grow concerned given the proximity of Pylos to Sparta itself; they were also facing difficulties in their invasion of Attica from a lack of food which was due to their invasion being in the early spring before the crops were ripe.[35]

Accordingly, men are sent to the island of Sphacteria, off the coast of Pylos, to protect against the Athenians landing there. When the Spartans attack, they land where Demosthenes had anticipated and the Athenians therefore succeed in driving Spartan ships out of the harbor, leaving 300 Spartans trapped on the island. The Athenians pursue further despite their already good fortune, defeating the Spartans and surrounding the island with their naval force. The gravity of the situation for the Spartans is clear; once they saw their men were trapped, they decide on negotiating an armistice, sending envoys to Athens to secure the return of their men from the island.[36]

The speech of the Spartan envoys is of particular relevance, as it is the only speech Thucydides allows us to hear of Spartans in Athens; it therefore corresponds to the speech of the Athenian envoys in Sparta. But it is also the only speech of unnamed Spartans anywhere in Thucydides.[37] As the Athenian speech at Sparta was most characteristically Athenian, this speech will be most characteristically Spartan.

While the Athenian envoys came forward on their own to defend Athens as the Spartans debated going to war, the Spartan envoys are sent by

35 In failing to observe the distinct nature of Pylos and invading Attica at a premature time of the season, the Spartans fail to correctly understand nature.

36 Scholars debate over the appropriateness of the Spartans' reaction, with most finding the Spartan speech following the disaster wanting. See, for example, Hornblower II pp. 168-69 and Westlake (1974), who will be discussed further below.

37 Hornblower II pp. 170-72 notes this speech has received little attention from scholars. This, despite another element that makes it unique: there is no reply presented. Unfortunately, Hornblower attributes the lack of the Athenian speech by Cleon (reported but not presented) as due to Thucydides' "attitude to Kleon"; thus "[t]he best we can say is that, where Kleon is concerned, Th.'s[ucydides] handling is more than usually irrational" (170). Gomme III pp. 459-60, discussing Romilly, rejects her argument that Thucydides approved of the speech because he failed to quote Cleon's response. Cf. Rood (1998) pp. 39-43 who presents Thucydides' many other motives besides simply historical accuracy (and thus a justification for only alluding to, while omitting, Cleon's reply to the Spartan envoys). On Thucydides' apparent bias, see note 47 below. Cogan (1984) pp. 73-77, however, praises the speech.

Sparta, but must depart from their usual custom and here speak at length, since the situation was "believed" (*dokeō*) by them to be a "major disaster" (4.15.1). Thucydides is silent on its severity and the men being captured; he may not share the Spartan view that the return of their men should be of the utmost concern.[38]

The Spartans urge the Athenians to use their good fortune in this situation to their advantage and to their "honor and reputation" (*timēn kai doxan* – 17.4). Ending the conflict between the two cities will gain the Athenians honor and reputation, as they will be viewed as its author (and thus presumably admired by the other cities as well). The Spartans know enough of the Athenians to understand that an appeal to their honorable side may tempt them to agree to peace. Besides, they continue, present prosperity should not lead the Athenians to be overly trusting that such conditions will continue forever. The Athenians should act "moderate" (18.4 – *sōphrōn*) in success given ill fortune may befall any city. One should be moderate in prosperity, as Thucydides contends the Spartans themselves are (8.24.2). The Spartans also anticipate the arguments of the Melians, who likewise attempt to persuade the Athenians that fortune in war may favor either side, it being not knowable how matters will fall out (5.102, 112.2). Similarly, the Spartans argue that one should not be led on by "hope" (*elpis*) and "grasping at something more" (*pleonos oregontai*) due to present good luck (4.17.4; cf. 21.2, 65.4).[39] The Spartans have only erred – they are no weaker than before. Good fortune only lasts for a time; eventually the Athenians will find themselves facing an unfortunate disaster which places *them* at a disadvantage. But since fortune has favored them now, the Athenians

38 Westlake (1974) does not share the Spartans' view either and believes Thucydides himself exaggerates the Spartan reaction. As he argues: "It is remarkable that Thucydides immediately after his account of the naval battle reports Spartan reactions to 'what had happened at Pylos' without referring to the Peloponnesian fleet or mentioning that its numbers had not been drastically reduced by its defeat (15.1-2). Any reader of this passage who has not paid close attention to the preceding narrative (14) might infer that the fleet had been virtually annihilated" (218). Westlake treats this episode largely from the point of view of military strength and how best to correctly assess the situation solely based on strategic considerations. But the Spartans have graver issues on their minds, as I will discuss below.

39 There is an interesting agreement here between the Spartans and Diodotus on the tendencies of the Athenians, and of human beings more generally. Thucydides also confirms the Spartans' judgment on the Athenians (4.21.2, using *oregonto*, "quite a strong word" as Mynott [2013] p. 247 notes).

should act moderately and thereby obtain a reputation for strength and wisdom (4.18.4-5).[40] While the focus on honor was a sound selling point at the beginning of the Spartan speech, it is not difficult to discern its limits. And in the Spartans turning to an emphasis on fortune and moderation, we can almost see the Athenians smirking among themselves.

Indeed, the speech reveals much about the Spartans' own self-assessment, albeit one characterized by reticence. They admit that the disaster on the island is a consequence of a failure in their judgment; but it was not due to a loss in "power" (*dynamis*) or "becoming arrogant" (*hubrizō*). This failure is one that may itself befall anyone (18.2). Thucydides partially supports these impressions with his description of the role fortune played in the battle, along with the successes of Demosthenes himself (compared to the opposing advice of his fellow commanders) and the Spartans' naval mistakes (11, 12.2, 14.3). The Spartans thereby imply the disaster they have suffered was due both to a failure in their judgment and also due to ill fortune. But they emphasize having not become weak, nor acting in a manner that would lead to punishment, i.e., they have not ceased from acting virtuously. Spartan failure is framed by them in terms of shame and nobility; they do not mention their own interests apart from these judgments. And they are indeed judged by the other Greeks based on the outcome of this battle, in particular the eventual surrender of their men (5.75.3).

The surest way to solve the enmity between the two cities, the Spartans continue, is for the Athenians to act with gentleness in their current dealings. However, the Spartans now quietly admit it may not have been

40 Placed in the middle of the Pylos narrative (4.3-41) is Thucydides relating an Athenian defeat at Eion in Thrace (4.7). This is after we hear of Agis invading Attica (4.6), a strategy his father, Archidamus, had also employed with little success (3.1-3; cf. 2.19-21). The narrative then turns back to Pylos, and the Thracian narrative does not return until 4.78, when it is Brasidas that leads the march, resulting eventually in the taking of Amphipolis, an incident that caused significant alarm in Athens (4.108). When we later consider the entire story of Brasidas as Thucydides presents it, this theme of fortune or chance will return – Brasidas is a piece of good fortune for the Spartans and he is, as a man, very much un-Spartan in many ways. Chance, in other words, does seem to change course for the Athenians later in the war. Thucydides introduces this to his readers with this seemingly out of place chapter, another reminder that we need to see the forest before chopping down what appear to be errant trees. It should also be noted that 4.24-25 reminds us of Athenian designs on Sicily, which will involve many shifts in Athenian fortune, and also as they do here, in the course of the war. Cf. Gomme III p. 441: "The whole episode [4.7] is of the smallest importance; Thucydides had it among his 'notes'."

only poor judgment or fortune that favored the Athenians – they should accept Sparta's offer to make a treaty on measured conditions since they have conquered Sparta also, or perhaps even predominantly, by means of "virtue" (*aretē* – 4.19.2). Measured conditions will ensure that each refrain from revenge and that the debt of shame will be placed on the Spartans.

With these considerations in mind, the Spartans urge the Athenians to agree to a peace now, "noble" (*kalōs*) as it would be for each city, to avoid being "forced" (*anankē*) into an "eternal hatred" (*aidion echthran*) of one another (20.1).[41] The advantages of peace are reputation and friendship for Athens and an alleviation of the shame of defeat for the Spartans (20.3). Yet why would Sparta be ashamed of defeat if they were bested by a better city and its men? No one would doubt Athens' naval superiority. Archidamus admitted as much before the war's outbreak (1.80.4). The true reason for Spartan shame becomes clear with their admission (almost in passing) introducing the possibility Athens is not to blame for the war, but instead Sparta instigated an unjust war. Or more cautiously, that Sparta broke the treaty by beginning the war without submitting to the stipulated process of arbitration (4.20.2). The Spartans view their bad luck as the reverse side of the Athenians' good luck, suffering due to beginning the war unjustly. This admission is especially striking, as the Spartans also claim that the Athenians will be considered "responsible" (*aitios*) for the peace should they now agree to Sparta's terms for a new treaty.

This is, indeed, *the* theme of the Spartan speech – mentions of or allusions to fortune, misfortune, good luck, bad luck, chance, and accidents are found nearly a dozen times throughout this relatively short speech (4.17.1, 17.4, 18.1, 18.3-5, 19.2. 20.2).[42]

---

41 See Gomme III pp. 457-58: "you will incur our eternal enmity, personal as well as public." Mynott's (2013) p. 246 translation "political enemies" does not clearly convey this and masks what seems important here – Spartan hatred. It is in keeping with the moral Spartans that they view enemies in this manner. Hornblower II p. 176, surprisingly, does not mention the passage.

42 As we noted above (note 29), Hornblower complains of this feature. Cornford (1907) understands the Pylos narrative as the embodiment (intended by Thucydides) of the place of luck in human life. Stahl (2003) p. 142 sees the speech, and indeed the Pylos incident generally, as "contributing to the reader's appreciation of the unexpected *situation of decision-making*" (emphasis in original). Stahl goes too far, though, in arguing that "[n]either the course of events nor the behavior of human nature displays here the faintest appearance of a *predictable* (calculable) 'constant'" (emphasis in original –144). Demosthenes' role in the Pylos narrative, it seems to me, belies this

The Spartan understanding of Athenian good fortune in this episode is a problem for them. While they attribute numerous events in the war to chance, they believe chance is governed by the gods should they choose to do so (recall Archidamus' speech before invading Attica – 2.74.2-3). Events resulting in misfortune (and failed policy or lack of experience) are understood by the Spartans to be punishment by the gods for injustices. The plague at Athens would have been understood by the Spartans as punishment for a transgression, as it was for some, or rather most, Athenians (2.54.1-4). Not surprisingly, then, the Spartans never mention the gods in this speech. Relatedly, the Spartans previously claimed the Athenians were unjust in acquiring empire and encroaching on Spartan territory and thus the Athenians do not deserve success because they are unjust men; yet chance favored them. The Spartans note this begrudgingly for two reasons: First, they believed the Athenians actually possessed an advantage in virtue and their capture of the Spartans at Sphacteria was not a matter of *mere* chance. Second, the Spartans in this context question who began the war. Far from academic, their question is who may be responsible (*aitios*) for the war (4.20.2). These admissions are related – if the Spartans had acted virtuously, i.e., justly, they would not have been "punished" with the misfortunes they now cannot help but recognize. Their belief in punishment implies a connection of virtue and outcome. They betray this without explicitly saying it because Thucydides imitates the speech of men who believe good fortune and just actions are inextricably bound together. Once the war turns very unfavorably for them (their view of this blockade of their men on the island), the Spartans necessarily question whether they may be at fault for the war itself. And though the Athenians' success is due to their virtue, i.e., the strategy of Demosthenes along with some simple chance occurrences that may indeed befall anyone in war, the Spartans begin to believe their fate at Pylos was deserved punishment for an unlawful breach of the treaty.

In fact, the Spartans may be giving the Athenians too much credit.

---

conclusion and Thucydides points to his mastery of a fortuitous event. Connor (1984) pp. 108-18 treats the narrative technique employed here (characterized by "paradox and surprise") as part of Thucydides' grander narrative strategy, noting that "the Pylos operation marks a major turning point in the *Histories*. It is the first sign of the grand reversal in which the war culminates...our first glimpse of the larger pattern" (111). It is because Thucydides employs these techniques, I would argue, that historians critique the Pylos narrative as lacking organization and information.

Thucydides' narrative of this event lends the impression of *Demosthenes'* virtue, not necessarily of the Athenians as a whole. But that the Spartans cannot help seeing this incident in grander terms is in keeping with the alignment we have just observed. Did the Spartans fairly evaluate their own situation? Or did they blame themselves in a manner that no other city would?[43]

It is tempting to reject this entire speech as the very definition of hypocrisy.[44] The Spartans ask the Athenians for fair dealing, including not only a treaty, but an alliance between the two. This despite the stated purpose of the war: to liberate Greece from Athenian imperialism and expansion. Yet this demand is not duplicitous or simply the begging of a bully who now finds themselves in the place of the victim. Already at this early stage of the war, we are aware that the Spartans themselves act as they now urge the Athenians to do – they are content with their present goods, so much so that they risk holding onto them into the future, and thus, at the expense of the future. To act is to risk injustice and a loss of good fortune. Fortune, as a centerpiece of the speech, sets the Spartans' silence on the gods into stark relief. Just as Archidamus had only alluded to divine justice when he doubted the morality of declaring war, the Spartans only allude to the gods, who for them are the arbiters of fortune, and barely admit that the Athenians won the battle by being better men. The Spartans want both to acknowledge *mere* fortune (to comfort themselves), but also distance themselves from the (impious) implications of their loss in this battle. Since the war turns unfavorably for them, they may begin to sense the need to admit

---

43 Westlake (1974) p. 222: "The strangely evasive tone of the whole speech suggests that the speaker is to some extent concealing the real feelings of the Spartan government." Contrasting with his military emphasis discussed above (note 33), this, in my view, better approaches the Spartan understanding of the disaster at Pylos. But in this context (222-24), Westlake speculates on possible earlier peace overtures by Sparta, despite none reported by Thucydides (on this, see also Gomme II pp. 390-91). Spartan evasiveness points, not to a diplomatic scheme long in the making, but to what the Spartans quietly admit: their guilt. Hornblower II p. 176 points to 7.18.2 (the passage confirming Sparta's guilt over starting the war, to be discussed below) in his comments on 4.20.2, but does not go on to suggest a broader significance to this parallel. He also mentions the Spartans' repeated references to "chance" (*tychê*) only in passing (p. 171). But for the pious Spartans, chance is never merely chance. What scholars fail to piece together is how the Spartans view the war, not from strictly strategic and clear-sighted assessment of interest, but from their perception of their own failure and guilt.

44 For example, Hornblower II pp. 170-72.

that the gods are not on their side; thus they only allude to virtue near the end of their speech (19.2), just as Archidamus had only alluded to the possible injustice of Sparta going to war near the end of his speech (1.85.2). This is a notable crack in the Spartans' moral armor.

The Spartans also believed, according to the editorial comment by Thucydides himself, that the Athenians were as interested in peace as they were (4.21.1). Archidamus also believed the Athenians were men like the Spartans (1.84.4).[45] But the Athenians read the situation for what it is: the men on the island are trapped and the Spartan speech certainly lends the impression they were anxious to come to terms with Athens. The Athenians notice, then, that a treaty could be made at their convenience; they reject the Spartans' proposals and "grasped at something more" (*tou de pleonos ōregonto* – 4.21.2). Sparta had warned Athens against precisely this because those who do so risk their good fortune. Those who have experienced good and bad fortunes understand how matters can change. Just as they blame the Plataeans despite their appeal to the necessities of subjugation to Athens, here they fail to fully appreciate what even the Corinthians claimed at Sparta – the relentlessly daring character of the Athenians (1.70.2).[46]

45 It is noteworthy that in both speeches, the Spartans appeal to what is common between the two cities, even as men; yet as the Helot revolt (1.102) and the Spartan preference for Dorians reveals (3.92; cf. 1.18.1), the Spartans are less than trusting of the Athenians, and other Ionians.

46 Orwin (1994) pp. 81-82 argues that the Spartans, based on their own argument regarding the fickleness of chance, ought not to surrender given such a relatively minor defeat. He characterizes the Spartan speech as abject and a betrayal of Sparta's allies (since it seeks no concessions other than the return of their men). In this context (pp. 75-86) Orwin is investigating Spartan justice and character, notably their conflation of justice and self-interest. See, especially, p. 85 where he levels the accusation of "hypocrisy" on Sparta, with the qualification that it may be "artful or artless." In my view, which qualifier one selects is essential in any analysis of Spartan character. Kagan (1969) pp. 231-37 cites scholars who all argue that the Athenians should have taken the peace offering from Sparta. Kagan also cites Woodhouse (1970), who argues (as does Kagan) that Thucydides himself favored peace. This latter line of thought, in my view, is mistaken in its *approach*: Thucydides here displays the character of each city for his readers to consider and weigh. The Athenians are grasping at more, while the Spartans are not interested in the broader war (despite their proclamation of liberating Greece). Thucydides' judgment on each city must be located, not simply in individual events, but in understanding the justifications given for certain policies and what the eventual outcome is in light of a city's justification. In other words, what is the political cost of "grasping at more"? What of the Spartans' fear and hesitancy? Thucydides' account of the war as a possession for all time is aimed particularly at this. If we want to weigh policy decisions, in this instance

Given the conditions Cleon, who is leading the negotiations now demands, the Spartans ask the Athenians to allow them to select counselors with whom they can discuss these conditions. Cleon responds by accusing the Spartans of having no just intentions and demands they speak in front of everyone, instead of conferring in private. But the Spartans realize they cannot satisfy Cleon's demands without upsetting their allies, especially if negotiations fail. And the Athenians are not willing to agree to what the Spartans view as "measured" (*metrion*) conditions (4.22.3). The Cleon-led Athenians realize of course the advantage of their position and make demands to which the Spartans cannot agree. These demands included the return of cities near Attica, cities the Spartans themselves gained, not recently, but in the Thirty-Year peace treaty when Attica was being attacked by them and Euboea had revolted from Athens (1.114-115.1).

Given the failure of these negotiations, the armistice between Sparta and Athens ends and hostilities are renewed at Pylos. The Athenians accuse the Spartans of an attack which violates the armistice, as well as other violations Thucydides describes as "not worth mentioning" (4.23.1). Thucydides thereby implies these violations directed at the Spartans are of questionable validity, that is, the Athenians led at this time by the violent demagogue, Cleon. In this, he sides with the Spartans who deny any "wrongdoing" (or "injustice" – *adikēma*).[47] Both sides now return to war with all their power

Thucydides' careful reader will not be surprised by the Athenians' rejection of the Spartan offer – not only were the Athenians always grasping at more, they are now no longer held back by Pericles' policy of no new conquests (2.65.7). And this assumes even Pericles could have held them back, should he have lived through the war.

47 Flower (1992) pp. 40-57 discusses Pylos only in terms of Thucydides' presentation of Cleon versus Nicias (4.27-29), that is, from the Athenians' point of view. Other treatments of Cleon in this episode include Woodhead (1960) pp. 289-317, Westlake (1968) pp. 65-75, and Marshall (1984) pp. 19-36. The widely held view in the scholarship, voiced by these authors, is that Thucydides disliked Cleon, and therefore presented, and judged him, negatively. It is worth presenting the contrary view: "[Thucydides] takes the most comprehensive and impartial delight in all that is typical in men and events and believes that to each type there pertains a quantum of *good sense: this* he seeks to discover…he does not revile or belittle those he does not like or who have harmed him in life. On the contrary: through seeing nothing but types he introduces something great into all the things and persons he treats of; for what interest would posterity, to whom he dedicates his work, have in that which was *not* typical!" (Nietzsche, *Daybreak*, aph. 168 – emphasis in original). Furthermore, only Woodhead places Thucydides' presentation of Cleon in the context of the overall situation at Pylos, including the Spartan motives in surrendering and seeking peace. Woodhead's conclusion is that "…out of tune with the democratic leader in

(or "strength" – *kratos*). We would expect nothing less from the Athenians. But is it not the Spartans who are inspired by their belief that the Athenian charge of a violation is false and now (finally) act with vigor at the perceived injustice of the Athenians' unfaithful negotiating?

Despite the Athenians' initially advantageous position at the moment they reject a possible treaty, the situation at Pylos now begins to press upon them. They are unable to reduce the men on the island and their ability to carry in food and water proves difficult. So poorly is their assault on the Spartans proceeding that they begin to regret not agreeing to the treaty previously offered (27.2). And it is Cleon who is held responsible for their rejection of the treaty, as he had urged the demos to reject Sparta's proposals or any further private discussions. Despite the Athenians' desire for a treaty at this point, Cleon also notices that he may be able to convince them to send a new expedition in an effort to push back the Spartan forces. He attempts to persuade them to send Nicias on the expedition given his "hatred" of him, but Nicias maneuvers the demos into placing Cleon at its head. And Cleon promises a quick result.

This elicits a perhaps surprising remark from Thucydides – the "moderate" (or "wise" – *sōphosi*) among the Athenians doubted Cleon's abilities, yet they were pleased with him leading this new expedition; for "either they would be freed from Cleon, which they greatly hoped for, or if disappointed in this expectation, would reduce the Spartans" (28.5). Despite the Athenians' daring character and grasping for more, Thucydides reminds us that there are moderate men at Athens, men of a more Spartan view.[48]

principles and temperament, Thucydides cannot help misunderstanding him, and the construction he gives to this scene has a distorting effect" (315). Yet, as we will see, this ignores the tension within democratic Athens that will later unfold; instead, this key episode blends (while contrasting) domestic political issues with foreign affairs. Both cities face pressures at home and the domestic dynamics at play have decided effects on how the aftermath of Pylos is handled.

48 The term is related to *sōphrosynē* (moderation). As Palmer (1992) p. 117 notes, this is the only mention of moderation in reference to any Athenian (or Athenians) in Thucydides. However, cf. 6.54.5-6. Hornblower II p. 188 argues: "Here the word does seem to be used in a favorable sense and without irony." Is there not an irony, however, in Athenians siding with a virtue we have seen Thucydides clearly identify as Spartan? Critiques by Woodhead and others (see previous note) ignore the domestic element of the narrative and the fact that Thucydides has already made clear domestic issues at Athens will prove harmful, if not fatal (2.65), to the Athenian war effort. It is in this spirit, in my view, that the remark on the moderate men in Athens must be read, rather than the standard scholarly view that Thucydides saw

And Thucydides' reminder arises in the context of his striking description of Cleon as "the most violent citizen at Athens, and at that time by far the most powerful with the people" (3.36.6). The Athenians are not a homogenous people; all cities have some kind of party or factional divide. These moderates in Athens desired the death of Cleon even *more* than the defeat of the Spartans; they preferred the death of a violent demagogue to a victory in this battle and perhaps even doubted the prudence of the ongoing war. We are reminded that it was the moderate Spartan king, Archidamus, who himself cautioned greatly against going to war.[49]

We learn something more, therefore, about Thucydides' claim that Sparta is moderate in prosperity – moderation in part means a concern for the regime more than a concern for victory in war, especially a war issuing from a desire for imperialistic expansion. Moderation is presented here as attentiveness to the health of the city, to domestic politics when that health is at risk from external pressures of war, pressures which in Athens allow for the ascent of an (at best) questionable statesman. Praise of Sparta, we recall from the beginnings, was not for their external actions (such as Athens' navy or its "adornments") but for their long-standing laws and thus for their stable regime.

Returning to the action and negotiations: Once Cleon and Demosthenes have the Spartans on the island at the point at which they could be overtaken, they send an offer to surrender. To no surprise, they do not surrender immediately; instead, they request to send messages to Sparta to ask what they should do, to which they receive the reply that "[t]he

---

fit to take out a grudge on Cleon via this episode. After all, Cleon's Athenian foil is Nicias and Thucydides, while offering qualified praise of Nicias' career and character, is also willing to point to *his* faults. Evidence of a grudge rests solely on Thucydides' military defeat and Cleon's possible role in his twenty-year exile from Athens. See, for example, Bowersock (1965) p. 139. Bowersock uses the evidence of Marcellinus (*Life of Thucydides*, 26) to confirm that Cleon had a hand in Thucydides' exile. Yet are we permitted to assume that this exile was the most important event in Thucydides' life and that his reaction would be to misrepresent Cleon? Scholars treat this bias as self-evident, without weighing that perhaps Thucydides portrayed Cleon in the manner he did because Cleon represents a departure from moderation. Thucydides' critique of Cleon is a critique of him as the most violent citizen, a designation no one could possibly assign to Nicias.

49 Thucydides places two chapters on the Athenian incursions to Sicily (4.24-25) between the Athenian rejection of the Spartan peace treaty (4.23) and the Athenian attack on Pylos (4.26). Sicily and Pylos are both instances of the Athenians "grasping at more," as the Spartans in the latter instance are aware of (4.17.4).

Spartans bid you to decide for yourselves so long as you do nothing shameful" (*aischros* – 4.38.3). But the Spartans on the island do surrender, to the surprise of all the Greeks; it was believed that not even "necessity" (*anankē*) would lead Spartans to lay down their arms rather than be killed in battle (40.1). The surrender is of nearly 300 men, including 120 Spartiates, Spartans from the first families of the ruling class.[50] This defeat causes their city its greatest distress.

It is in this context that Thucydides makes two observations. First, the surrender of the Spartans was the most surprising event in the war. None of the Greeks could believe that a Spartan would do anything but die in battle (40.1-2). Second, this Spartan decision elicited a mean-spirited remark from an Athenian ally, asking one of the prisoners if those who had died were "noble and good men" (the implication being that only the dead were true men [*kaloi kagathoi*]).[51] The Spartan prisoner answers shrewdly and laconically that "[t]he spindle – that is, the arrow – would be worth a great deal if it could tell good [or brave] ones (*tous agathous*) from the rest" meaning, as Thucydides adds "...that the killed were those whom the stones and the arrow happened to hit" (40.2).

Is Thucydides' explanatory remark here not redundant? Or at least

---

50 The number of men, 300, reminds us of the Spartans who did not surrender to the Persians at the battle of Thermopylae, which Thucydides alludes to in this context (4.36.3). Hornblower II p. 191 notes a reversal from 1.23.1, where the Persian War is diminished.

51 This translates as "noble and good ones," or colloquially, "gentlemen." In Greek, *anthrōpos* translates as "human being" implying "mere human being." *Aner* is "man" by way of distinction. Cf. Strauss (1964) pp. 221-22 who notes Thucydides' employment of these terms in this context. Hornblower II p. 195-96 remarks on possible ambiguities in the term. See Gomme III pp. 480-81 and (1953) for discussion of the term. Crane (1998) p. 232 states that "[t]he surrender at Sphacteria is not an exception, but a true indication that the Spartans are not the inherently heroic, self-denying figures that the rest of the Greeks assumed." This denies the very simple fact that, first, Thucydides presents the Peloponnesian War as greater than previous wars, and thus nothing that either Sparta or Athens had previously experienced. Second, it ignores entirely the issue of blame, i.e., the perceived cause of the war and what effect it had, psychologically, on the combatants. Thucydides shows that the Spartans overcame their guilt for the original breach of the treaty as the result of Athenian actions *preceding* their victory at Mantinea (7.18.3; cf. 4.23.1), a victory won by "courage," and which restored their reputation throughout Greece. The estimation of Spartan character by the other cities was not mistaken; it was, rather, incomplete, failing to weigh both the grandeur of the war and not fully comprehending Spartan fear of injustice.

an additional emphasis that raises the question: Why relate this exchange at all? The Athenian ally who uttered the remark, intentionally or unintentionally, allows us notice something about Sparta – intentionally if he understands a Spartan's view of chance; unintentionally if he does not. For is it not the case that a Spartan might believe one *deserves* to die? Do they thus not comfort themselves in their defeat by suggesting that it is *merely* chance and not rather something else, i.e., their own injustice, that is to blame for their capture? As we observed, the Spartans can barely come to admit the Athenians are better men, or more precisely, that Sparta lost the battle and thus must be, in their minds, less virtuous men. And if it was believed that no necessity could cause the Spartans to surrender, are we not forced to say that the Spartans lost spirit? And if so, why?

The remark by the Spartan is a deflection from the fact that to admit a diminishment of their virtue, their worth as *kaloi kagathoi*, is to admit a defeat greater than simply loss in a particular battle. Notice their reply drops "noble" (*kalon*) from the formulation and only responds that the spindle cannot distinguish good (or brave – *agathos*) men. For a Spartan, surrender is never noble. And it returns us to the reason, the reason expressed, reservedly and in passing, in the Spartan speech: The question of who is to blame for a war among the Greeks. Despite their attempt, for the Spartan, chance is not wholly separable from divine justice, the gods' judgment on who *should* win; not surprisingly, therefore, the Spartans avoid admitting defeat, nor do they satisfactorily find comfort even in the apparently unfortunate character of that defeat.[52]

And Sparta's troubles continue. A short while later, the Athenians send ships to the island of Cythera, off Sparta's mainland of Laconia. As Thucydides' narration details, the persistence of the Athenians in their prosecution of the war is something the Spartans were simply unprepared for.[53] Cythera,

52 Jordan (1986) p. 139, drawing on Homer and Hesiod, notes that chance (Tyche in its personification) has always been understood as a child of the gods.

53 Westlake (1974) challenges Thucydides' view, arguing instead that "…in the opinion of the Spartan government, six years of war had shown its declared aim, namely the destruction of Athenian power, to be unattainable" (221-22). We must remind ourselves, though, of the "declared aim" versus the truest pretext (1.23.5-6), and ask whether the Spartans ever truly expected to achieve their stated goal of liberation (2.8.4; cf. 1.69). Westlake's view is arrived at largely by doubts about Thucydides' knowledge of the Spartans' motives. Yet Westlake himself attributes motives to the Spartans: "[t] the officials seem to have concluded, rightly or wrongly, that no military action of any kind by their forces at Pylos would provide successful…" and "[t]

an island of strategic importance, is overtaken, Pylos is still being held, and the Spartans fear domestic revolution (i.e., a possible Helot revolt). Add to this their naval struggles (Pylos and Cythera being accessible by sea), their belief that fortune was continually turning against them, and the Spartans now lacked "daring" (*tolma*) more than ever and were crippled from acting, fearful of making errors in what was for them an unprecedented situation (4.55.1-4). As Hornblower notes, this is one of six excurses occurring from Book Four through to the deaths of Brasidas and Cleon (and thus the peace treaty at the beginning of Book Five – 5.16) on the morale of both Spartans and Athenians as the war presses on and each city faces the unexpected.[54]

This rather short passage on Cythera (even including its context – 4.53-56) strikes at the heart, by way of prelude, of issues Sparta will continually face and for which they will need to adjust. That the Cythera narrative is immediately followed by the speech of Hermocrates, the Syracusan, in his call for Sicilians to unite against an Athenian threat (59-64), taken together with Thucydides' later remark that the Syracusans were the most capable at combatting the Athenians (8.96.5), only places Spartan troubles into the starkest relief.

Sparta's Attempts at Peace

After their failure to secure a treaty with Athens, or at least the return of their men, the Spartans begin to admit to themselves that they are involved in a war for which they are at least legally responsible, and which has dragged on despite their initial fears, predictions, and strategy. Mistakenly believing at Pylos that Athens desired peace as much as they did, the Spartans offered terms they hoped would end the war, bestow honor and nobility on Athens, and offer an alliance of the two cities. But the Athenians are

---

here is a possibility that the crews, almost all of them allies, were demoralized by their defeat..." (219). However, "their conclusion that the situation was hopeless seems to be indefensible if, as has been suggested, there was a reasonably good prospect of rescue by military action of some kind" (221). Westlake's emphasizes on the fleet size ignores Thucydides' emphasis: namely, the issue of moral responsibility, quiet yet noticeable in the Spartans' assessment of the situation in the overall war (4.20.2). Cf. Rood (1998) pp. 50-51 who identifies linguistic and narrative parallels between the Spartan defeat at Pylos and the Athenian disaster in the harbor at Syracuse.

54 Hornblower II pp. 218.

always "grasping for more" and, precisely for this reason and the advantages they held during the negotiation at Athens (not to mention other possible reasons), they reject any treaty and alliance.

But Book Four concludes with the Spartan commander, Brasidas, continuing the Spartan war effort under the official banner of liberating Athenian subjects from their empire. Despite the events at Pylos, Brasidas undertakes expeditions of his own and is successful in inciting Athenian subject cities across Greece to revolt. As these revolts continue to gain momentum, and after news spreads of their defeat at Amphipolis, the Athenians now become alarmed and discouraged (4.108.1). Brasidas was "measured" in his conduct and advertised to Athens' subjects that he had been sent by Sparta to free them from the Athenian empire (108.2). And despite Spartan reservations about Brasidas' activities, his efforts produce a one-year truce between the two cities. Such a truce was now appealing to each city: Athens wanted to end Brasidas' movements and institute a general peace, while Sparta wanted reconciliation, their men from the island returned, and a treaty for a longer duration (none of which was secured after the Pylos incident). Thucydides (again) emphasizes the Spartans were particularly concerned about the return of their men (4.117.2; cf. 108.7). They thought they would most be able to achieve this while Brasidas' "good fortune" (*eutuchei*) lasted. The Spartan view, that chance affects the course of war, is again confirmed. Through the actions of Brasidas, the fortunes of the Athenians have now changed, and the Spartans are able to negotiate for the return of their men, something they were unable to do so long as Athens was in a position of strength.[55]

55 There is a great deal of scholarly debate surrounding 4.117.2. The text is as follows (Mynott [2013] translation): "It was the men of course that they wanted back above all, since Brasidas was still enjoying a run of success. If he went on to yet further successes and brought about a more equal balance of power they still stood to lose them, even if in carrying on the fight on an equal basis they would have a better chance at final victory." Many commentators believe the passage to be corrupt, including Hornblower II pp. 361-62, who details the debate and various solutions put forward by Classen/Steup (German edition), Gomme (in his *HCT*), and the Budé (French edition) of Thucydides. The meaning of the Greek, according to Hornblower is: "they attached more importance to getting their men back, because of the continuing success of Brasidas." Hornblower comments: "This is an odd thing to say." In my view, there are two ways to understand this statement: first, as a reminder of what Thucydides has already stated – the Spartans' priority on securing their men. He mentions this at 4.15.2, 40.3, and 108.7. We hear about it, further, at 5.14.3 and 24.2. Second, could Brasidas' successes, should they continue, not push the Athenians

Brasidas succeeds where previous Spartan leadership had failed, defeating the Athenians at Amphipolis and Delos. These losses harm Athens to such a degree they sue for peace to stop their cities from going over to Brasidas (4.108.1-2, 117.1). Brasidas makes peace possible for Sparta. Unlike the Spartan strategy of ravaging the countryside of Attica and other allies of Athens, Brasidas successfully brings over Athens' subject cities under the promise of liberating them. The Spartan doubt about the justice of their cause does not seem to have affected Brasidas in his conduct; Brasidas wages the war of liberation Sparta proclaimed as their cause at the war's outset, but has been unable or unwilling to undertake. Yet there is a problem here for Sparta: tension between Brasidas' good fortune and the perceived need of the authorities at home to end the war. Perhaps we could say that it is not Spartan good fortune – plagued by guilt, ending the war is still their priority, despite Brasidas placing them in an amazingly advantageous position.[56]

The Athenians themselves also desire peace, something almost unthinkable and something Archidamus and previous Spartan attacks had not been able to achieve. Both cities at this stage find themselves in uncharacteristic territory. But regardless of Sparta's newfound situation, the Spartans still just wanted to go home – there is a psychological tension between their prowess in battle and their fear of fortune, represented in their belief that the capture of their men was most serious. Clearly, not all cities would understand this situation as they did. Yet this is more than simply poor

---

into an *all-out* war effort to thwart Brasidas, therefore eliminating an opportunity for the Spartans to get their men back? (Gomme III pp. 594-95 reads the passage this way, although still seeks emendations). After all, Thucydides notes that the Athenians were hoping to stop other cities from revolting after Brasidas successfully took Amphipolis. By stopping Brasidas' activities via a concession to Sparta (the return of their men) Athens could avoid having to face rebellions across *all* of Greece (4.108-109.6). In this same context, though, Thucydides judges that the other cities intent on following Amphipolis' example were miscalculating Athens' strength. This implies that, if the Athenians *had* focused on putting down revolts, they would have been able to do so. Overall, the sense of the passage is clear: the Spartans wanted their men back above all else. As Hornblower himself notes, the word *eutuchei* (from *eutucheo* – to be fortunate or prosperous) occurs both here, and at 5.16, where Brasidas is again mentioned and where, again, Thucydides reminds us of Brasidas' role in placing Sparta in a much better position to negotiate for the return of their men. As we have seen, the motif of fortune and chance has characterized the entire Pylos narrative, including Brasidas' place in it.

56 Brasidas, the events alluded to here, and his relation to Sparta are discussed in detail in Chapter Four.

policy; or rather, Thucydides forces us to question why the Spartans view the Pylos incident as they do. We recognize, of course, that calculation of their interests is affected by their understanding of those interests, what *they* view as the most urgent aspect of the situation. If the return of their captured men was not top priority for the Spartans, but rather, say, how this battle could be used to advance their interests in the larger war, then perhaps those men could be sacrificed to that end. But for the Spartans, this was never on the table. Thucydides gives no indication Sparta was still focused on the larger war in light of the capture at Pylos. This incident is a striking example where the interests of a city, what *they* view as a necessity, is in fact a choice based on a calculus that from another point of view is most imprudent or perhaps even foolish. Yet such an example must be acknowledged; such decisions cannot be understood simply as a cost-benefit analysis, but rather as a moral one, influenced by the Spartans' newfound guilt.

In one way, this guilt should surprise us given the response of the Delphic oracle, the god Apollo, signaling support for the Spartans in the war (1.118.3). This is to say nothing of the inconsistency between this guilt and the Athenian thesis. However, Spartan guilt arises with their misfortunes and the greatest misfortune for Sparta was the capture of the Spartiates. This makes sense of the fact that the Spartans did not consult the god again before concluding a truce with Athens because they believed they breached the solemnly sworn Thirty-Year treaty (4.117.3). No consultation with the god would seem fitting given such circumstances (although the usual oaths and libations consecrated the truce between Sparta and Athens, and the treaty begins as such – 118.1). They can only hope to end a war for which they were responsible in an attempt to appease the god for their unlawful action.

Following the one-year truce, Cleon and Brasidas engage again at Amphipolis. At the same time, both Sparta and Athens now desire peace beyond their limited one-year truce. The Athenians regret their decision not to reach an agreement after the capture of Sparta's men at Sphacteria; now even they attribute their own success *merely* to good luck, not the skill or strategy of Demosthenes (5.14.1-2). The truce, intended to afford each city time to secure their next move given the difficulties each faced, has become a treaty.

Domestically, a few key incidents reveal the cities' respective moods.

With Cleon now dead, Nicias emerges as Athens' most prominent general and convinces the city to agree to terms (16.1).[57] During the peace, Sparta accuses their own king, Pleistoanax, of bribing the Delphic priestess as a means of ensuring his return to Sparta and accession to king (16-17.1). Pleistoanax had been exiled from Sparta on suspicion of corruption when he invaded Attica, but failed to proceed further (1.114.1).[58] The peace has not wholly alleviated the Spartans' concern with their own breach of the treaty and perhaps they suspected that even Apollo's supposed support for their war effort was similarly due to bribery. The Spartans now blame Pleistoanax for *all* their misfortunes; and while Thucydides is silent on the truth of this charge, he allows us to observe the weight the Spartans placed on oracles (reminding us, of course, of Delphi and the Cylon pollution). While Thucydides states in his own name that the only oracle that came true related to the length of the war (5.26.3), he does not disregard the significance of oracles as such – oracles affect the Spartans' prosecution of the war.[59]

The manner in which this treaty arose, however, hints at how tenuous it is. Both Athens and Sparta suffer from factions within their cities, and at this stage of the war, certain individuals favor the peace while others oppose it. Cleon and Brasidas both favored war: Brasidas due to the success and honor he obtained; Cleon due to the crimes for which he was responsible and wished to hide (5.16.1). Pleistoanax, the Spartan king, sought peace since he had been accused of bribing the priestess at Delphi, and he believed no harm could come to him during peacetime, and because the return of the Spartiates on Sphacteria would ensure he could suffer no further blame for all that had befallen Sparta in the first ten years of the war. Nicias also supported peace; however, he desired both to guard his own "good fortune"

57 This treaty (5.18-19) is the so-called Peace of Nicias. Nicias is discussed in detail in Chapter Four.

58 For further background, see Rahe (2019) pp. 222-27 (with p. 284n46) who draws additional evidence from Diodorus Siculus and Plutarch. Thucydides' account of Pleistoanax is detailed in Chapter Three.

59 Hornblower III p. 45 argues that the mention of the oracle is "inconsequential." But is Thucydides not perhaps saying that while he, Thucydides, does not look to oracles for guidance, for the Spartans (and others) oracles and other divine matters are very important? Rejecting oracles, as this example makes clear, may introduce political problems when they *do* come true, whether by coincidence or divine intervention. Insofar as oracles appear to come true, their influence over how human beings interpret significant events will always be a part of the story of that event.

as well as relieve the troubles "for himself *and* his citizens" (16.1 – emphasis added). Only Nicias seems to have a motive in pursuing peace which is not wholly guided by his own interests. And the dissolution of the peace and beginning of the second half of war similarly will be the result of certain individuals in each city (as we will detail below) guided more by private ambitions than service to their cities.

Sparta also faces further difficulties: Their treaty with Argos is set to expire, their men are still barricaded on the island, and the potential for their allies on the Peloponnesus to rebel and go over to the Athenians is a fear Thucydides himself confirms (14.4). But in Thucydides' repetition of these concerns, he only mentions the return of the prisoners, who he now identifies as Spartiates from the first families in Sparta (14.3-5, 15.1). Thucydides' silence on the Argive matter in his repetition imitates the Spartans – the return of their men at this point in the war was their only true concern. The larger purpose of the war is dropped.[60]

Thucydides also now reveals that the beginning of the war was Sparta's invasion of Attica (20.1).[61] This despite his earlier claim that the events at Plataea were an overt breach of the treaty (2.7.1). But there he did not

60 Strassler's edition of Thucydides (1996) on 5.34.2 (p. 321n2b) brings out the common argument among scholars: The Spartans wanted their men back due to the number of Spartiates, Sparta's most elite citizen, having been reduced significantly since the time of Herodotus (see, for example, Hornblower II p. 194, Cawkwell [1983]; cf. Cartledge [2002] pp. 263-72 and Rahe [2016] pp. 129-31 for further scholarly debate and conjectures on these calculations). If the number of Spartiates was of the utmost concern to the Spartans, Thucydides makes no mention of this. Instead, we have seen Thucydides' focus: the gravity of this disaster, and in the negotiations at Pylos with the Athenians, the Spartans quietly raising another issue – who is to blame for the war. As I have argued, *this* concern is Thucydides' explanation, especially if we also consider his later statement that the Spartans came to believe *they* were to blame for starting the war and the effect this had on their war effort (7.18.1-3). Thucydides is interested in the psychological or moral explanations and less concerned in this instance with possible "material" explanations; he of course mentions other such practical considerations that affect strategy and conduct, but refrains from doing so in this case (cf. 7.27.3). This moral explanation, perceived guilt over committing an injustice, is in keeping with Thucydides' claim that his account of the Peloponnesian War is to be a possession for all times, so long as the human condition remains the same (1.22.4).

61 "...from the first invasion of Attica *and* the beginning of this war." (5.20.1 – emphasis added). For debates on this passage, see Hornblower II pp. 490-93. Cf. Rawlings (1979) who (partially) defends Thucydides' statements at 2.1 and 5.20 against widespread scholarly rejection of Thucydides' dating on the start of the war. See Chapter Three note 3 below.

indicate clearly that it was *Sparta* who breached the treaty. Thebes had invaded Plataea and Sparta came to assist their allies (while Athens also began to prepare for war). The beginning of the war is precipitated, though, by this act; yet as we have observed, the Thebans were invited in by a faction of Plataeans. And the war between Sparta and Athens was already forecast, given Sparta and its allies had voted for war.

If the action of Thebes does not constitute the beginning of the war, we may consider that the part allies and neighboring cities play in the cause of any war is difficult to determine. And even if Sparta is unjust by beginning the war, this itself does not imply that Athens is exculpated. Athens is at most here only exculpated legally, i.e., they did not breach the terms of the treaty at the beginning of the war. Sparta breached the treaty with its failure to allow for arbitration of differences; but this is also merely a legal breach because Thucydides' explicit judgment states Sparta was *compelled* by Athens to wage war. If fear is a valid compulsion, as the Athenians themselves admit, we must say that breaches of treaties, i.e., acts of illegality viewed as injustice, will always happen should the compulsion be perceived as sufficiently great.

But it is the Spartans who are ridden by *their view* that they breached the treaty in the first part of the war; the relevance of their efforts here at ending the war thus become clear. Thucydides reveals that Spartan guilt had an adverse effect on their conduct. They came to believe that they had violated the treaty with Athens through their involvement with the Thebans' attack on Plataea and due to their refusal to submit allegations to arbitration, as the Athenian envoys had offered; thus they "deserved" (*eikotōs*) the misfortunes that befell them in the war, including the loss of their men on the island (7.18.2). Treaties were solemnly sworn, and oaths taken to ensure compliance; and the gods were held to support such oaths. The misfortunes in the war for the pious Spartans could not help but be seen as divine punishment. "Fortune" is the will of the gods intervening in human affairs as reward and punishment for those that act justly or unjustly. Later, Thucydides notes that the Athenians breached the treaty and alliance agreed to at the outset of the 14th year (5.20-22); they will aid the Argives when the Spartans invade their territory in the 18th year (6.105.1). Taken together, we now notice a pattern: Each side breaches a treaty but in the second part of the war, justice will be on the side of Sparta, not Athens; the Spartans, coming to recognize this breach and particularly attuned as to whose side the just cause fell, will expect the war to proceed in their favor and will be full of "eagerness" (*prothumos*) in resuming it (7.18.3).

Sparta's Uneasy Alliance

Regardless of the agreements, maneuverings, and expectations of the two major players, and despite Spartan pressure, their allies, including Boeotia, Corinth, Elis, and Megara, refuse to sign this new treaty (signed in the war's 10th year) on the "pretext" (*prophasis*) that the treaty could have been more "just" (*dikaios* – 5.22.1). The allies complained, expecting to receive back (in any resolution) what they were in possession of before the war had begun. Sparta's chief worry is to muster support as protection against Argos, the third most powerful city in Greece and an old enemy (28.2, 29.1). Argos was strengthened by their ability to maintain neutrality thus far, but the Spartans correctly fear that they desired to gain supremacy of the Peloponnesus for themselves.[62] This is the Argives' motive in listening to the Corinthians' complaints, who condemn Sparta's alliance with Athens. Argos could gain an alliance for itself from Sparta's disgruntled allies, who themselves hoped to form an alliance with Athens (24.2). The view of Corinth is that Sparta must have their own designs on the Peloponnesus given this new alliance. As a result, Argos welcomes any Greek city desiring to ally with them, Mantinea being the first to come over out of fear of Sparta. Many other cities in the Peloponnesus were considering following, assuming Mantinea had a good reason for leaving the Spartan fold. Thucydides allows us to notice, however, that Mantinea's actions were less calculating than emotive: they were fearful of Sparta and "angry" for being included in the treaty with Athens (29.2). The Mantineans act based on their belief that Sparta would engage in controlling the Peloponnesus now that they were not at war with Athens and due to the perceived injustice of the treaty; their "reasons," upon which they act, are both their own and false.

Nevertheless, the fear of Mantinea becomes the fear of the other cities as well. Sparta and Athens had a clause in the treaty allowing for either city to alter the agreement, so long as it did not breach their oaths (29.2). The cities of the Peloponnesus now fear Sparta and Athens will act in concert to

62 Only great strength seems to allow for the neutrality of a city, as in the case of Argos (5.28.2). Or perhaps weakness; cf. Melos.

subjugate them. The liberation of Greece from the Athenian empire seems but a distant memory in the minds of the other cities, replaced by the possibility of an Athenian-Spartan one. Liberation had been Brasidas' motive or rhetoric, and while he suggested he spoke for Sparta as a whole, this Spartan reversal in signing an alliance with Athens presents a striking rebuttal. Contra Sparta's now disgruntled allies, Thucydides has not indicated this was in fact Sparta's intention. While the allies assume Sparta has empire of its own in mind, this was not its aim. Misperception by Sparta's allies is both understandable, but also revealing of how odd Sparta's actions are in the aftermath of Pylos.

Confronting this situation, the Spartans attempt to bring their suspicious allies back to their side and into the alliance; they accuse the Corinthians in particular of violating their oaths, since the treaty had stipulated the majority's vote as binding on all others. The Spartans correctly observe that it was the Corinthians who instigated discontent and prodded the other allies to join into an alliance with Argos (30.1), a clear treaty violation. The latter respond to this allegation by claiming they cannot breach their other past allegiance to the Thracians, with oaths sworn on trust in the gods. The gods were the only basis on which oaths of a treaty could be violated, given they could interfere, standing in the way of a city complying with treaty conditions.

We do not hear any Spartan response to this Corinthian argument, despite the fact that Thucydides openly states the Corinthians merely used this "pretense" (*proschēma*) as a means to justify their failure to abide by their agreements with Sparta (30.2). The Spartan envoys leave to return home. The Spartans' silence here is telling – they do not even attempt to argue with the Corinthians. The Spartans do not reply, as the Corinthians had done on an earlier occasion, that the gods view compulsion as an excuse for breaches of oaths (1.71.5). On both occasions when Sparta's allies use the language of divine justice, the Spartans are ineffectual, rendered silent (5.22.1, 30.4).

And there are other problems with establishing peace as well. During the initial stages of the alliance, Athens and Sparta dispute the conditions required of each side for its fulfillment. Athens, in particular, accuses Sparta of failing in their obligations and becomes generally suspicious of them. The agreement between the two included bringing allies into the treaty, and the two cities were to unite in "compelling" those who refused to accept it

(35.3). The Spartans argue, however, that they are unable to restore Amphipolis as the Athenians had requested – it is not in their "power" (35.5). They reiterate their promise to negotiate with Boeotia, Athens' interest here lying in the return of Panactum which was held by the Boeotians. The Spartans undertake these negotiations, but the Boeotians will not give them access to Panactum without making an alliance. Such an alliance, however, would be a breach of the existing treaty between Sparta and Athens, both having agreed to act together in *any* actions of peace or war. And while the Spartans have recovered their prisoners on Sphacteria through the alliance, the Athenians still hold Pylos itself (located, we recall, on the Peloponnesus) and will not return it without Panactum. The Spartans ally themselves with Boeotia to gain Panactum, even though they are aware that this would be "to do wrong" (*adikeō*) towards Athens (39.3). Thucydides makes clear that this breach follows from the Spartans' principal interest – the restoration of Pylos, which he repeats twice (36.2, 39.2).

Clearly, though, the Spartans (and we might add, all cities) find themselves in an irreconcilable position: demands from allies or potential allies cannot both be met. Thucydides presents the Spartans as negotiating in good faith with both Athens and Boeotia. Sparta assures the Athenians they are attempting to fulfill all the conditions of the alliance. Thucydides presents no ill dealing here on the Spartans' part. But regardless of the claims of either side, Thucydides notes that *neither* had given back all they were required by the treaty (26.2). And both sides will be involved in battles throughout Book Five (a supposed peacetime), culminating in the Athenians' restatement at Melos of their imperial view.

But Spartans are not Corinthians nor Athenians, and the bulk of Book Five will reveal a much more hesitant and cautious Sparta, a manipulative Corinth, and an enterprising Athens. It seems that while the treaty and alliance serve as a means to end the war for the Spartans, it is only a means for the Athenians to find themselves in a more advantageous position to renew hostilities. It is Athens that will eventually breach the alliance by an *overt* act leading to renewed open war with Sparta (6.105.1-2). This is not to deny that both cities were in violation of treaties and alliances throughout the war – neither side was wholly just.[63]

---

63 See Hornblower II pp. 113-18 on the extensive scholarly debate over Thucydides' inclusions of the treaty texts from 5.18-19, 22-24. Hornblower rejects extreme positions, such as those that seek to dismantle late Book Four and most of Book Five,

This does not detract from the movement towards peace animating the Spartans at this time in the war. That Sparta was acting with certain designs in mind is only supported by Thucydides' remarks that a faction within Sparta swayed certain decisions, what I will call the "war party." The Spartans' guilt and their doubt about who started the war support the view that they were interested in maintaining peace, not in continuing aggression. Faction within Sparta at this time, though, is revealed in the Sparta-Boeotia narrative – the Spartans wished to obtain Panactum in order to exchange it with the Athenians for Pylos *and* (as Thucydides adds) because the party of Xenares and Cleobulus (Spartan ephors) wanted to dissolve the treaty between Athens and Sparta and carry on the war (5.39.3).

The Spartan-Boeotian alliance thus concluded, the Boeotians take it upon themselves to raze Panactum. When the news of these matters arrives at Athens, the Athenians blame the Spartans. Thucydides reveals that ancient oaths had been exchanged between Athens and Boeotia regarding Panactum; neither city's inhabitants should occupy it, the Boeotians razing it so that it would remain common land (42.1). This oath and the actions of the Boeotians did not involve the Spartans directly, but led the Athenians to blame the Spartans, nonetheless. Once again, the Spartans have been unable to control their allies; they repeatedly fail in their actions abroad and the belief amongst the Athenians is that this is due to Spartan complicity and injustice.

The Athenians' conclusion, as Thucydides has alluded to, is subject to one key objection we might perhaps overlook: The ephors in Sparta have changed and the war party has ascended to power. Cleobulus and Xenares were both directly opposed to the treaty and sought to dissolve it; their party pressed for the alliance with Boeotia, *knowing* this would be a breach

---

and sides (with reservations) with the view that Thucydides could indeed "innovate" in his writing and, therefore, the section (beginning with the agreements at 4.117 and leading into Book Five) could mark a transition in Thucydides' narrative since the truce, alliance, and treaty negotiations mark a transition in the war, from war to peace (as Stahl [2003] p. 138 observes). Hornblower cites Connor (1984) as a corrective to the Separatist view, which provides the arguments for dismantling this portion of the text, as I will discuss further in Chapter Three. Connor (1984) p. 145-47: "The concern with the composition of the *Histories* has impeded attention to the literary role of the documents." In other words, the listing of signatories, treaty terms, and lack of speeches in Book Five signals, I will argue, something unique about the Book as a whole, rather than evidence of its incompleteness, and contributes to the story Thucydides aims to tell.

of Sparta's agreement with Athens (even leaving aside Panactum) and thus would likely result in renewed hostilities (36.2, 39.3). The terms of the treaty were agreed to *before* Xenares and the war party came to power (36). As Thucydides will present more overtly later in Book Five, "Sparta" and "the Spartans" no longer refer to a unified approach to the war.

Despite a looming Athens-Argos alliance (the result of Sparta's own alliance with Boeotia) Nicias is able to persuade the Athenians to attempt again to negotiate with the Spartans and fulfill some of the conditions of the treaty and alliance. Nicias, in contrast with other Athenians, wants friendship with Sparta even though Athens need not be friendly given their position of strength from which to negotiate.[64] The conditions Nicias seeks include Sparta relinquishing its alliance with Boeotia; otherwise, Athens will finalize its own with Argos. The Spartans refuse and Thucydides *repeats* that this is due to Xenares and his party (46.4). The refusal of conditions aimed at preserving an alliance, and more importantly, cessation from hostilities, is not a typical Spartan action. An Athenian-Argive alliance is thus concluded due to the "anger" (*orgē*) of the Athenians at Spartan "injustice" (*adikeō* – 46.5). Apart from the continued Athenian refrain of acting only with a view to their interests, the Athenians' anger betrays, perhaps surprisingly, their expectation that Sparta act according to the terms of justice. Despite these disagreements, the treaty between Athens and Sparta was not officially renounced (48.1).

Xenares dies during a battle at Heraclea and Agis (son of the former Spartan king, Archidamus) will now lead Sparta in the war.[65] Although treaties and alliances are still in place, two key figures arise that help guide the trajectory of the next phase of the war: Alcibiades pushes the Athenians forward by finding pretexts for continuing hostilities against Sparta and its allies. And Agis' command of Sparta and its allies (along with their other king, Pleistoanax, to a lesser degree) culminates in the largest battle between the two sides and a pivotal event during the central years of the war (the peace officially stretching from the 10th to the 18th year). It is in these years that Thucydides reveals more details of Sparta – the internal

64 Nicias, in contrast to Alcibiades and the war party in Sparta, is interested in preserving the current treaty and alliance. His view of the war is closer to Sparta than to Athens.

65 This confirms Archidamus' fear that the war would last into the following generation (1.81.6).

order of their city, their regime – as their domestic situation obtrudes, or rather dictates, foreign affairs, compelling us to consider the city itself more closely. The division between the Spartans seeking peace and those who supported the party of Xenares reminds us of Book One – the king, Archidamus, and the ephor, Sthenelaidas, differed on a declaration of war. In other words, Thucydides introduces here, early in Book Five, the Book on Sparta, that the stable, long-lasting regime that was the source of the city's power is not without troubling tensions within.

The Athenian thesis has been strengthened by the Spartans' admission that they may have been responsible for starting the war. Far from acting according to justice, the Spartans now appear exposed to the accusation of being a self-serving city, even if one preaching justice – a Sparta of the most obvious hypocrisy. But the Athenian thesis is still faced with a problem: Sparta repeatedly justifies its interests as well as its shortcomings, and therefore hides from itself the tension between self-interest and morality. This tension begins to become apparent, only to them, through their guilt. That cities view their interests clear-sightedly, as per the Athenian thesis, is a problem. Sparta's interest would seem to be a large-scale effort against Athens, to say nothing of the stated purpose of the war: liberating Spartans, Peloponnesians, and their allies from Athenian domination. Brasidas pursues this strategy with notable success. But the Spartans engage in no such effort, seeking only an unsatisfactory, strategically questionable, end to all hostilities.

While the trans-legal cause is exculpatory according to the Athenian thesis, Spartan guilt results in seeking a treaty with Athens to end the war despite their admittedly weak position from which to negotiate. The Spartans fail to act according to that thesis, because this guilt, arising from the capture of a relatively small number of their men, derails not only their stated purpose in the war, but even a negotiation on measured terms. Sparta views its interests more in maintaining their city, its domestic cohesion, than winning foreign wars.

This in turn points to a more fundamental consideration, beyond the particulars of Sparta-Athens: What is the end or goal or purpose of the city itself? Is it preservation or glory? What is required of each? Is the former possible without the latter? Is the former necessarily at odds with the latter? And which goal presents the city with its most compelling "necessities"? Sparta seeks to preserve its city, its way of life, against the encroachments of an "Athens." Athens seeks its preservation in its greatness, a greatness motivated by love of glory. In the next stage of the war, Thucydides shows clearly that Sparta's protection of the city at home and their ability to prosecute the war, even when in a position of strength, are not unified ends. In these upcoming years, we will locate characteristic differences between Sparta and Athens, only some of which we have observed in Thucydides' war narrative thus far.

Chapter Three

Sparta and The Primacy Of The Regime

Thucydides' preliminary and most visible judgments on Sparta highlight the city's success in putting down tyrannies, maintaining good laws and a stable regime that protected the city against civil war (*stasis* – 1.18.1), thus combining moderation and prosperity (8.24.4). These judgments, along with Athens' on-going instability post-Pericles, direct the reader to the question of what differentiates Sparta from Athens. Domestic politics figures into Thucydides' account over the course of the war, notably with Periclean Athens and the plague, along with oligarchs and democrats fighting for control of various other cities; but the internal workings of Sparta, despite some evidence, have remained a relative mystery up to this point.[1]

Here in the central years of the war, Thucydides' above cited observations, occurring in Books One and Eight, are rendered problematic by Book Five.[2] This Book also shows us a peak of Sparta's war effort we have

1 Some scholars deny or downplay Thucydides' presentation of domestic politics. For example, Romilly (1963) pp. 102-103 claims that Thucydides "refuses to see any primary connection between home and foreign policy" and thus for Thucydides "imperialism belonged to the realm of foreign policy, and he allowed no other considerations to enter into his study of it." As the title of this chapter indicates, I disagree with this view and will argue precisely the opposite: The foreign policy of a city cannot be understood independent of its regime and attendant domestic politics. Most accounts of domestic politics in Thucydides, and Greek political thought in general, only focus on Athenian democracy. On domestic politics more broadly, consider Fleiss (1959), Orwin (1994) pp. 172-92, Jaffe (2017b). On tyranny in Thucydides, see Palmer (1982). Connor (1984) pp. 220-29 discusses Athenian oligarchy and democracy in Book Eight, although unfortunately does not draw parallels to Sparta in Book Five. Forde (1989) pp. 116-75 details Book Eight and Alcibiades. Rood (1998) p. 205 notes: "...the tension between Athenian qualities at home and abroad is central to Thucydides' explanation of why Athens lost the Peloponnesian War." Price (2001) treats Thucydides' presentation of *stasis* as a model for understanding both the Peloponnesian War and future wars.

2 On the potential significance of Thucydides placing arguments in the center of a larger whole (as part of a ring composition), see Ellis (1991) p. 348 and context. See also Strauss (1964) pp. 222-23 and (1983) p. 95 on Book Five. Thucydides himself

not yet witnessed, but in so doing reveals Sparta's failures in strategy, along with outright errors arising from tensions within the city. Foreign and domestic policy come together. The Spartan virtues leading to the good domestic order Thucydides praises do not foster success, as the end of Book Four and early Book Five attest, in dealing with both allies and enemies in their apparent war of liberation.

Sparta's difficulties prosecuting the war direct us to a closer investigation of the Spartan "regime" (*politeia*) and comparisons Thucydides expects his reader to make. Only through his two paradigmatic depictions of *stasis*, the transition from Periclean to post-Periclean Athens and the Corcyraean civil war, can we fully appreciate Thucydides' assessment of Sparta. It is precisely the Spartan regime that protects it from the cancerous civil strife (and all-out civil war) we witness these other cities suffering. Thucydides' statements and presentation of the functioning of various cities at war are revealing, then, of regime types, not presented taxonomically as per Aristotle, but as we witness these regimes (along with the characters of their differing citizens) in action.

Evidence of foreign policy differences between Athens and Sparta abounds in the first four Books. But in the first ten years of his account, Thucydides has not been as forthcoming regarding domestic Sparta. In this chapter we will consider how internal regime dynamics bear on Sparta's foreign policy as they navigate the nominal time of peace underway during Book Five; weigh the regime breakdowns in Athens and Corcyra as they undergo *stasis*; detail the Spartan regime by canvassing the disparate evidence Thucydides scatters across his account; and finally, discover how, for Thucydides, the regime (*politeia*), its peculiar laws and customs (*nomoi*), bear on Spartan psychology – the characteristic citizen Sparta produces.

Thucydides has detailed more of Athens in the earlier parts of his account – we witness the rise of a beautified Athens in the naval and monetary themes of the Archaeology; we are allowed to hear the Athenian envoys at Sparta describing the motivations of Athenian empire and the justifications for it; we hear Pericles extol the noble character of Athens and the Athenians. If the Athenian empire and its understanding of itself contributed to the internal discord within Athens late in the war (as Thucydides

signals this is the central period of the war: "As for the agreement that intervened in the middle [*mesos*], one would be quite wrong to think that this period did not count as a state of war" (5.26.2 – Mynott [2013] translation).

signaled in his summary of Periclean Athens – 2.65.7-13), then the strongest case to be made for Sparta rests not on their success in the Peloponnesian War, but on Athens' failure to secure victory. Athens could have succeeded were it not for the factions fighting for control of their city. This is strengthened by Thucydides' statement that the best Athenian regime of his time was the regime of 411, a "measured mixing" (*metria xynkrasis*) of oligarchy and democracy, the few and the many (8.97.2). And in addition to Athens, Thucydides allows us to witness *stasis* in Corcyra and the factions in Athens late in the war. On the other hand, Sparta appears, at least initially, to have suffered none of this internal discord. Their city survives the war.

Book Five: Thucydides' Neglected Spartan Narrative

During the nearly seven years of tentative peace, Sparta is more fully revealed than anywhere else. At this point in the war, in the time of an official alliance between Sparta and Athens, there is as much action as ever. Sparta must deal both with Athenian complaints of Spartan failure to fulfill certain stipulations of the treaty, as well as their prosecution of the war going forward (when the tentative character of the peace becomes clear). Sparta does in fact "commit wrong" against the Athenians by allying themselves with Boeotia, who refused to give back Panactum, a city Athens demanded as a condition of the treaty. Sparta had already pleaded they were doing everything possible to fulfill this condition. But there were strong parties in Sparta on either side of the war debate, some in favor of ending the war with Athens, others seeking to continue it despite the alliance in place. These parties also had to contend with ongoing complaints from their allies, not only due to what they viewed as an unjust alliance between Sparta and Athens, but especially as fighting continued amongst the allies on both sides. Accusations, complaints from the other smaller cities, maneuvering for what each side sought to achieve, along with parties in both cities for and against reigniting the war, characterize this period. The official alliance and peace between the two major cities did not, therefore, resolve all the differences that had arisen during the course of these first ten years; nor did most of the other Greeks truly view the peace as signaling an actual end to future hostilities.

Before considering Thucydides' narrative during this period, we must establish how the 11th to 18th years of the war figure into his account as a whole.[3] The significance of these years is signaled by Thucydides himself, in his digression near the beginning of the 11th year (5.26), his so-called Second Preface.[4] Here he argues that the Peloponnesian War, despite

3 Despite the fact that the eight-book structure is today generally regarded as the correct one, there is still some scholarly disagreement. See Bonner (1920) on the sources that argue for eight, nine, and thirteen book versions of Thucydides. Marcellinus' *Life of Thucydides* (a work of the 5th or 6th century A.D. and only recently translated into English by Burns [2010]) argues that the eight-book division was the most common, even in antiquity. Regardless of whether one is able to settle this debate, we must also be alert to Thucydides' own division by years, i.e., according to the natural changes of season, since he directs our attention to *this* division as the one employed in his account (5.20.2-3, 26.1). Thucydides states that the war lasted 27 years in total; thus, part of the period in Book Five during which the war is not officially being engaged in is during the central year of the war (14th). Thucydides' praises of Sparta occur at the beginning and end of his account (1.6.4, 18.1, 8.24.4), while Book Five complicates these praises. This, it seems to me, is further evidence of Thucydides placing the burden on the reader to weigh all the speeches and actions, along with his presentation of them, to construct his complete Spartan portrait. Cf. Hornblower II pp. 490-93, III 48-49 on objections to Thucydides' dating and use of seasons. Hornblower notes problems with Thucydides' calculations, since he does not tell us certain events by which he makes such calculations. It is hard to believe, though, that Thucydides would be so sloppy. Hornblower, in this context, does not weigh the effect of leaving the beginning and end of the war as somewhat indeterminant, something Thucydides has already done. For example, on 5.20.1, Hornblower II p. 490 argues the reference to the Spartan invasion of Attica should be removed from Thucydides' text. For an explanation (and defense) of this passage, see Chapter Two note 58 above.

4 On the Second Preface, see also Connor (1984) pp. 142-44: "On this passage...hangs much of the Separatist criticism of Thucydides." Rood (1988) pp. 84-88 also addresses the long-held view of this portion of Thucydides' text: "The second preface is a careful transition which marks out the first war as a discrete unit, and argues for its place within the whole when it is relevant. It does not support the view that book v is a hurried attempt to fill in the years between the peace and the Sicilian expedition, demanded when Thucydides arrived at his final conception of the war." Cf. Hunter (1977) (also cited by Connor) who draws Separatist conclusions based on evidence amenable to other interpretations (especially her view that the incompleteness of Books Five and Eight is obvious). After all, the peace between Sparta and Athens *was* an official treaty (which Thucydides details – 5.17.2-19) and a pause in the war (at least between Sparta and Athens – 5.25). Moreover, among other literary effects, this new stage of the war makes intelligible Thucydides' Second Preface, which, it seems to me, has a clear, explicitly stated purpose: to note the unity of the Peloponnesian War and its duration, while signaling it as officially a time of "peace." In other words, it does nothing less than lead the reflective reader to weigh the fundamental question of when cities are at war versus when they are at peace.

treaties and alliance during this period, is not two wars, but one. The limitations on truces, fighting amongst allies (even when Sparta and Athens were not involved), and wars in Epidaurus and Mantinea are his proofs of this contention (26.2). For Thucydides, it appears adherence to treaties is the only time when cities are not openly at war. The importance of agreements and their corresponding oaths is not illusory though – as Thucydides shows at its outbreak, pretexts are required. How each city understands the war and justifies it to others and, perhaps more importantly, to itself is part of what distinguishes them. Not all cities assess war and peace alike. Hostilities occurring during the Sparta-Athens alliance observable throughout Book Five, for example, begin to show more clearly the relationship between Sparta's domestic politics and its influence on their handling of both enemies and allies.

While factions within each city were divided along proponents of continuing the war and those that favored peace, the deaths of Brasidas and Cleon, as well as strategic losses for both sides, help bring about an alliance. Reasons for the alliance, though, differ: While Cleon's death aided Athens in securing support for a treaty arising from the influence of Nicias, the situation for Sparta is more complex. Brasidas, while a proponent for war because of his support for Sparta's cause to liberate Greek cities from Athens, was not viewed favorably by Sparta's leading men. Nevertheless, the ephor, Xenares, led a charge at Sparta to continue war with Athens for reasons Thucydides does not make clear. Perhaps he viewed the injustice of Athens as cause for continuing or perhaps he felt little for the cause of securing the return of the Spartiates from Sphacteria. It was Sthenelaidas, also a Spartan ephor, who argued vehemently for the war before its outbreak, in contrast to the king, Archidamus. With the death of Brasidas, Agis, the current Spartan king, will lead the city during the cessation of open hostilities. But Sparta's allies did not view this alliance as having any good end and began to fear an empire of both cities over the rest. Corinth, in particular, leads this charge; but their inability to procure support for a counter-alliance against Sparta forces them to move to Argos in an attempt to protect themselves, despite Thucydides' indication that no such imperial designs existed under the new agreement (5.27; cf. 5.22.1-2). The Corinthians fail to recall their own portrait of Sparta as a city that seeks above all to avoid the risks of war (1.70.1). Nevertheless, Corinth's courting of Argos will prove significant, precipitating the unfolding of key events for both Sparta and the Peloponnesian War as a whole.

Thucydides thus quietly reminds us that political decisions are often based on misleading, false, or misinterpreted information; but these decisions are no less decisions and lead to irremediable actions regardless of the basis of the city's knowledge. And since Corinth, along with the allies of both Sparta and Athens, continues to lodge complaints, the Spartans find themselves compelled to provide some support and avoid potential revolts. The allies, as we will see, complain to Sparta on more than one occasion, but as their customary religious sacrifices before leaving on an expedition prove unfavorable, the Spartans are unwilling to leave home. When conditions worsen, however, including Alcibiades securing an alliance with Argos, they finally march on Argos, Thucydides making no narrative comment on whether the sacrifices were favorable when they finally *did* act (5.57.1). While we could perhaps assume by this silence a favorable sign, we must wonder whether the Spartans quietly decided they had no choice but to depart from their customary practice or justify action regardless of the outcome. Thucydides could easily have mentioned the sacrifices were they favorable. If the Spartans ignored this practice in this case from a perceived necessity to protect their interests, we still need to explain this inconsistency; for they *do* obey the sacrifices and other signs on other occasions throughout the war. With notable repetition, Thucydides highlights this practice in Book Five. While the Corinthians see ill-dealing and conspiracy at every turn, the Spartans feel the weight of the gods.[5]

This inconsistency in the Spartans' relations with their allies and

5 This is the first of numerous mentions of sacrifices during the years of official peace. While this is clearly not the first act of Spartan piety Thucydides allows us to see, it is another pious practice we are only now made aware of (5.54.2, 55.3, 116.1). Kagan (1981) pp. 84-85, citing Busolt (1880), argues that: "We must agree with Busolt that the unfavorable frontier sacrifices were merely 'pretext by which the sudden withdrawal was explained to the army'" despite Kagan's willingness to entertain genuine Spartan piety. Rood (1998) pp. 106-108 also notices religion used as a pretext, but his examples, interestingly, are all cities *other* than Sparta. Flower (2017) p. 429 notes: "It may be significant that only for Sparta do we have evidence for the border-crossing divinatory sacrifice called *diabatēria*." See Xenophon, *Regime of the Lacedaemonians* XIII.1-5 with Proietti (1987) p. 72. Proietti's interpretation of Xenophon's presentation of Sparta argues that sacrifices performed by the king led to greater obedience to him on campaigns. Parker (1998) pp. 157-58 also discusses Xenophon's account. Powell (2009) offers a response to Parker's account of Spartan religion and dyarchy. See Rahe (2016) pp. 43-44 with n23 for further detail on the king and campaign sacrifices.

enemies reminds us of the beginning of the war. Ignoring a potential breach of the treaty by not submitting to arbitration, the Spartans still sought a pretext for commencing hostilities against Athens. The tension between their possible breach of the treaty and their belief in the injustice of the Athenian empire left them searching for further justification; they seemed to have doubts their cause was just, or at least justifiable, for war. Thucydides' later remark (7.18.2) that they came to view their breach of the treaty and thus the start of the war as the cause of their guilt implies, despite these doubts, that the Spartans viewed this cause as sufficiently justified in their own minds. This does not mean this cause was sufficiently justified according to Thucydides, for he fails to make *any* remark on their claim to be liberating Greek cities from the Athenian empire. What appears as hypocrisy and obvious motives of self-interest to others does not explain the Spartan mind. Thucydides had stated his opinion on the cause of the war before this – the Spartans acted out of fear and thus did not require a justification for an act of self-preservation. Despite Thucydides' statement, however, the Spartans could neither admit this (for strategic reasons) nor did they believe it; their eventual admission (that is, to themselves, as Thucydides presents it – 7.18) indicates that only later did they hesitatingly acknowledge their cause was not on the side of justice. The necessity of defending their interests, interests they feared would be compromised by an expanding Athenian empire, is not for them a sufficient justification for action. Although the interests Sthenelaidas appealed to did offer such a justification (while also castigating Athenian injustice), the Spartans ultimately hold they were responsible for the treaty's breach. Necessity does not allow one to act against the dictates of justice in the Spartan mind (including the express stipulations of a treaty requiring arbitration of disputes) and thus the Spartans believe they were rightly, even divinely, punished for their actions.[6]

To fully understand the Spartans' pious practices (and exemplification

6 The word Thucydides uses at 7.18, *paranomēma*, may be translated "unlawful act," "injury," or "offense." But Hornblower III pp. 573-75 prefers Jowett's "transgression" since it retains the pious tone of the Greek. Relatedly, see the verb *enthumeomai* ("take to heart"), which is used by Thucydides in the context of Delos, the eclipse at Sicily, and the Athenians' assessment of their misfortunes at the hands of Brasidas. Thucydides' language here signals, in tone, the pious implications the cause of the war has for the Spartans, and confirms Archidamus' warning that Sparta risks being dragged into a war that would, despite the accusation of Athenian injustice, be their fault, both officially (as per the treaty) and divinely (as per the gods). See notes 91 and 92 and context below.

of their belief in divine justice), along with its source, we must consider what Thucydides reveals here in Book Five not disclosed previously (and why it is only disclosed now). In the lead up to the largest land battle in the Peloponnesian War (at Mantinea), Thucydides closely tracks details of the Spartan regime's effects on their foreign campaigns. This feature of Book Five has only one other parallel – the domestic turmoil at Athens found in Book Eight. Book Five also stands out since it contains no speeches after the alliance between the two cities – the reader's attention is focused on the *actions* of the war; it appears, in its particular mood, in keeping with the Spartan distrust of speeches (cf. 1.86.1). As Tim Rood argues "the lack of speech tellingly points to a pattern of repeated failure: talk was plentiful and unproductive." Spartan distrust of speech is a reminder of problems of political speech more generally and imitates this portion of the war, animated by a sweeping, yet tentative peace deal, one not supported by the numerous other cities also drawn into it, and thus characterized by distrust and secret maneuvering. Nor can we assume, as all but a few scholars do, that Book Five is incomplete simply because it lacks the usual speeches, since, as Rood continues, "[t]reaty texts can themselves include narratives" and "[g]rappling with the terms of treatises helps readers to construct their own narratives."[7] Nor, I would add, do actions fail to shed light on Thucydides' overall presentation of the war, simply because this portion of his narrative is not punctuated with speeches of the combatants. And we cannot of course ignore the fact that perhaps the most (in)famous speech in Thucydides closes the Book: the Melian Dialogue. We cannot, therefore, assume Book Five as it stands does not contribute to Thucydides' stated goal of presenting the truth of the Peloponnesian War and of leading the reader to the truth of politics as such.[8]

---

7 Rood (1999) pp. 91-92.

8 Lack of speeches and the focus on treaties, including ones Thucydides cites at length, are key justifications given for a rejection of Book Five as a complete Book. Hornblower III pp. 53-57 notes that there has been something of a revival by Westlake, Connor, and Rood to accept Book Five; yet Hornblower also notes that this is possible for a literary approach only. Historiography has difficulties with chapters 27-83 (from the Second Preface to the Melian Dialogue), since we have little non-Thucydidean evidence of Greece at this time, from 421-416 B.C. Cf. Rood (1999) pp. 83-130 who spends an entire chapter considering some of the arguments still rejecting this Book, finding them unfounded, particularly if one weighs Thucydides' larger purpose in presenting this period of the war in a unique manner. Connor (1984) pp. 142-43 notices linguistic parallels between 5.25.3 and 1.23.6 where Thucydides expressed his

For are treatises and their breach not a key and complex element of politics today, as it was then? Is the analysis of treaties and their implications not fundamental for political actors and observers to understand? Do cities' actions not also reveal, perhaps even more truly reveal, their intentions and designs in spite of what is contained in their speeches? Can we assume cities did not deliver speeches during these years? Or is it not rather a clear literary device on Thucydides' part in refraining from long quoted speeches here, signaling to his reader something significant about his presentation in Book Five?

The pace and, as it were, action of the first four Books may leave some readers disappointed over the movement of Book Five. And since this Book culminates in the Melian Dialogue, often taken to be *the* Thucydidean statement on the harsh realities of politics and empire, it is easy to dismiss the remainder of the Book precisely when it seems to conform to our preconceived expectations, those in line with the Athenian thesis. But why should those expectations include a desire for grand speeches, moving narrative, and the action-packed pace of Books One to Four? Is it not Thucydides himself that has set us up to expect as much? Instead, as I will argue, the character of Book Five imitates the character of the Spartans themselves – laconic, distrustful of speech, and circumspect. It also reminds us of the boring, trivial, and mundane, even during a grand war. This form of presentation is a hint to its most revealing contents, Book Five and the 14th year of the war being the portion of Thucydides' narrative focused on his investigation of Sparta.[9]

---

view of the truest cause of the war. It seems, in other words, that Thucydides' literary devices must eventually come to bear on one's interpretation of the text. See note 12 below for further discussion of this point.

9 And of course, we cannot forget that in Thucydides' Second Preface, he reminds us that his exile from Athens resulted in him spending time with the Peloponnesians (5.26.5). This is yet another hint, I believe, that Book Five is going to be Thucydides' opportunity to delve deeper into the puzzle that is Sparta. In fact, Thucydides provides a number of hints regarding the uniqueness of Book Five: it begins with the Athenians' purification of Delos (a pious matter that opens, closes, and lands in the middle of the text and with which the Athenians reveal persistent concern – see 1.8.1, 3.104, 8.108-109) and it ends with the Melian Dialogue, the only "speech" in Thucydides with a dialogic structure, an exchange in which questions of divine justice figure prominently.

Sparta at War Reconsidered: Kings versus Ephors

A foundational part of this investigation reveals the following: The divide in Sparta between those in favor of war and those opposed to it is an indication of the degree to which Spartan actions move towards those of the Athenians (cf. 8.2.3). Sparta will become more clearly imperialistic after the defeat of Athens and the end of the Peloponnesian War.[10] That the Spartan regime begins to shift in this manner is best understood as one consequence of the scale of the Peloponnesian War – the extreme necessities into which this war drove all cities is evidence for the view of the Athenians rather than of the Spartans. But as we have seen, not all Athenians supported continuing a drawn-out war of ever-increasing scale, risk, and damage. Yet the views of those such as Archidamus and the moderate men at Athens are not successful in practice, and it is those most Athenian in character, the Syracusans, who according to Thucydides were most successful in combating them (8.96.5). Necessity operates on the Spartans, as the Athenian thesis makes clear, but only very reluctantly do they move away from pious strictures and moral hesitations as they understand it. And only some of the Spartans begin to recognize necessities bearing down on their city. The changes within the regime are thus not sudden, full-scale political or social ones. Rather, certain individuals initiate a movement away from Spartan tradition, fueled by pressing necessities of war on the one hand, and private desires on the other. Unsurprisingly, this sets up in-fighting within the city, evidence of which first arose with Archidamus and Sthenelaidas, but became apparent with Xenares and the war party. The hereditary kings and the elected ephors were often at odds. The Peloponnesian War brings to the fore this struggle. The changes are almost imperceptible but become clearly consequential as the war marches on.

Witnessing on-going strife despite the official peace, the Spartan king, Agis, is sent to lead the Spartans and their allies into battle near Argos against that city and its allies. Alcibiades had aided in securing Argos' alliance to Athens, creating a pretext for hostilities by arguing Sparta had breached its oaths (5.56.3). The battle is thus set to commence with the Spartans having surrounded the Argives' contingent with a large force including a vast number of their own allies. But the Argives, despite believing themselves to

10 As portrayed in Xenophon's *Hellenika*. But intimations of this imperialistic direction are also observable in Thucydides' account.

be in the superior position, sue Agis for arbitration of the cities' complaints against one another. And while the Spartans were in truth vastly superior in position and strength, Agis agrees. He is offered "just and equal" (*dikas... kai isas*) arbitration and thus grants the Argives a four-month truce (59.5-60.1). Thucydides notes that even if another ally had been added to Argos and their allies, Sparta would *still* have been in a notably superior position (60.3). Considering this remark in its context, Thucydides implies that even if the Athenians were present (which they were not due to a delay in arriving to support their allies – 59.3), the Spartans would still have had the upper hand.

Agis is severely "blamed" (*aitia*) by the Spartans and their allies for this truce because of the "beautiful" circumstances in which they found themselves, Thucydides confirming that this was the "noblest" (*kalliston*) Greek army brought together up to this point in the war (60.2-3). Nevertheless, Agis' withdrawal is obeyed by the army and Sparta's allies in accordance with "law" (*nomos*). Agis' actions here are clearly puzzling, Thucydides emphasizing it was Agis' own decision to accept the truce (60.1). Given the advantageous position of Sparta, recognized by the Spartan army and their allies, this suggests Agis did not shirk from battle due to cowardice or ignorance of their advantages. The only possible motive we have appears in the language of the truce: Agis seems to place the apparent "just and equal" character of arbitration above the potential benefit to Sparta in winning this battle and thus weakening Athens' allies. Notable is the fact that this near battle occurs just *after* Thucydides' mention of the death of Xenares, one of the key proponents for the war party in Sparta. It seems that Agis, son of King Archidamus and belonging to the peace party, was not interested in pursuing such a large campaign and battle against the Argive-Athenian (or any other) alliance (a policy position Brasidas also continually ran up against).

These years of the war, being the low point for Spartan morale previously noted, resulting from their defeat at Pylos, is a sign justice may not be on their side. A possible hesitation rooted in fear of misfortune (and hence the possible impiety of breaching the oaths upon which treaties were sworn) is further strengthened by Thucydides' mention here, for the first time in his account of the war, of the Spartans' customary sacrifices before going out on a military campaign (54.2, 56.3). The Spartans would refuse to cross a frontier into enemy territory should these sacrifices prove to be unfavorable. Rooted in their adherence to pious customs, this practice signaled to them whether the gods favored a particular campaign, just as they had consulted the Delphic oracle at the beginning of the war (1.118.3).[11]

Despite arriving late, the Athenians still attack Orchomenos where Sparta had placed hostages. The blame of Agis thus becomes more severe when he returns to Sparta. The Spartans depart from their usual hesitancy to punish their own leading citizens by declaring they will be razing Agis' house, as well as fining him. Agis pleads his case, promising to recompense for his past failure by taking the field again and doing a good service for his city. Instead of punishing him as planned, the Spartans now instead make a new law requiring Agis to be accompanied by ten Spartiates as counselors when going on a campaign (5.63.4). For the Spartans, kings both led the army into battle and were in charge of the sacrifices before engaging in campaigns, to say nothing, of course, of their hereditary position within the regime. While the Spartans and their allies could have advanced the cause of the war with a victory over the Argives and their allies, Agis preferred to accept an offer of arbitration. Agis, seemingly in contrast to those at home who blamed him, preferred peace to war.

Yet what precisely is the blame directed against Agis? For the offer of just and equal arbitration would appear to be in keeping with Spartan justice (and caution). That the Spartans could have potentially defeated the formidable third city, Argos, but failed to do so as a result of Agis' decision, confirms their anger was due precisely to his failure to strategically succeed in prosecuting the war. But it is in this very context that Thucydides allows us to notice both that Agis is leading the army by law (60.2) and that the Spartans institute a new law to direct him in battle. Spartan law is the source of obedience for the Spartan; but law is also the only means by which

---

11 The first mention of Agis is at 3.89.1 where he abandons an invasion of Attica due to numerous earthquakes. In this context, Thucydides offers his explanation of inundations which were particularly common at this time – the land is overtaken by the sea, killing those who lived there. According to Thucydides, earthquakes were the "cause" (*aitia*) of these inundations. When Agis reappears at 5.54, he is again held back, now due to the unfavorable sacrifices. For the Spartans, earthquakes, as with sacrifices, could portend the gods not favoring certain actions. See Gomme IV (Andrewes) p. 74 and Hornblower III p. 143, both of whom note that this pious practice was *exclusively* Spartan. On Agis' motives, consider Rahe (2020) pp. 272-74 and context. Rahe suggests both that Agis may have been given to caution, aware of the role of fortune in large battles; but he also argues that a long-term peace deal with Argos could prove advantageous to Sparta well into the future.

Sparta determines how to secure their interests abroad. Agis' failure to look to Sparta's interests as victory in battle is perhaps not due to the Argives' offer itself or any lingering guilt arising from the affair at Pylos, but rather from the general hesitancy Spartans habitually display in going to war, placing themselves as it does in the hands of potentially unfavorable fortune. In keeping with this habituation, Agis' desire to compensate quickly for his failure is especially motivated by the severe blame directed toward him, a shame even a king shows himself susceptible to. Agis' attempt to repair his reputation now leads the Spartans to act with uncharacteristic immediacy and haste (64.2). But we wonder whether the Spartan authorities at home, through their new law, have solved the true cause of their disappointment.

Facing further revolutions and a potential loss of allies to Argos, the Spartans again leave on a campaign with a force that Thucydides notes for its numbers (64.1). As they enter the territory surrounding Mantinea, Agis immediately brings the army within dangerous proximity of the Argives, who had taken up a strong position after observing the Spartan advance. An older man points out the position of the enemy to Agis, believing the latter's resolve to prove himself has left him unaware of the current situation (65.2). Thucydides leaves it somewhat ambiguous whether it was due to this old man or because Agis changed his own plans (65.3), but the Spartans and their allies now retreat and do not engage. If the old man is one of the ten Spartiate counselors, then Sparta's new law seems to succeed to the extent that Agis pulls back after being alerted to the enemy's positional advantage. Furthermore, the following day the Spartan army is greatly surprised when they return to their previous encampment only to find the Argives and their allies already in position. Agis is able to direct the troops into battle order according to law. Spartan law dictates how the troops are to be arranged and this order is directed by the king's commands to his various ranking officers (66.2-4). The laws which governed the Spartans within the city also governed the manner in which they conduct themselves in their land battles. The army would obey the king, both in his exercise of the traditional pious sacrifices, as well as leading them into battle. Yet this power granted to the king leaves the entire army in the hands of the decision-making of one individual. One could of course note that in the case of Athens as well, expeditions are led by a single commander. But with Sparta, it is unclear their statesmen are up to the task. At the same time, the use of laws to arrange one's battle order is never mentioned by Thucydides in relation to any other city (to say nothing of the new legal restrictions placed on the king). While this is a particular feature of Sparta and seems to be one reason for their strength in past battles on land, the Peloponnesian War, and the battle at Mantinea in particular, tests Spartan strategy.

In the prelude to this battle, which Thucydides states was the greatest to occur in some time and among the most remarkable cities (74.1), he details the forces on either side.[12] Thucydides admits that the number of forces was difficult to determine given the secrecy of the Spartan regime and other men bragging about the forces of their own city. But he immediately

12 Connor (1984) p. 144: "No other battle in the *Histories* approaches this one in the detail with which it is presented." Connor interprets the singularity of this description to the place of the battle in Thucydides' narrative – this was officially a time of peace and yet hostilities continued, thus Thucydides' "love of paradox" led him to place this battle here. This interpretation acknowledges that the detail of the battle draws our attention to the treaty and alliance between Sparta and Athens and thus stands out by contrast to any other battle narrative. Connor does not mention the fact, however, that Thucydides focuses on Sparta in particular in this portion of his account. And despite the apparent purpose of simply drawing our attention to this contrast, Connor's notion that Book Five is incomplete due to its style, and thus did not receive complete revision by Thucydides, presupposes he did not have an intention for presenting his account of this period of the war in a different manner than other periods. As Connor himself notes, this is the interval between the Peace of Nicias and the outbreak of renewed, open hostilities due to Athens' breach of their treaty with Sparta. And he further confirms that Thucydides is able to present details of the war in a manner differing from other parts of his narrative, should he choose to do so. But the conclusion he draws from denying the Separatist approach (i.e., the claim that differences in Thucydides' style are due to differing times of composition and even that he changed his mind on certain interpretations of events) only focuses on the contrast between the treaties and the actions of the cities. Thus, we must consider, for example, whether the unusual features of Book Five (the lack of speeches along with Thucydides' focus on alliances, treaties, battles, and the restoration of Sparta's renown due to the victory at Mantinea) are intended to hint that these details, centered as they are on Sparta, are to teach us something about that city and therefore the war, that he had not previously disclosed. Hornblower III notes that Books Five and Eight "have traditionally been regarded as scrappy, provisional, and problematic, and thus as lacking the final authorial hand." And while Hornblower challenges this position, to a degree, in his judgment "the problems of bk. 5 are greater and more numerous (but have been much less studied in recent years) than those of bk. 8" (pp. 1-2). Nevertheless, he does later note that Mantinea (5.63-75) is in fact "the most highly elaborated and worked-up sections" of Book Five (pp. 163-64). As I argued in the Introduction, modern scholars deny, explicitly or implicitly, that Thucydides is an able enough writer to change his "style," despite the Peloponnesian War now entering a unique phase. Gomme (1937) pp. 132-55 defends Thucydides' account of Mantinea against the (extreme) attack by Woodhouse (1933).

offers a calculation of the Spartan forces based on the noticeable order of their army; on the other hand, he does not offer an estimate of the forces of the Athenians and their allies (68.1-2; cf. 74.3). The bragging belongs to others, not Sparta. And this bragging leaves Thucydides silent on the number of the Argives and their allies. Bragging disguises the numbers of men better than Spartan secrecy; this secrecy fails because their order is so precise and thus the scope of their forces becomes knowable (68.3). Since the Spartan battle order and numbers of troops is directed according to law (cf. 4.128.1), the very law in Sparta requiring order and secrecy fails in its intended purpose, while the bragging of cities regarding their troop numbers succeeds in hiding information from the enemy about their strength. Sparta's battle order is impressive, but also a problem.

After detailing the contingents of the Spartan army, Thucydides reports the exhortations of each side. While the Mantineans, Argives, and Athenians exhort their troops, appealing to the desire for empire, to avenge injustices, and the glory they hope will accompany a victory, the Spartans call on their troops' memories of what they have learned from their long discipline in war (5.69.2).[13] Not trusting in noble speeches as an exhortation to virtue, they trust in this discipline to secure their safety, including their march into battle itself. While the Argives and their allies proceed with haste and anger, the Spartans march to the music of the flute players, measured, and keeping order in their formation.[14] Thucydides' purpose in relating the preparation for this battle becomes apparent with the outcome – despite errors in their battle formation and Agis' attempt to correct it, the Spartans win a victory due to their "courage" (*andreia*).[15] While the Argives and their allies bested the Spartans in "experience" (*empeiria*), the Spartan

13 This exhortation bears comparison to Archidamus' praise of Spartan virtue (1.84.3). Despite their defeat at Pylos, the Spartans do not doubt their education and the virtues it inculcates (4.40.2).

14 Thucydides notes that this practice was not due to piety, that is, "for the sake of the divine" (*ou tou theiou charin*). Aside from the kinship between law and piety, Thucydides is focused here on the Spartan order and its relation to their conduct in battle. He provides sufficient indication of Spartan piety elsewhere (Spartan sacrifices – 5.54.2, 55.3, 116.1; Spartan celebration of festivals – 4.5.1, 5.75.5-76.1, 82.3). As Jordan (1986) p. 123 argues: "Thucydides was so aware of Spartan religiosity and its profound role in Spartan life that he found it necessary to explain that for once a custom had a purely practical purpose."

15 Connor (1984) p. 144 and Price (2001) p. 13 treat Mantinea as an instance of hoplite warfare Thucydides wished to detail; but this overlooks the narrative significance of

virtue of courage secures their victory (72.2). The Spartan order, based on law and including their new law, is not as decisive at Mantinea as their old virtue. Their laws had the purpose of attempting to instill good order, but this order failed. While this may be due to Agis' loss of authority from the previous engagements near Argos, it seems rather that Agis' attempt could be viewed as a failure because the polemarchs did not have time to react to his sudden commands, as Thucydides suggests (72.1). The Spartan king makes errors in his commands and thus their order breaks down in the midst of the battle. Since this breach resulted from the fear affecting all armies (71.1), Thucydides implies *both* the Spartan battle order, and Agis' commands, failed. But it is especially Agis that errs since he (unlike Thucydides) seems unaware until the moment before engagement that such fear will cause a breach in the ranks.

Spartan laws and customs do, importantly, inculcate the courage shown at Mantinea; but they apparently fail to educate the Spartan commanders and generals to the level of experience and skill shown especially by the Athenians. While the laws cultivate or enforce courage, they cannot cultivate the judgment or intelligence of the statesman. Nor can the laws that guide life within the city guide strategy in war (including battle formations that may well require modification). And this tension, which manifests itself in their king and his agreement to arbitration with Argos, is not visible to the Spartans themselves – their blame of Agis for his failures, failures rooted in his hesitation, caution, and possible concern with fairness he displays in this agreement. The Spartans are blind to their regime's inability to cultivate the virtues of a commander at war. It is the daring and boldness of Brasidas that was able to liberate Athens' subjects from that empire and bring about the Peace of Nicias. And we must wonder whether the courage that won Sparta a victory at Mantinea is not a Spartan manifestation of "Athenian" daring. A long Spartan discipline has not inculcated intelligence for command; Agis is still under the sway of a Spartan education. The Spartan regime does not breed the intelligence and art or skill of other regimes, particularly Athens.[16] Sparta's laws direct everything for the Spartan. Their lack of innovation in battle, to combat an opponent such as the

---

this passage, Sparta's reputation after this battle, and changing relations with their allies.

16 Consider 4.55.

Athenians, is in keeping with their lack of innovation in laws (1.18.1, 71.3).[17] That Sparta was *the* noteworthy Greek land power is unquestioned; that the Peloponnesian War placed Sparta (and Athens) in battles that tested their previous successes is indisputable.

Tension existing between customary practices and innovation is reinforced by Thucydides' remark that the new law created before Mantinea was unprecedented in Sparta (5.63.4). Sparta did not make new laws. The laws of Lycurgus (Sparta's ancient legislator), which were never changed until Sparta found itself in the middle of the long Peloponnesian War, were sanctioned by the god at Delphi.[18] Spartan obedience to laws, and even to their hereditary king's ill-timed commands, were rooted in the divine approval of these laws, and therefore in the authority of the city itself.[19] While Spartan law is harmful, or at the least a potential liability to Sparta's foreign policy and war aims, to breach these laws "was not only unlawful, but unholy."[20] Thus these laws were unhesitatingly obeyed, both at home and abroad, enforcing a moderation that fostered the domestic stability, exemplified in Thucydides' praise of Sparta's prosperity. Thucydides offers no account of the Athenians (or any other city) conducting affairs abroad guided by particular laws. It is precisely a *lack* of such laws that forms a key part of Pericles' praise of Athens (2.37.1-3).

In this way, the battle order and the new law of the king brings together domestic and foreign politics; it is unique to Sparta, is the source of both their power and weakness. If this is the case, we observe the implications of Thucydides' detailed description here: The Sparta regime produces a weakness abroad, and there may be no resolution to the strain this creates. Conversely, this is the reverse side of the problem we witness in Athens: Their success abroad begins to undermine their domestic stability at home (under Pericles), and the expansion of their empire corresponds to chaos at home, including intrigues and political infighting among the citizens (in post-Periclean Athens, as we will detail below). Athenian imperialism does not rally the troops and present a united front; it divides the city.

Regardless of the shortcomings of Sparta's laws, their reputation is regained by the battle at Mantinea. Fortune (*tychē*) was viewed as the

17 Aristotle, *Politics* 1269a19-23.

18 Xenophon, *Regime of the Lacedemonians* VIII.5.

19 Plato, *Republic* 431d8-e6.

20 Xenophon, *ibid.*

cause of the Spartans' previous failures. Thucydides reports that Sparta's allies blamed them for "weakness" after the affair at Pylos or generally for "bad counsel and slowness" (5.75.3; cf. 2.8.4). These causes are distinct; they had been perceived as weak given their unprecedented surrender at Pylos (5.28), but were broadly blamed for the manner in which they carried on with allies and prosecuted wars (1.70).[21] And even though their reputation was restored, this restoration is immediately followed by further inaction – Epidaurus is taken by the Eleans and Athenians while the Spartans are celebrating a festival at home (5.82.3). Only once this festival is over (a festival that is exclusively Spartan) do they go out to Argos and secure a treaty and eventual alliance. The restoration of their reputation is unwarranted: Mantinea is followed by inaction and the battle was only won by courage; Agis or the ten new counselors, even if they had affected anything, were still dictated in their actions by ineffectual laws.[22] There is an irony in the restoration of Sparta's reputation because the problems with Spartan character highlighted by the Corinthians will continue. The other cities' impressions of Sparta, after Pylos and Mantinea, are not shared by Thucydides.

The cause of Spartan slowness and bad counsel is not resolved by the restoration of their reputation; these flaws follow from the fundamental characteristics of their regime – its strict obedience to the laws.[23] Slowness, as one part of their moderation, was inculcated into the Spartans through this obedience. Other cities fail to see this cause of Sparta's inaction. For even in the arguments of the Corinthians before the outbreak of the war,

---

21 While the Corinthians' claim is borne out by the course of the war, Thucydides only confirms this judgment in his own name late in his narrative (8.96.5). This is the only instance when Thucydides himself calls the Spartans "slow" (*bradeis*). It seems that he intends to suggest that while the Corinthians are correct, we as readers can only confirm their judgment after understanding Book Five.

22 Nichols (2015) p. 100n30 observes that "Spartan innovation in the law has the effect of constricting, rather than opening up, possibilities."

23 Crane (1998) pp. 86-87, 233-34 treats Mantinea in terms of the restoration of Sparta's reputation, but argues that this restoration was an incorrect assessment by the other cities because the Spartans' weakness was their inability to innovate. This inability is understood by Crane to mean their reliance on hoplite warfare rather than adapting to the Athenians' superiority at sea. The Spartans' resoluteness was, according to the other cities, the same. They were blamed for weakness, bad counsel, and slowness. This interpretation is correct in noting that the view of the other Greeks was "incomplete," but the source of its being incomplete is due rather to Spartan guilt that their injustice started the war. The only Spartan virtue called into question by the other cities is their courage, not their justice.

their criticisms of Sparta are correct only so far as the Corinthians understand them; they do not locate the *source* of Sparta's deficiencies.[24] And Thucydides imitates this only partial understanding of Spartan character by not allowing us to see this aspect of Sparta until Book Five. But as Thucydides slowly reveals the source of Sparta's deficiencies, he also reveals the beginning of changes within the city itself. Sparta's laws are a problem at war because they do not allow for innovation – in the case of Mantinea, Agis seemed correct to attempt to move the troops due to the fear that naturally arises in battle, a fear the law regarding battle order (in its rigidity) appears to neglect. And while Agis may ultimately be deficient as a commander, Sparta's victory at Mantinea reveals that the creation of Sparta's new law to remedy this deficiency fails.[25] Both Sparta's laws and Sparta's ability to prosecute this war, as they have habitually prosecuted all their wars, initiates reforms that will take root in the city later in the war.

Thucydides' narrative further demonstrates Sparta's caution: the Spartans are victorious at Mantinea, but only win the battle and attempt nothing further. They do not seem to be fighting to win the larger war; they fight until the enemy retreats but fail to pursue a complete victory (5.73.4, 75.1; cf. 4.55). While this may appear to be a function of this period of the war being one of peace, the Athenians, by contrast, do not hesitate to harass Spartan interests (5.59.3, 61.1-5). While perhaps appearing moderate, acting merely out of self-interest in avoiding potential harm, Sparta's lack of eagerness is in fact at odds with their broader advantage. Their own intention in renewing hostilities was to support Epidaurus; yet they fail to hold it after winning the battle at Mantinea. And their other king, Pleistoanax, does not proceed further once he is informed of the Spartan victory, while their other allies coming from Corinth and surrounding areas are dismissed (75.1-2) and the Spartans themselves also return home.[26] This allows the

24 See the Athenians' claim at 1.77.6.

25 Woodhouse (1918) defends Agis. Cf., however, Kagan (1981) p. 115.

26 Sparta, we recall, had in fact two kings, both of whom came to their position via heredity. See Chapter One note 43. Thucydides (and Xenophon) intimate, but do not advertise, this fact. Aristotle's *Politics* 1271a20-25 is critical both of hereditary kingship and of the conflict necessarily entailed with two kings holding office. As all three authors intimate, the relationship between the kings and the ephors is a significant aspect of how the Spartan regime functioned. Thucydides depicts as much with Archidamus and Sthenelaidas in Book One, as well as Agis and Pleistoanax (versus authorities at home) in Books Five and Eight (discussed below).

Eleans, Mantineans, and Athenians to surround Epidaurus, build a wall, and maintain forces there (75.4-6). Sparta fails to take back revolting cities, and to form and maintain new alliances (particularly with Argos), alliances that could strengthen their position going forward.

And, finally, Thucydides presents one further consideration in his conclusion of the 14th year of the war. When their new (but short-lived) ally, Argos, calls on the Spartans for aid, since democrats in the city were plotting to overthrow the Sparta-supported oligarchs, the Spartans again fail to act. Waiting until the Spartans were again occupied with a festival, the democrats attacked the oligarchs within the city. The Spartans eventually arrive, but finding the oligarchic party defeated, they return home. Envoys from Argos and the now-exiled oligarchs arrive at Sparta to plead their case and the Spartans decide that the democrats had "done wrong" (82.4). Yet despite determining that justice was on the side of the oligarchs, those whom the Spartans had signed a treaty and alliance with, they continually delay in marching out to provide assistance (82.5). While the stipulations of their treaty and alliance do not include any provisions in the event of faction or civil war within the city, the oligarchic party *is* the ally of Sparta (76.2). Did the Spartans even need to determine that the democratic faction had harmed the oligarchs? Both in maintaining a regime favorable to Sparta and in deciding on the issue of injustice, the Spartans nevertheless fail to offer support, losing Argos to the Athenians as a result, the democratic party naturally allied with Athens now able to gain hold of the city (82.5-6). Spartan inaction resulted from their celebration of another festival, directing our attention back to customary, meticulous Spartan piety, and a drawn-out, procedural justice.

Some Spartans, however, do not seem wholly unaware of this weakness. Before the outbreak of the war, Archidamus argued both that Sparta should be cautious in going to war because they were not prepared to do so *and* that to declare war against the Athenians, who had offered arbitration, would be unlawful (and by implication, impious – 1.82, 85.2). Even assuming their cause was just, Archidamus implies, does not establish their preparation for war with Athens. And the opposite also holds: preparations do not equal the justice of Sparta's cause. In fact, Archidamus doubts the Spartan position (to which he cautiously objected) in *both* cases.

Here in the 14th year, in Thucydides' first mentions of frontier sacrifices, we noted previously that he did not reveal whether the sacrifices were favorable once the Spartans decided they had to act to stop the continued assaults on Epidaurus and the attempts by its other allies to revolt, in contrast to the previous sacrifices restricting their engagements abroad. The Spartans, then, seem to be selectively just; their actions are inconsistent because they sometimes recognize, if only half-consciously, that they are compelled to defend interests abroad rather than avoiding risks by staying home. The necessity to engage in foreign wars had to clearly threaten Spartan interests, i.e., to appear *to the Spartans* that it threatened their interests. The Athenians at Melos are therefore correct in noting that Sparta conflates its advantage with justice. And they note in that context that the Spartans are "most virtuous" (*pleista aretē*) concerning their city's laws (5.105.4). The Athenians imply they do not make this mistake, instead aware of their interests, and not masking these interests behind proclamations of justice.

The Athenians are unaware, however, that the Spartans are not attempting to be duplicitous in aligning Sparta's interests with justice – the Spartans believe in their own press. Their identification only seems false to the Athenians because they, unlike the Spartans, question this identification.[27] Nor are the Athenians clear on the fact that Sparta's interests are even *harmed* by pious strictures. The conflation of justice and interests is not truly to Sparta's advantage: the Spartans miscalculate. Or more precisely, Spartan devotion to virtue masks and clouds their awareness of political necessities the Athenians proudly proclaim. This identification is the root of the Spartans continually fighting battles, that even when victorious, see them fail to push forward, eagerly and with daring, for the sake of securing potentially decisive victories. And it is precisely these victories that would further their mission (only half-heartedly supported by them) to liberate Greece from Athenian tyranny. The Spartans wished to believe, in initiating the Peloponnesian War, to be liberating not only themselves, but their allies, from unjust, imperial tyranny. Not only did they become aware of the dubiousness of their own justice, but after Pylos, their abilities also came into doubt. Slowness, caution, and lack of daring action is deeply instilled into Spartan character.[28]

27 Bruell (1981) p. 27. That the Athenians' accusations against the Spartans arise in the context of their incorrect belief that the Melians share their own views (5.89, 111.3) reminds us to consider how the Athenian thesis bears on the domestic politics, the civic virtue, of Athens itself.

28 For other instances of Sparta's slowness, consider Archidamus at the beginning of the war (2.18); the revolt of Mytilene (3.27.1, 3.29.1, 31.1-2); their failure to aid Melos

Despite the shortcomings of Sparta's laws with respect to their foreign policy, magnified as it is with the scale of the Peloponnesian War, obedience to the regime and their rulers was a fundamental part of Spartan moderation. And this moderation, a city preserving its way of life at home during war, appears in stark relief when set beside the all-out strife that afflicted numerous other cities, including their opponent, Athens. Whatever may be said of failures in Spartan foreign policy, Athenian *stasis* throughout the war is ultimately at the root of Athens' defeat (2.65.11-12).

Periclean and Post-Periclean Athens

Athens' domestic situation during the war provides a clear juxtaposition to Spartan moderation. Stepping back from our Spartan narrative to analyze *stasis* in Athens and Corcyra will set Sparta's domestic policy in relief. While Archidamus' praise of Spartan moderation has shame and obedience to law as its centerpiece, Pericles' policy decisions in the early stages of the war reveal a novel view of Athens and its character, one rooted in daring (*tolma*). On the surface, Thucydides separates Pericles from his successors (2.65). Drawing out the implications of Pericles' new vision for Athens, however, reveals the resounding effect that vision had on the regime changes in Athens after his death, changes culpable for Athens' loss in the war. Thucydides' account of the Peloponnesian War all but ends with Athenian civil strife (8.66, 96); it does not end with a definitive victory of a superior Sparta. Carefully considered, therefore, Thucydides' eulogy of Pericles presents a puzzle for the reader to solve, rather than an unqualified praise of Periclean Athens and a critique of his successors. Attribution of Athenian greatness to the present generation necessarily diminishes the previous one, Pericles daringly calling into question traditional Athenian life, both in his view of Athens and even through specific policy recommendations. This is in stark contrast to Archidamus' praise of Sparta. In Thucydides pointing to, even focusing, on the domestic implications of Pericles' vision and policies, the costs of continued Athenian imperialism (and by association, the

(5.115.2, 116.1). For instances of Sparta's lack of eagerness, consider the Corinthians' exhortation (1.71.6); the criticism of Archidamus (2.18.3). Cf. their sudden eagerness after coming to believe that the Athenians were guilty of injustice (7.18.3).

Athenian thesis) come to the fore, costs from which Pericles himself, I will argue, cannot be entirely divorced.[29]

Pericles' view of Athens is presented by Thucydides in three quoted speeches and one reported speech, as well as Thucydides' own "eulogy" or commentary on Pericles himself. With Pericles' first speech, we noticed the strategic question of how Athens should proceed with the war. Let's summarize what we noted in Chapter One: Pericles warns the Athenians that, should the Spartans be victorious, Athens will be losing their allies through revolution; Athens must not acquiesce to any demands or threats from Sparta, lest they appear weak; Athens needs to utilize its sea power and avoid battles on land. The Athenians must treat themselves as islanders, rather than attempting to defend the city, ports, and countryside comprising Attica (1.143.4). Homes and land of the Athenians are not fundamental, but rather each individual Athenian. Pericles almost goes so far as to suggest the Athenians display the lack of importance of Attica, their countryside, to the Spartans by destroying their own homes themselves (143.5).

Pericles' policies are decidedly practical – abandoning land for sea appears sound strategy, playing to Athens' strength and avoiding Sparta's own. Yet this foreshadows a problem: Land is lost, and this means homes, not simply physical property. In Pericles' next address, which Thucydides reports in indirect speech (2.13), he reiterates his policies regarding the conduct of the war by Athens, as well as adumbrating Athens' financial situation he alluded to earlier. His reiteration returns to the issue of land and property; the Athenians are to move from the country into the city and utilize the public funds found in the temples for their "safety" (*sōtēria*) should they be needed, including the gold from the statue of the goddess herself (13.5).[30]

At this point, Thucydides narrates a striking digression disclosing the origins of Attica and the founding of Athens as a city (15), a description of

29 Others who have noted Thucydides' critique include Forde (1986), Orwin (1994), Monoson and Loriaux (1998), Foster (2010), Diduch and Hadley (2016).

30 Fustel De Coulanges (1980) pp. 32, 53; Bruell (1981) p. 25. See also Foster (2010) pp. 174-82, Diduch and Hadley (2016) pp. 47-51. Foster (2010) pp. 165-72 highlights how Pericles' reported speech (2.13) converts religious objects and resources into money for the current war effort (including Athens' supplies of gold). The statue in question is of Athena. There may be an irony, therefore, in Pericles' (or Thucydides') use of *sōtēria* here; the word, in certain contexts, has pious overtones. Consider 1.65.1, 2.60.4, 61.4, 7.71.3.

the city's founding bearing comparison to the Archaeology, the movement from rural peoples to seafaring cities. We may overlook, however, that for the Athenians, a reliance on their navy was not initially an abandonment of Attica. Nor can we help but be reminded of Sparta when Thucydides relates that the unification of Athens as a city by Theseus was "administrative": inhabitants throughout rural Attica still lived independently. Rural Attica still exists, and is populated, despite a flourishing "urban" Athens. Immediately following Pericles' reported speech and before detailing Athens' founding, Thucydides had noted that, while the Athenians followed Pericles' advice to move into the city, this move was "difficult" (*chalepos*) for most Athenians, "accustomed" (*ethō*) as they were to living outside the city (14). Thucydides' juxtapositions, used throughout his presentation of Pericles, are on display here: Pericles' strategy, with its emphasis on money and war funding, is followed by Thucydides' account of the founding of Athens, an account replete with references to Athens' traditional gods (15-16.1).[31] And in leaving the countryside now, under Pericles' injunction, Thucydides states in similar terms (and for a second time – cf. 2.14) a startling outcome of Pericles' advice (16.2):

> It was oppressive and difficult (*chalepos*) to be leaving their homes (*oikias*) and the ancestral temples (*hiera*) which had come down to them from the ancient regime (*archaion politeias*) of their fathers (*patria*), and to change their way of life, each leaving behind his own city (*polis*).[32]

Indeed, Pericles violates an oracle (proclaiming the ground surrounding the Acropolis may not be occupied) by moving the Athenians into this area due to the lack of space within the rest of the city (17.1-4). Thucydides does note that this was done out of "necessity" (*anankē* – 17.2), this policy being, as he argues, with a view to defending the city and utilizing Athens' navy (13.2). Moving the rural citizens into the city appears necessary given that defense of the countryside is risky and would take away from their ability to use their "judgment" (*gnōmē*) as a naval people to prosecute the war.[33] Sparta

31 I have discussed the background on Athenian piety as it bears on this episode previously: see Diduch and Hadley (2016) pp. 49-51, 58-64.

32 This passage is difficult to translate. I have consulted all available English translations, along with Foster (2010) pp. 174-82.

33 This policy itself needs to be assessed in light of Agis and the Spartans holding the countryside of Attica late in the war (7.27-28). See note 55 below.

was, as Pericles has noted, superior on land, battles there favoring them. We are also thereby reminded that Sparta remained rural; there is no movement into a consolidated "metropolis" as at Athens (cf. 1.10.2).

But we must ask precisely what kind of necessity this is; it seems only to follow from Pericles' original policy of abandoning the countryside. And in calculating his naval-based strategy, Pericles appears unaware of any possible domestic implications of this policy, including the customary tie of "most" (*pleiōn*) of the citizens to the countryside, their homeland (2.16.1). This means, though, that Pericles is not wholly cognizant of their tie to Athens itself, as a city for which a citizen would willingly sacrifice his life.[34]

With this speech as a preliminary, Pericles' own vision for Athens, and

34 Reeve (1999) p. 443 argues Pericles governed in a moderate manner by satisfying the interests of the few and the many within Athens. Reeve's contention is based on the observation that Pericles himself was not "overcome by ambition or *pleonexia*" despite Pericles' repeated exhortations to both daring and the desire for glory. But in Reeve's praise of Pericles, where he cites 2.65.1-10 as proof of his contention that Pericles "governed in a moderate way," he leaves three sentences (65.2-4) out of his quotation. In these sentences Thucydides directs our attention (again) to the suffering Pericles' domestic policies caused the demos and thus their need to level a fine against him to alleviate their anger. Further, Thucydides' claim that Pericles governed in a "measured" (*metrion*) way is qualified – Pericles governed in a measured way "during peace" (65.5). Thucydides leaves us to consider, then, both the soundness of Pericles' policies with regard to the domestic accord within the city and also whether these policies could have remained unmodified during a prolonged war. Balot (2001) pp. 136-78 similarly highlights Pericles as a moderating force, unifying the tension between self-interest and the common good. Private greed, Balot argues, was directed outward from the city via empire and thus preserved internal cohesion. Pericles' successors were unable to continue this Periclean skill of promoting the self-sacrifice of the Athenian citizen to the city's common good. Greed thus directed itself back into the city, when these successors sought aggrandizement for themselves at the cost of the city's need and aims. The unification of self-interest and the common good that Pericles celebrates is achieved, according to Balot, via Periclean rhetoric, an ennobling if idealized vision of Athenian democracy. It seems to me, however, that Pericles' rhetorical skills did not diminish the tension and hardship felt by the many, rural Athenians. Pericles preaches unity through self-sacrifice, but undermines it once the rural Athenians lose tangible attachment to *their* true "Athens" – the countryside. In other words, Pericles' reforms differ from those of the past, and Pericles himself relies on the latent trust the Athenian citizen granted to the (older) foundations of their city. The decay of Athens occurred not simply through unleashing the greed of the few, but with the dismantling of tradition that is a theme throughout all of Pericles' speeches – questioning the need for land; treating temples and statues as mere property; questioning the value of Homer and the tradition; in a word, by arguing away the poetic and divine foundation which attached the Athenian citizen, not rationally but emotively, to the polis. Cf. Palmer (1981) p. 38 and context.

what is expected of each citizen for the city's success, is most clearly articulated in his Funeral Oration. Pericles offers an account of the growth of Athens, including how the city has come to its present state as the leading city in Greece. While seemingly showing respect for tradition by beginning with the generations preceding the present one, Pericles' view of Athens is in fact what we may call a "progressive" one – while Athens has inherited what was left to it by the previous generations, it is the current generation that has rendered the city "self-sufficient" (or "independent" [*autarkes*] – 2.36.3). Reverence for Athenian tradition can only be qualified reverence: the past generations were not a golden age of heroic Athenians.[35] Indeed, the Funeral Oration begins by calling into question the very "law" (*nomos*) demanding such a speech be given to commemorate the death of the men who died defending Athens, despite the fact that it is regarded as "noble" (*kalon*) to do so.[36] Pericles understands the deeds of the men who have died to be sufficient indication of their nobility, but will acquiesce to the law he has just called into question (35.1-3). Pericles' questioning of Athenian law in delivering the oration is thus at one with his recommendation to move the people into the city: Pericles' view of Athens, and emphasis on strategic considerations for the war, demonstrates a depreciation of customs, laws, and more generally, Athenian tradition.

Through this depreciation, including past generations and no less than Homer (41.4), as well as his later admission that the Athenian empire is "so to speak" a tyranny (63.2), Pericles has reduced the citizens' tie to Athens

---

35 Pericles may be referring here, in part, to the time of the Persian War when an alliance between Athens and Sparta (at least in the beginning) fought off Persia's advances (1.96.1). We might also wonder, though, if Pericles is not perhaps referring to himself. See Orwin (1994) pp. 13-39 for a detailed analysis of the Funeral Oration. See especially p. 16n3 where he emphasizes Pericles' diminishment of early Athens as a means to elevate the current generation. Cf. Balot (2001) pp. 173-74 who sees Pericles' praises of past and present Athens as having equal weight.

36 Hornblower I p. 292: "The public funeral was more of a religious event than would be guessed from Th.[ucydides]'s narrative: the dead were in fact given a heroic cult." It seems that Thucydides chose instead to contrast the Funeral Oration with the plague; it also appears in keeping with the overall tenor of the speech, a praise of present-day Athens, that Thucydides is silent on details of the individuals for whom the speech is given. Thus, Hornblower continues, while scholarly debate exists on the oration as a "genre," it "is likely enough...that Th.[ucydides] makes Pericles concentrate to an unusual degree on the present rather than the past, avoiding the traditional themes" (295). Not surprisingly then, it seems to me, Thucydides "secularizes" this (Periclean) version of the funeral.

to the extent that justice and piety strengthen this tie.[37] And as we know Thucydides is wont to do in his order of presentation, Pericles' Funeral Oration is followed by the plague. Thucydides *does* remark that the plague also spread to other cities, specifically the most "populous" (54.3). This is in keeping with his attempt to provide a natural explanation for it. But in sparing the Peloponnesus, we must notice what *the Athenians themselves* attributed its causes to, particularly by those who suffered from it most: Bringing such great sufferings on the Athenians, they recalled an old oracle proclaiming that with a Dorian war would come a plague, as well as recalling the more recent oracle proclaiming the Spartans would win the war with Apollo's support (54.3). If Athens had acted in an unjust and impious manner through the acquisition of their empire, did the gods who are the guarantors of justice bring the plague as a punishment for Athenian daring? Most Athenians certainly weighed this possibility.[38]

Thucydides' own explanation for the cause and spread of the plague, one divorced from divine justice, does not negate his awareness of its effect on most Athenians. What is certain is that the plague undermined traditional Athenian beliefs in noble and shameful actions, evidenced by the resulting lawlessness and pleasure-seeking Thucydides describes (53.1-4). The move into the city proves to be much more than a simple geographic migration from rural to urban life – the very basis of what it means to be "Athenian," particularly for those accustomed to living outside the city, begins to change. It is nothing less than a foundational shift of the regime, a move away from the independence enjoyed by the rural population, even after Theseus' unification compelled all those in Attica to live under Athens as a city. Pericles goes further than Theseus: He abandons all traditional bonds joining his Athens to its original founding, severing the Athenian psyche from the moral justifications for their regime, and thus from their distinctly Athenian way of life.

37 Undermining traditional Athenian piety includes the demos' trust in both Pericles' leadership, and later statesmen, including Nicias and Alcibiades, as will be discussed below. Deprecation of Homer, it is worth noting, also means a depreciation of traditional education; cf. Plato, *Republic* 362e-363e. For Plato and Thucydides on democracy and trust, focusing on democratic deliberation, see Mara (2001). For the importance of public trust to a democracy, and the role piety plays in undergirding this trust according to Thucydides, see Diduch and Hadley (2016).

38 In contrast to Archidamus' account of Sparta (1.84.2-3), Pericles never mentions moderation, but does indeed extol daring (*tolma* – 2.39.4, 40.3, 41.4, 43.1).

Taken together, severing Athenians from tradition severs them from public devotion to the city, thereby liberating what we might call the private realm. Pericles, however, does not seem wholly unaware of this problem. Private interests of those in the city would be restrained, Pericles argues, since noble deeds are of greater importance to the man of pride; even bad men could be made good by "public-spirited benefit" they bestowed upon the city (42.3). This is his attempt to balance private and public. Only by service to the city does one act virtuously and nobly, Pericles implicitly denying a virtue of man as man apart from his city. In this, he sounds positively Spartan: A citizen dedicated wholly to defending their city is a virtuous citizen and a virtuous man. But Pericles also acknowledges the attraction to Athens and her greatness is tied to the Athenian regime – Athens is a democracy affording freedom and equal treatment of private individuals (37.1-2, 43.4).[39] Dedication to the empire, contra Sparta, must be freely chosen by each and every Athenian. But where does this leave *the* public sacrifice, dying in battle, as the men for whom the Funeral Oration is held have done? Unlike Spartans, Athenians are afforded a freedom and equality which allows, and even encourages, private pursuits, aims of the individual apart from the city. In this very speech, Pericles is silent on whether dying for one's city is good for the individual, quietly suggesting, in fact, that death is bad and to be avoided (43.1). And the plague's effects, graphically detailed by Thucydides, cast doubt on Pericles' reliance on noble actions freely chosen to stem this tension between private interests and those of the city (43.2, 53.3).

Pericles' appeal to honor and nobility, as that which makes a man willing to die for his city, is predicated on the supposedly permanent nobility given to those who have died in battle (44.1). More specifically, in urging the Athenians to "become lovers" (*erastai* – 43.1) of Athens' power, Pericles roots the Athenians' desire for nobility in Athenian imperialism, the hopes *it* promises to fulfill. Later, in post-Periclean Athens, the Athenians "fell in love" (*erōs empitnō*) with the voyage to Sicily; they did not simply make

39 Pericles' understanding of wisdom, or one's love of it, is that it serves the city (2.41.1-3). Cf. Bruell (1981) p. 29. On the question Periclean Athens as a democracy, consider Andrews (2004) and Connor (2018).

sober calculations of the city's interests and their empire, but looked to what *they* hoped for in the faraway and the future (6.24.3).[40]

Willingness to die for one's city (so ingrained among Spartans that those at Pylos hesitated even to consider surrender – 4.38.1-3) reminds us that a hidden theme of the Funeral Oration is death. Hidden because Pericles betrays having thought about mortality, showing an awareness of death, but one also suppressed or denied by him. Our half-conscious admission to, and confrontation with, the fact of death and the resulting fear of this fact leads to attempts to find ways to overcome it. *Erōs* drives hope, leading human beings to contrive means to conquer any dangers or terrors (3.45.4-5). Hope for the honor rewarding noble actions seems to promise precisely this overcoming; but one can only overcome the fear of death if one believes this honor is immortal (2.64.5-6). The Athenians' hope for immortal glory from noble pursuit of empire (evidenced by Thucydides' presentation of the Sicilian expedition) agrees then, in an important respect, with the Spartans' hope that their virtue will be recognized by just gods. That the Athenians believe they are deserving of a reward for what they view as a (relatively) measured empire (1.76.2-3) implies a hope in divine justice, gods rewarding such virtues; for without such gods, there could be no certainty of the correspondence between one's virtue and just reward. If by "piety" we understand actions rooted in our concern with immortality, this motive has a hold on all human beings, even among those who deny it. For Thucydides, there is something in human nature that drives us to morality, to be moral beings, even when we may also be self-interested calculators.[41]

But instead of the divine rewards for virtue, Pericles explicitly relies on the human recognition of noble deeds. Yet while maintaining that such noble actions will always be recognized, he also admits that "everything naturally declines" (2.64.3). But if everything naturally declines, do the memories of noble deeds not decline as well? Pericles questioned the need

40 On citizens as *erastai* and this metaphor as it relates to reciprocity, consider Monoson (1994). Cf. Forde (1984) pp. 439-42 and Diduch and Hadley (2016) pp. 54-57 on the tensions and confusions latent in Pericles' attempt to make love of the city the citizen's preeminent longing. See also Mynott (2013) p. 402n1 on *erōs* and related terms. Hornblower III p. 361 on 6.24.3 notes that this is a "famously poetic expression."

41 Strauss (1964) p. 229 suggests that "there is something reminding of religion in Athenian imperialism." Ahrensdorf (2000) p. 590 argues: "By claiming that the Athenians *deserve* the reward of eternal glory, Pericles expresses the belief or hope that they will get what they deserve and hence that the world is such that human beings get what they deserve" (emphasis in original).

for Homer's poetic praises, yet how else will a city's heroes be commemorated? Pericles' own Funeral Oration, a customary celebration of those who have died for their city, focuses more on the greatness of the city than the individual men for whom the speech is taking place, men Pericles fails to ever mention by name (41.5, 42.2).[42] While arguing that noble deeds on behalf of the city also bestow nobility on the individual, certain individuals may have considered whether one could secure the honor attending noble deeds by acting apart from Athens. Pericles' allusions to death cannot help but foster and grow into a desire to overcome it. More than this: The freedom afforded by Athens, a freedom unthinkable in Sparta (cf. 1.84.3), unleashes the individual, the individual's private interests and pursuits (those driven by hope and *erōs*) on the city. And if this honor is what the individual desires, it is not clear private interest serves the city's own. Rather than sacrifice oneself for the sake of the city, the private individual may be led, through Pericles' exultation of honor, to sacrifice the city of Athens to their *own* ambitions. Those individuals may seek to become themselves self-sufficient.[43]

Thucydides' own remarks point in this direction: His eulogy of Pericles ends by noting decay in Athenian public-spiritedness, the care and attention to the city's needs Pericles argued would be freely chosen by the demos.[44] Since Pericles occupied a singular position within Athens' democracy by acting as its "first man," and had the ability to hold together the tension between private and public, those who sought to lead Athens after his death

42 In keeping with this silence, Pericles only mentions death once (43.6) and here the gravity of it as a fundamental human concern seems dismissed. Pericles denies the pain of death, which would seem to include the pain that accompanies the fear of death. See Nichols (2015) pp. 36-37.

43 Strauss (1964) pp. 193-94, Forde (1986) pp. 438-40, Orwin (1986) pp. 81-82.

44 Pericles' "eulogy" (2.65) is one of the most debated passages in Thucydides. A few controversies relevant to note here: First, it is clear evidence Thucydides lived until past the end of the Peloponnesian War; it thus bears importantly on the supposed incompleteness of his text. Second, it reveals to the reader that Thucydides did not view Periclean Athens simply as the best possible regime. Finally, and most importantly, it contains direct observations on post-Periclean Athens, its domestic life, to which Thucydides attributes Athens losing the war. Not simply or only the actions of Sparta and Persia, but the domestic politics of imperial Athens at war led to changes after Pericles' death that cast the city into *stasis*. Cf. Hornblower I p. 340 who argues that "Th.[ucydides] here implies, surely wrongly, that there was a radical difference between the style and methods of Pericles and those of his successors." See Chapter Two, note 25 on differences between Pericles and Cleon.

were forced to appeal to the demos' private longings to such a degree that even during the ambitious Sicilian expedition (when so to speak everyone felt the gravity of the undertaking and its risk to the city itself) political infighting within Athens occupied the city more than soberly considering the best strategy for victory (2.65.11-12). Thucydides' eulogy of Pericles and his observation on the decline in post-Periclean Athens are often treated as evidence of Thucydides' exultation of Pericles and his policies. Yet one could just as easily ask whether it was not Pericles' policies that contributed to Athens' decline and whether even Pericles could hold together Athens if he lived through the war.[45]

Domestic strife arising from a desire to rule in Athens during the time of the Sicilian expedition radically harmed Athens, resulting from what Pericles *himself* undermined most – piety.[46] Indeed, Thucydides' comments on the causes of Athens' loss in the war (65.6-12) along with his description of the lead-up to, and passions for, the Sicilian expedition (6.30-32) bear comparison for any consideration of his views of the city, the regime.[47] For these comments reveal that the Athenian piety Pericles undermines, through his denigration of tradition generally, only suppressed a piety the Athenian thesis could not erase. And this thesis, we might suspect, was promulgated only by a few "enlightened" Athenians and not by the demos

45 As Foster (2010) p. 214 observes, Pericles dies at 2.65.6, seemingly separating 2.65 into two parts, the demos' view of Pericles and Thucydides' own.

46 Monoson and Loriaux (1998) discuss "moral norms," "human morality," "social cohesion," and "norms and law" in what they identify (correctly) as Thucydides' subtle critique of Pericles; yet surprisingly, despite detailing Periclean Athens, the plague, the migration from rural countryside into the city, and Corcyra, they do not mention piety, gods, divine law, or religion generally (2.53.5 is quoted, with its reference to "fear of gods," along with a passing reference to the Athenian purification of Delos, but neither is discussed [pp. 289, 291]). This silence covers over *the* key to Thucydides' teaching on domestic politics, the regime (and hence his critique of Pericles): "norms of moral conduct" that attach human beings to family, friends, city, and fellow citizens through trust in the way of their ancestors, along with the gods overseeing human conduct, cannot be divorced from piety.

47 Consider Strauss (1964) pp. 199-209. Cf. Hornblower III p. 381-82 who denies "the scene described was abnormal in kind." Perhaps this description of the preparations for Sicily was part of the Athenians' "usual departure rituals" but it has no parallel in the pages of Thucydides. Hornblower looks to Pindar and Herodotus, but that seems only to beg the question as to why we find no trace of other such rituals by the Athenians before an expedition. Taken with the pious context (6.53), and considering the motives stated for the expedition (6.31-32), the impious character of Athenian imperialism appears to be the central question Thucydides poses for his reader.

itself. Certainly, there was no place for the Athenian thesis among pious Spartans.

Immediately preceding the expedition, the mutilation of the herms (statues related to the god Hermes and his cult), an impious act, looms large in Athens: it was interpreted by the Athenian demos as an ill omen for both the potential success of the expedition as well as for the democracy itself (6.27.3). The demos feared tyranny, as Athens moved back and forth between democracy and oligarchy. Unlike Pericles, the other statesmen were unable to rule with his same prominence and were highly mistrusted (as both Cleon and Diodotus were forced to contend with during the Mytilenian debate). Perhaps due to their own realization that they acted out of private interests, the demos feared demagogues were merely seeking their own. But while the demos feared for democracy's slide into tyranny, Thucydides' own judgment on regimes other than Athenian democracy is not unfavorable. In the context of discussing Alcibiades, one of, if not, *the* key individuals feared by the people as a possible tyrant, Thucydides digresses to correct a misinterpretation, accepted by the Athenians, of the Peisistratus tyranny. Contrary to widely held Athenian belief of its harsh character, it was in fact gentle, promoted virtue among its citizens, and was outwardly concerned with piety by attending to the sacrifices and temples. It was only due to a private quarrel resulting in an (incorrectly) perceived assassination attempt on the tyrant that the tyranny *became* distrustful of its citizens, leading to increasingly harsh measures against them (54-59).[48]

Thucydides' digression on the Peisistratus tyranny warrants our own: This is Thucydides' second telling of the Harmodius and Aristogeiton story; this retelling is, therefore, significant.[49] We recall in Book One, he introduced this story as an example to support his contention that most human beings generally accept traditional accounts of the past without scrutiny (1.20). In this case, the Athenians were confused over who's who in the killing of Hipparchus. But Thucydides' first telling of this story does not mention *why* Hipparchus was killed, leading us to assume it was a political

48 Consider Strauss (1964) p. 196: "[T]he admiration for the Athenian tyrannicides of Harmodius and Aristogeiton was an important part of the manner in which the Athenian democracy understood itself."

49 Compare Hornblower I p. 57 where he discusses the meaning of this repetition, suggesting both that it adds something to Thucydides' previous relation of the story, but also that it would be seemingly necessary for Thucydides' immediate (Athenian) audience only to remind them of the story. My view accords with the former.

assassination plot (Hipparchus being a tyrant). So here, when he includes new details, we learn that it was not from a politically calculated motive, but an "enraged lover" (or "pained lover" – *erōtikōs perialgēsas*) that was the cause, the murder being a daring, rash, and uncalculated, i.e., emotional, act (6.54.3. 59.1). The origin of Athens, and thus the storied or mythological basis of the city, particularly its democratic government, is in fact a falsehood. That basis is a noble notion of democracy as the best regime, one which overcame oppressive, tyrannical rule; but the revolt against what only *became* a "harsher" (*chalepotera*) tyranny disguises the causes and thus glorifies democratic revolution (59.2). And what is more, it is in this story, twice told, that Thucydides reveals tyranny, this tyranny, as a good regime, animated as it was by "virtue and intelligence" (*aretēn kai xynesin*), all while upholding established, traditional laws and piety (54.5-6).[50] Placed in the context of the Sicilian expedition, and thus in the context of the question of what has changed from Periclean to post-Periclean Athens, the Peisistratus tyranny compels the reader to compare these not insignificant praises of the regime, presented in Thucydides' own voice, with his assessment of Periclean Athens and its decline. And for our purposes, and in light of Spartan piety, Athenian piety and its effect on their regime takes on added importance.

The denigration of Athens, both in its past and, as we will observe with the Sicilian expedition, is the prominence of private passions, the more dangerous as they move away from a long-standing bond of the citizen to the city, a union achieved through law-abidingness and pious customs. By contrast, the prominence of Alcibiades in post-Periclean Athens was of grave concern as the source of potential tyranny. Alcibiades was attacked by the demagogues who feared him taking over rule of the city and was suspicious to the demos due to his undemocratic and unlawful way of life. Alcibiades' private conduct, unlike Pericles', led his opponents to successfully accuse him of responsibility for acts of impiety that dominated the demos' imagination at this time (6.28.2, 53.1-3, 61.4).[51] Indeed, Thucydides

50 For a discussion of the scholarship (and comparison with Herodotus' telling of the story) see Hornblower III pp. 433-53. As Palmer (1982) p. 107 observes, this is Thucydides' only attribution of virtue (*aretē*) to rulers.

51 Once we are aware of Thucydides' critical assessment of Pericles, the return of piety in Athens becomes clear: it was due to their fear that the Sicilian expedition, as a further expansion of the Athenian empire, may be unjust and impious (see 6.27.2-3, 31.1, 32.1-2). Therefore, the Athenians' concern with finding those responsible for

confirms through his narrative that Alcibiades' private ambitions were his dominant concern and cast suspicions on him; yet at the same time, his abilities as a general and commander seemed to recommend him (2.65.11, 6.15.2-4, 53.2). What this means, of course, is that such a man as Alcibiades had difficulty ruling in broad daylight because both the demagogues and the demos suspected he would use his superiority against them for his own political gain. This contrasts with Pericles, whose key skill was quieting this angry demos (2.65.8-9). Not surprisingly, Alcibiades found a means to honor and glory apart from the city of Athens by betraying Athens in his aid to Sparta after his exile.[52]

Thucydides' depiction of Athenian democracy hones in on this tension between private and public interests, a tension especially strong in democracies, where liberty of the individual citizen is a point of pride (2.37.2, 38, 40.1-2). For this reason, Athenian democracy also directs our attention toward civic virtue more broadly, those qualities tying a citizen to their city. Pericles argues civic duty is freely chosen; but Thucydides' praises of Sparta for their regime, its long-lasting laws and moderate character, appear in stark contrast to the immoderation at Athens during its (post-Periclean) decay. It was Sparta that Thucydides states was able to combine moderation and prosperity, its regime never experiencing the domestic political problems that plagued Athens and led to its eventual defeat (8.24.4).[53] Further, it is Thucydides' judgment that Athens was "well-governed" (*eu politeusantes*) for the first time in his lifetime under the regime of 411, being a "measured" (*metrion*) regime comprised of "the few and the many" (*tous oligous kai tous pollous* – 8.97.2), rather than the dominance of the demos soon after

the mutilation of the herms was a pious attempt to "appease the gods" (Ahrensdorf [1997] pp. 258-59). Compare Strauss (1983) pp. 103-104 on the oaths used by both the oligarchs and the democrats as Athens' regime fluctuated between factions late in the war, including "the greatest oaths" (*tous megistous horkous* – 8.75).

52 Forde (1987) p. 127 argues that Alcibiades' pursuit of honor, separating him from service to any particular city, was a problem for Athens. We will see this problem for Sparta as well, especially visible during the campaign of Brasidas.

53 Strauss (1939) p. 524: "According to the view of the classical thinkers, one cannot assert that war against other cities is the aim of the life of the city without being driven to assert that war of individual against individual is the aim of the life of the individual." Strauss argues in this context that Xenophon views peace as the goal of political life, not war. Part of Xenophon's criticism of Sparta's legislation (and thus Lycurgus) is that it is dedicated to war. Cf. Plato, *Laws* 629b8-630e5; Aristotle, *Politics* 1333b38-1334a10.

Pericles' death, to say nothing of Thucydides' judgment of Periclean Athens itself.

Immediately before the establishment of this regime late in the war, and thus the return of measure or moderation to Athens, their domestic situation was indeed bleak – their fleet at Samos was in revolt; almost their entire navy had been destroyed, along with the death or capture of many men; they were at war with one another; and they had lost Euboea (the source of their provisions) since Attica was controlled by the Spartans through their post at Decelea (95.2, 96.1-3).[54] This control of Decelea by Agis and the Spartans meant holding the very Athenian countryside Pericles had urged them to abandon. And this strategic decision, while not originating from Alcibiades (5.17.2), was only carried out by the Spartans with the aid of Alcibiades' persuasion (6.91.6-7, 93.1, 7.19.1-2), proving effective in harming Athens externally at a time when they were also suffering from faction within (7.27.3).[55]

Love of victory and daring, born out of Pericles' cultivation of noble longings, longings in full bloom in Alcibiades, led to the persistence of imperial designs, mixed with fulfillment of private desire, all absent of

54 In both of these passages from Book Eight, Thucydides uses the verbal form of *stasis* (*stasiazō*). This further reinforces or confirms his earlier judgment (after Pericles' death) regarding the reasons why Athens lost the war. This is not to deny, however, that Sparta could have done more here (and elsewhere) to harm Athens; but Thucydides makes both judgments with knowledge of Spartan character, in particular their lack of daring. For debates and other sources on the regime of 411, see Hornblower III pp. 1033-36.

55 See 7.27.3-5 for Thucydides' statement that the loss of the countryside became a serious problem later in the war, strategically harming Athens. This statement occurs in the context of new preparations for Sicily, after the Spartans and Syracusans had won a battle in the port of Syracuse. The Spartans began again to attack Attica to distract the Athenians, while the latter attempted to send troops and supplies to reinforce their increasingly desperate situation in Sicily. Both Alcibiades and Thucydides point to the loss of money as the reason this Spartan initiative could (and did) harm Athens (6.91.6-7, 7.18.1, 27.3-5). The Spartan presence at Decelea, therefore, led to financial problems *because* the Athenians had no countryside and needed to import all their supplies, importation being costly since all transport could happen only by sea, rather than across their own (now occupied) land. Needless to say, this is a noteworthy development in light of Pericles' adumbration of Athens' apparently vast financial resources (2.14). Further, the Four Hundred are also able to rule Athens due to the constant presence required of most Athenians to guard against a Spartan incursion from Decelea toward the walls of the city (8.69). And finally, this preoccupation resulted in the loss of Euboea which caused even greater panic than the disaster in Sicily (96.1-3).

piety. Pericles attempted to replace Athenian tradition with citizens' freely chosen commitment to the city; but by emphasizing individual freedom, Pericles pulls citizens away from long-standing attachments that fostered trust, civic obligation, and sacrifice – the family, the traditional laws and customs, the previous generations who built Athens to greatness, Homer, and the gods: in a word, the way of life of most Athenians. Thus while some wish for further elaboration from Thucydides as to the precise causes of Athens' decline, he has left clues for readers, notably his emphasis on the "private" (*idios*) in the elevation of quarrels and desires above the good of the city (2.65.7).[56] A city divorcing citizens from their moral, and we could add, emotional attachment to it (an attachment necessarily founded on ancestors and the gods and even the trust Pericles himself enjoyed), opens up daring and immoderate ambitions corrosive to the city's true interests. This was *the* recipe for Athenian decline and their demise (6.31.4-5).

Civil War at Corcyra

Athens loses the Peloponnesian War as a result of faction within the city. Private ambition took the place of pious reserve and moderation, and although the city itself was not destroyed, Athens narrowly avoided a collapse into civil war. While the example of Athens is therefore instructive for Thucydides' view of domestic political health, Corcyra is the gravest statement in his work on the loss of moderation. Our appraisal of the Spartan regime may only be complete by detailing this loss. Thucydides' description of civil war (*stasis*) leaves a clear impression that it is the worst of all political events in its destruction and harm to human beings.[57] War

56 Both Gomme II pp. 191-92 and Hornblower I pp. 342-44 remark on Thucydides' lack of precision in this sentence.

57 *Stasiazō*, the verbal form of *stasis*, begins Thucydides' narration of the events at Corcyra (3.70.1). However, it should be noted that *stasis* is introduced in the Archaeology and continues as a theme throughout the work. For our purposes, we note that the first mention is in the context of Thucydides' initial remarks on the Spartan "founding" (*ktisis* – 1.18.1; cf. 1.6.4). Views on the best translation of the term vary, since *stasis* need not indicate full-scale civil war (therefore, "strife," "discord," etc.). In this regard, consider Connor (1984) p. 96. Most scholars and commentators agree on a few issues in these chapters: 1) *Stasis* has a range of meanings; thus, most simply retain the transliteration of the Greek, as do I. 2) That 3.84 has long been, and should be regarded as, an interpolation not by Thucydides (not to be confused with

at home means all political stability has been lost; all laws and judgments upon which the regime rests and flourishes collapse or are called into question. Similar to the plague at Athens (to which it bears comparison), *stasis* is the political version of a natural disaster.[58]

While cities may abandon or adjust principles of justice in conducting foreign relations during a war, domestic stability can still exist at home. Thucydides' praise of moderation (a praise of Sparta – 8.24.4) as *the* quality of a sound regime, and account of the loss of trust among the citizens (a critique of post-Periclean Athens – 2.65.11), is seen most clearly in the extreme consequences resulting from its loss and is relevant for any consideration of his overall political teaching. Archidamus praised Spartan virtue, but how this is constitutive of a healthy city cannot be fully understood until we know what its absence entails. By presenting *stasis* in the longest passage in his account in his own voice, Thucydides lends gravity to what occurs at Corcyra. While Spartan moderation, its rest from the ills of civil war, is the stability or "restful growth" (*hesukhasasan auxethenai* – 1.12.1) required for a city to become prosperous, the revolution at Corcyra is a "motion" (*kinēsis* – 3.75.2) that destroys the city by destroying virtues tying a political community together.[59]

In Thucydides' order of presentation, the revolution at Corcyra begins to take shape only one chapter after the events at Plataea (3.70.1). Oaths, gods, and fatherland all figured prominently in the Sparta-Plataea-Thebes debate; so too in the instigating events at Corcyra. The stand-off between the oligarchs and democrats initiating *stasis* is mired in accusations of

---

Separatist critiques). 3) That the importance of this section is signaled by it being the longest section in Thucydides' own voice in the entire text. Scholarship on Corcyra's *stasis* that should be consulted includes: Edmunds (1975), Macleod (1983) pp. 123-39, Connor (1984) pp. 95-105, Orwin (1988) and (1994) pp. 175-92. See also Ahrensdorf (2000) for a comparison of Hobbes and Thucydides on anarchy (3.82-83 discussed at pp. 587-91). Strauss (1964) pp. 146-47 and context for a discussion of *stasis* placed within important remarks on Sparta.

58 Strauss (1964) p. 147: "The depravation caused by civil war, that man-made plague, resembles the depravation caused by the plague proper." Saxonhouse (1978) p. 472: "Thucydides uses the same word, *metabolai*, upheavals (2.48.3; 53.1; and 3.82.2) to describe the plague and the rebellion (*stasis*) at Corcyra. Both the political and physical upheavals serve to illustrate human nature freed from the restraints of the *nomoi*."

59 Strauss (1964) pp. 146-47; Orwin (1994) p. 183; Price (2001) pp. 208-10.

sacred violations by each party against the other (70.4-6).[60] What unfolds at Corcyra is thereby related to the Spartan view of the war: Thucydides sets up comparison of Spartan and Athenian foreign policy (at Plataea and Mytilene, respectively), but places this comparison in the context of a new and easily overlooked domestic "variable" – *stasis*.

Stasis is more likely the result of foreign wars due to incitement by such parties within the city who seek "to innovate" (*neōterizō*), that is, to revolt.[61] Factions can call in allies to change the regime in favor of either side, while during peace there is neither "pretext" (*prophasis*) nor wish. Democrats called in the Athenians; oligarchs called in the Spartans. Calling in outsiders is motivated by two goals: arranging the city with a view to one's own advantage *and* harming one's adversaries (82.1). Since all cities in Greece were some mixture of the few (the oligarchs) and the many (the democrats), these factions battle for control of the regime, of the type of government favoring the one side or the other. For Thucydides, faction always exists, even during peace; but a relative stability or balance is struck that is more likely to be upset by a larger war. Revolutionary parties can gain support by a foreign presence; barring a larger war that offers such opportunities, these parties tend to be small and relatively powerless. This stability, though, is also based in part on the type of the regime: revolutionaries demanding radical change is always a danger for democracies. In this case, the Corinthians used the return of prisoners from the battle at Epidamnus to help instigate a revolt within Corcyra, hoping to bring the city over them. Sparta, then, is a noteworthy exception – its unchanging laws, observed over a great expanse of time, were strengthened by the authority of tradition and the institutional arrangements of the city (1.18, 5.63.4).

The characteristics and motives of these parties during the Peloponnesian War are not those particular to civil wars during this time – for Thucydides, the dangers of *stasis* are permanent so long as "human nature" remains the same.[62] Cities and private individuals have "better thoughts"

60 Hornblower I p. 469 on Thucydides' introduction of Corcyra: "…the *amount* of detail remains surprising" (emphasis in original).

61 The prefix of *neōterizō* is related to the word *neos* or "new." Civil war is the result of attempts at something new, or more precisely, political innovation. See also Price (2001) pp. 22-26 for this term and for a more detailed breakdown of Thucydides' language at 3.82.1-2; cf. 6.27.3.

62 Pouncey (1980) pp. 143-45 argues there is "almost" a permanent condition of human nature, but that Thucydides has "overwritten" his claim to its permanence.

during times of peace; but confrontation with necessities arising during a foreign war leads to denigration of the virtues holding the city together.[63] War is a violent teacher because it takes away the ease of daily life and thus affects the character of human beings (3.82.2).[64] Thucydides' emphasis here is on the individual, on human psychology, not simply on offices or "institutions."

Yet even in the horrors of civil war, where necessity places the greatest strain on conditions within the city (particularly the compulsion to face death), there are qualities or virtues that are held in honor. Human beings do not abandon moral judgments altogether; rather, they redefine those qualities – thoughtless daring is courage, moderation is unmanliness, and generally, the only ones trusted were those who proposed extreme measures (82.4). Despite the conditions of civil war, in which pretexts or justifications would not seem to be needed given this tendency to extremism, pretexts are nevertheless sought and actions justified. Even in the violence and hatred of civil war, human beings seek to *justify* their actions, not in terms of self-interest (which would seem to preclude any concern with justifications at all), but through changing the meaning of terms designating what is considered just and noble; thus, names change their meaning in a manner that is not arbitrary; the concerns of human nature are fundamentally moral, and language expresses these concerns. Virtue is redefined, human beings still seeking to pass judgment on what is just and unjust, noble and shameful,

---

This argument, however, focuses only on *fear* as the dominant human motive. By reducing human actions in civil war merely to fear, Pouncey does not recognize a core Thucydidean observation: human hope. It is hope's ability to overcome the greatest fears that allows human beings to strive forward – for justice, for immortality, for vengeance – precisely in the midst of the most dire circumstances (3.45.7, 7.28.3, 56.2, 59.2, 70.7). For a comparison of human nature in Hobbes and Thucydides, see Johnson (1993) pp. 63-71.

63 Thucydides emphasizes the pressure of necessity brought on by war by modifying *anankē* with the term *aekousios* ("against one's will": Liddell Scott [1889] p. 15). Translations include Mynott (2013): "Forces beyond their control"; Hobbes (1989): "Necessity of doing anything against their will"; Crawley (1996): "Imperious necessities." Scholarship also offers its own renderings; for example, Ostwald (1988) p. 59: "Involuntary necessities"; Orwin (1994) p. 176: "Falling subject to overwhelming necessities."

64 This statement is ambiguous in the Greek. It can be translated either as "a violent teacher" or "a teacher of violence" (*biaios didaskalos*). Connor (1984) p. 102: "I believe both are intended."

good and evil; in a word, proclaiming a new morality, the best way of life within the city.[65]

That justice and nobility remain a dominant concern during *stasis* is brought out by Thucydides noting that ties of party took precedent over even those of kinship and family. These party relations (*hetairikos*) were based on "greed" (*pleonexia*) and ignored the "established laws" (*tōn keimenōn nomōn*). "Trust" (*pistis*) no longer rested on "the divine law" (*tō theiō nomō*) but on mutually "transgressing the law" (*paranomeō* – 82.6).[66] Acts of justice rooted in the divine law no longer exist; instead, unjust acts are the bond of those belonging to each party. Trust between the members of the city was previously based on expectations that all would comply with the established laws and the divine law. Just and noble actions followed from this adherence, its basis being a lawful "reverence toward the gods" (*eusebeia* – 82.8).[67] For Thucydides, family, kinship, the laws of the city, and the divine law are the bonds of the city because these legal and customary ties foster civic trust. In better times, the divine law restrains passions liable to undermine that trust.

Arising from greed (*pleonexia*) and love of honor (*philotimia*), the "cause" (*aitia*) of the especially brutal violence and circumstances of *stasis* is the desire for rule, a desire not simply driven by safety and self-preservation, advantage and interest. Rather, as Thucydides notes, a "love of victory" (*philonikeō*) among the parties meant ruling over others and gaining honor from one's party for revenges and transgressions of the law; this

65 Orwin (1994) p. 177n10 notes that the root of these concerns and their expression in language is not merely conventional; rather, it is due to fundamental human concerns. The changes in language are a reflection of permanent moral passions Thucydides locates as the cause of the particular viciousness of civil war. Edmunds (1975) focuses on "the ethical concept of inversion." Connor (1984) pp. 95-105 also provides an excellent discussion of the role of language in this episode.

66 Surprisingly, neither Gomme nor Hornblower mention "the divine law" at 3.82.6, despite this being Thucydides' only use of the term. Marinatos (1981) p. 33 mentions the term, but does not attempt to provide it with content, other than noting the association between morality and religion. As Strauss (1983) p. 96 observes on divine law (and "the divine" at 5.104-105), Thucydides is hardly clear "about the precise meaning of the expressions." Macleod (1983) pp. 128-29 emphasizes law, but not divine law. Orwin (1994) p. 178 equates divine law with oaths. Price (2001) p. 66 insists divine law does not mean "transcendent, immutable law."

67 *Eusebeia* is dismissed by Gomme II p. 380 and Eatough (1971) p. 242 as lacking pious meaning. Cf. Hornblower I p. 486 who defends the term, citing Marinatos (1981) p. 44n9.

was of the utmost concern (82.8). Surprisingly, even in the depths of a civil war human beings do not seek simply to provide for their safety; in the face of extreme necessities, rather than hopelessness or nihilism, acts of revenge actually bred hope. Fighting on behalf of one's party (and thus implicitly, on behalf of a particular cause that one views as just and noble) is cause for hope. One is not devoted simply to one's own interests or advantage, but instead to the agenda and goals of one's party.[68]

The "fair speeches" of each side were, then, not simply pretexts to justify continued violence. Each party has its own "platform," as *the* proper and fair arrangement of the city, an argument for a specific regime. Democrats call for political equality for the many; oligarchs for a moderate aristocracy of the few. And while such proposals, in creating an enemy out of the other party, may not benefit the city, each party implicitly made claims to do precisely that (82.8).[69]

Yet this itself is not simply a form of the hypocritical posturing we have seen the Spartans accused of – the greed and honor of each party is rooted

68 Cogan (1981) pp. 185-89, by contrast, presents Thucydides' account of human nature as "almost identical" to that of Hobbes, arguing that "[t]his selfish, appetitive nature is, for Thucydides, the cause of crimes of all descriptions" (187). Connor (1984) pp. 95-105 presents Corcyra as "...the dissolution of the human basis for morality... the only principle is the calculation of self-interest." "It is Hobbes' *bellum omnium contra omnes*" (99). This is odd, though, since Connor goes on to note: "...it is clear that Thucydides traces the origins of the *stasis* back to psychological factors such as self-aggrandizement (*pleonexia*) and ambition (*philotimia*)" and "...is a manifestation of a tendency within human beings that can take especially pernicious forms" (102). This is a richer description (as is Connor's account of Corcyra as a whole) than is the former statement. Ahrensdorf (2000) pp. 587-90 focuses on the hope for immortality and, convincingly, details the similarities and key differences between Thucydides and Hobbes.

69 See Orwin's (1988) p. 838 critique of Cogan (1981) pp. 149-54, who argues that the extremes of civil war are rooted in "ideological orientation." According to Orwin, Thucydides "would not have us assign the excesses he describes to the misguided zeal for the public good." This may, indeed, be the case for some party members. But can we speak of the motives of all members of each party as identical? Some were more extreme than others, as Thucydides implies (3.83.3). While many recognized *stasis* as mere pretext to act out long pent-up hatred, some may have believed their cause. Even while *stasis* releases human nature from the constraints of law, we are not licensed to assume that justice as understood by each party was entirely divorced from their particular laws and regime, that is, their "ideology" (3.82.8). Some extremes, even or especially those that attacked the other party, may have been understood, if not by the leaders, possibly by the participants, as conducive to their version of the public good.

in their sense of *deserving* to win victory over the other. Each party justifies their own actions. Even in overthrowing traditional laws and family ties (by redefining the virtues such "social" institutions inculcated), fighting for the sake of one's party is animated by a view of justice binding the party itself together. Most found themselves on one side or the other during the civil war; it was not a struggle of every man against every man.[70] Contrary perhaps to our expectation that the violence of civil war would alleviate the tension between justice and interest, what we notice is the opposite. Revenge, which one believes redresses past injustices (and hence is motivated by justice), was actively undertaken apart from any concern with self-preservation. While each side claims, and even may believe they act for the good of the city, they instead seek control of the regime for the sake of rule *itself.* Gaining political power becomes a goal, absent any reference to the good of the city. Victory over one's enemies becomes an end in itself, as there is no unified city to speak of, and thus, no common good. Each side becomes enemy of another, with the victor able to impose their regime on the defeated. Victory allows for (and in Corcyra resulted in) such acts of revenge. It is not enough to rule; one must also punish. And there is pleasure itself in these acts, an outlet for the pent-up envy of the weak.

And even more striking is what individuals and parties would do to justify their acts of revenge: Those involved in the war *allowed* an injury to occur for the sake of providing themselves with an injustice that could *then* be redressed (82.7). While the established laws and thus piety no longer tie citizens (or even family) together, the motive to redress injuries demonstrates the passion for justice is even stronger during *stasis*. Parties during its extremes having no manifest hope for survival, Thucydides presents this passion – a striving for something higher, something transcendent – as stronger than the supposed necessity of self-preservation itself. Each party did not merely seek their own private advantage under the fair words of justice; revenge harmed both their own advantage and the common good of the city.

Those not animated by revenge did not fare well. Failing to involve

70 Thucydides' indication that some refrained from involving themselves in civil war at Corcyra, and that those who were involved tied themselves to a particular party, renders problematic Pouncey's Hobbesian claim that civil war is "the beleaguerment as one of every man for himself" (1980, p. 147). Precisely the opposite: Human beings unite through a shared sense of justice and righteousness, thereby more easily giving themselves over to, and being eager to commit, the worst kinds of atrocities (3.82.6).

oneself with one party or the other often resulted in death. Ironically, those who refused to join the extremes were killed out of "envy" (*phthonos*); it was thought they might escape and hence survive (82.8). Yet this also confirms party members punished outsiders because they believed their party was on the side of justice; refusal to participate was *de facto* injustice. But this obsession with apparently just punishment for outsiders masked from the parties their still-existent concern with survival. Self-preservation does not entirely disappear; self-interest instead becomes moral. Envy by extremists toward moderates who might escape the ravages of *stasis* betrays a realization, if only half-conscious, that self-sacrifice for one's party's cause would not fulfill the deeper desire driving acts of revenge – to overcome one's own assured death. To partake in revenge, as an expression of justice, is to seek to participate in something higher, something beyond death itself. More than this: It implies that even though the parties were silent on piety, and actively overturned divinely established laws, they did not truly abandon the divine, or more precisely, a certain implicit theology. As the Spartans expect just or unjust actions to be rewarded or punished, favored or hindered by the will of the gods, so too did the parties (and each individual) expect that to "redress" an injury would be to partake in an act of justice which somehow protected them from the vicissitudes of fortune.[71] Each party's cause, its "justice," replaces the abandoned divine justice. Party becomes god.

Traditional virtues being not abandoned but redefined thereby points to deeper moral concerns. For to act "virtuously" (in this instance, carrying out revenge) means foregoing one's advantage or interest for the sake of adherence to virtue, thus making oneself worthy of the gods' favor. As the Athenian envoys implied, pursuing one's interest is not an indication of one's worth; only sacrificing interests could bestow such worth (1.76.4). Only through noble actions could one hope to become worthy of overcoming one's own assured death.[72] By their very participation in the extreme measures occurring during civil war, as opposed to pursuing a measured course, those who directed the political parties betrayed a longing to achieve something greater than survival itself, a longing only to be fulfilled by a divine or cosmic power they themselves had rejected or ignored.

71 This reminds us of a version of Spartan justice, justice as revenge, promulgated by Sthenelaidas, Cleon, and Alcidas. See Chapter One's "Sparta's Debate For and Against War."

72 Ahrensdorf (2000) p. 590.

For Thucydides, Corcyra's *stasis* places human beings' permanent attachment to justice and piety, to morality, on display. Piety and law are the safeguards standing between *stasis* and *polis*, Corcyra and Sparta offering paradigmatic evidence for each. Perhaps we can even say that "reverence for the gods" (*eusebeia* – 3.82.8) is a necessity for any city to avoid descending into *stasis*.

And these pious safeguards are particularly needed to protect against daring (*tolma*).[73] Daring is that aspect of human nature that can only be answered by *nomoi*, both human and divine – shame, reverence, and fear of the gods. Sparta's laws kept the possible causes of civil war in check, by both suppressing, and channeling, desires for victory and honor. Directing citizens toward service to the city moderates a daring and lawless striving for power by individuals or distinct factions within the regime. Even the Spartan regime had internal competition. But the tension Thucydides has highlighted between the hereditary kings and the elected ephors is contained both by the hereditary, divinely sanctioned source of each king's power (5.16.1-3), along with the laws to which the ephors had to defer (1.132.1). Obedience to the laws is a form of moderation, stifling challenges which "grasping for more" present. Human nature's permanent tendencies are not one homogenous expression defined only by nature, but may be tightened or slackened, strengthened or weakened, depending upon the constitution of the *polis*; therefore, political life as humans construct it can be better or worse, as Thucydides' description of *stasis* (which, importantly, was not limited to Corcyra) shows. In fact, its cruelty and violence were made worse as cities learned from others that experienced *stasis* before it (3.82.1-2). And, we must add, made worse by the greater or lesser susceptibility to *stasis* arising in the first place.

To be sure, *stasis* erupted (so to speak) everywhere, as the Peloponnesian War offered opportunities for daring action against one's domestic enemies. Still, it would be remiss to ignore both the parallels between the plague at Athens (the result, in part, of questionable policy) and Corcyraean *stasis*, on the one hand, and the comparison we are intended to make between Athens and Sparta, on the other. Book Eight is not the story of an organized, daring, and strategically flawless Sparta; to be sure, certain Spartans *do* improve in all these respects (as we will discuss). It is instead centered

73 *Tolma* is thematic in the description of the Corcyraean civil war (mentioned three times at 3.82) and the plague at Athens (mentioned three times at 2.40-42).

on the story of an Athens in decay, daringly overextending its empire and allowing factions to tear apart domestic peace, fostering intrigues and distrust enveloped by impiety. *Stasis* reminds us of the human capacity for cruelty; but it thereby also reminds us of the conditions occasioning its rise and thus the human capacity for morality. It reminds us that we, as social and moral beings, live together, and differ in *how* we live together. Clearly this is part of the significance of Sparta, if not a key revelation for Thucydides. Even for the Athenians, it is the Spartan regime that lends the city its notoriety (5.105.4). No other city is so thoroughly a unity; nowhere is a citizen so thoroughly a citizen; nowhere are the private interests of the individual so noticeably absent. Yet the Spartan regime requires closer consideration; for while Thucydides lauds Sparta for its civic qualities, the precise functioning of the regime, and implications of its peculiar character, are still unclear.

The Spartan Regime: Imperialism Versus the Helots

Thucydides' striking narration of *stasis* is his most prominent statement on the needs of the city. The relation between regime change, or destruction, and external war is shown most clearly in the growth and destruction of Athens and the civil war at Corcyra. With this as comparison, readers may now better appreciate details of Thucydides' Spartan narrative. By resurrecting not only Book Five, but also piecing together other seemingly minor or passing events presented in different contexts throughout, Thucydides accounts for the growth of Sparta from its beginnings, including the manner in which it wielded influence over other cities (1.18.1, 19), along with the virtues that saved it from internal destruction (84.1-4). Sparta's relative domestic stability cannot be divorced from its founding; but nor can its founding be divorced from other details we might miss, those we can now (retroactively) better understand: its own empire; the slave population from neighboring Messenia (the Helots); and Sparta's quietly continuing colonization of important areas of Greece, all of which shed light on understanding Thucydides' initial statement of Spartan power: its regime (10.2-3, 18.1). Thucydides offers hints, beginning in his Archaeology and running up to what we have detailed of the Spartan regime in Book Five, that readers must note while weighing comparisons between Sparta and the other cities.

Sparta put down tyrants in establishing their empire, and Athens also involved itself in civil disturbances when they could install a regime friendly to their interests and empire (115.3). In fact, they charge the Spartans with precisely those same actions, arranging the affairs of the Peloponnesus as they saw fit. Indeed, as Thucydides presents it, the Spartans *did* in fact involve themselves abroad, putting down tyrannies and stabilizing against the factional conflicts characterizing the fertile Peloponnesus in those times (1.18.1). This liberation from tyranny was the beginning of *Spartan* imperialism; but it was an imperialism of a limited sort. Sparta only arranged affairs among those mainlanders who were within their reach, thus establishing itself as the leading city in the region. In this context of his early narration on the Spartan regime, Thucydides makes a passing remark about these tyrannies that reminds us of Sparta itself – nothing great proceeded from them because they had to be attentive to matters at home (17). The focus of the tyrant is to maintain control of their city by not being absent from it on military campaigns; they could not pursue that greatness known as empire (cf. 3.45.6). Indeed, however strong and feared Sparta was as a city, they did not possess the abilities to control as vast an area as naval Athens did. Yet as Thucydides reminds us in the context of the capture of Pylos and the Spartans on the island, the area of Messenia formerly belonged to the Messenians who spoke the same dialect as the Spartans. Messenia is evidence of Sparta's early imperial founding (4.3.3, 41.2).

This detail sheds light on the Archaeology – between the Persian and Peloponnesian Wars, the Messenians were located in Naupactus. When (in the Pentecontaetia) Thucydides relates the story of Sparta's Helots – a slave-farming population within Sparta that revolted during the occasion of an earthquake (approximately 465) – he notes that these Helots were allowed safe passage out of the Peloponnesus due to an oracle from Delphi commanding the Spartans to do so. These Helots were themselves Messenians, driven out of their country near Sparta during the First Messenian War (generally thought to be circa 8th century B.C. – 1.101.2). Now, during this Third Messenian War, the Spartans complied with the oracle and the

Athenians received the exiled Messenians and placed them in Naupactus because of their hatred of the Spartans (103.1-3).[74]

Before the Helot revolt, Sparta and Athens were allies, Athenian supremacy not yet having transformed into what would become the Athenian empire (97.1-2, 99.1). The Spartans ask for aid from Athens to subdue Helots during the initiation of their revolt; the Athenians arrive, but due to their "daring and innovating" character they are sent away by the Spartans. This resulted not only in the Athenians becoming deeply offended; it also led to the dissolution of their post-Persian War alliance. Besides this event being a precipitating reason for the division between Sparta and Athens (and therefore important for Thucydides' explanation of the lead up to the war we have discussed), for our purposes here it is instructive of Sparta's fundamental focus – their regime. Fearing the Athenians because they viewed them as so fundamentally different from themselves, the Spartans believed they might attempt to incite a revolution within their city (102.3). While any city may fear the presence of others, it is Athenian character that fostered acute Spartan distrust. The Spartans themselves were neither daring nor innovative. Nothing great proceeded from Sparta just as nothing great proceeded from the tyrannies at this time in Greece. Both Sparta and these tyrannies lacked the "daring" necessary for empire (1.17). But Sparta's moderation is not simply due to their cautious, un-daring character – the Spartans were compelled to stay at home and guard against such potential Helot revolts, keeping the city attentive to itself.

Thucydides confirms this relation between moderation and necessity in Book Eight – he praises both the Chians and the Spartans for being moderate while prosperous (8.24.4).[75] Yet in this context, both cities are also noted

74 Not unimportant for the Spartans was the fact that this revolt occurred along with the great earthquake of 465/4 and lasted for a decade (1.101.2). See Cartledge (2002) pp. 186-91 for a comparison of Thucydides' account with that of Diodorus Siculus. For background on the earthquake and Helot revolt, see Hornblower I pp. 156-58 and Rahe (2019) pp. 125-33.

75 Romilly (1963) p. 225n3 argues that this statement by Thucydides indicates a quality of the Spartans that "no one ever thought of denying" and thus "the admiration implied in this unnecessary remark indicates a frame of mind closer to that in the speech on Pylos than to that in the Funeral Oration." This footnote occurs in the context of Romilly arguing that Books Five and Eight are incomplete, are "early" versions akin to how the other books would have appeared before completion, and thus "composed with less care" (p. 226). Along with my initial remarks (see Introduction note 14 and context), Romilly's argument does not acknowledge that the praise

for having the greatest number of slaves (40.2). Sparta was unable to pursue "the greatest things," especially empire (1.10.2, 3.45.6), because they were more concerned with safety at home than daring enterprises that would have kept them abroad and thereby place the entire city at risk, should those at home view this as an opportunity to rebel. Thucydides implies that only necessity will restrain and moderate cities from expanding. And even Sparta did possess a certain empire; they expanded to a certain degree or limit because, unlike Athens, the land surrounding their city possessed rich soil that led to faction (*stasis*), those in possession of land accruing great power for themselves (1.2.3). All cities are compelled to expand, go to war, and rule others. Perhaps this explains Thucydides never passing judgment in his own name on the Spartans' claim to be waging a war of liberation. The Spartans (and Chians) were moderate because they faced the necessities of war at home – revolt and *stasis* or peace.

The gravity of Sparta's Helot problem is further confirmed by the harsh measures the Spartans undertook to guard against potential future revolts.[76] During the affair at Pylos, the lowest point for Sparta in the war, the Athenians took advantage of the Messenians now located on Naupactus, to engage in a campaign against Laconia, the countryside surrounding Sparta. Warfare against an area so near to their city caused the Spartans the greatest fear, including a fear of another revolution (4.41.1-3). It is in this context Thucydides emphasizes the extent of this fear: The Spartans asked the Helots to make a proclamation amongst themselves as to who was most distinguished in war, under the "pretext" (*prophasis*) of granting them their freedom. Once this portion of the Helots (two thousand in total) had been

of Sparta's measured or moderate conduct, whether at war or among themselves, is never stated by Thucydides himself until this instance. Moreover, the speech at Pylos was given by the Spartans according to their view of the situation (4.21.1-2). As for Pericles' Funeral Oration, it suffices to simply recall that Pericles' praise of daring is most at odds with Spartan moderation, which comprises part of Thucydides' praise. Cf. Strauss (1964) p. 148. See Hornblower III p. 819ff. on this as a rare authorial statement on the Spartans. This remark is all the more striking for occurring in the context of the domestic turmoil in Athens, along with Thucydides' additional remark later in Book Eight praising Athens' regime of 411 (8.97.2). It reminds us of what we have learned of Sparta; but it is also a reminder to us to go back and reconsider Thucydides' presentation of both cities. Thucydides' text requires we move forward and backward, reconsidering stages in the war, to understand fully each city's character and its bearing on the lessons we draw from the Peloponnesian War.

76 See Rahe (2016) pp. 11-12. For further background on the Helots, see also Cartledge (2002) pp. 138-53, 299-307.

selected, however, the Spartans killed them, fearing these would be most likely to rebel against the city (80.2-4). Spartan justification of such harshness was rooted in Helots not being citizens and thus not sharing in the equality and prerogatives full Spartan citizenship enjoyed.[77]

Thucydides remarks here that the Spartans always had to be focused on guarding against the Helots.[78] This remark is reinforced immediately preceding the treaty and alliance between Sparta and Athens after the first ten years of the Peloponnesian War. Both cities, as we have seen, were weakened by problems they encountered as the war dragged on, among the Spartans' greatest concerns being the Helots, and others located on the Peloponnesus, engaging in their "former" (*proteron*) attempts at revolution (5.14.3). Thucydides thereby further reminds us of early Spartan imperialism: they did indeed possess an empire on the Peloponnesus, an empire maintained as the superior land power able to contain other cities, along with a reputation that stoked fear. Their empire was limited or "moderate" because of the on-going war within the city and within their region.

It is not only in their founding as a city, however, that Sparta attempted to expand and exert their influence. During the Peloponnesian War they also attempt the founding of a colony at Heraclea (3.92-93).[79] The Malians and the Dorians sent to Sparta for assistance. The Malians were hoping for Sparta's assistance and security after a war with their neighbors and the Dorians also joined for the same reason. The Spartans decided to grant their request because they wanted to be of assistance, but also because Heraclea was strategically located near Euboea and therefore would allow them to maintain a fleet nearby to harass this principal source of Athenian revenue (Sparta now compelled to exert their influence also by sea).

While Thucydides had mentioned that the Malians were composed of three distinct tribes, when he relates the Spartans' decision to send out a colony as assistance, he only mentions the Trachinians. Further, the Spartans also sought to aid the Dorians, who Thucydides notes were originally from Sparta and seemed to have settled near Heraclea some time ago. Indeed, it was the Dorians who were the first to settle Sparta itself (1.18.1).

77 On the differences between Helots and other Greek slaves, see MacDowell (1986) pp. 37-42.

78 Cf. Aristotle, *Politics* 1269a37-39. This was due, in part, to clear numerical superiority. See Rahe pp. 11-12 with 152n21.

79 This is not Sparta's only colony, but the only one Thucydides describes in detail. Cf. 4.53.2, 7.57.6.

Despite the strategic reasons for the Spartans' decision, they were also motivated in founding Heraclea with a preference for certain tribes or "peoples" (*ethnos*) over others (3.92.5).[80]

Only after consulting the god at Delphi and receiving a favorable response did they send colonists to Heraclea, led by three Spartans to be its founders: Leon, Alcidas, and Damagon. They also invited other Greeks to join and settle at Heraclea, with the exception of the Ionians and some other peoples. And many peoples did join the colony from the belief that any place established by the Spartans would be prosperous. Yet this belief is disappointed. The nearby Thessalians harassed the new colony and reduced its population to ensure it would not become a powerful neighboring city. But most notably, the Spartans themselves harmed their own efforts by governing the colony "harshly and in some cases not nobly" (*chalepōs te kai estin ha ou kalos* – 3.93.2; cf. 5.52.1). The Spartans both failed to protect their new colony from the Thessalians and were unable to rule the colony in a manner that would make it prosperous. They were unable to govern with any gentleness, despite the fact that holding a colony near Euboea would be advantageous to them in the larger war. Indeed, it was their ability to control the flow of Athens' resources much later in the war that caused significant harm to that city (8.96.1-2).

Thucydides' mention of Alcidas as one of the three commanders of the colony at Heraclea is a reminder of this harshness toward others. Alcidas was the Spartan commander who was urged by Sparta's allies to refrain from harming Athens' subjects, who were only so by necessity. To continue would have led to Sparta creating more "enemies" than "friends" (3.32.2). And as Thucydides subtly hints with his narration of the founding of Heraclea, the Spartans preferred only one of the Malian tribes and their own

80 Consider 7.57.2 where Thucydides lists the cities allied with the Syracusans or the Athenians. While he notes the divisions of cities, and the peoples to whom each city belonged (Dorians, Ionians, and Aeolians), he first states that it was not justice or kinship that led to the alliances as much as interest or compulsion. The exceptions seem to be the Corcyraeans, fighting against their colonial city of Corinth due to "hatred" (57.7). Those from Argos, being Dorians, also fought against the Spartans due to hatred as well as private interest (57.9). Thucydides thereby implies that hatred and the resulting desire for revenge *did* affect their decision, even when it also served their interests. See Orwin (1994) pp. 139-41 and (2017) pp. 364-66 who instead emphasizes self-interest. Compare Hornblower III pp. 222-23 on the importance of kinship for the Spartans (see, for example, 1.107.2). Fragoulaki (2013) offers the most detailed study on kinship in Thucydides.

peoples, the Dorians, over foreign tribes and Ionians. Not only Alcidas, but the Spartans generally, drew a hardline between friends and enemies, offering assistance to their own while treating others harshly and as foreign. And this treatment harms one of their own intentions – to expand their influence abroad with a view to causing Athens some trouble; indeed, the Athenians were originally alarmed by the new colony (93.1).

Thucydides only quietly presents Spartan imperialism and, in this way, seems to imitate the manner in which other cities viewed that imperialism – we do not hear any blame of Sparta by other cities for this empire, but only for their lack of eagerness in prosecuting wars and supporting allies. It is Athenian imperialism that receives blame because it is visible to everyone, or more precisely, the Athenians do not even attempt to disguise their ambitions. Yet even with the threat of the Helots, the Spartans also needed to establish stability on the Peloponnesus. Domestic order within Sparta presupposes control over the region so far as to ensure they would not be constantly under threat from their neighbors. Rest or peace, as the opposite of motion or war, requires controlling an empire that does not place the city at risk of invasion or of attempts by outsiders to incite a revolution within Sparta among the Helots (1.21.1). Thucydides warns of the possibility of external wars inciting civil wars because every city, to varying degrees and kinds, has factions within the regime. Yet this raises a question: Was it the *necessity* of staying at home (the Helots) or the *character* of the Spartans (their pious caution) that led to this limited imperialism?

Thucydides states that the Spartans did everything with a view to the Helots at home (4.80.3). This then was the cause of Spartan moderation, casting doubts on any genuine piety and justice of the people; Sparta is not an expansive imperial power only because its most pressing war is at home, among a hostile population apt to revolt (1.102). Sparta offers us, then, confirmation of the Athenian thesis – Spartan moderation was compelled by their internal security problems: the Helots.[81] Yet Thucydides' Spartans undoubtedly view politics through their pious customs and rearing, and Book Five thus supplements the Corinthians' preliminary observations on Spartan character (1.70). A version of the Athenian thesis holds: calculated interests guide any city's policy. But does this mean all motives are *reducible* to self-interest? Did the Spartans fail to cross frontiers on military expeditions aiding their allies merely as a pretext to deal with their Helot problem

81 See Orwin (1994) p. 85 and context.

at home? If so, then this fails as genuine piety. If not, then the Helots, while imposing a form of necessity upon the city, did not determine all strategic calculations. All cities balance risks versus rewards, and the Spartans did march out on campaigns. Indeed, it is an oversimplification to say Sparta avoided all occasions to aid their allies: their Dorian kin were of notable concern to them.[82]

A further issue in determining best policy is that self-interest itself is often unclear – the distinction between what appears to be advantageous at a given moment and what is in fact so is often murky. In this vein, we might note that Sparta's necessary attention to the Helots harmed their foreign policy by constraining them where other courses of action would have provided beneficial (Thucydides' striking claim, for example, that had they been more enterprising late in the war, the Spartans could have marched *right into the Piraeus* – 8.96.3-5). And then there are Spartan decisions that appear wholly un-Athenian, confounding simple explanation – Sparta's colony in Heraclea revealed a preference for fellow Dorians, for their own, their kin (3.92-93), despite Thucydides' apparent view that kinship ultimately bows to necessity (7.57.2, 5, 9); Alcidas attacked Athens' subject cities seeking to come over to Sparta (3.32); and finally, the possession of Heraclea, near Euboea, would have been most advantageous to Spartan interests should they been able to hold it earlier in the war.

All of these actions, however, could be understood as motivated by fear. And if the Spartans do act out of fear, fear is a motive recognized by the Athenian thesis as compelling. But if fear is compelling, must it lead to imperial expansion, as Athens did in responding to their fear of Persia? And does the Athenian thesis not state that cities with power will always expand (1.76.2-3)? But what cities are those? Athens as hegemon, and then imperial tyrant, is the exception among cities (99). Since most other cities are weak, or near equal to their neighbors in power, considerations of justice and moderating one's expansion, will indeed factor into consideration. Cities do act with a view to justice, manifested as treaty obligations, oaths, and other agreements to prevent war with their (near equally powerful) neighbors. Yet since Athens is superior, it must surely act with no such concerns in mind. Delos, Mytilene, Pericles' punishment after the plague,

82 See Hornblower III p. 222 who notes in the context of discussing the Melian Dialogue (citing 1.107.2 and 3.92.3) that the Spartans "were prepared to go a long way, literally and figuratively, in defence of their own 'metropolis'."

the preparations for the Sicilian expedition, however, all serve as examples of *Athenians* acting from justice and piety, not calculations of advantage. We might even ask: Is the Athenian boast of possessing a measured empire not in fact partially true? Did they not restrain themselves, not due to any advantages of restraint itself, but out of a sense of honor or even justice? Did they not seek to administer a milder empire, contra the Persians, because to do so is noble, a moral dictum that Greeks do not rule Greeks as barbarians rule barbarians? Are these decisions in keeping with the Athenian thesis?

The Athenian thesis itself becomes merely a means to exculpate Athens for choosing empire. This is, not surprisingly, how Sthenelaidas, the Spartan ephor, reacted to it; this is how Sparta's allies reacted to it. It is a novel attempt to ground morality in the language of nature, self-interest as natural necessity; and while it offers reflections on human nature, especially in Diodotus' expression of it, Diodotus' version of that thesis is notable for pointing to the *barriers* to calculated, rational self-interest: Cities and individuals cannot always escape hopes and *erōs* coloring calculation, fortune or misfortune vindicating success and failures, and other incurable passions that law and gods cannot wholly restrain (3.45.4-5). Motives that are moral, justice and piety, kinship and hatred, cruelty, and even love and goodwill (7.57.10, 86.4) are part of Thucydides' political psychology.

To return to the Spartans: Human nature, educated by the Spartan regime, resulted in the Spartan understanding of the Helots, i.e., as foreign, something to be feared, something to be harshly governed. Moral qualities present in human beings, to greater and lesser degrees given their regime, affect *how* they respond to necessities all cities face (including their own internal ones). For if this were not the case, all cities would approach war in the same manner; but the Athenians strive forward where the Spartans retreat (8.2.4; cf. 8.92.3, 106.5). And while for the Athenians this striving is due to their drive for nobility and the honor that attends it, the Spartans hold nobility to be service to their city – praise and blame strongly motivates their actions, fear of acting shamefully in disobeying the laws, which included their defense of Sparta, inculcated near unwavering obedience (4.19.3, 5.9.9, 5.104). The laws of Sparta, being sanctioned by the god at Delphi, are the foundation of their fear; this includes sacrifices before campaigns and adherence to the oaths consecrating treaties.

The regime's relevance for Thucydides' assessment of war is signaled by the fact that Sparta wins the war because of Athenian ambition; and this ambition is of questionable piety. While the Athenians believe they have the support of the gods as well, it is because the gods excuse human beings in cases where necessity rules (4.98.6). The gods would not blame the Athenians for pursuing their interests because it is a "law" set down that all human beings obey. If this "law" directs human nature itself, then one cannot be blamed for acting in accordance with it (5.105.2-3). But for the Spartans, the gods are not subject to necessity: Human nature is able to navigate fortune through moral acts. Human life is fundamentally susceptible to fortune and thus the gods that control fortune will reward those who act justly (2.74.2-3). And justice at home means adjudicating disputes between citizens by lessening human nature's ambitions, moderating those most likely to fuel *stasis*, a moderation only achieved through Spartan-like strictures: the pious *nomoi* foundational to the regime.

Sparta's Preeminent Men: The Cases of Pausanias, Agis, and Pleistoanax

Fearing the gods and being highly susceptible to shame among their fellow citizens, the Spartans possessed a strong moral attachment to their city. No individual was elevated above the city; however, this did not wholly prevent some from trying. And when such attempts were made, even when impropriety was suspected, punishing a fellow Spartan placed the city in a difficult position, so strong were the restrictions of the laws.[83] The problem that certain individuals create for Sparta is the sting of a Spartan who is able to attain honor outside of the city, freeing himself from the praise and blame rooted in the laws, and from the radical equality (among full citizens) these laws sought to promote and protect (1.6.4). Since their domestic order depended on these laws, the possibility of an individual acting outside of the authority of Sparta abroad could lead to the diminishment of authority within the city itself.

Three such Spartan individuals require our attention, to better

83 Consider Rousseau, *Considerations on the Government of Poland*, Chapter 2: "The Spirit of Ancient Institutions." Spartan laws affected every stage of the rearing of children, future citizens of Sparta. See MacDowell (1986) pp. 52-70 and Rahe (2016) pp. 23-30.

understand city and citizen, and thereby domestic influences on policy and strategy: Pausanias, a Spartan commander (and regent) before the Peloponnesian War accused of conspiring with the Persians; Pleistoanax, the exiled Spartan king accused of bribery; and the other Spartan king during Pleistoanax' time, Agis, who despite the failures we detailed surrounding the battle of Mantinea, will have some success pressuring Athens late in war, precisely because (as with Brasidas) he departs from customary Spartan policies.

Beginning before the outbreak of the Peloponnesian War (circa 478), the Spartan authorities at home were forced to confront their commander, Pausanias. While Pausanias was successful in his military capacity, ably pushing back the Persians, his conduct on campaign cast suspicion on him. Eventually recalled back to the city for his violence, actions more in keeping with a tyrant, Pausanias contributed to the ascendancy of Athenian imperialism Thucydides details in the Pentecontaetia. Those cities liberated by Sparta and Athens during the Persian War initially sought Athenian rule precisely *because* of Pausanias' harsh conduct (1.95.1-4) and the hatred it caused (96.1).

And while Pausanias was indeed recalled to face these accusations, the Spartans only found him guilty of injustices against private individuals, not of the charge he was conspiring with the Persians against the city itself. Thucydides himself states this latter charge was in fact the most evident (95.5); yet the Spartans initially demur. Fearing others might be corrupted in this manner, they instead refuse to send any other citizens out of the city to lead their foreign endeavors across Greece (95.7).

Pausanias does not allow this recall to quell his ambitions, however, going out of Sparta as a private individual to renew his relations with the king of Persia. Thucydides allows us to witness the truth of the most serious charges against Pausanias, that he had sought (and was now again seeking) to rule over all of Greece with the aid of the Persian king (128.3). While this ambition was fueled by the support Pausanias was granted by the leading Persian, it was also due to the great "worth" (*axiōma*) placed upon him among the Greeks for the victory at Plataea over the Persians themselves (in 479 – 1.130.1). After believing himself to be in a position where he could direct Greek affairs as he saw fit, Pausanias further adopts Persian customs and again returns to his violent and harsh treatment of others.[84] Thucydides

84 Cf. Plato, *Republic* 573d2-5.

repeats that it was this violent temperament that led the freed cities of Greece to turn to the Athenians (130).

Pausanias' ambitions, and the manner in which they manifest themselves, break with Spartan customs and way of life. While we have seen instances of harshness by the Spartans for the sake (as they believe) of Sparta, Pausanias' violence is seen by the Spartans as a threat to themselves – it is a striking contrast to the measured way of life the Spartans adopted from early on, a way of life intended to foster (and enforce) a common good by reducing differences between the few and the many (1.6.4). But the honor Pausanias received from his victory at Plataea, although furthering Spartan interests and influence abroad, fueled his own ambitions, ambitions which could not be restrained away from Sparta and which placed the city at risk as he sought to act privately, taking command of it for himself.[85]

In his narration of the Spartans becoming aware of his conduct, Thucydides notes why this is a uniquely Spartan problem – to punish a member of a Spartan first family was difficult and required the most trustworthy of evidence to proceed (132.1). Specifically, the ephors needed evidence against their commander (who was of royal lineage) to exercise their authority over him. Eventually they discover that in seeking to distinguish himself, Pausanias had engraved his own name on a pillar intended to commemorate the cities which had fought with Sparta to defeat the Persians; the Spartans had to correct this pillar to read "Sparta" along with the other cities. It was further discovered that Pausanias was conspiring with the Helots by promising freedom and citizenship if they aided him in rising up against the city, the always present and potential enemy faction within the city posing a danger men such as Pausanias could seek to exploit. Pausanias' actions fairly clearly demonstrated he was acting contrary to, and was contemptuous of, the things established by these laws, and thus the charges were indeed very serious (132.2).

Yet the Spartans, still mistrustful of this abundance of evidence, acted slowly and delayed (132.3-5). The Spartans' customary caution and slowness affects even domestic affairs. Where we noted their suspicion of the Athenians and fear of possible innovation to their laws during the past Helot revolt, even the laws in place directing the ephors to protect the city by guarding against the office of the king (one of the ephors' key functions)

85 Cf. Aristotle, *Politics* 1333b31-35. See also Rahe (2019) pp. 70-73 for other details of this story.

seem ineffective.[86] And when they finally sought his arrest (only after overhearing Pausanias incriminate himself), some ephors nevertheless signaled to him as they approached, allowing him to escape to a temple where he could not be retrieved without the Spartan authorities committing an act of impiety. Thucydides notes that these ephors acted out of "kindness" (*eunoia*) to Pausanias (134.1), unwilling to act against one of their own.

While the Spartan laws attempted to moderate the ruling offices, these laws could not wholly protect the regime. The honor Pausanias received in war could not be satisfied within Sparta, where no one individual could distinguish themselves above all others. But obedience to these laws and education in them, as in all *nomoi* Thucydides presents, did not restrain all ambitions. And the Spartans themselves seem at least partially conscious of this shortcoming, fearing to send Pausanias (and any others) abroad again on a campaign. And while Thucydides is clear that he was in fact guilty of the charges against him, doubts can be raised as to the charges against others blamed by the Spartans for succumbing to bribery or corruption. Pausanias was not the only Spartan to fall under suspicion.

Early in Book Five, Thucydides reminds us that Sparta had two kings. Pleistoanax, King Agis' counterpart, desired peace after the deaths of Brasidas and Cleon (5.16.2-3). Pleistoanax, we recall, had been exiled from Sparta (during hostilities between Sparta and Athens after the Persian War) for advancing toward Attica but failing to invade the countryside nearest to Athens. The opinion of the Spartans (one of their perennial fears) was that he had been bribed (1.114.2, 2.21.1: by Pericles, as Plutarch contends).[87]

Despite the detail in Thucydides' narration of this incident, he does not

86 Pausanias was the guardian (or regent – *epitropos*) of his first cousin, Pleistarchus, who was still a minor and thus could not hold his inherited position as the Spartan king (1.132.1; Herodotus 9.10.2). As Rahe (2019) pp. 13-14 aptly notes: "His success at Plataea [in 479] had given Pausanias a measure of prestige that he would not have attained. But it did not alter the fact that he was not himself a king. He was, in fact, nothing more than a stand-in – destined to be superseded when Pleistarchus came of age – and everyone knew it, including, of course, Pausanias himself." See White (1964) for details on the Agiad, one of the two family lines of Spartan kingship (the other being the Eurypontids). See Rahe (2016) pp. 69-72 for the lineage of each royal house. On the history and sources for Sparta's dyarchy, including its divine sanction, see Millender (2017). On Pausanias versus Spartan authorities at home, see Rahe (2019) pp. 33-52.

87 Speculation among scholars also points to the "bribery" as possibly being nothing more than his youth and inexperience at this time, and thus, he simply made a bad deal with Pericles. See White (1964) pp. 140-41 and Rahe (2019) pp. 225-26.

offer any explicit judgment on the charges against Pleistoanax (as he had in the case of Pausanias).[88] As the son of this shamed commander, the Spartans may have been suspicious of him simply because of his family relationship. The questionable character of these charges against Pleistoanax, though, is also a reminder of the Spartans' earlier blame of Archidamus and, later, Agis. The blame of Agis before Mantinea is in keeping with that of Archidamus at the beginning of the war.[89] Archidamus was accused of weakness, lack of eagerness, and even of siding with Athens (2.18.3). And we suspect this must have been due to his caution in declaring war, weary of potential injustice of breaching the treaty, the same kind of caution Sparta seems to show in allowing for the return of Pleistoanax, despite their suspicions. In all these instances, their kings are blamed for failing to take advantage of potentially significant opportunities in battle and, generally, to victoriously prosecute the war.

Despite this Spartan king's seeming irrelevance to the overall war, Thucydides goes further in detailing Pleistoanax' case: When he was in exile, he built his house inside the precinct of Zeus, sacred ground ensuring he would escape further punishment. The Spartans, in contrast for example to the Athenians at Boeotia, would not attempt to attack him here (5.16.2-3; cf. 4.97-99). However, despite his exile, Pleistoanax was able to restore himself to the kingship at Sparta during the Peloponnesian War. In fact, the Spartans restored Pleistoanax with the same pious customs, including the dances and sacrifices practiced when kings were instituted on the first foundation (*ktizontes*) of Sparta (16.3).[90] Yet this restoration is *itself* accompanied by severe blame, the Spartans believing Pleistoanax had

88 Westlake (1968) p. 94 notes Thucydides' detailed presentation of Pleistoanax despite his lack of importance to the overall war. This would seem to support the view that Thucydides relates these details on a Spartan in the portion of his narrative where he most clearly elaborates that city and its individuals. For background detail on this episode, see Hornblower II pp. 465-67.

89 Cnemus, a Spartan commander, also incites the anger of the Spartans for the loss of a naval battle at Acarnania. While they accuse him of weakness or cowardice, Thucydides' description of the battle (and Sparta's angry response to its result) implies a lack of familiarity with naval maneuvers that allowed the Athenians to attain victory (2.84.3, 85.1-3).

90 This term is used at 1.7, in the Archaeology, in reference to the cities founded during the times of piracy, but before seafaring became more prominent. Sparta's founding, in other words, pre-dates even Thucydides' attempt to portray the foundations of Greek cities as such (1.18).

done so "unlawfully" (*paranomeō*). This new accusation against him (and his brother) was that they had now bribed the prophetess at Delphi to give a favorable response to his political restoration (since the Spartans of course went to consult her). As a result, they further blamed Pleistoanax for every loss befalling them at this time of the war. Let us return to Thucydides' initial statement when relating this incident (5.16.1):

> Pleistoanax [wanted peace] because he was maligned by his enemies about his return from exile, who were always insisting, to the Spartans' misgiving (*enthumia*), that whenever losses came their way, they were to be attributed to his unlawful (*paranomeō*) return.

I have translated this passage in an attempt to retain key terms, notably of *enthumia* as "misgiving." What English translation cannot reveal is the pious nature of this word. None of the available translations bring out a stunning fact: *enthumia* is used here, and only here in Thucydides, and by no other author.[91] Hornblower notes its similarity to the verbal form *enthumios*, which Thucydides uses at 7.50.4: his narration of the eclipse during the Sicilian expedition. Nicias' interpretation of this eclipse (based on the soothsayers) proves, as we will discuss below, disastrous. But despite Nicias' decision, most Athenians "expressed misgivings" (literally: "took to heart" – *enthumion poioumenoi*) about the eclipse and urged the commanders to remain in Sicily (despite the previous resolve to leave immediately). For our purposes, there is an etymological link to another key passage as well: the Spartan expression of guilt (*enthumeomai*) after coming to view themselves as the cause of the first half of the war (7.18).[92] Why does Thucydides digress to relate, in detail, the Pleistoanax incident? And why here?[93]

Thucydides' language seems to provide the hint. This language expresses

91 See Liddell-Scott (1889) p. 263. The term is translated "scruples" by Jowett (1881); "sensitivities" by Mynott (2013) (who notes its rarity and pious overtones); Hobbes (1989) maintains the sense of guilt without directly translating *enthumia*; Crawley (1996) and Lattimore (1998) leave it out. See Hornblower II pp. 462-67. Consider Dodds (1951) pp. 28-63 (including n46, which refers to 5.16.1) on what he describes as "guilt-culture."

92 Cf. Hornblower III pp. 573-74 where 5.16.1 is referenced. With *enthum-* words at 7.18.2 and 7.50.4, Hornblower III p. 642 notes these words are a part of a "powerful and interesting group."

93 Gomme III p. 664 also asks why Thucydides' narrative of Pleistoanax is placed here, rather than, in keeping with chronology, in Book Three.

a pious guilt: If pious misgivings are internalized, transformed from simply the outward commands of laws and customs, actions proceeding from dictates of piety do not originate in calculated self-interest, or even with a view to one's apparent good. Rather, it is through this internalization that human motives become, or can be understood as being, compelling. Contrary to the Athenian thesis, which designates human fears, passions, and hopes as natural necessities of the human being (1.76, 5.105), Thucydides presents the human condition (1.22.4), comprised of both our nature (*physis*) and the laws or customs (*nomoi*) that mold this nature, as difficult to overcome.

This is not to deny glimmers of realization among some Spartans. We are reminded of Archidamus' hesitation in undertaking the war, a hesitation borne out of fear of the war's injustice (1.84.2). And here, in the story of Pleistoanax, the Spartans appear to implicitly recognize the potential misuse of piety for the private ends of a Spartan individual; yet it seems they cannot tear themselves away from the priestess' prediction – they will suffer famine, i.e., divine punishment, as a result of *not* restoring Pleistoanax, their hereditary king (5.16.2). The Spartans seem almost compelled to obey such commands despite their suspicion, restoring him with the most pious customs yet blaming him nonetheless. And in blaming Pleistoanax, are they not in fact blaming themselves for being unable to act outside of these customs when it may seem prudent to do so, torn between committing an impious act and allowing one of their own to violate a most sacred matter, the hereditary office of the king?

The passage points to Sparta's domestic, internal politics and reminds us that the kings hold office by birth. Given its link with 7.50.4 (the eclipse during the Sicilian expedition), "natural" disasters such as earthquakes and plagues are brought together with Spartan piety. Are we to think, therefore, of the Athenians as well, and Pericles being blamed for conditions in Athens, affected as they were by both the plague (exacerbated by earthquakes at the time – 2.59.2) as well as the Spartan destruction of the countryside in Attica, the land outside the city that Pericles' policies forced rural Athenians to leave? Sparta's domestic situation, which as we have seen Thucydides details through the narrative of Mantinea and the other Spartan king, Agis, is introduced as a theme of Book Five. It is in this very passage introducing Pleistoanax that Thucydides has noted Brasidas, Cleon, and Nicias wanted peace, for their own individual reasons.[94] Brasidas, despite his successes, also finds himself at odds with the Spartan authorities at home who were only aiming at the return of the men from Pylos and a cessation to hostilities, if not a treaty to end the war entirely.

As for Pleistoanax's motives, as Thucydides presents them at 5.16.1, who precisely are his "enemies"? The hereditary king had to contend both with the other royal house, and also with the ephors, an elected body that sought at times to constrain both kings' authority. After all, it is Archidamus that advised against the war, while Sthenelaidas won the vote of the Spartans for it. Their policy preferences were at odds. Even in Sparta, the city is never wholly unified; and the tensions within the regime are laid bare through the pressures of the Peloponnesian War. Pressures of a great war compelled Sparta to act; but these actions did not always accord to the good of Sparta, but to its harm. And far from seeking to rule other cities, they strove to avoid it, whether this was strategically prudent or not.[95] Fundamental to Thucydides' account of Sparta, then, is the coming apart of the city from within, and it is the divide over conduct of foreign policy that arises as a repeated source of tension.[96]

Kings are sons of Zeus, as the priestess at Delphi reminds the Spartans

94 Hornblower II p. 462, citing Ste. Croix (1972) p. 153 and Kallet (1993) pp. 179-80, notes that "the motives given by Th. in this para. are purely personal." This passage, 5.16.1, has been a rather contested one, scholars wanting to delete or emend Thucydides' text. See Gomme III pp. 661-62 and Hornblower II pp. 462-63. But the main reason for desiring emendation is due to Thucydides' argument: that in *each* city there was a battle for political power, scholars refusing to believe this was the case *in Sparta*. Yet Thucydides states that Pleistoanax and Nicias were "more eager than ever" (*pollō dē mallon prouthumounto*) to make "peace" (*eirēnē*) and also provides the individual motives of each statesman. Why we should be surprised by Pleistoanax's desire for peace is unclear to me (aside from him being introduced rather abruptly: see Hornblower II p. 463). After all, we have already witnessed Spartan hesitancy with Archidamus, and the narrative of Brasidas (as we will detail in Chapter Four) highlights his un-Spartan willingness to aggressively prosecute the war. Pleistoanax's desire for peace is thus a reminder of the uniqueness of Brasidas, along with Thucydides now highlighting, as I have argued, the domestic elements of each city affecting their foreign policy. This includes tensions within Sparta by those seeking to direct it. That Thucydides then digresses on Sparta, in particular, signals that the Spartan narrative is the centerpiece of Book Five.

95 The moderate men at Athens (who we may recall in this context where Cleon is mentioned) sought to balance victory in war with ridding themselves of Cleon's poisonous popularity at home (4.28.5).

96 See Chapter Four note 78 and context.

on their consultations of her.[97] Despite the accusations against Pleistoanax, accusations apparently powerful enough for him to remain in exile for over 18 years, he is not only returned from exile; his return is a return to the very foundations of the city itself.[98] Fear, as we have observed, manifests as slowness, caution, and reserve, the very characteristics inculcated by Sparta. Yet as Thucydides implies here, the source of Sparta's greatest fear is the gods. Is this fear compelling in the same manner in which their fear of the Athenian empire compelled them to war? Is fear of the gods, of being guilty of an injustice, not a motive for Spartan action, a necessity *for them*? Is this not as much a compulsion for the Spartans as fear of the Persians compelled the Athenians to acquire, hold, and expand their empire? After all, the very foundations of Sparta itself rest on, and remind Spartans of, their divinely sanctioned regime, their very way of life.

This habitual caution and risk-aversion even manifests itself among the best of the Spartans, men such as Archidamus. During the attack on Attica early in the war, that led to accusations against him, the Spartans were seeking a "quick" (*tachos*) advance for the sake of harming the Athenian countryside (2.18.4). But Archidamus' delay was not simply due to his caution, nor any corrupt intent to aid the Athenians. Thucydides notes that Archidamus had *reasons* for delaying at Oenoe and later at Acharnae; he believed the Athenians would not let their land be wasted and therefore waited for them to come out from the city to defend it; and Thucydides himself confirms that Archidamus *was* correct (20.1-2, 21.2-3). Pericles incites the Athenian demos' anger and is blamed for his policies, the Athenians realizing just how close the Spartans were to their city. Archidamus' strategy forced the Athenians to watch while the Spartans destroyed their homeland.

Spartan blame of their kings and commanders for poor policy decisions, bribery, and weakness is based on an inconsistency in the Spartans' own understanding of themselves. While the laws of Sparta could not restrain a man of the ambition of Pausanias, those laws at the same time failed to cultivate daring akin to the best of the Athenians, a *need* for which

---

97 For a discussion of oracles in Greek politics, see Parker (1985). On Delphi and Lycurgus, see Chrimes (1949) pp. 475-89.

98 In the Archaeology, Thucydides observed that the older regimes were "hereditary kingships" (*patrikai basileiai* – 1.13.1). On the founding of Sparta, see Malkin (1994) p. 15.

the Spartans implicitly yet unknowingly acknowledge in their criticisms of their own kings. And near the end of the war, Thucydides reminds us (again) both that the Spartans typically seek peace and that a capable Spartan must act apart from Sparta to serve Sparta.

Following the Athenians' disastrous defeat in Sicily, Book Eight opens with the Spartans hoping for a quick and noble ending to the war, leaving them in secure hegemony of Greece. For the Spartans did not desire a war such as the Peloponnesian War, nor did their education and regime prepare them for it. Thucydides states, for example, that they were "compelled" to adopt a navy (*anankē* – 8.2.3). After Athens' defeat in Sicily, however, they had good hope for this "noble end" (*kalōs teleutēsantos* – 2.4). But, yet again, the Spartans are all too ready to cease prosecuting the war before it is complete; for Thucydides in this context notes that the Athenians, despite their Sicilian defeat, were again preparing themselves for war (4, 15.1-2). Agis, Sparta's king, is left to act; but he arranges matters differently here than in Book Five.

Perhaps due to his enmity with Alcibiades (12.2), and despite the protests of Sparta's allies, Agis compels the Peloponnesians to provide money for a fleet and brings them into alliance with Sparta (3.1).[99] And when Euboea and others seek to revolt from Athens, Thucydides notes emphatically that Agis himself sets this in motion and all of it was done *without* authority from home (5.3): Agis had the "power" (*dynamis*) to send out troops and levy money and men.[100] The result is Sparta's allies obeyed him more than Sparta itself; he now showed himself to be feared. Before the near battle at Argos in Book Five, Agis had received the blame of both the army and the Spartans at home (5.60.4, 63.1). But here, in acting on his own authority, he is able to secure allies (via compulsion), expand the Spartans' overall forces, as well as incite revolts among Athens' subject cities. It was Brasidas who also employed this strategy, leading the Athenians to agree to a truce

99 One of Archidamus' main policy objections to going to war with Athens was due to Sparta's monetary deficiency to carry on such a war (1.83.2-3).

100 Hornblower III p. 763: "The negative formulation…is emphatic, and is the prelude to a narrative which is more forthcoming about division inside the Spartan elite than anything since 5.16." Is it perhaps not a prelude, but rather, a culmination? Details of the tensions within Sparta were already revealed with Sthenelaidas securing a vote for war (contra Archidamus' advice), Xenares and the war party during Brasidas' campaigns, the Mantinea campaign and Agis' controversial generalship, and later, with the ascent of Gylippus (to be discussed in the Nicias' narrative in Chapter Four).

and subsequent alliance after the first ten years of the war. And as there, so here, Agis is only able to do this apart from, and despite, his city; thus, in Book Eight, Thucydides' Spartan narrative begins to treat Spartan individuals, and the city itself, as distinct (8.8.2). When the Corinthians delay accompanying Agis and his allies on an expedition to Chios because they are celebrating a festival, Agis proposes that he undertake the expedition himself as a private action (9.1). It is Agis that holds Decelea at the time the Athenians also lose Euboea to the Peloponnesians, a loss Thucydides notes as especially troubling precisely because Attica was now, finally we might add, held by the Spartans (95.2).

Agis' newfound readiness for war first arises, however, only after Thucydides notes that the Spartans no longer felt guilt for breaching the treaty and beginning the war (7.18.3, 19.1).[101] And this initiative, along with the power he holds for himself, follows on Thucydides' statement that the Spartans believed Athens to be on the brink of defeat and thus Sparta hoped the war would soon be over (8.8.2). Lastly, the following summer as Agis is holding Decelea and the Four Hundred in Athens sue for peace (70.2), he first rejects any peace agreement, hoping either that the appearance of the Spartan force would frighten the Athenians into surrendering, or that the city might surrender due to the internal discord happening at that time. Agis wants to take Athens without encountering any risks. But the city remains calm, and the Athenians only engage against a small number of Agis' men; thus, when the Four Hundred again sue for peace, Agis now agrees and sends envoys to Sparta to negotiate, using his reputation to pursue Sparta's interests (71). His caution in the first part of the war gives way to his forceful prosecution after Athens' official breach of the treaty and alliance between the two. The justice of Sparta's cause was initially as important for Agis as it was for the city, for the Spartan psyche; Agis is still fundamentally Spartan.

101 "...the Spartans came to believe that the very same transgression [*paranomēma*], for which they had previously been guilty [*hamartanō*], had turned around [*periestanai*] to the Athenians, and therefore were eager [*prothumos*] for the war" (7.18.3 – my translation). This is a loaded passage: Hornblower III pp. 573-75 notes that Thucydides both recalls earlier episodes of his narrative (which, I would add, forces the reader to look back) and uses language revealing of the Spartan point of view. "Transgression" maintains the pious overtones of the Greek. "Turned around" expresses the change in the war, but especially the complete reversal, according to the Spartan view, of their prospects, being now uncharacteristically "eager" for war. Spartan action, in other words, follows on Spartan morale.

If this is the case, Thucydides' narrative of Agis, a Spartan king, provides insights into his view of Spartan psychology. Despite being raised, as it were, in the Spartan cave, the contrast between Book Five and Eight is notable: Agis *begins* to separate himself from his city and pursue policies (i.e., troops and money) advantageous to it, policies that could have aided Spartan interests and aims earlier in the war. Agis is portrayed by Thucydides as demonstrative of Spartan justice, yet eventually led to confront war's necessities and thus compelled to act apart from the restrictions placed on him by the city, for the city's own military success. It may also, however, be for his own ends; although Thucydides gives no explicit statement of Agis' possible motives, he signals as much by mentioning his enmity towards Alcibiades (8.12.2), suggesting the seed for the growth of private interest, interests apart from Sparta's perceived or true interests as a city.

If Agis was ultimately directed by such interests or believed Sparta's cause was now justified in prosecuting the war (or both), we notice the result is the same – only now does a Spartan king utilize the means necessary to successfully lead a full-scale Spartan war effort. Thucydides' account of Sparta reveals not simply the shortcomings of Spartan law, but the changes to a Sparta now compelled to face the necessities of a foreign war. The necessity to innovate in the art of war, to accommodate for the demands required for victory, leads to innovations directly bearing on the structure of their regime. We are thus reminded of the Spartans' decision with Brasidas (at the end of Book Four) – his successes in the war led, not to a new law (as in the case of Agis), but to the Spartans disobeying one of their own laws (4.132.3). And in this case, the disregard of their law was for the sake of maintaining authority over cities newly liberated by Brasidas. With both Agis and Brasidas, Thucydides hints at what would be required for the Spartans to truly challenge the Athenians. Thucydides also clearly states that with more "daring" the Spartans could have sailed into the Piraeus late in the war, initiating strategic possibilities that would have led, one way or another, to Sparta and its allies possessing the whole Athenian empire (8.96.4).

Sparta will ultimately fail, strictly speaking, to defeat Athens on their own. More than this, we cannot fail to notice that its peculiar power, its regime, did change, unable to maintain strict control over itself when confronted with a war of such a scale. What surprises us even more, though, are the causes for Spartan failure: oaths, treaties, earthquakes, sacrifices, and festivals have kept the Spartans at home.[102]

---

102 Balot (2015) pp. 17-35, in reviewing Orwin's (1994) Thucydides, takes issue with his account of necessity, particularly as it relates to human nature – whether we are compelled by the natural tendencies inherent in being human or whether we have agency over our own actions; this also includes pious motives as they relate to our understanding of necessity. On Balot's view, Orwin presents human nature as compelling (especially in the case of Diodotus). Drawing on Aristotle, Balot argues instead that: "If our character in general is subject to self-formation through our own habitual practices, then, as Aristotle argues, our characters, too, along with our actions, are voluntary: they are up to us, provided that they are chosen by us in awareness of the relevant circumstances" (30). Yet I would suggest that there could be limits on that formation. Practicing good things, for the sake of overcoming or "auditing" our apparent good, as Balot argues, is hindered (in the case of Sparta, severely hindered) by *nomoi* – the laws and customs of the city. This is Plato's teaching with his cave, just how *restrictive* the cave can be in forming our notion of the good. Thus, while Balot is correct in arguing that change and growth are possible for human beings – and that this is indeed central to Thucydides' own goal of educating a reader's understanding of the human good – this does not lead, it seems to me, to the conclusion that it may be achieved by most people, most of the time. Balot does not distinguish what Plato's Socrates regularly distinguishes – the differing natures, and thus differing potential, of his interlocutors (a distinction Thucydides also apprises himself of – 1.22.4, 138.3), thereby denying natural and conventional limitations bearing on the human condition. While Thucydides does not endorse the Athenian thesis as his characters state it, he does present fears, hopes, and miscalculations all leading human beings astray in choosing their own good, and politically, in pursuing objectively best policies given particular political circumstances (evidenced notably by Spartan piety). Nor can I agree on a related issue: namely, that "Athenian piety differed from Spartan piety in at least a single important respect: that the Athenians, unlike the Spartans, accepted responsibility even for acts that they committed under life-threatening duress" (24). The Spartans blame themselves for the war, despite Thucydides apparently exculpating them (1.23.5-6; curiously, Balot later acknowledges this fact). And this blame, as we have noted, manifests itself in grave guilt for their breach of the treaty, thereby breaking solemnly sworn oaths they had taken with the Athenians (7.18). To be sure, the Spartans *do* attempt to justify their failure at Pylos by treating the men killed as victims of bad luck (when provoked by the enemy – 4.40.2). But Thucydides never presents the Spartans as convinced by their own attempt – they sue for peace with Athens precisely because such a defeat signals to them their own failure, a failure they cannot help but view in moral terms, seeking as they do to be good, virtuous men (4.18.2, 19.2). Balot points to Thucydides' view of the Athenian thesis as "the quintessential sign of Athenian dishonesty" and, similarly, "the Spartans, too, like the imperial Athenians, show themselves to be dishonest and hypocritical when it comes to the "greatest things."" Yet this language of dishonesty (Balot concluding his essay in promoting honesty as a "cardinal element of the good life") attributes the moral confusions and inconsistencies of the cities (and individuals) to a conscious hypocrisy, implying both Spartans and Athenians could have overcome this dishonesty

Thucydides' critique of Sparta is directed not only towards the city acting as a whole, but against Spartan individuals, against the men themselves. Spartan moderation, originating in the laws and regime of the city itself, its constitution, imparts a distinct character to the citizens. And this moderation leaves most Spartans either constrained by the weaknesses of their education or ineffectual for the city because their ambition strays from it. What we have seen of the Spartans thus far is nothing exceptional – Pausanias' ambitions do not materialize, Agis' vigor for war still gives way to caution, and even if Pleistoanax bribed the Delphic priestess, he only did so to restore himself in Sparta from the initial (and doubtful) bribery charges. Pleistoanax' exile and restoration might appear comical in light of Alcibiades' exile and restoration, given the severity of the latter's charges and potential punishment. For Thucydides, what makes Sparta unique as a city is its psychological and moral characteristics. The cave matters; yet we immediately note that these are not exclusively the preserve of Spartan citizens (consider, for example, the Athenian demos), nor are the Spartans a homogenous group. Beyond the Spartan kings, Thucydides highlights three characters to illuminate the Spartans and the "Spartan" type, as well as revealing more clearly than anywhere else his praise for, and critique of, the "Spartan" element in man-made *nomoi* and in human psychology.

---

and acted otherwise. To know whether this is possible, we would need to answer the question of the degree to which the human condition (constrained by both *physis* and *nomos*) affords the pursuit for, and attainment of, the highest good.

Chapter Four

Spartan Characters

In signaling the characteristics of the "Spartan" and "Athenian" early in the war (via the Corinthians' speech – 1.68-71, among other instances), Thucydides establishes an initial dichotomy for understanding the actions of the principal participants in the war. But more than this: Thucydides signals to his readers that the *permanence* of his account requires using the evidence he has provided to construct our own psychological portraits of what drives the human condition.

Of Thucydides' "characters" three recommend themselves for our consideration of Spartan psychology. First is the city of Melos and its spokesmen, whose speeches and actions demonstrate their unwavering commitment to justice, kinship, and the gods. No other city in Thucydides' account of the war states as directly their belief in the power of divine justice. Second is Nicias, an Athenian commander eulogized by Thucydides, but who prosecutes the war in a Spartan manner, with caution, pious fear, and circumspection. Third is Brasidas, Sparta's most worthy commander, who rises through the ranks of the Spartan army and does significant harm to Athens' interests under the banner of liberating subject cities from their empire. Brasidas is one of the most highly praised individuals in Thucydides' entire account, bearing comparison to other commanders and to the city he represents. Educated in the Spartan cave, Brasidas is nonetheless marked by his eagerness and daring, his vigorous prosecution of Sparta's war of liberation, and despite or because of these un-Spartan traits, is their most successful commander. Working through each of these three characters, Thucydides' initial dichotomy starts to betray further distinctions and shades. The Melians, Nicias, and Brasidas are hardly the same men; yet they all share something of the "Spartan." Thucydides' view of Sparta as a city, and as a psychological study, is only complete through a consideration of these three different manifestations of the Spartan view.

The Melians: Divine Justice and Kinship

As brutal, uncompromising, unflinching, unforgiving the power politics of Athenian imperialism may appear, Thucydides' articulation of it in the Melian Dialogue, for our purposes, is secondary to the *reaction* of the Melians. The Melians are "the most conspicuous spokesmen for justice in Thucydides."[1] Their dialogue with the Athenians is of course significant for eliciting the boldest and most frank statement of Athenian imperialism in Thucydides' account, especially striking when set against the surprisingly moral tone of the Melians.[2] While the Athenian thesis can obscure moral motives, as it does in the easy rejection of Spartan righteousness, this dialogue offers the strongest contrast, as the Athenians themselves imply, of Sparta and Athens. But the infamy of the Dialogue lay in its result: the Melians' unwavering belief that the justice of their cause will allow them to persevere against the significantly stronger Athenians leads not to their victory, but to their demise.[3] The Melian Dialogue is therefore *the* essential contest of the Athenian thesis with the Spartan view of the war since the Melians take the Spartan view to its utmost conclusion – hope in the gods and trust in the just actions of their own kin to secure the Melians' own self-interest. Or in terms the Melians would understand: gods are guarantors of justice and the Melians are just; kinship is an unbreakable bond and the Spartans are kin.

But the Melians' moral psychology reveals as much about the Athenians' own as it does of themselves – they are not the rational calculators, weighers of necessity, and tough realists they present themselves as, and as they seek to be. Diodotus' assessment of hope and trust is on display here and thus confirms a key difference between his thought and theirs – an ability to see the hold these affections have on human beings as they reason through even the seemingly unavoidable necessities of survival and self-preservation. Viewing the Dialogue in this way, "Spartan" psychology, the moral and religious expectations of human beings, clearly expand beyond that original Athens-Sparta dichotomy with which Thucydides began.

1 Bruell (1974) p. 15.

2 The Melian Dialogue, having taken place on a rather far off island, has led to speculation that it is entirely Thucydides' invention. See Hudson-Williams (1950) pp. 166-69, Romilly (1963) p. 297. For those critical of denying its historicity, see Amit (1968) pp. 225-28, Kagan (1981) pp. 149-51, Orwin (1994) pp. 99-100, Seaman (1997) pp. 409-11.

3 Disgust at the Athenians is most forcefully expressed by Grote (1851) p. 156.

As the Melian Dialogue is the only speech of its kind in Thucydides' text, it is easy to ignore the context. Even if Book Five was filled with speeches, it would be a striking departure. But given the Spartan focus in Book Five, along with long passages of treaty terms, battles, and the detailed narration of this nominal peace, this exchange stands out all the more. Nor can we ignore that Book Five began with the Athenians' purification of Delos, mentioned again by Thucydides (5.1; cf. 1.8.1, 3.104.1-2, 8.108.4-5). Lost in interpretations of the Dialogue are its unparalleled observations on piety, on the possibility of divine justice. In fact, the contribution the Melian Dialogue adds to the Athenian thesis, and its opposite, is precisely its treatment of the issue of the gods (or "the divine").

While the envoys at Athens, Diodotus, and others (notably, Hermocrates in Book Four) had expressed versions of that thesis, as well as observations on justice versus necessity, the Melian Dialogue brings the gods out into the open. And by the gods, we mean here the pious, sacred or holy, the divine, and thus the question of virtue itself: What do the gods expect of human beings? And if human beings act as they are instructed by the gods, what can they expect in return? For while all notions of justice deal with reward and punishment for just or unjust actions, the Melian Dialogue is not simply focused on breaches of treaties or the laws of this or that city; it deals with requirements for, and limits placed upon, the pious individual himself.

Second, the differing views of the Spartans, the character of the Spartans as allies and combatants, is itself a focal point of debate between the Athenians and Melians – the last third of the debate focuses on Spartan character. Indeed, as Hornblower correctly notes, the structure of the Dialogue is, broadly, Athenians/gods/Spartans. After all, the Athenian thesis stated here does not prove convincing to the Melians, and the Melians reveal a decidedly Spartan view of the world.[4]

Scholarly debate still surrounds the question of whether the Athenians at Melos articulate a version of the Athenian thesis differing from that of other Athenian speeches Thucydides presents. Some contend the Athenians at Melos present a much harsher version of their thesis, evidence

4 See Hornblower's introduction to the Melian Dialogue (III pp. 216-25). Generally, scholars have approached the Melian Dialogue as Thucydides' study of imperialism and empire. For example, Andrewes (1960). See also Johnson Bagby (1995) on the use of Thucydides by realism and neorealism, with notable reliance on the Melian Dialogue as evidence of Thucydides' own views.

Athens has succumbed to a moral decline, harming any justified claim to their empire.[5] For example, while the Athenians at Sparta before the war claimed they rule with justice, or a certain measure of restraint, and are therefore worthy of their rule (1.76.3-4), at Melos no such justifications seem to be advanced; in fact, such speech is criticized as merely "noble words" not worth mentioning (5.89). Additionally, the result of the discussion at Melos is the slaughter and enslavement of its citizens (along with Athenian colonization), while at Mytilene (by comparison) the Athenians spare all but those who initiated the revolt from Athens.

Other scholars, however, argue there is no fundamental change in the Athenian thesis; rather, the Athenians at Melos differ in tone and in what they explicitly state, but this can be attributed to the specific situation in which this speech is given – the Athenians at Sparta state their view of empire before the Spartans and their allies; later, Euphemus' appeal to Athenian fear finds expression at a moment when the Athenians are in a less than favorable position (6.83.3-4).[6] Further, the salvation of the Mytilenians requires the speech of Diodotus, an individual in Thucydides who is noted by nearly all scholars as singularly rare. Besides, even Diodotus' amazing speech barely saves Mytilene (the second vote being extremely close – 3.49.1). And lastly, the Athenians at Melos could not claim to rule justly or with measure or appeal to their worthiness to rule for precisely the reason that they had prohibited the Melians from invoking such moral claims.

Most notable for our interest in the Athenian thesis (and its contrast to the Melians' view of justice), however, is that its statement here did not anticipate the outcome – the Athenians are genuinely surprised at the Melians' decision (5.113), expecting only the many, the people, would be susceptible to what the Athenians see as the Melian ambassadors' delusion (85). But this Athenian failure to understand their staunch refusal to submit is of importance for our consideration of Sparta because it is in keeping with their failure to understand the Spartans as well.[7] While the Athenians correctly predict Sparta will not intervene to aid Melos, they fail to notice

5 Cornford (1907) pp. 182-85, Romilly (1963) pp. 286-90, Pouncey (1980) p. 92, Cogan (1981) pp. 92-93. However, cf. Johnson Bagby (1995) p. 178.

6 Bruell (1974) p. 13, (1981) p. 28; Connor (1984) pp. 151-53; Bolotin (1987) p. 14; Forde (1989) p. 51 n46; Orwin (1994) pp. 111, 113-14; Ahrensdorf (1997) pp. 236-37.

7 Cf. Machiavelli, *Florentine Histories* I.10.

the revelation of their own self-deception in their proud assessment of both the Spartans and the divine. Nor are they aware that their critique of the Spartans, the inseparability of Spartan justice from Spartan interest (which the Athenians qualifiedly praise), reminds us again of the tension between an imperial foreign policy and domestic, civic virtues.

As for the Melians, they will place their city in the hands of fortune, determined as it is by the justice and injustice of a city. The Athenians are the unjust attacking a just and neutral city, Melos being a colony of Sparta, yet not providing any material support nor having been involved to this stage in the Peloponnesian War.

The Athenians

The Melians begin by proposing a discussion between their leading men and the Athenians' own (5.84.3). The Athenians concur precisely so both sides may be frank with one another. To speak instead before the people is to resort to arguments merely persuasive, i.e., not true in whole or in part. By speaking only with the leading men, the Athenians imply both sides need no such arguments (85). But this Athenian expectation is disappointed.

The Melians object, not to a discussion amongst only the few, but that the Athenians have arrived in force. The negotiations appear dubious – the only possible outcome being war or slavery (86). The Melians' basis for this claim is notable: If they cannot convince the Athenians of the justice (*dikaion*) of their cause, they will refuse to submit; if they surrender, slavery (*douleia*). But as the Athenians reply, the only issue should be Melos' immediate "safety" (*sōtēria* – 87). Discussion of terms with the Athenians should proceed based on the obvious threat and what can be done to avoid that threat. The Melians concede as much. But since the Melians have already alluded to the fact that justice matters, it becomes clear they do not truly believe the only issue is their safety, or that safety may in fact be secured through other means.

The Athenians, sensing the psychological turmoil the Melians hint at, frankly state they will not offer "noble words" (*onōmatōn kalōn*) to support their right to empire. Noble words are claims about justice or morality and *all* such claims have no place, justice only being a question among equals and clearly Melos and Athens are not equals. The Athenians immediately allude, however, to precisely such arguments – a right (*dikaion*) to empire based on their defeat of the Persians which freed all Greeks from that war (89); and the fact that Melos is a colony of Sparta and thus could be construed as their enemies. The Melians, for their part, should not claim they have maintained neutrality, nor that they have committed no wrongs against Athens. Rather, in cases of obvious inequality, the strong exact what they can (as much as they can) and the weak yield (*synchōreō*).[8]

Despite denying justice has any place in an Athens-Melos negotiation, these remarks taken together imply both that Melos deserves to be conquered because they are a colony of Sparta *and* that the Athenians deserve their empire because they were left to finish the war against Persia. Despite dismissing justice, the Athenians cannot help but mentioning what they deserve. In the very instance they prompt the Melians only to concentrate on safety, Thucydides compels us to question whether the Athenians soberly contemplate their city's motives (and interests), apart from moral considerations.

Yet, as noted, scholars have begun to notice (contra Thucydidean "realism") that the Athenians do not claim "might makes right."[9] Athens' strength does not render their actions in attacking Melos as just; rather, justice is not a consideration because Melos lacks the strength from which to counter any conditions Athens seeks. Justice is a consideration among equals because justice's power lies in the strength of each city to compel the other. After Sparta's defeat at Sphacteria and Athens' loss of Amphipolis, neither city had sufficient strength to threaten the other by use of a compelling force which could not be matched, and thus used as a counterthreat; instead, both cities sought a treaty to establish a period of peace (the Peace of Nicias – 5.16, 46).

8 Mynott (2013) critiques Crawley's (1996) famous (and often quoted) translation: "the strong do what they can and the weak suffer what they must." But Mynott's "accept" in place of "suffer" is, in my view, too weak. The verb *synchōreō* means "to yield or make way," retaining the notion of submitting to superior power without necessarily accepting it (Liddell Scott [1889] p. 756). In the Pentecontaetia, Thucydides makes clear that some cities submitted to Athens willingly, but this soon led to others becoming part of the Athenian empire who did not (1.98.4-99.3).

9 The Athenian arguments, and their tone, have of course given rise to the interpretation that "might makes right." More and more, commentators and translators have noted that this is simply not the case. See Romilly (1963) pp. 299-300, Bolotin (1987) p. 18, Orwin (1994) p. 99. Mynott's (2013) recent translation of the text also corrects this misinterpretation.

Yet, as the Melians demonstrate, expectations of justice are not merely rooted in the recognition of necessity's compelling power. The Melians would speak of justice if they could; and they attempt to. Seemingly turning to expediency, they argue the common good of Melos and Athens involves justice – if the Athenian empire should fall, others would exact the worst revenge upon an Athens that itself rejected justice. Issues of justice will arise for Athens once they are in a position of weakness. Here the Melians argue the Athenians should consider *their* safety, their future safety, since revenge will be taken upon them.[10] This is in disregard of the Athenians' earlier remark that the Melians should not consider the future, but only their immediate safety. By presupposing the Athenian assault on Melos is unjust, arguing instead that the Athenians may commit acts answered later with acts of revenge, the Melians are again neglecting the current threat (90). The apparently immoral character of the Athenian attack is the Melians' true focus.

The Athenians do not even respond to this warning of revenge; they only indicate they are willing to take risks for the sake of their empire. In fact, the Athenians hint that they do not wholly believe their empire will decline ("*if* it should end" – 91; emphasis added).[11] And in response to the Melians' claim of a common good between the two cities, the Athenians offer a contrasting account of the interest of each – the conquest of Melos is in the interest of the Athenian empire, and the safety of Melos is in the interest of Melos. The preservation of Melos is the *true* common good, preserving Melos from destruction while adding another city to the Athenian empire.[12] But here we are reminded of a flaw with the Athenian thesis: Melos – a small island out of strategic distance from either the Peloponnesus

10 Thucydides' Athenian narrative has long been considered tragic. Consider Cornford (1907) and Macleod (1983) pp. 140-58. All scholars must weigh Athens' fall, notably if it is foreseen and predicted by the Melians' remark here. This consideration, however, takes one outside of the Dialogue itself and brings one back to the causes of the Peloponnesian War, and we could note, of war generally. Answers require interpretation of Thucydides as a whole. Certainly, the tragic view is closer to the Melians and the Spartans and is a question we will return to with Nicias.

11 This reminds us of Pericles' claim that all things by nature decline (2.64.3). Yet Pericles also argued for the Athenian empire bestowing everlasting glory on those who served the city's own glory. Pericles and the Athenians appear confused about both imperialism and nature, their "lifespan" we might say, pointing to a belief that glorious deeds overcome what we perceive as the regular order of nature.

12 Not as beautiful as Sicily (6.31.3), but an addition nonetheless.

or Sicily, whose resources cannot be significant enough to influence the Athenian navy, and moreover, who have been neutral to this point in the war, more than sixteen years along – does not seem to serve Athens' interests.[13]

Of more immediate significance, though, is the Melians' response, asking how it is as useful *for them* to serve Athens as it is for Athens to rule. The Athenians offer no justifying reply: submission ensures Melos not suffer a worse fate; the city is of no benefit to them in this case, Athens' interest being an extension of their empire. The Athenians deny Melos' continued neutrality because their failure to reduce the island would be taken by their subjects as a sign of weakness: perception of their power matters, perhaps especially in light of the Brasidas-led revolts pressing Athens to agree to peace with Sparta (97). Besides, Athens extracts tribute in money and ships from their allies and, assuming Melos has something to contribute in this regard, this concession has some use. Either way, strength is the only means by which one can live independent of Athens, thus Athens' subject cities will believe those who live autonomously to have resisted the Athenians. The security of the Athenian empire is strengthened by the subjugation of Melos because it signals to those other subjects that no city (especially islanders, as the Athenians note) can escape the reaches of their empire (99). And Melos' weakness is additional proof of Athens' strength, this weakness being not less significant but more. For why should Athens fail to conquer so weak a city?

Questions arise, however, as to the soundness of this argument. The Athenians contend that failure to subjugate Melos will be interpreted as weakness, harming Athens. But the Peloponnesian War's outbreak was caused by the significantly stronger Sparta (in comparison to Melos) and

---

13 Andrewes (1960) pp. 1-2 speculates on possible causes for the invasion noting, however, that we lack clear evidence for a precipitating event. Seaman (1997) pp. 392-93 rejects the notion of an antecedent cause, emphasizing instead (I believe correctly) that the Athenian reference to wrongdoing early in the debate (5.89) is a rejection of the subject of justice, not an implication of previous Melian injustice. Pouncey (1980) pp. 96-97 argues that the Athenian claim of conquering Melos due to fear is an example of the Athenians smuggling in "fair words" (despite their previous prohibition against it). Orwin (1994) seems to argue both that Athens feared their subjects and possible revolts (pp. 101-102), and also that the Athenians conquer Melos "because it is there" (p. 116). He ultimately sides with the latter view that the strong expand to (or beyond) the limits of their empire, perhaps without sound consideration of these limits.

its allies being fearful of Athens' continued encroachments. The Athenian empire, in other words, was *already* sufficiently feared; their subjugation of Melos does not add to this fear. And even the revolts of their subject cities were only possible with the support of Sparta, or rather, the tremendous and unforeseen successes of the very un-Spartan Brasidas. Athens' strength is unquestionable. Perhaps not surprisingly then the Athenians' extension of empire, in light of Melos, appears limitless in character, does not shore up revolts that have already begun, nor is in keeping with their interests. Not compulsions such as fear, but honor (and profit) drive Athenian imperialism. The Athenian thesis is certainly correct that these are human motives; but for the Melians (and Spartans) such motives fail to excuse (cf. 1.86).

The Melians have failed in their attempt to locate a common good. The good of each city is at odds with one another and thus no arrangement between the two could serve the interests of each, given the Melians' rejection of being subjected to the empire. To be subjected to Athens, however mild the terms, is to lose their autonomy. Failing to mount a defense of their city, the Melians argue, would be base and cowardly because such failure would not allow them to live freely. Melos should be willing to venture risks for their freedom since the Athenians themselves risk much to retain their empire (5.100). In setting up freedom as their goal, as their ultimate good, the Melians signal what will be their fundamental refusal to acquiesce to terms.

For the Athenians, though, refusing to acquiesce would not be to deliberate "moderately" (*sōphronōs* – 5.101). Honor and shame, they concede, do exist, but like justice only amongst equals. No shame would fall on Melos for agreeing to what the Athenians will later refer to (twice) as the "measured" (*metrios*) terms of subjugation, terms that would of course include what should be their primary concern: their preservation (111.4). The Athenians thereby leave open the door for honor and shame to play a role in the action of cities, moral strivings beyond, if not inimical, to safety. For even if honor is a "compulsion" along with self-preservation, as the Athenians themselves argue, it may only be pursued prudently (cf. 8.27.2-3). The Athenians of the Melian Dialogue suddenly come to light as preachers of *sōphrosynē*. Herein lies a problem: No one reading Thucydides will overlook the sequel to the Melian Dialogue, the Sicilian expedition. We may, however, overlook such Athenian statements, focused only on the Melians' eventual decision. But Thucydides sets up confusions in the

Athenian thesis itself in this first section of the Dialogue, and the remaining two sections on the divine or gods and on the Spartans, to reveal further just what comprises both Melian hopes and Athenian confusions.

The Divine

While acknowledging the difference in strength between the two cities is great, the Melians rebut by appealing to "fortune" (*tychē*) and "hope" (*elpis*) for the first time in the Dialogue (5.102). Neither the Athenians (nor anyone) can deny fortune has some place in war; but the Melians' particular overreliance on it appears in the Athenians' response: Only a great hope could expect fortune to overcome the material disparity the Melians themselves recognize. The Athenians are aware that the "nature" (*physis*) of hope is such that it provides support for those in danger; but it also leads entirely to reliance upon it. The Melians must avoid this, and thereby not abandon "human" (*anthrōpeia*) means to preserving themselves. Those that rely on hope turn away from such means altogether, blindly following prophecies and oracles, things "invisible" or "unseen" (*aphanēs* – 103.2) that lead to their destruction.

For since the Melians have recognized Athens' superiority, they are tempted to look to non-human means – the Athenians introducing the issue of "the divine" (*tou theios*) in human life, first with their reference to prophecies and oracles, and then explicitly (105.1-3).[14] Hope and fortune

14 Strauss (1983) p. 96 notes that "the gods" is not used in the Melian Dialogue, but instead "the divine." Strauss leaves it to the reader to see that Thucydides here avoids the noun and only uses the broader adjective. The Greek adjective *tou theios* means "the divine" or "of or belonging to the gods," while *to theos* is the noun conveying the anthropomorphic "god" or "gods." It seems the issue under discussion, as Thucydides presents it here, is the question of human beings' understanding of the relation between themselves and the cosmos. The use of "the divine," in contrast to "the gods," goes to the heart of the Melian-Athenian debate – whether human beings are compelled to rule or are compelled in some way to place limits on this pursuit. But to answer this question means to answer whether nature (including human nature) is directed by knowable necessity or whether "nature" is directed by something that we cannot know and thus itself is fundamentally unknowable. Related is the fact that the only mention of "the divine law" by Thucydides is during the *stasis* at Corcyra, and there the term refers to the effects of its loss within a city (3.82.5-6). This could indicate that the relations governing citizens within a city are directed by the laws and that these laws receive divine sanction – Thucydides mentions the "established

belong together for the Melians because their hope rests on divine favor, standing up against the unjust encroachment on their autonomy.

The Athenians' rejection of hope receives the Melian reply that they place "trust" (*pisteuō*) in the divine, as just men contending against unjust men. Divine attention accompanies human efforts. But apparently only to fortune in war; the Melians also add that such efforts will be supported by the Spartans. The Spartans will be "compelled" (*anankē*) by "shame" (*aischunē*) to aid Melos as their own kin (*xyngeneia*); therefore, their confidence is not "irrational" (*alogōs*). Hesitant to place their hopes entirely in the divine, and compelled in the discussion by the Athenians to speak of their manifest means for safety (103), it appears material power required for war will come from the Spartans (104).

This turn to fortune and justice requires us to step back and summarize the Dialogue thus far: The Melians, like the Spartans, do not view fortune as merely chance occurrences that may befall participants in war. Fortune is directed by the divine, in accordance with justice. But then the Melians must also provide an account of precisely what constitutes Athenian injustice. From the discussion thus far, their view of this injustice includes the Athenians' unwillingness to negotiate without the presence of force; the Athenians refusing the Melians their autonomy; and that Melos has remained neutral in the larger war, despite belonging, broadly speaking, to the Spartan tribe. Yet on all points the Athenians have had a response:

---

laws" of the city immediately before noting that "the divine law" was transgressed. It is certain that while the result of transgressions of the divine law is civil war, the result of the Athenians' view of the divine is not necessarily war; yet Thucydides continually directs our attention to a kinship between piety and domestic concord, shared beliefs regarding fundamental human concerns among those living together. The divine law appears to be limits required for human beings only within which they may live peaceably together. After all, it is "trust" (3.82.6 – *pistis*) among citizens in particular that divine law supports, something post-Periclean Athens notably lacked. If this is the case, then the statement of their views on the divine by the ambassadors at Melos differs from Thucydides' own. For debate on Thucydides' views, see Eatough (1971) and Marinatos (1981). The former attempts to diminish Thucydides' (only) use of *eusebeia* ("reverence" or "piety") at 3.82.8, thereby eliminating its role in *stasis*. Eatough thus concludes that "[w]e should be wary of reading into the [Melian] dialogue at this point any hint of assent to, or sympathy with, the Melian case" since "[t]o expect tangible rewards from the gods for one's piety is...unreasonable" (250-51). Marinatos (as well as Hornblower I p. 486), by contrast, defend Thucydides' serious attention to religious matters, which must include, I would add, the case presented by the Melians.

The situation cannot be considered apart from Athens' superior forces; all cities that rule look to their interests; and the common good of Melos and Athens can only be those terms set out by the Athenians; finally, these terms are in fact in the interest of both cities – Athens wants to preserve Melos as a city to become a tributary paying ally and Melos wants to preserve Melos.

The Melians, however, cannot free themselves from the view that to submit in *any* manner to the Athenians is shameful: they should take any and all risks to preserve absolute independence from Athens. This view, perhaps more than any other, raises doubts about the sobriety of their hopes.

Yet we must immediately add that it is also a view we are most familiar with – autonomy and freedom at any cost. The hill upon which one will die. Death before dishonor. Hope, as the Athenians argued, is by its nature at odds with viewing danger for what it is. But is not the hope for autonomy from empire not the reverse side of hope for great glory from holding an empire, an empire that could expand to so to speak everywhere should the Athenians possess the requisite daring (as Pericles claimed)? The Athenians cannot deny the appeal of risk itself and the hoped-for glory from its conquest. Freedom and empire are the greatest things for which cities, and perhaps also individuals, are willing to fight to the death to obtain (3.45.1-7).[15] Directly after the Athenians allude to risks they take maintaining their empire, the Melians themselves raised, for the first time in the discussion, the prospect that failure to defend their autonomy may be not only shameful, but "great baseness and cowardice" (*pollē kakotēs kai deilia* – 5.100).

Returning to the Dialogue: With the divine now openly invoked, the Athenians' reply is striking for what it reveals of their "theology." The Athenians believe they may also expect the goodwill of the divine; they do not claim as their right, nor act contrary to what human beings "hold" (*dokeō*) regarding the divine or want for themselves. The Athenians believe of the divine and know of human beings that according to "natural necessity" (*physeōs anankaias*) they rule (*archō*) whenever they can. This "law" (*nomos*) was not made by the Athenians nor are they the only ones to act upon it. All that have the power to use this law use it; it is, therefore, reasonable not to fear the gods (105.1-3).

According to this new articulation of the Athenian thesis, human beings

15 Not surprisingly, this is another connection of the Melian Dialogue to the Sicilian expedition.

rule when they possess the power to do so. To rule is to act according to nature and nature is governed by necessity; no one it seems, city or individual, can act contrary to this. And the Athenians go even further, implying the divine is also subject to this necessity. Contrary to the Melian-Spartan view, gods do not govern the cosmos; necessity does. If this is so, then both human beings and gods rule and considerations of justice, while appealed to by human beings in need, do not hinder this rule. Ruling, including especially Athenian imperialism, is not unjust since it is simply to act, or perhaps, to be acted upon, by the compelling necessities of nature.

If the Athenians are correct, then what are we to make of sacrifices, oaths, pollutions, etc., including those the Athenians themselves participate in (notably, purification of Delos which opens Book 5)? How are we to understand these fulfillments of (supposedly) divine commands in light of the view that nature compels us, compels us to what others would view as hubristic acts? The Athenians present themselves not as impious, but nevertheless denying any power to justice, a claim wholly foreign to the Melians.

The Spartans

In response, the Melians now refrain from speaking of the divine and only focus on the Spartans (5.106). As with Archidamus and Sthenelaidas before the outbreak of the war, they do not respond when the Athenians directly justify their imperialism based on its apparently compulsory character. What are we to make of this silence? Is the Athenian view airtight? Can it receive no other reply than silence? In both defending their empire in moral terms, and in presuming to know the gods such that they serve as further justification for imperial action, the Athenians do indeed leave themselves open to critique. Neither the Spartans nor Melians appear capable of supplying this critique.[16] As pious peoples, both cities' spokesmen,

16 Cf. Strauss (1964) p. 190: "There is no debate in Thucydides' work in which the Spartan or Melian view defeats the Athenian view." It is worth noting that while Thucydides' Athenians observe what is "clearly knowable" (or "manifest" – *saphōs*) regarding human nature, they merely "believe" (*dokeō*) what they state about the divine; nevertheless, they do not act on this distinction, and therein, it seems to me, lies their hubris: rejecting piety based on their "enlightened" observations on human nature, the Athenians excuse that nature while shortly thereafter praising themselves for their apparently honorable restraint. Athenian hubris lies in its radical undermin-

even when pressed by war's necessities as the Melians are here, and as the Spartans were at Pylos, speak only in the language of justice; necessity is foreign to their way of thinking. The best the Melians appear capable of, it seems, is to turn to the issue of advantage. In this instance, advantage for the Melians is secured, though, not by the gods but by the Spartans, who will lose their allies' trust if they fail to aid the Melians.

The Melians' turn to offering manifest support for their safety implies the Athenians have compelled them, in the argument, to recognize at least partially that they must offer a defense of their position not relying simply on hope for divine justice. But a striking aspect of the Melians' response is how they frame their appeal to "necessity" (*anankē*): the Spartans will aid them out of necessity, but it is a necessity rooted in "kinship" (*xyngeneia*) and "shame" (*aischunē* – 104). As the Athenians imply in their response, the Melians thereby do not abandon justice; since the Spartans will have to take risks in aiding Melos, and while security accords with advantage, the Melians trust in their support. The Spartans, the Athenians argue, being more cautious than most cities (supported, for example, by the claims of Archidamus that Sparta needs time to sufficiently prepare before declaring war) are hesitant to get involved aboard (107). Nevertheless, the Melians do not view it this way. Interest and justice belong together; in supporting their friends, the Spartans will not lose their fellow Greeks' trust (*apistos*); therefore, the Melians place their own trust (*pisteuō*) in the Spartans to aid them (108).[17]

The Melians' reply to the Athenians' rejection of trust, in particular, sketches what they believe are the strategic possibilities for Sparta to harm Athens' interests (110). Perhaps most interesting of all is the Melians' mention of Brasidas, his successes in bringing over Athenian allies to Sparta. Attacking Athenian allies, along with Attica, would harm Athens. In this the Melians are correct. And while Brasidas did not live to continue this strategy, Agis' attacks on Attica late in the war do cause significant harm to Athens' movement of supplies as they attempt to defend the city while also

ing of their city's foundational *nomoi* via its claim to fully comprehend *physis*. Cf. Orwin (1994), especially pp. 104-106 (citing Macleod [1983] p. 62).

17 This passage contains some ambiguity in the Greek. Gomme IV (Andrewes) p. 176 glosses it. Hornblower III p. 245, however, notes the issue. It is not clear if the Melians mean the Spartans share their interests (due to kinship) or share the same views (and are thus faithful or loyal – *pistos*) to those views.

invading Sicily.[18] The irony of the Melians' mention of Brasidas, though, is their ignorance that Brasidas' exploits were not supported by the Spartans at home, nor is Brasidas typical of Spartan war policy.

Either way, the Athenians correctly note the Melians' argument rests on hopes and the future rather than the present, straying again from consulting for their immediate safety. According to the Athenians, therefore, the Melians would show "great irrational thought" (111.2 – *pollēn te alogian tēs dianoias*) if they do not judge the present more "moderately" (or "prudently" – *sōphronesteron*) than they have done thus far. Exhorting the Melians not to be overtaken by the notion they will act "shamefully" (*aischros*) in considering their safety, the Athenians argue it is shameful to engage in what all must recognize. Shame is so powerful a motive that one may act more shamefully when in error, rather than simply accepting misfortune; if the Melians "deliberate well" (*eu bouleuēsthe*) among themselves, they will not view as shameful their submission to "the greatest of cities" but will accept the "measured" (*metrion*) terms Athens offers (111.4). Noting the dangerous appeal shame can have for human beings, the Athenians continue to exhort the Melians to avoid it.[19]

As the foregoing makes clear, the Athenians mention "shame" (*aischunē*) repeatedly in this sequence.[20] Is Thucydides perhaps reminding us not to simply gloss the Melians' reasons for resistance? It is easy to follow the thrust of the Athenians' argument, and by now, the reader surely recognizes the Melians' refusal to put forward a sound, sober, calculated plan for handling the present situation in which they find themselves. But the Melians' sense of shame cannot be ignored; nor, relatedly, do we understand the Melians' position if we miss their reference to the Spartans as their kin (*syngenēs* – 108).[21]

Trust is rooted in kinship. But for the Melians it is also a shared interest that comes from possible future need. This unites the first and second parts

18 See Chapter Three note 53 above on 7.27.

19 As Nichols (2015) pp. 119-20 notes, though, the Melians *had* resisted a previous Athenian attack, although (importantly) one led by Nicias (3.91).

20 Gomme IV (Andrewes) pp. 178-79 and Hornblower III p. 248 note there is no parallel in Thucydides of this concentrated use of *aisch-* (shame) words.

21 The term used here is related to that at 5.104. See Fragoulaki (2013) p. 33 and context. As she notes, the Melian Dialogue also uses other terms to refer to kinship ties and, generally, the Dialogue is "heavily preoccupied with intercommunal *xyngeneia*" (p. 41).

of the argument put forward by the Melians at 5.108 – that the Spartans, should they need Melos on their expeditions abroad, can rely on them, and they can rely on them being they are kin.[22] Yet we fail to understand this fundamental political affection if we ignore the Melian view: they trust in their friends, their colonists, and their kin. These bonds are both natural (kin) and partly conventional (colony). After all, the Greeks, both Athenians and Spartans, fought together to quell the Persian (barbarian) threat before the Peloponnesian War. At the same time, the distinction between Spartan and Athenian cannot neglect the Dorian and Ionian origins of each city, respectively. Even if the Archaeology, and the ancient times in general, exhibited more preference for, or importance placed on, kinship, Thucydides signals its significance again before the Melian Dialogue's sequel: the Sicilian expedition.[23]

While kinship in Thucydides can often be ignored, it in fact figures largely in the narrative, especially for all non-Athenians. It was Sparta who sent away the daring and innovative and un-Spartan Athenians (1.102); it was Sparta who founded a colony in Heraclea only to favor their fellow Dorian inhabitants over others (3.92); it is Sparta that has problems with its foreign policy precisely because it treats its own, its kin, differently from those who are not Spartans, and especially, not Dorians; it is Sparta that was so trusting of its own they could not see Pausanias' treasonous activities (with the Persians, no less) for what they were (1.132). Aiding one's kin in time of need promises to be returned in the future, trusting as one does that kinship is a better predictor of reciprocation than agreement with those who are foreign. This is the key basis of the Melians' reliance on Sparta: that they will be ashamed not to aid their own kin and colony when the Athenians press Melos into an "alliance."

Terms of the Melians' surrender are now made clear by the Athenians; but the preservation or safety of Melos was the driving consideration from the beginning and, therefore, the Melians could not have misunderstood

---

22 Any Spartan fleet travelling the east Aegean Sea *would* find Melos the nearest stopping point, even though the island is otherwise far from Sparta. Both Gomme IV (Andrewes) p. 176 and Hornblower III p. 245 observe that the Melians' claim has some merit, Hornblower referring to 8.39.3 where a Spartan fleet *does* in fact stop at Melos.

23 Consider 1.2.6, 6.1, 12.1-4, 18.1, 89, 3.92; cf. 7.57 and see Chapter Three note 80 above. Appeals to kinship are present in speeches by Brasidas (5.9) and Gylippus (reported – 7.5.3-4).

alliance as destruction or enslavement.[24] And yet they have. In fact, the Athenians no longer abandon moral considerations (those "noble words" they argued were unnecessary), compelled, it seems, to appeal to shame and nobility to assure the Melians that submission is honorable, as well as providing for their safety. Safety and honor come together once the Athenians realize an appeal only to expediency or interests will fail. In this, we are reminded of Diodotus who united justice and advantage to deceive an Athenian demos unable to abandon justice. According to the Athenians here, Melos' submission to Athens is to bear oneself in a "noble" (*kalōs*) manner with their superiors, while those who are "measured" (*metrios*) with their inferiors act correctly, the Athenians now implicitly patting themselves on the back for doing something they claimed was not possible – acting freely and with choice (5.111.4; cf. 105.2).

The Athenians withdraw and, after the Melians discuss the matter among themselves, they reiterate their view (despite the conditions stipulated): to surrender without fighting is to relinquish their "freedom" (*eleutheria*); their city enjoyed this freedom, since first inhabited (*oikeō*) 700 years ago; and the Melians will save (*sōzō*) themselves, trusting (*pisteuō*) in the fortune owing to the divine (*tychē ek tou theiou*), along with relying on the help of humans (*anthrōpōn*), namely the Spartans (112). For the Melians, it is Athenian encroachment that decides the matter. Submission is shameful.[25] Despite the Athenians seeking only that the island city no longer remains neutral, the Melians cast the conditions of their decision in terms they began with, terms of freedom and slavery (5.86), moral terms. Their language is an appeal to tradition: their homeland, the gods, their kin. These will sway the fortunes of war.

The Athenians respond with bewilderment: the Melians alone regard the future as more apparent than the present (113). Trusting in Sparta, fortune, and hope will lead to their ruin, the Athenians implicitly denying

24 Athens' terms are noted at 5.111.4: Melos would be required to provide monetary support ("tribute" – *hypotelēs*). This contrasts with the regime change required by Sparta's "allies" (1.19.1), a policy which would appear to be more akin to a loss of autonomy than tributary payment. It is also notable that the terms at Melos are those Athens has always demanded, or at least accepted, from their "allies" (1.99.3). This fact should be added to considerations of Athens' supposed "moral decline" often attributed to their speech and deeds in, and following, the Melian Dialogue.

25 Consider Crane (1998) p. 249 on the comparison between Thucydides' Melians and Herodotus' Athenians (drawing on Herodotus 8.143.2).

being moved by such beliefs.[26] But neither claim is true: the Athenians betray the hopeful belief that their empire will last forever, that their actions are acceptable to a divine power who recognizes the necessities supposedly compelling human action, necessities the Athenians both appeal to and deny. For to act shamefully or honorably, as they try to teach the Melians, must be a matter of choice, of human decision. But others, including the Melians, do not see it this way. Only the Athenians apparently look to the present more than the future; yet the Athenians have been looking to the future – Sicily has always been the prize they seek. And one of their own, Diodotus, understanding hope and *erōs* as constitutive of human nature itself, is thus less certain than other Athenian speakers of his countrymen having overcome its delusions.

The Aftermath

With the decision of the Melians announced, the Athenians commence attacks but do not press forward vigorously, since most of their force returns to Athens. Thucydides, however, does not relate the conclusion of the affair at Melos immediately. The narrative, instead, is interrupted to remind us of other on-going hostilities. Notably, the Athenians at Pylos were pressing the Spartans, resulting in the latter's proclamation to their allies that any who wished could attack the Athenians; the Spartans themselves, however, still refused to openly engage them, seeking to avoid a breach of the treaty still officially in place (5.115.1-2). Thucydides' mention of Pylos reminds us that it was in the speech following that incident that the Spartans had intimated they were to blame for initiating the war, a belief arising from their defeat and capture (4.20.2. cf. 7.18.2). Thucydides reminding us of Pylos in the context of Melos reinforces the similarity between the Melian and Spartan view. And in another interruption by Thucydides (before relating the outcome of the Melian affair), a single sentence separating a Melian attack and their destruction, the pious Spartans intended but refrained

26 Cornford (1907) pp. 184-85 notes the irony throughout the Dialogue of the Athenians counselling the Melians against hope, only to be taken in by it with the sequel: Sicily. Orwin (1994) p. 110: "That [the Athenians] fail to persuade the Melians suggests that the envoys' project of 'enlightenment' itself rests on unreasonable hopes." However, cf. 2.65.12.

from invading Argos because the sacrifices they carried out before crossing into enemy territory were again found to be unfavorable (5.116.1).

Domestic politics emerges, if in a subdued manner, in the Melian narrative. After all, the Athenians frankly state their controversial views once it was agreed that they were speaking, not to the Melian people, but to the few (5.85); they offer a criticism of Spartan foreign policy rooted, as they imply, in Sparta's civic virtue; and they offer frank and stunning observations on the failures of piety to act upon the priority of necessity, inheriting Pericles' blindness to piety's importance for the city itself. With a reference to the Spartans' customary adherence to frontier sacrifices and Pylos, their reason for failing to aid Melos becomes clear: Sparta just retrieved their soldiers trapped on the island and (nominally) ended a war they no longer were certain to be on the right side of.[27]

What domestic factors possibly influenced the Melians' decision? What would happen were the few to submit? What is the view of the many? Did a separate faction, one opposed to the few, turn Melos over to Athens (116.3)? The Athenians were angered at Pericles when he allowed their countryside to be burned by the Spartans. Whether his policy of abandoning it was the best war strategy or not, the demos did not share that view, or at least refused to accept the consequences of his policy, destroying as it did their ancestral homeland.[28] In other words, by reminding us of domestic political issues and all that was destroyed by *stasis* at Corcyra, Thucydides leaves us to consider how such issues figure into the situation that the Athenians, in their emphasis on safety, fail to consider. This is not to suggest the Melians' decision was prudent or sound; what it notes are the psychological motives behind a decision that seems, as the Athenians claim, illogical.

As the Spartans' guilt originated from their belief that injustice will lead to deserved misfortunes as punishment, the Melians believe they will persevere as just men fighting Athenian injustice. Reward and punishment, in the form of victory and defeat, is decided by the gods. The Athenians

---

27 Scholars blame Sparta for not coming to the rescue. Macleod (1983) p. 64: the narrative reveals the "Peloponnesians' egoism and incompetence." Connor (1984) p. 153: "We know...that neither the gods nor the Spartans will intervene to help [the Melians]." Orwin (1994) p. 110 "The second thread of the [Melos] narrative...is...the indifference of Sparta."

28 Before the war, during the plague, and before the Sicilian expedition, at least some, if not most, Athenians were susceptible to prophecies and oracles (2.8.2, 2.54.2-5, 6.32.1-2; cf. 8.1.2)

surely feel no guilt for their imperial actions, and the Melian Dialogue reminds us why: they have a justification, not rooted in divine justice, but based on an account of nature. Contrary to that thesis, the Spartan-Melian view contends that human beings must refrain from acting unjustly; necessity does not exculpate one from morality. It is not clear whether the Spartan-Melian view holds that the gods are also just among themselves; what is clear is that the gods are at least *concerned* with justice among human beings (along with adherence to related pious practices) and intervene in human affairs on this basis.[29] And should it be the case that gods themselves rule where they can (and perhaps even unjustly), the Melians and Spartans never argue human beings are compelled to imitate the gods.[30] Compulsion has no place in their understanding, even if when pressed by the Athenians they implicitly admit it in speech (5.87-90).

But does this admission, implicit or not, mean the Melians support the Athenian thesis? For the Melians also immediately argue it is not good for their city to submit to Athens (92), an encroachment on their absolute freedom that must be defended because it would be shameful (*aischros*) to fail to resist. Even in recognizing necessity, this "recognition" is colored by fear of shame. And here, the Athenians' rhetoric cannot be ignored: They do not reassert any claims suggesting they are worthy to rule and thereby fail to potentially dissuade the Melians from resisting. They do, however, avail themselves of "noble words" (87 – *onomatōn kalōn*), appealing to the Melians' longing to act nobly in defending their island (111.4). But for the Melians, any terms, no matter how mild or moderate are shameful – submitting *at all* to an unjust aggressor would be a failure to stand up, not simply for themselves, but for the *cause* of justice itself. In defending themselves, they defend their belief in the power of justice. Practicing justice *is* the means to their salvation, and it is in the divine that they expect a victory of justice against the hubris of injustice.

If this is how the Melians view their cause, we notice the consequences for the Athenian thesis: a failure of that thesis to take seriously the necessity of confronting other peoples with differing moral expectations from their own. And by failing to recognize this, they fail to recognize their thesis will

29 As is evidenced in the Greek poets: Homer, Hesiod, and later, Pindar.

30 Orwin (1994) p. 105 notes that the Athenians pick up on stories of unjust, even tyrannical gods, especially Zeus. Yet, as he also observes, Greek piety prohibited imitation of gods by human beings.

never be the only (or even predominant) view – justice and its demands are at odds with the apparently exculpatory strictures of necessity because justice denies precisely that any human action is fundamentally necessary. In the Spartans, the Athenians fail to recognize their blindness or justification in conflating self-interest and justice; for while the Spartans do not distinguish justice from service to their city, the Athenians do make such a distinction.[31] And since even the Athenians refrain from claiming certain knowledge of the divine, the Melians' decision is not entirely baseless. But this lack of knowledge also means the Melians base their safety on hopes, hopes the Athenians believe all cities, at least their rulers, should be immune to. Thucydides allows us to hear the bewilderment in the voices of the (obviously) militarily superior Athenians after the Melians abide by their original decision to resist. Yet this bewilderment reveals Athenians too hasty and self-assured in believing other cities will dispense with justice.

Considering the beginning of the war, however, we note a divergence in Melian and Spartan views. While the Melians refuse to turn over their city, even in the face of the external compulsion that is Athens, the Spartans were willing to go to war. And as Thucydides states (as his own judgment), Spartan fear was decisive in this declaration. The Melians assuage their fears where the Spartans do not; and some Spartans were less certain of the justice of going to war against Athens, revealed in Archidamus' hesitation

31 Orwin (1994) p. 110: "Reluctant to stir against Athens, despite manifest cause…the Spartans fully vindicate the envoys' assessment of them." The Athenians were correct, but not due to the assessment they state. This assessment claims that supposed Spartan justice is merely Spartan advantage. In Thucydides' narration of the entire Melos episode, however, he intrusively reminds us of the frontier sacrifices proving unfavorable *and* the Spartans' reluctance to violate the treaty still in place (5.115-116). The Spartans were preoccupied with Argos, a city on the Peloponnesus with whom they had a long enmity (1.102.4) and which was far closer to Sparta than Melos, as Thucydides reminds us of immediately preceding the Melian Dialogue (5.82-83). These factors, it seems to me, cannot be divorced from the Spartans' failure to arrive to aid Melos. Like all cities, including Athens, they must weigh pros and cons, risks and rewards, of policy decisions. To reduce each and every Spartan decision to their *key* domestic issue, the presence of the Helots, is counter to the fact that the Spartans did go to war, leave their city, and used the Helots as troops when they needed both to go abroad, while nevertheless also fearful of this threat from within (4.80.5, 5.57.1). Nor can we ignore that adherence to the treaty was far from advantageous to Sparta, given the Athenians were continually harassing Spartan interests, including Pylos, control of which is of on-going concern. Treaty obligations and pious observances, in the Melos episode and throughout Book Five, are precisely at odds with the advantageous policy the more maneuverable Brasidas, for example, was able to deliver.

on its legality. Even though the Spartans hid this fear from themselves and proclaimed the liberation of Greek cities from Athens was their aim, their departure from arbitration as per the treaty is in keeping with their fear that Athens' continual growth would encroach on the Peloponnesus and eventually Sparta itself. The Melians, however, do not take this step; their view is entirely governed by "Spartans, fortune, and hopes" (113).

In neither case do the Athenians comprehend these deeply held convictions. Daring not only at war, but also in their thought and frank statement of it, they claim to know human nature and its responses to the necessities of war (and human life), at the same time failing to recognize that human understanding is inseparable from justice and piety. And if recognizing when avoidance of shame is prudent (111.3), what about the reverse side, striving for honor excessively pursued? Athenian daring carries them too far in the sequel to the Melian Dialogue, the Sicilian expedition, where Athenian neglect to thoroughly weigh their own thesis becomes apparent. They doubt their own empire is susceptible to decay and neglect the possibility other cities may seek to punish them should the Athenians find themselves in a position of weakness. It is the Syracusans, as Thucydides presents, who were first motivated by fear, but later by glory, once they believed that they could stave off the Athenians attempting to invade their island. Once defeated, the Athenians *were* punished, a treatment that could perhaps be described as unduly harsh (7.87). Glory, like justice, can drive cities to harshness and excess. Glory and justice seem to unite in the righteous indignation of the victor, the victor who overtakes his previous ruler. Arguing their empire was more measured or just that it needed to be, the Athenian envoys at Sparta imply a comparison with an empire previously defeated – the Persian empire.

But does their own contention of a harsh Persian empire not lend support to the Melians' view, that those who rule may not do so exclusively with a view to sober, calculated, defined interests? That a desire for revenge, such as the Athenians themselves displayed in their treatment of the Mytilenians, might very well take hold and guide their manner of ruling? That demonstrating their abundant strength to obtain the honor, such strength leaves their empire susceptible to overreach, and itself fosters hatred? Athenian daring in thought and their stated thesis is confused, its forcefulness and assuredness disguising from its proponents this very confusion. The

Melian Dialogue works out these confusions, revealed both in the case of the divine and the Spartans, the Athenians' Achilles' heel.

For Thucydides, Melians and Athenians are in their own way daring where moderation is called for: The Athenians immoderate in believing they know the gods (and human nature), the Melians in relying wholly on the gods and not on what men can know (and achieve) themselves. For the Athenians, these tensions and confusions in the Athenian thesis unfold in the lead-up and execution of the Sicilian expedition, an action unimaginable among Spartans. With this episode, Thucydides shows Athens at its most daring, yet alongside (and thus by way of contrast with) its most cautious, public-spirited, and "Spartan" commander, Nicias.

Nicias: Athens' "Spartan" Conscience

Nicias is a reminder that for Thucydides, "Spartan" and "Athenian" are not merely citizens of particular cities, but character types he has crafted into psychological portraits. Thucydides' presentation of the Athenian commander and statesman signals his proximity to the Spartan view of the war, implying as Nicias does that a life of just and pious actions towards men will result in a favorable outcome. Thucydides' "eulogy" on Nicias' life notes that he least of all deserved his death (having been one of the generals of the failed Sicilian expedition and dying at the hands of his captors) since he lived his life in accordance with law-bred or "customary virtue" (*aretēn nenomismenēn* – 7.86.5).[32]

Those customary, traditional virtues are the ones we have seen in Sparta and even among moderates in Athens: moderation, piety, and observance of the dictates of justice. Thucydides goes further here, though, than with the Spartans or Melians in exploring especially the issue of divine justice. With the Spartans, their success (as we will later see) is dependent on Brasidas, and they have not been clearly favored by the gods in the war (on their own view). With the Melians, their failure cannot help but be seen as their own inability to assess the circumstances before them. But with Nicias, we

32 I use the term "eulogy" with some hesitation. Thucydides' final remark on Nicias appears initially as praise; the reader should be aware, however, that this praise raises questions given Thucydides' presentation of the Athenian thesis and its doubts regarding divine justice.

find something of a middle road – Nicias is both responsible for significant strategic errors that a more "Athenian" mind (say, an Alcibiades) would not commit; but he is also more aware, and his life an exploration of civic (and pious) virtue from within a regime that has openly articulated a thesis of self-interested human nature.

As some scholars have noted, Thucydides' assessment appears to present Nicias' life as a tragedy – striving for virtue, Nicias suffers a fate that he does not deserve.[33] Yet if Nicias did not deserve his eventual fate, then Thucydides casts doubt on divine justice and his portrait of Nicias, including his eulogy, is a puzzle. The Spartans believed their losses in the first part of the war were due to their breach of the treaty with Athens; thus, in the second part of the war, they gained confidence their injustice had been punished by the capture of their men on Sphacteria and expected to be successful (especially given the Athenians' subsequent breach of the agreement bearing Nicias' name – 7.18). If Nicias' fate was not deserved, however, we must decipher why, weighing both the character of Nicias' virtue and the incidents that led to his death.

Most scholars quite naturally focus on Nicias' conduct in the expedition to Sicily, on strategic errors he makes during its prosecution, while also arguing Nicias is a rare instance where Thucydides notes the "psychological" motives of one of his characters.[34] In addition, though, we must add that Thucydides presents Nicias in an unparalleled manner; there are numerous mentions of him *before* the Peace of Nicias and Books Six and Seven (his most noticeable involvement in the war). These earlier mentions are notable features of Thucydides' presentation that receive little or no scholarly attention.[35] Further, Thucydides' eulogy on Nicias' life is unique;

33 Most notably, Cornford (1907). See also, Lloyd-Jones (1983) pp. 137-44.

34 Pouncey (1980) pp. 117-30 and Connor (1984) pp. 200-209 focus on Nicias' errors. Westlake (1941) p. 59 argues that it is unusual for Thucydides to focus on the "private virtues" of one of his characters. In his later work, Westlake (1968) p. 96 argues Thucydides' reasons for this focus are obscure and "speculation on the problem would be unprofitable." But this is unsatisfactory given the importance of Nicias – Thucydides' assessment of him is among the most noticeable of any character and is especially relevant for his view on divine justice.

35 For example, Westlake (1941) pp. 59-60 argues that before Nicias' appearance in the debate over Pylos, he is invoked in "operations producing no important result." The exceptions here are Pouncey (1980) and Strauss (1964). Pouncey (1980) pp. 118-19 notes that these actions of Nicias are generally overlooked, but he only provides a list of them without explanation. I follow Strauss (1964) pp. 200-202 who persuasively

for in the case of Brasidas, Thucydides does not remark on whether his death was deserved or not (5.11.1). Only in the case of Nicias does Thucydides reveal an opinion on the justice or injustice of one of his characters' deaths.[36]

And as we have seen throughout, Thucydides' presentation is always purposive. Striking it is that Nicias' last speech is the last speech quoted in Thucydides' text and it states most clearly the Spartan view of divine justice. If Nicias' life and the manner in which it ended was undeserved, Thucydides either strongly condemns divine justice (as it fails in Nicias' case) or doubts it altogether. Nicias' life and death would then be a culmination, and it seems, a refutation, of the Spartan view of the war as Thucydides presents it. Yet Thucydides allows us to notice numerous errors in Nicias' prosecution of the war, raising doubts about how precisely Nicias' fate was undeserved. This is even more striking in light of the fact that Nicias' most infamous error is his failure to leave Sicily due to an eclipse and the subsequent interpretation of it by the soothsayers, when the Athenians still had an opportunity to escape successfully.

These initial observations raise doubts specifically about the relation between Nicias' piety and his prudence. We are reminded of the Melians and wonder whether Nicias shares their hopes; or perhaps Nicias himself was a victim of divine justice for being involved in the Sicilian expedition. His death follows on the Athenians' slaughter of the Melians, raising the question of whether the Athenian defeat at Sicily was not punishment for their continual expansion, a punishment that the Melians themselves had

presents each of the seven actions of Nicias prior to Book Six as significant for understanding Thucydides' complete portrait of his character.

36 Both Pouncey (1980) pp. 129-30 and Westlake (1968) p. 209 argue for a diminishment of Thucydides' remark at 7.86.5. Pouncey claims Thucydides' remark is an "irrelevant anachronism" and Nicias stands "out of pace with the war." Westlake argues Thucydides' focus is only on Nicias' "virtue" which is a "moral term" indicating Nicias' "goodness." However, Westlake does not elaborate on what he understands by "goodness." Both appear to minimize Thucydides' remark because they focus, not incorrectly, on Nicias' strategic errors. These errors, it is argued, form the basis for our judgment of Thucydides' view of him. Yet Thucydides could have refrained from this remark and, despite their attempted diminishment of it, scholars confront it because it is so noticeable – this is one detail of Thucydides' account he does not attempt to disguise. That Nicias' errors are also both apparent and significant draws our attention to the puzzle or problem of how these errors relate to Thucydides' overall assessment of him.

forecasted.[37] Through his eulogy and the manner of Nicias' death, Thucydides brings Nicias together with both the Spartan view of the war and with the actions of the Athenian empire – Nicias appears to share characteristics of *both* cities and we are compelled to wonder if his view of the war sheds light on the shortcomings of the Spartan and Athenian views.

Thucydides' Introduction of Nicias

Although Nicias' initial appearances in Thucydides' account are brief, each is purposive when considered in light of his more noticeable involvements late in the war. Thucydides' first mention of Nicias is at Minoa when the Athenians are attempting to free up a passage between an island and the mainland (3.51). This incident is related by Thucydides in one paragraph that falls between the Athenians' decision on Mytilene (i.e., their salvation) and the surrender of Plataea to the Spartans (i.e., their destruction). Nicias' first appearance is between two of the most striking events in Thucydides, each depicting Athens and Sparta in dealings with now hostile cities resulting from the outbreak of the war. Nicias' next appearance occurs in an Athenian attempt to subdue Melos (3.91). Nicias is unsuccessful in forcing Melos to submit, while Athenians without Nicias are later successful. It would not be remiss to note here that Nicias is never described by Thucydides as "daring," the characteristic most often noted of the Athenians. The third incident involves Nicias and Cleon debating a resolution on how to handle the Spartans trapped by the Athenians on the island of Sphacteria (4.27-28). The antagonism between the two leads Nicias to retire his command once he notices the Athenians are hostile to Cleon. Thucydides notes that the Athenians in question are the "moderate" men in Athens, who are more interested in ridding the city of Cleon than of capturing the Spartans (28.5). The moderate men are on the side of Nicias, not Cleon

37 Many scholars view the Sicilian narrative as displaying Thucydides' tragic view of the war, e.g., Westlake (1941) p. 59, Rawlings (1981) pp. 136-39, Macleod (1983) pp. 140-158, Lebow (2003) pp. 115-67, and especially Cornford (1907). Cf. Connor (1984) pp. 207-8 with n57. In the context of discussing Thucydides' description of the suffering of the Athenians as they leave their camp in Syracuse to begin their final attempt at escape (7.75), Connor is cautious in his interpretation of the possibility of divine retribution arguing that "[t]he passage seems to me to raise the question of theodicy but to leave it quite open."

(who was most popular with the people but also most violent). The preference for moderate policy at home versus victory in the larger war, favored by the moderates in Athens, reminds us of Sparta.

Following on this preference, the next action of Nicias is at Corinth (4.42), when he hastily claims victory over the Corinthians and their allies. While Nicias defeats one contingent, he allows others to escape. As a result, when a reinforcement of Corinthians arrives, the Athenians are forced to flee, leaving behind the bodies of two of their men. Nicias later ensures these two bodies are retrieved after a truce is agreed to by the two sides – the retrieval of bodies was a pious duty of those in command, although during the Sicilian expedition, necessity will force the Athenians to leave their men behind as they attempt to escape Sicily, both the wounded and the dead (7.75). Further related to later events in Sicily, in this context, is the fact that in this present skirmish the Athenians prevail over the Corinthians in the first part of the battle due to their cavalry. In preparation for the Sicilian expedition, Nicias will argue that the Syracusans' "chief superiority" over the Athenians rests with their cavalry (6.20.4); yet when he is consulted again on preparations, after attempting in vain to deter the expedition, Nicias fails to mention the cavalry at all. Through this preliminary comparison of Corinth and Sicily, Thucydides quietly suggests Nicias' error by noting immediately that the Athenians granted the commanders sent to Sicily complete autonomy (*autokrator* – "one's own master") to arrange matters as they believed best for Athens. In his obvious dismay at finding himself susceptible to fortune given such a dangerous expedition, Nicias fails to note in his advice on the preparations for Sicily that it must include a cavalry to match this notable Syracusan strength (25.2). And while Thucydides sometimes tempts his readers to overlook strategic and material details of the war (particularly given his remark after the death of Pericles on the cause of the fall of Athens and its connection to Sicily) in this instance he offers a competing, or perhaps complementary, if not openly stated, explanation.[38]

38 Strauss (1964) p. 201 and Liebeschuetz (1968) pp. 296, 301 both notice the significance of cavalry. Instances of the cavalry abound once we are attentive to them: 6.70.3, 71.2, 98.4 (Athenian cavalry defeats Syracusan cavalry); 6.101.4-5, 7.4.6, 5.2-3 (cavalry of no use and thus close combat ensues with the Athenians winning the battle; Gylippus admits strategic mistake related to misuse of cavalry); 6.2-3 (Gylippus wins due to cavalry, routing the Athenians); 7.13 (Nicias notes problem of cavalry); 7.24 (defeat at Plemmyrium leads to problems for Athens' access to supplies; cf. 7.4.6 and 7.13);

The fifth action of Nicias is an attempt to subdue the island of Cythera, a colony of Sparta (4.53-54). The Athenians are prepared to expel the Cytherans from the island, located as it is near Laconia (the inhabitants of the island also being Spartans). Nicias becomes involved in negotiations with a faction within the city and offers an agreement with terms more advantageous (*epitedeios*) than the Athenian plan of expulsion. Nicias offering terms more favorable than the Athenians reminds us of both Archidamus and Brasidas (2.73.1, 4.114.2). Thus, in this case, Nicias and the Athenians find themselves at odds over foreign policy. And, most interestingly, Nicias' negotiations with the Cytherans do in fact aid Athens in subduing the island. Later during the campaign in Sicily, Demosthenes and Eurymedon will agree to remain in Sicily because Nicias appears to have some information they lack. As Thucydides relates, Nicias is in secret negotiations with a faction within Syracuse that seeks to end the war with Athens. This faction leads Nicias to hope for a resolution, despite the desperate situation of the Athenians, as well as the other commanders pressing Nicias to agree to an Athenian evacuation from Sicily (7.49). Nicias' strategy of negotiation is successful at Cythera, but his hope for a successful negotiation in this instance leads directly to Athenian delay and a failure to depart from Sicily, while Nicias himself will only endorse this attempt shortly thereafter. Similar to his generous plan in dealing with Cythera, when the city of Mende revolts from Athens, Nicias aids in negotiating gentle terms (4.129). This is in contrast to the treatment of the city of Scione, where the citizens are slaughtered on the advice of Cleon after inciting a revolt from Athens.[39]

The seventh and final action in Thucydides' introduction of Nicias involves negotiations with Sparta for peace (resulting in the so-called Peace of Nicias – 5.18-19) and the enforcement of their subsequent alliance. Nicias acts as an envoy to Sparta, as he attempts to fulfill the terms of the existing treaty between Sparta and Athens. Here again, Nicias wants to maintain peace while the many Athenians were angry with the Spartans, in particular for their refusal to relinquish their alliance with Boeotia. Nicias argues peace is in Athens' interests because Sparta would seek war to restore its

---

7.55.2 (horses are mentioned, along with ships, in enumerating similarities between Athens and Syracuse); 7.78.6, 84.2, 85.1 (cavalry severely hinders the Athenians' attempted escape by land).

39 Burns (2011) p. 222n13. We are reminded that the brutality of the incident at Scione precedes that of the Athenian siege of Melos.

reputation. And while Sparta sought a treaty with Athens after the death of Brasidas, the ascendancy of the war party led by Xenares wants to dissolve the treaty (5.39). Therefore, while the Athenians agree to allow Nicias to negotiate with the Spartans, Xenares and the war party refuse Nicias' terms, and he is compelled to return to Athens without having achieved his objective. Nicias is blamed by the Athenians for this failure, and they immediately sign an alliance with Argos instead, creating decisive problems for Sparta and its allies. The Athenians' tendency to blame their generals and statesman when their hopes are disappointed will also be a consideration for Nicias in his decision to remain in Sicily – part of his argument for delaying a departure is to avoid charges of bribery and incompetence leveled by the Athenian demos. Despite this blame for Nicias' failure to secure the treaty conditions sought by Athens, his demands and attempts do not seem unreasonable – Thucydides does not comment on the negotiations directly, but does note that the war party was decisive in Sparta's refusal of Nicias' proposals. Preceding these negotiations and the cause of them, Thucydides had also noted the change of key individuals in each city (5.16).[40]

With the deaths of Brasidas and Cleon, Nicias becomes the leading man in Athens. In contrast to the other men mentioned (motivated as Thucydides argues by private interests), however, Nicias was *both* motivated by private honor *and* by a concern with the other citizens (*kai tous politas* – 16.1). Nicias sought to maintain peace because his own reputation was already well-established and he had been the most fortunate Athenian general to date; he did not want to risk his reputation or safety by continuing the war, nor did he want to place his city at war. It therefore appears that the private interest of Nicias and the public interest of Athens are in agreement.

Yet the Athenians do not share this view and the alliance between Argos and Athens will compel Sparta and its allies to march out in response to Athens' renewed hostilities. Thucydides leads us to wonder whether continued peace would not have been of interest to Athens as well. However that may be, it is also significant that Nicias here suffers bad fortune for the first time. Previously, Thucydides stated that Nicias had been the "most fortunate [or successful] commander of his time" (*pleista tōn tote eu pheromenos*

40 I do not number this mention of Nicias in the actions currently under consideration. Thucydides' comments on Nicias' motives at 5.16, however, belong together with his attempts at maintaining the treaty at 5.46.

en stratēgiais – 5.16.1). Misfortune joins Nicias to the Spartans – the Spartans were favorably disposed toward Nicias due to the peace he helped author, including the return of the Spartans held on Sphacteria, which, in the Spartan view, was their greatest misfortune during the Peloponnesian War (7.86.3).

Given the striking similarity between these early episodes involving Nicias and later events during the Sicilian expedition, perhaps the significance of Nicias is hinted at by the particularly artful manner in which Thucydides presents him. Taken with Thucydides' remark on Nicias' virtue, these initial actions present his "Spartan" character. Nicias prefers peace to war, his focus on the city and resulting policies are in keeping with the moderation Thucydides praises in Sparta, and even the seeming passing mention of Nicias retrieving the bodies of Athenian soldiers exemplifies his piety in adherence to this customary practice.[41] But the mention of Nicias' private or psychological motives, specifically his admitted concern with private honor and preeminence within the city, is at odds with what we have seen in Sparta. We are reminded of Sparta's king, Agis, and the faction arising between himself and the ephors, leading to the new law that the king must be accompanied by overseers on any foreign campaign. This is in contrast to the unfettered autonomy granted to Nicias and the other generals before departing for Sicily. And as we have seen of the Spartan regime, no one individual was able to gain preeminence, nor was Spartan moderation wholly separable from the Helot population. Nicias comes to light as sharing the Spartan view of the war, while also in a qualified manner replacing Pericles as the leading statesman in Athens.

Nicias may then offer a corrective to the problems of Sparta, particularly the lack of outstanding statesmen able to conduct the war. For Nicias' ascendancy in Athens is partially the result of the deaths of Cleon and Brasidas, and Brasidas was the only Spartan who (alone) furthered the possibility of either peace or victory for Sparta over Athens. But Brasidas' policies, though successful, were not supported by his city and incurred the envy

41 Strauss (1964) p. 202n68 argues that Nicias "is the representative *par excellence* of moderation in the city of daring," while Connor (1984) p. 206 concurs arguing "Nicias has, moreover, been a spokesman for and a representative of the cause of self-restraint and moderation so strongly, if tacitly, articulated in many of the earlier parts of the *Histories*." The connection, then, to the Spartan king, Archidamus, is obvious. But so too is the relation to his foil, Brasidas. Perhaps we could say Brasidas is the representative *par excellence* of daring in the city of moderation.

of the leading men despite being the only statesman to further the Spartan war cause of liberating Athens' subject cities. In turning to the Sicilian expedition, Nicias will immediately depart from Spartan habit by openly stating his own private motives, while also defending his policies with a view to the interests of Athens and gaining the Athenians' trust as one of its commanders. Nicias reminds us of Pericles through his influence over the Athenian demos; yet Nicias' influence over the city is not clouded by the problem we have observed of Pericles' depreciation of law and tradition, of the old Athens (2.35.1, 36.2-4, 43.3, 45.1-2, 46.1). Nicias' piety, generosity, and dedication to his city strike the reader as novel, as un-Athenian, particularly at this point in the war – perhaps Athens has never been led by such an individual.[42] Nicias may offer an instance of the public-spirited individual most able to benefit his city. But with Nicias' Spartan view of the war comes the question of how this view will be received among certain Athenians and manifest strategically in the war's prosecution. From what we observed of the Athenian thesis at Melos and throughout Thucydides' account, Nicias' moderation, piety, and justice cannot but be at odds precisely with this thesis.

Nicias' Un-Athenian View of the Sicilian Expedition

Nicias' advice to the Athenians during the assembly debating the Sicilian expedition is, as he admits, not related to the assembly's preparatory purpose but rather urging them to refrain from the expedition entirely (6.9.1). Nicias had been one of those chosen to command despite disagreeing with the expedition's aim – for Nicias it is based on "slight and fair-seeming pretexts," while actually being undertaken for the conquest of Sicily (8.4). The intention of Nicias' first speech is, therefore, to dissuade the Athenians from Sicily, or more generally, from the imperialism that has driven much of Thucydides' account of the war. But this attempt immediately encounters difficulties.

Nicias first must dispense with the possibility that some may accuse

42 This judgment presumes the reader has begun to notice problems with Periclean Athens. But even without this insight, Thucydides leads readers to notice Nicias' prominence as one approaches the Sicilian expedition more than Pericles, Demosthenes, and without the difficulties, and violence, which Cleon presents.

him of having private motives, advising Athens based on his own interests and not with a view to the good of the city (9.2; cf. 3.42.3-6). Nicias acknowledges this objection by noting he would gain in "honor" (*timē*) by leading Athens to Sicily, if indeed it succeeds. And he even contends one may still be a good citizen while also concerned with one's own person and property; for Nicias these concerns appear to be united. Nicias has been a successful (and fortunate) commander and therefore his honor is derived from these successes. If Nicias is victorious in the Sicilian expedition, he will further gain honor for himself; if he fails, he will be blamed like he was blamed for not ensuring the terms of the treaty with Sparta were enforced (5.46.4-5). Although Nicias may well accrue honor from a successful conquest, we will later confirm that he nevertheless disagrees it is best for the city, genuinely skeptical it serves the common good of Athens.

Nicias now admits, however, that the Athenians are unlikely to listen to him due to their "character" (*tropos*) – the Athenians refuse to keep what they have and willingly take risks for uncertain and future things (6.9.3). This reminds us of the reverse trait of the Spartans, as the Corinthians noted – they are satisfied with what they possess and thus are slow to act and lack daring (1.70.2). Nicias is advising the Athenians as if they were Spartans. Nicias and Athens are at odds in spite of Nicias' argument that his private interest, honor, is in service of Athens' supposed public interest, conquest of Sicily. But since Nicias is satisfied with what *he* possesses, his private interest is no longer in agreement with Athenian daring. Indeed, according to Nicias the expedition does not serve the public good; he argues instead that the Athenians should not place their current empire at risk for the sake of conquering Sicily, as their characteristic daring threatens to do (10.5). As he admits, he can only show the Athenians their ill-timed haste and the difficulty of what they desire.

With a view to deterrence, Nicias first reminds his countrymen of the war at home, still a danger since peace with Sparta is not secure. Nicias correctly notes that Sparta's allies have not accepted the terms of the treaty (10.2-3); knowing this, Athens should not seek a new empire (seemingly in an echo of Pericles — 1.144.1) Yet Nicias' policies are even more cautious. Pericles' exultation of imperial glory and the unlimited capabilities of the Athenians to conquer any land would have supported, in principle, the Sicilian expedition (even though practically he argued, in anticipation, against it). Nicias, though, continues in this speech to emphasize the dangers Sparta poses, particularly given the treaty inducing the Spartans to shame (6.10.2, 11.6); he expects Spartan honor to rouse them to reengaging in open hostilities. Thucydides, though, has continually narrated Spartan caution and slowness – the very peace named after Nicias was the result of the Spartan desire to end the larger war, despite the relatively small number of men captured. Not surprisingly, Nicias and the Spartans got along rather well (5.46.1).

In keeping with Nicias urging caution, along with preservation and maintenance of the existing Athenian empire, he criticizes the Athenians for grasping at another one. Some allies have openly revolted, and others are only precariously obedient to Athens; the Athenians are wrongly focused on Sicily while allowing other injustices to go unpunished. The Athenian pretext for going to Sicily is that Egesta is an ally of Athens and has been treated unjustly (6.10.5). But this is also the reason Thucydides reports as the basis for Nicias' objection to the expedition (8.2). At least part of Nicias' objection to the Sicilian expedition appears to be precisely its injustice: The Athenians are merely using the Egestaeans' appeals to achieve their *main* purpose, conquering Sicily for the expansion of their empire. Nicias will also refer to the Egestaeans as "barbaric" implying, it seems, they are not worthy of Athenian aid, and thus (perhaps unknown to himself) that the oath of the Athenians need not be kept (11.7). What Nicias reveals in these objections is striking – while he explicitly argues the expedition is not in Athens' interest (their continued expansion ignoring other compelling interests closer to home), he also betrays his deeper belief of the expedition's injustice. As such, this charge of injustice quietly becomes the theme of the remainder of Nicias' speech.[43]

Continuing Nicias' accusation is his thinly veiled criticism of Alcibiades' role in the expedition. Alcibiades, he argues, has only his own ends in view, a desire for private profit to support his extravagant way of life. Further, Alcibiades is too young and would endanger the city – Alcibiades lacks the wisdom bestowed by age (reminding us of Archidamus' appeal to his own age and experience – 1.83.1). Nicias thereby appeals to the older men (we presume some of whom are the moderate men in Athens – cf.

43 It is significant (at least rhetorically) that Nicias fails to address the issue of the oaths the Athenians had made, presumably in their alliance with Egesta (6.6.2). Strauss (1983) p. 97 notes that both Alcibiades (18.1) and the Egestaeans (19.1) remind the Athenian assembly of these oaths.

4.28.5) not to be "cowardly" (or "soft" – *malakos*); they should speak up against the expedition as ill-advised. Is Nicias himself one of these men? Does he fear appearing cowardly and is this why he ultimately partakes in the expedition?

Nicias does not attempt to retire his command, as he had previously (4.28). Instead, he now states that he disagrees with the expedition because the Athenians are affected by "sick *erōs*" (*dyserōtas)* and success does not proceed from this desire (6.13.1).[44] Indeed, this desire has led to the greatest danger Athens has ever faced. Even Nicias, noted for his law-bred virtue, is willing to possibly breach the law against the assembly reversing previous decisions if the Athenians are willing to reconsider (14.1). And if the expedition risks Athens itself, an Athens Nicias is dedicated to and has displayed a genuine concern with, then the sick *erōs* of the Athenians is counter to the public interest or common good of Athens – from the point of view of the city, as embodied in Nicias, this Athenian desire is a further injustice. Nicias certainly believes he himself is free of this sick *erōs*.[45]

This passion manifests itself, in Nicias' view, as pursuit of private interests, particularly profit. Both his blame of Alcibiades and the demos reveal this. And Thucydides himself confirms the demos' desires were for private ends and not with a view to the good of the city (24.3). Nicias is aware, then, that Athens risks extending its empire to a point it can no longer hold onto what it has. Nicias believes the empire is unjust because it is driven by desire; that said, the "noble ruler" (*kalōs archai*) ought to benefit their "fatherland" (*patrida*) as they are able (14). We cannot help but notice that Nicias perhaps views himself as such a ruler.

This observation allows us to understand how Nicias can admit to his own private benefit from the expedition, but then chastise Alcibiades – Nicias urges the city to seek its safety and thus advises caution, while Alcibiades recommends the expedition only for profit and private glory. If we

44 The term Thucydides uses is *dyserōs* (*dyserōtas*, cited above, is the plural, thus referring to all Athenians). It is used only here and by Nicias in particular. See also Hornblower III pp. 335-36.

45 Diodotus would simply call this *erōs*, led on by accompanying hopes (3.45.5). Nicias' usage thus implies a problem with the Athenians' desire, i.e., that the Athenians need to purge themselves of it. We also note that Nicias further implies that being possessed by this desire will result in harm to Athens, i.e., that they will be punished for it. How this punishment is assured is only fully revealed by Nicias' later actions and speeches in the war.

consider Nicias' motive of honor, however, his urging of caution to the Athenians appears to be congruent with this interest – he was already an honored commander and thus his argument for avoiding the expedition is also in his own private benefit; he seeks not to place *himself* at risk. Yet is Nicias aware of this? Does he seek simply to avoid command under the guise of impugning both Alcibiades and the Athenians? Does Nicias hypocritically replace the private interests of other Athenians with his own?

Nicias *is* correct to claim that the expedition is a risk to the city (6.8.4). And by impugning the desire directing the Athenians toward Sicily, Nicias insinuates his genuine motive. Nicias refuses to accept the Athenians' "sick *erōs*" because he expects or wishes that they were not possessed by this affliction. And his hesitation in openly claiming that the Athenians are acting unjustly reminds us of Archidamus. With Nicias, however, the problem of Athenian injustice is more complex. Archidamus feared that Sparta could commit an injustice by not submitting to arbitration; but Nicias fears he himself is implicated in this injustice along with the city – his first speech is indeed genuinely public-spirited.[46] And as we have observed with Sparta, the needs of the city domestically, along with the needs of the city at war, differ yet intertwine in such a manner that the city cannot wholly abandon justice when at war. We are reminded of Thucydides noting Alcibiades' problematic relationship to Athens – thereby agreeing with Nicias' appraisal of Alcibiades' motives – in a comment made before we are allowed to hear Alcibiades' response (15.1-4). Yet despite Nicias' objections (that the Athenians are proceeding with an expedition that neither is beneficial nor proceeds from public-spiritedness, the virtue Nicias endorses), neither Alcibiades' character nor anything revealed about him in his speech were able to deter the Athenians. Alcibiades' speech and the Athenians being reminded of their oaths by the Egestaeans made the city more "eager" for the expedition, not less (19.1).

Nicias introduces his response to the Athenian decision by granting it the success that "we wish" for (*boulometha*). But Nicias will nevertheless offer his judgment on it and the speech abounds with references to himself ("I" – 20.1, 23.3), revealing more clearly the tension between his view and the Athenians' own. Yet Nicias does not refuse command; he will only resign if the Athenians fail to heed his advice. Nicias appears both to desire to lead the expedition and for it not to go forward. This confusion

46 Burns (2011) p. 221.

animates his first two speeches – what he was supposed to offer in his first speech, an assessment of what is needed for success, he now offers in his second speech.

But Thucydides notes in his own introduction to this second speech that Nicias *still* believed he could sway the Athenians from the expedition if they were only made aware of its great scale and risks: great cities such as Syracuse will not be ruled (20.1); it is an expedition unlike any other (21.2); the Athenians will be wholly independent and have no reliance on others since they are entering a "land of strangers" (21.2, 22, 23.2); the Athenians will, therefore, need "good counsel and even more good fortune" (*eu bouleusasthai, eti de pleiō eutukhēsai* – 23.3) to proceed along the "safest" course (*sōtēria*); being "mere humans," they place themselves at the greatest risk (23.3). Such arguments, Thucydides reminds us, were ones Nicias had already attempted to use, without success, in his first speech (6.9.3, 10.5, 11.1-3, 13.1). Thucydides reports that Nicias believed either the Athenians would be deterred from the expedition *or* they would equip it such that they would proceed safely, with the preparations Nicias thought requisite for success (19.2). But in highlighting the extravagance, risks, and difficulty in ruling the Syracusans, Nicias offers little deterrence to Athenian *erōs*. Rather than quelling their ambition with his implicit appeal to the daring needed for success, Nicias reinforces it (and thus its attractiveness to the Athenians) by presenting it in the manner he does. While Pericles had intentionally urged the Athenians to fall in love with their city, Nicias unintentionally leads the Athenians to falling in love with the Sicilian expedition (24.2-3).

Nicias' own motivations for his speeches are, therefore, ambiguous or even confused – he seems uncertain whether he wants to truly avoid the expedition or not. Nicias perhaps still desires the honor of its potential success so long as it can be undertaken safely.[47] With these confused motives, Nicias come to light as straddling Athenian and Spartan views. We also note that in his second speech Nicias only focuses on the material conditions he believes are necessary for success – nothing is said about the

47 Orwin (1994) pp. 119-20 suggests that Nicias may have been fearful of the political ascendancy of Alcibiades. Alcibiades perhaps reminds Nicias of his past contest with Cleon, who was able to elevate himself with his capture of the Spartans at Pylos. If this interpretation is correct, it further reinforces the view that Nicias is concerned not merely with himself, but with the possible dangers of an Athens led by Alcibiades.

command of the expedition; specifically, he does not attempt to deter the Athenians from sending Alcibiades.

The results of Nicias' speeches prove problematic. His intention had been to frighten the Athenians by the scale of the expedition or to bring large enough preparations to ensure their safety. But the Athenians only "became more eager" (*epithumios*) than before because they trust his advice – with the proper preparations, the danger of the expedition could be averted entirely. Thus, *erōs* fell upon all for the expedition – even the older men viewed it as possible and the younger men longed to see and consider "absent sights and spectacles" and had "good hope" that they would return from it "safely"; further, the demos and the military not only expected to earn their wages in the present, but also that the power gained from their conquest would allow their wages to continue *forever*;[48] and with "this desire of the many"[49] others remained quiet and would not speak up for fear that they would be seen as speaking against the city (24.1-4).[50]

Nicias' appeal to safety required emphasizing the danger and risk of the expedition. Instead of a deterrence, this appears to have contributed precisely to the Athenians' *erōs* for the expedition because it also appealed

48 This account of the Athenians' response to the speeches of Nicias and Alcibiades, stated by Thucydides in his own name, appears to confirm that the Athenians did not believe their empire to be susceptible to failure or "death." In their speech at Melos, the Athenians are only able to *conditionally* agree when the Melians point out precisely this possibility (5.91).

49 Connor (1984) p. 168 argues that *pleonōn* ("the many") at 6.24.4 could refer to the majority *or* to Athenian *pleonexia* ("grasping for more"). Hobbes translates this as "vehement desire" but Crawley (1996) renders the phrase as "enthusiasm of the majority" ("enthusiasm" translating *epithumia*, perhaps distancing the reader from Thucydides' use of "love" [*erōs*] in describing the Athenians in the preceding sentence). Given the context, perhaps we could argue both that this desire applies to the majority, but also that this desire was vehement, resulting as it does from both hope and *erōs*. Woodruff's translation (1993) p. 122 "this vehement desire of the majority" thus renders both possible interpretations of the passage, as does Mynott's (2013) "extreme passion on the part of the majority." Mynott notes the ambiguity Connor observes, citing Hornblower III p. 363.

50 On the motivations for the expedition, Thucydides comments on four parts of the city: the older men, the younger men, the demos and military, and those who feared to speak against it. This contrasts with 4.28.5 where he speaks of "the Athenians" and "the moderate [men]," the latter siding with Nicias against Cleon. Nicias' appeal to safety in preparing the Sicilian expedition perhaps reduced the number of moderates within Athens if we presume that the moderates mentioned at 4.28.5 included the older men in Athens who now favor the expedition. Cf. 1.83.1.

to their noble confrontation of these risks. The Athenians are not wholly unmoved by fear, though, and therefore the safety of Nicias' involvement (given his good fortune along with the good counsel of Alcibiades) was the strongest endorsement *for* the expedition. The Athenians are able to combine their hopes with their safety (while concerns with justice and piety were not absent). They were more hopeful for the expedition *because* it had the counsel and presence of Nicias, the lucky general who preached service to the city (24.3). Nicias' virtue is attractive to the demos. Nicias appears to them as he presents himself: genuinely serving his city.

In this way, Nicias' speeches seem utter failures. Thucydides does confirm some of Nicias' arguments against the expedition. That Nicias is wrong about Athenian character raises problems, though, for the attempt in his speeches. These speeches were part of an assembly considering the expedition's preparations; yet it had already been decided upon. And it had already been decided that Alcibiades and Nicias would lead the expedition, with unlimited powers, together. When Nicias therefore assaults Alcibiades' character, despite Thucydides' partial agreement with his assessment, he thereby assaults the commander he will be sharing command with on an expedition of no small risk and danger, rendering it even more risky. That the expedition's preparations were beautiful and especially pious (6.32.1-2) reminds us of the latent Athenian piety that presents itself especially in times of danger (2.21.3, 54.1-5; cf. 2.16.1-2), a danger Nicias emphasized. The safety Nicias' speeches offered, as well as his noble and pious character, appear to belong together in his fellow citizens' reaction to his advice.

Set between the Athenians' decision to prepare for the expedition and its commencement, Thucydides relates the recall of Alcibiades from his position of command to face charges of impiety (6.27-29). With the mutilations of the herms occurring in Athens, Alcibiades is implicated due to his private way of life (61.1-4). Thucydides provides enough evidence for the reader to doubt the charges, but their relevance is nonetheless weighty – regardless of guilt or innocence, the belief of the demos signals Alcibiades' problematic private ambitions. Trust the Athenians place in Nicias is the result of his observable public-spiritedness; but since Thucydides argues that the recall of Alcibiades ultimately harmed the expedition, we are led to the view that Nicias is in part responsible for this recall, even if only because his speeches confirmed the demos' fears of Alcibiades.[51] Nicias was unable

51 Strauss (1964) pp. 203-4; Orwin (1994) p. 126.

to refrain from blaming Alcibiades; Alcibiades lacks *his* virtue because he does not serve the city in any manner. Thucydides, by contrast, implies Alcibiades' abilities would have secured victory over Sicily, and perhaps beyond (6.15.2; cf. 2.65.10-12). Whatever blame Nicias casts on Alcibiades, he possesses talents Nicias lacks. But Alcibiades' foreign policy skills are both suspicious to the demos and harmful to the city domestically; thus, the demos' recall, along with trusting Nicias' counsel, confirms the manner in which the Athenians were affected by Nicias' speech.

We are reminded of Pericles. Trusted by the demos, Pericles himself derived honor from the glory of Periclean Athens. Pericles gave himself to the city because his virtue depended on the city. Pericles sought honor as Nicias did. They appear then to share the same political stature within Athens. By abandoning what Nicias believes to be Athens' interests, however, the Athenians are abandoning the virtue on which Nicias prides himself. And, therefore, Nicias' blame of the Athenians begins to appear as the realization that in pursuing Sicily, they are acting shamefully – he urges those like himself, i.e., those possessing law-bred virtue, not to be ashamed to speak against the expedition since it is only Athenian *erōs* that leads them on. But the problem for Nicias is the law-bred character of Athenian virtue had already begun to decay in Pericles' openly expressed doubt of established law (2.35.1). If the Athenians' desire for Sicily is thus in tension with Nicias' virtue (and more generally, with a not-so-distant Athens, an Athens still visible in the rural Athenians who watched their fatherland being burned by the Spartans early in the war – 2.21.1-3) and Nicias has come to see this, then the union of Nicias' private interest with Athens' public interest begins to fall apart.

While we are aware of the great defeat awaiting Athens, we must not neglect Nicias' exhortations without consideration of their merits. Thucydides confirms the passionate character of the expedition in the preparations undertaken as it is set to depart. These preparations were animated by both hope and fear (6.30.2) as the risks became more apparent (31.1). Thucydides' description particularly emphasizes the Athenians' concern with its appearance – it was the "fairest looking" (*euprepes* – 31.2-3), an attempt to display Athens' power, and accompanied by "daring" (*tolma*) and a "great hope" (*megistē elpidi* – 31.6). On the eve of the riskiest attempt to expand their empire, the Athenians are more affected by the nobility, the beauty, of the expedition than by a sober calculation of their interests in the war at hand, a war presumably still being waged against Sparta.

Nicias' Initial Errors in Sicily

After a digression on the tyranny of Peisistratus and his sons, presented in the context of the Athenian demos' fear of Alcibiades and his recall to Athens on charges of impiety, Thucydides' account turns to the Athenians preparing to attack Syracuse. In the debate preceding Alcibiades' recall, Nicias argues for securing funds for their force, and generally, weighs how to settle affairs in Sicily without endangering the Athenians (6.47). Lamachus (the third commander of the expedition) argues that the Athenians ought to sail to Syracuse immediately, before the Syracusans are able to fully prepare, with the purpose of creating panic among them. Lamachus' entire strategy rests on surprise (49.1-3).

With the recall of Alcibiades, the Athenians are now divided into two forces (62.1). Nicias' force sails to Egesta and is able to receive money he had gone there to secure, but then sails to the city of Hybla and fails to subdue it (63.2). In the following winter, when the Athenians are finally prepared to attack Syracuse itself, the Syracusans had regained courage from the Athenians' failure to engage them immediately. Initially, the Syracusans had both feared and believed the Athenians would do so. Since Lamachus had advised a strategy of surprise, Thucydides intimates that Nicias was author of the Athenians' delay, a strategy that was his alone. But we also recall that Nicias himself, in his second speech, had argued Syracuse must be attacked immediately if the Athenians hoped to overtake the country (23.2). And while the Athenians do secure a victory over the Syracusans, they are unable to continue an assault on the city given the apparent difficulties of doing so during winter (71.2). In this context, Hermocrates exhorts the Syracusans by noting their defeat was due to strategic errors and not the result of cowardice or fear; he implies that had the Athenians done more to harm the Syracusans' resolve, they may have been less eager to receive Hermocrates' advice. That advice included his urging the Syracusans to use the winter for additional preparations against the Athenians (72.4). Given the Athenians' failure to follow through on their attack, the Syracusans are able to commence with these preparations, including sending to Sparta for aid.

Under the influence of the now Athenian-in-hiding Alcibiades, the Spartans agree to send forces to both Syracuse and Attica (93.2). We are meant to notice, of course, that Thucydides only states that it did not *seem* possible to fight against the Syracusans in winter. When the able Demosthenes later arrives in Sicily, he decides on his own strategy against the Syracusans in direct contrast to Nicias' own. Indeed, Thucydides confirms in this context that it was Nicias who initially believed Syracuse could not be attacked in the winter (7.42.3).[52]

Remaining in Catana for the winter, Nicias' decision to delay was seemingly justified by the need for cavalry to match the Syracusans' and to secure other supplies for a future attack. After his defeat in the initial debates and with the expedition being prepared, Nicias' counsel was sought on the forces required. Yet despite Nicias' previous emphasis on the superiority of this Syracusan cavalry in his second speech (6.20.4), he only mentions triremes, hoplites, archers, and slingers, along with allies in his adumbration of the required forces (25.1-2). Nicias' oversight has now harmed the Athenians and seems to compel his delay at Catana. While Nicias was correct to note the disadvantage of Athenian cavalry, his delay to recompense for this disadvantage only created additional problems by strengthening Syracusan morale and also affording them further time for preparations. Nicias allowed both the fear of the Syracusans to dissipate (expecting the Athenians to attack immediately) and to send for Spartan aid (effecting the arrival of the Spartan commander, Gylippus); neither would have occurred otherwise. The Syracusans initially believed, incorrectly as Thucydides presents it, that they could fend off the Athenians on their own (7.42.3). We cannot help but being reminded of Nicias' focus on the overall safety of the expedition as well as his continued strategy, notable for its lack of daring.[53]

Nicias' policy of safety continually leads to errors: He underestimates

---

52 Thucydides does not initially state precisely why the delay in Catana (staying the winter there) occurred – there is no mention of Nicias in particular (6.63.1-3); however, the mention of the cavalry and the issue of supplies and money echoes Nicias' speech before the expedition departed (6.71.2; cf. 6.22). When Demosthenes arrives, Thucydides reveals that it *was* Nicias who caused the delay in Catana (7.42.3). Demosthenes seems to have had little or no concern with supplies – he only wanted to ensure that the Athenians strike fear in the Syracusans and their allies, something Nicias failed to do (6.63.2).

53 Pouncey (1980) pp. 124-25; Westlake (1968) pp. 174, 192-94.

the reinforcements led by Gylippus and fails to attack the disorganized Syracusan army Gylippus was attempting to organize before engaging the Athenians (a continued problem for the Syracusans throughout Thucydides' narrative – 7.3.3-5). Before Gylippus' arrival, the Athenians had been successful in building a siege wall to surround Syracuse and cut off access to supplies, placing the city in a desperate situation. Due to Gylippus' land forces, however, and the building of a counter wall to block the Athenian wall, Nicias moves the Athenians' supplies to forts on Plemmyrium (across the harbor from the city itself – 4.4). Yet this strategy will later prove to be a failure – Gylippus attacks the forts while the Athenians are occupied fighting the Syracusans at sea, leaving them unguarded. Thucydides notes that this loss of Plemmyrium (and thus a loss of supplies) is Nicias' error and the "greatest and foremost" (*megiston te kai en tois prōton*) cause leading to the ruin of the Athenian army (7.24.3). And Nicias' contempt for Gylippus' force (6.104) and characteristic delay only provided opportunity for Gylippus' eventual success.

During the building of the counter wall, Gylippus also continued to attack the Athenians by land. He fails in his first battle as the result of a strategic error hindering, and thus rendering useless, the important Syracusan cavalry. But Gylippus corrects his own mistake, the Syracusans and their allies proving successful in their next engagement (7.5-6.3). This subsequent victory of the eager Gylippus cuts the Athenians off from completing their siege walls, allowing the Syracusans to complete their own counter wall. And Gylippus is also successful in later raising more forces (again) for strengthening Peloponnesian land and sea capabilities. Ironically, it is the Spartan Gylippus who learns from his mistakes and shows a certain vigor in conducting the war, while Nicias is becoming even more cautious and reserved than the Spartan commander he is facing. We also note that the cavalry Nicias failed to recommend in his preparations for the expedition shifts the battle from a near defeat of the Syracusans to securing them a significant victory (7.4.6, 7.5-7.7).

With this defeat and newfound difficulties for the Athenians, Nicias sends a letter to Athens recommending either a recall of the expedition or to provide further reinforcements. Even given reinforcements, though, Nicias' purpose can no longer be the splendid victory the Athenians had hoped for – Thucydides mentions twice in his introduction to the letter that Nicias was only concerned with safety (8.1) and avoiding danger (8.3).

The daring expedition to Sicily which would require a daring commander (read: Alcibiades), now has at its helm Nicias, who seeks to avoid danger through a defensive military policy characterized by delay and safety; this has left Athens with consequential losses. Nicias reminds us of Thucydides' Spartan narrative of the war: continued delays and incomplete measures in battles, inability to provide for supplies and allies, and most notably, lacking vision and strategy to secure a victory in the overall war.

Apart from the strategic issues Nicias betrays in his letter to the Athenians, his concluding remarks are particularly striking. Nicias again blames the Athenians themselves, proclaiming: "For your natures are hard to rule" (*chalepai gar hai hymeterai physeis arxai* – 14.2); the Athenians desire to hear the most pleasant things rather than the truth (*alethes*), and blame (*aitia*) the bearer of bad news for disappointing their expectations (14.4); therefore, Nicias will tell the Athenians the truth as the safest course. Given the issues the expedition is facing (including the problem of supplies and cavalry, along with desertion by foreigners who came to Sicily for the promise of pay – cf. 6.24.3), Nicias argues the Athenians need to allow for a retreat *or* send reinforcements and replace him as commander (because of his current illness). Nicias returning to Athens would occur given either option, but the Athenians refuse his resignation.

Nicias' analysis of the Athenian plight, and his proposed solutions, further highlight the strain between his preference for safety and the Athenians' hoped-for outcome. According to Orwin, "By now [Nicias] really ought to know which of these options [the Athenians] will adopt."[54] While this interpretation of Nicias is certainly plausible, Orwin's "ought" raises a potential difficulty – Nicias, in his letter's stark complaint, is not wholly able to *accept* the difficult natures of the Athenians. Referring to a lack of knowledge, "oughts" imply that we expect human beings never to choose actions or view the world colored by their own moral prejudices or blind spots.

But Thucydides, in the case of another "Spartan," Nicias, has been presenting an opposing view. Nicias wants to be able to subdue the Athenians' stubbornness and therefore hopes they will take his advice – writing a letter was to avoid misunderstanding and blame. For why would Nicias send the letter if he *truly* believed it would not be convincing to the Athenians? To accept their difficult natures, rather than attempt to sway the

54 Orwin (1994) p. 121.

Athenians to his view, would be to undermine Nicias' own belief in the possibility of virtue. Nicias' hope means that he *wishes* the Athenians to act contrary to, or to overcome, their natures, i.e., in service of the city, as Pericles had also admonished the Athenians to do. And by implication, Nicias seems to believe that he deserves to be removed from the expedition now because it no longer conduces to his safety; it is an ill-begotten (not to say potentially immoral) escapade, driven by the Athenians' sick *erōs*.

Considered in light of his concern with safety, Nicias' proposed resignation seems rather self-serving. For if Nicias was also concerned with the safety of the Athenians and was convinced of the desperation of their situation, he would not have allowed those in Athens to decide the issue, potentially leaving his men stranded in the circumstances they now find themselves. On Nicias' own assessment of the circumstances, both here *and* before the expedition, merely sending more ships would not suffice. Nicias appears, therefore, to be duplicitous or "hypocritical" in calling for reinforcements from Athens as a tenable strategy, while proposing a return for himself. Fear resulting from the potential consequences of acting against the Athenian assembly at home is something that Nicias knows well (5.46.4-5; cf. 4.65.3). Nicias is fearful of being blamed for the failure of the expedition and thus refuses forthrightly to recommend his recall to Athens. Bringing more men to Sicily would not seem to alleviate the current Athenian difficulties and, therefore, safety would only seem to reside in a return to Athens.[55]

And in his failure to acknowledge his own errors leading to these difficulties, Nicias instead blames the natures of the Athenians – the problem of telling the Athenians the truth looms large (6.14.4; cf. 3.42.1-6). Nicias' advice seems most motivated by the fear he has of being blamed for *any* decision; avoiding this, he offers *the Athenians* a choice rather than stating a decision himself. Nicias appears utterly concerned only with saving himself at the cost of failing to save the Athenian forces already beleaguered in Sicily.

But in the context of blaming the Athenians, Nicias also offers a justification for his recall – he has proven dedication to Athens in the past with his good service. Nicias hopes the Athenians will allow for his recall now that he is ill and can no longer carry on his duty. Nicias' apparently obvious hypocrisy in failing to recommend the best way to save his men (yet able to

55 Strauss (1964) p. 205; Burns (2011) pp. 226-28.

recommend the best way to save himself) is complicated by his belief that his virtue should be recognized and rewarded by the Athenians. Believing he deserves recompense for his past service, Nicias' request for his return to Athens is not intended by him to hide his errors and subsequent blame; it indicates his own lack of awareness of these errors and of placing himself above his troops. His expectation that the city serves him now contrasts with, but appears also to be informed by, his stated claim that he has served the city. Nicias' confusion stems from the tension we have noted between his private interests and those of Athens. Appearing to exhort the city to safety, Nicias is in fact exhorting Athens to act for *his* safety. That he is unaware of placing his private interest above his men is signaled by appeal to his own public service. His concern with virtue and its reward disguises from himself his placing private safety above that of the city.[56]

There is also a further complication in Nicias' view. In his blame of the Athenians in his letter, we are reminded of his blame of the Athenians before the expedition. And if we are correct to understand the cause of that blame as owing to the injustice of the expedition, then Nicias' letter states his continued disagreement on this basis. Nicias may have wished he could counsel the Athenians to return from Sicily, but he is unable to combat their natures, which includes not only protecting against their hopes not being disappointed (as Nicias fears doing to them here) but also their unjust desires. Indeed, while Nicias' errors in prosecuting the expedition have led to problems, these errors were the consequence of his caution and lack of daring. The counsel of safety that led *the Athenians* to trust in Nicias (and not in Alcibiades) is therefore *itself* in part to blame for the expedition's failure. And Thucydides reinforces Nicias' initial objection to the injustice of the expedition by following Nicias' letter with a detailing of Sparta's renewed prosecution of the war – the Spartans became encouraged from the belief that the Athenians had acted unlawfully and thus breached the treaty (7.18.2-3). As we know, the Spartans were slow and very cautious in their prosecution of the war, most notably after they stated openly the possibility they were to blame for originally breaching the treaty (4.20.2). That Nicias has also betrayed his belief in the injustice of the expedition appears to

56 Burns (2011) pp. 226-27 argues Nicias hides the unpleasant truth of his own errors from himself. We must say "hides" in the sense of being unable to fully confront and accept them.

have motivated both his initial lack of eagerness, as well as contributing to further poor decisions leading to its ruin.

Nicias' Hopes and Athens' Defeat

In response to Nicias' letter, reinforcements arrive from Athens. Demosthenes as commander (along with Eurymedon) believes he has only one chance to shift the advantage in the war, but this opportunity fails (although through no fault of Demosthenes). After this serious defeat at Epipolae, with Gylippus and the Syracusans gaining a victory through both their "daring" (*tolma* – 7.43.6) and "success" (*eupragia* – 46.1), the Athenian commanders consult on what has transpired and also on the condition of their men. While Demosthenes counsels for a return to Athens – including carrying on the war against the Spartans in Attica, one of Nicias' original objections initially in leaving Athens – Nicias now votes against it. Despite the arguments of his letter, Nicias has hope from the arrival of Demosthenes and because he is in contact with a faction inside Syracuse that wanted Athens to take the city (48.2). This strategy, as we recall from Thucydides' previous hint (4.53–54), had been successful at Cythera. Nicias is also hopeful given the large costs the war is placing on Syracuse (7.48.5). These causes of hope are perhaps connected, if we assume that Nicias is in communication with those few within the city who are funding the war.

More striking, though, is Nicias again stating his trepidation about the Athenians at home, how they will judge of his conduct should the commanders vote to return to Athens – Nicias fears the soldiers would report home that the commanders had been bribed; hence Nicias declares that he did not want to die by an unjust verdict but "privately" (*idios* – 48.4). In other words, Nicias accuses other citizens of injustice – the Athenians blame commanders should they return without securing victory, just as they are suspicious of the private motives of those who seek to counsel the city. Whereas the Spartans could hardly believe or admit private motives existed among their first men, the Athenians could hardly believe or admit a commander acted with a view to the good of the city, possessing the quality all cities must inculcate – public-spiritedness.

Yet Nicias' apprehension signals more than his objection to the Athenians' judgment on their commanders; it reveals Nicias' deeper distress that his own death may be an unjust one. For to die "privately" in this instance means to die in battle, courageously, fighting for one's city during war, and thus in an honorable manner. On the other hand, to be sentenced to death on bribery charges in Athens means to die a very shameful and public death. In his stated preference, Nicias is again focused on himself above the possible safety of his troops. This is a problem we have seen before, and it cannot but shine a bad light on Nicias. Yet we only understand Nicias' psychology if we seek to understand the expedition from his point of view: Nicias is not simply malicious in his decision; for he *also* had hopes the enemy was weakening and his secret conferences with certain Syracusans would be successful in ending the war. For Nicias, these hopes *justify* his judgment to remain in Sicily despite the difficulties facing the Athenians.

Strategically, Thucydides' own objection to Nicias' decision is perhaps contained in Demosthenes' response to Nicias' hopes – Nicias, in contrast to Demosthenes, relies on others within the city and not on himself or what he can manifestly affect (7.49.1-3). But Thucydides is more intent on allowing us to notice that Nicias' policy is based on these particular hopes, hopes covering over his fears and confrontation with them. Nicias again disguises difficulties and inconsistences in his own views from himself, elevating his just death above saving his men and thus possibly his city.

Nicias' demand for a just death, by succumbing to the false judgment of his city, is in keeping with an appeal to his public service in his letter to Athens. To retreat would be to risk appearing as weak or cowardly, something Nicias had specifically exhorted the other elder Athenians not to do. Nicias fears he will be judged lacking in civic virtue by returning to Athens. Despite knowing that the "Athenians' nature" (48.4) is prone to suspicion and skepticism, and that the soldiers are liable to protect themselves from the accusation of acting cowardly by accusing the commanders of bribery, Nicias is more disturbed by the thought of being judged unjustly by his city. Despite his implication that the Athenians are unjust judges, Nicias still fears the shame such a judgment would bring on his own life. After all, Athens is *his* city.

Nicias' openly stated objections to Athenian imperialism, as a policy issuing from Athenian *erōs*, come together with his fear of the city's blame should he disappoint their hopes. This results in delay, his vacillation on which policy to pursue.[57] If the Athenians attempt escape, Nicias may be punished in Athens. But even Nicias glimpses the suffering of his men as well as his own. His fears of an unjust death in Athens conflict with his hopes, not only for his own escape, but also for that of his men. Yet by failing to act decisively either way, Nicias' vacillation results in failed strategy. It results in a delay in any possibility of the Athenians escaping Syracuse. When matters worsen and additional troops arrive to join the Syracusans, even Nicias cannot deny the dire circumstances.

Most of the Athenians, however, were impressed with the eclipse now occurring and Nicias refuses to consider the worsening circumstances in accordance with an interpretation of the soothsayers. Thucydides remarks here that Nicias was "too attached to superstition and the like" (*ēn gar ti kai agan theiasmō te kai tō toioutō proskeimenos* – 50.4). Despite their piety, the Syracusans did not interpret the eclipse in the same manner (51.1). Reminding us of Sparta's sacrifices before leaving on foreign campaigns, the Athenians' interpretation of the eclipse becomes justification for further delay, implying any action would risk a vengeful response from the gods. Nothing could be in starker contrast to the Athenian thesis as stated at Melos. Thucydides thereby signals a shared piety of Nicias and the Athenian demos, i.e., those who do not expound the Athenian thesis (cf. 5.105; 2.14, 16.2). Nicias is trusted by the demos because of his piety and public-spiritedness; the demos is distrustful, however, of so to speak everyone else who distinguishes themselves from the city.

Due to the Athenian delay as the result of the eclipse, the Syracusans attempt to "compel" (*anankē*) the Athenians into a naval battle. Successful, the Syracusans gain a decisive victory. The "great hopes" of the Athenians are now gone; they had lost their "vigor" (or "spirit" – *athumia* – 7.55.1).[58] Seeing this, Nicias delivers a speech, the last quoted speech in Thucydides' text (77.1-7). He has become "eager" (*prothumia*) and serious about reaching as many men as possible with his words, his intention being to benefit as

57 Pouncey (1980) p. 126 observes Thucydides' numerous mentions of "delay" in characterizing Nicias' actions during the debate regarding whether to remain in Sicily or attempt an escape (7.47-50).

58 Throughout the Sicilian narrative, Thucydides uses *prothumos* ("ready," "eager," or "willing") to characterize both the Syracusans and the Spartan commander, Gylippus (in fact, Book Seven begins as such – 7.1.4). In using the related *athumia* here, Thucydides signals a reversal for the daring Athenians and punctuates their defeat. See also note 49 above.

many as possible. Nicias remains hopeful in face of the Athenians' "unworthy misery" (77.1). As Nicias must admit, however, despite his previous good fortune, his fate is now that of the other Athenians, including the "meanest" (*phaulotatois* – 77.2) among them. While Nicias has lived his life with piety and justice toward gods and men, what the Athenians may suffer will befall him as well. Fearing punishment for the injustice of the expedition, Nicias turns again to hope, offering his views on the gods. If the Athenians offended the gods, they have already been sufficiently punished with their previous defeats. Implicitly, Nicias suggests the gods recognize necessity, only judging human beings based on what they reasonably deserve – an act of injustice followed by a punishment human beings can understand as proportionate to the transgression. While the expedition may have been unjust, punishment via the Athenians' current suffering has been meted out by the gods. Despite this, though, Nicias seems reluctant to wholly exculpate himself or the Athenians from possible further punishment – he does not wholly deny that the Athenians (and himself) face potentially graver dangers in their attempts to escape (the success of which Nicias qualifies – "if" at 77.7). That Nicias admits to fear, if only for a moment, and to hope because his fate rests on his own virtue, is to admit that his fate has been brought down to that of other men, those who desired the expedition for profit and from a sick *erōs*. And he now may suffer as they do. But Nicias is still hopeful because he does not accept, despite raising the possibility, that he himself has been unjust.[59]

Nicias' admission to his fears of further punishment from the gods is a particularly troubling claim. For if there is a correspondence between living a pious and just life and receiving favorable or just treatment from the gods, then Nicias should not be fearful. Only if he has been unjust should he fear punishment. Both his belief that the Athenians have been punished and his fear that they may be punished further implies that Athenian injustice is also Nicias' injustice. Recalling the tension between Nicias and Athens, the virtuous life of the pious and just man who serves his city honorably finds itself at odds with an Athens that can only, at best, vacillate in its uneasy acceptance of a man such as Alcibiades. In conflict with the city he has dedicated his life to serving, Nicias is a more complete portrait of what remains only germane in Thucydides' Sparta – the tension between a virtuous citizen and his regime. But for Thucydides, Nicias lacked the virtues

59 Burns (2011) pp. 228-29.

required to conduct the foreign policy of a daring city. Nicias' lack of daring harms Athens. We are left, though, with the difficulty that the Athenians could not trust a man like Alcibiades, one who does not attempt to disguise his private interests and ambitions and possesses none of the traditional virtues a man such as Nicias displays. Alcibiades appears as a manifestation of the Athenian thesis, a thesis unleashing grave problems *within* the city.[60]

Returning to Nicias: One cannot help but sense Nicias' nobility in his surrender on the condition that his men are allowed to live (7.85.1). And despite the fact that his surrender to Gylippus, in particular, was a calculation based on "trusting" (*pisteuō*) that Spartan (and thus appears to be a decision with a view to his own safety), Nicias proceeds from the belief Gylippus would judge him more justly. Indeed, Nicias was particularly "beloved" (*prosphilēs*) by the Spartans because he had "eagerly" (*prothumos*) worked to secure the peace treaty and the return of the Spartan men imprisoned on the island (86.3). Gylippus believed it would be "his noble prize" (*kalon to agōnisma*) to return to Sparta with their greatest Athenian friend. But the Syracusans and Corinthians both feared Nicias; he was put to death against Gylippus' wishes. Notice, however, that Thucydides renders these specific reasons for Nicias' death of little significance – "it was said" (*hōs elegeto*) that the Syracusans he was conspiring with feared him revealing them; "for these or the like were the causes of his death" (*kai ho men toiautē ē hoti engutata toutōn aitia etethnēkei* – 86.4-5). Thucydides distances us from Nicias' *actual* death because his eulogy of Nicias is intended to direct us to the *manner* in which Nicias lived his life and how precisely his fate was undeserved.

This returns us to Thucydides' eulogy: Nicias "least of all deserved his

60 Bruell (1974) p. 15 argues that Thucydides' praise of Nicias is related to his view of the Corcyraean civil war and corresponding praise of Sparta – it is from the point of view of the needs of the regime. In other words, the virtues of Nicias and the Spartans are both law-bred, whereas the Athenians of post-Periclean Athens lack such laws, seen especially in the regime changes in Book Eight based on private interests. The piety of Nicias and the Spartans issues from their obedience to laws, while Athenian piety reappears preceding their expedition to Sicily, suffering as they do from fears reminding us of cautious Nicias and the Spartans. Athenian *nomoi* from the past linger, returning in vehement form despite attempts of the Athenian thesis to separate justice from piety, or more specifically, to reduce the gods to the observable necessities the Athenians claim to have comprehended.

death since he lived his life in accordance with law-bred virtue" (86.5).[61] Nicias possessed virtues the city endorses and educates its citizens to through its laws. Nicias is the Athenian reminding us of Sparta because he is a representative of the old Athens, i.e., the pre-Periclean Athens at odds with the openly stated Athenian thesis. The people – the many in the city who cannot be said to adhere to the Athenian thesis nor understand its full import – trusted Nicias because he was law-abiding, pious, and upheld traditional virtues; he may pursue private honor, but he also serves the city; he is not suspected of tyranny as Alcibiades because his private habits do not strike fear in the demos. And from the citizen's point of view, adherence to virtues beneficial to the city is evidence one has abandoned, or at least moderated, thoughts of one's own private good.

When Nicias admits openly that he is not unconcerned with benefiting himself as a private individual, the benefits he receives are in union with his public service to Athens. While adherence to virtue may require a sacrifice of one's private good, virtue also promises rewards, the public benefits one receives. The Athenians who die in the trenches of Syracuse after their capture gave up their own private lives in Athens for the imperial ambitions of their city. Along with this sacrifice and the demands and duties it places on one's life, though, are the rewards by gods and men, including the honors of the city and the just judgment of the gods. Nicias himself reveals this expectation when he solicits the Athenians to allow for his retirement from the Sicilian expedition; Thucydides therefore reveals this expectation in his eulogy of Nicias.

But as commentators have noted, we cannot help but draw the conclusion that Nicias' belief in virtue or his theology "is refuted by his fate."[62] What Nicias expected from being a pious and just man, a man who lived his life according to virtue, was not death in battle. In turning himself over to Gylippus, he hoped for a just judgment on his life, i.e., he expected that Gylippus, being a Spartan, would reward him for the manner in which he had previously benefited Sparta (a just judgment). Nicias' unawareness,

61 On the difficulty of translating what seems to be Thucydides' intentional ambiguity in this passage, see Hornblower III pp. 741-42. Compare Mynott (2013).

62 Strauss (1983) p. 101. Connor (1984) p. 205n53 concurs arguing that Thucydides is "emphasizing the failure of Nicias' own expectations" (see Connor's footnote for scholarly debate on the passage). Romilly (2012) p. 92n62: "The narrative is, in fact, a contradiction of his speech rather than a confirmation of it." Burns (2011) p. 230 uses the same phrase as Strauss.

or partial awareness, of his own competing views of deeds and fate, is an important part of understanding him as a human being.

Whereas the law-abiding Spartan did not seek to distinguish himself from the city (cf. 86.2), Nicias did, even while also serving the city. That service to each came into tension cannot hide from us the fact that Nicias hoped for their perfect union. Brasidas, meanwhile, offers a striking contrast. Thucydides certainly intends the comparison – for while Brasidas also perishes in battle fighting for his city, Brasidas achieves honors Nicias is unable to achieve. But Brasidas does not appear to suffer from the same hopes Thucydides locates as the basis of Nicias' strategic errors in battle. Brasidas does share, though, the aims of "prosperity and honor" (*eutuchein te kai timasthai* – 5.16.1) and therefore the honorable wartime actions he undertakes (apparently on behalf of Sparta but also on behalf of himself) raises the question of whether he too perhaps shares Nicias' view of human life. Thucydides thus reveals another facet of Spartan character through their most noteworthy commander.

Brasidas: Sparta's Liberator

Despite Brasidas' pivotal role in Thucydides' narrative, and his unique relation to the city of Sparta, scholarly accounts are rare. Remarks on Brasidas often note Thucydides' striking praise, but ultimately conclude that Brasidas does not receive enough commentary to distinguish his importance. Indeed, Brasidas dies early in Book Five and the narrative covering his involvement in the war is largely (though not entirely) concentrated to a portion late in Book Four. [63]

63 Connor's (1984) pp. 127-40 narrative account offers many important observations on this period of the war. While Connor is correct to note the importance of understanding Spartan liberation and the reaction of the cities in the northern Greece region to it (p. 138), he hesitates to explicate Brasidas' motives and culpability for the revolts of Athens' subject cities. Heilke (2004) investigates Brasidas as an instance of Thucydides' narrative, educative as it is for potential statesmen. Similarly, Wylie (1992) seeks to appraise Thucydides' "account of Brasidas' military career and of the operations in which he was a protagonist." However, he admits in a footnote that "[u]nfortunately we have no other major source on Brasidas' career except Diodorus Siculus (12, 43, 62, 67-68, 72-74), who adds little to Thucydides and indeed appears to have used him as his authority (cf. Diod. 12, 62, 1-5 and Thuc. 4, 11-12)." Wylie concludes pp. 92-93: "What strikes us most forcibly in reviewing Brasidas' military

Yet it would be a mistake to rate importance in this manner; after all, Pericles dies in Book Two. Brasidas also resembles Nicias in a few ways:

---

career is not so much his gifts - which were considerable, and almost unique among Spartans - as his limitations." Yet by focusing only on the military aspects of Brasidas' actions, Wylie does not develop an overarching interpretation of Thucydides' Brasidas, nor of his place in the overall Spartan narrative. Cartledge and Debnar (2006) p. 573 make a similar effort. As I noted in the Introduction, they claim Thucydides does not impute motives to Brasidas apparently because he lacked information. This is odd since Thucydides states directly that Brasidas desired success and honor (5.16); and, I would argue, shows through the narrative a great deal about Brasidas. Hornblower II Introduction pp. 38-61 sees Thucydides' presentation of Brasidas as Homeric, seeking to compare him to Achilles (and history to epic poetry). Burns (2011) p. 508n3 correctly notes the general lack of scholarly attention to Brasidas. His account is one of the more recent, focusing on how Thucydides' Brasidas contributes to an analysis of moral virtue and its potential limits. Burns contrasts his account with Heilke by arguing that Heilke begins from the realist assumption that political actors cannot refrain from pursuing their self-interest. By beginning at this point (an assumption that proves problematic), Heilke arrives at the conclusion that Brasidas' virtues fell short of achieving the success he desired. But Burns argues, correctly I believe, that Brasidas' concern with his own private interests is far from clear – Thucydides praises Brasidas for his measured or gentle conduct and his justice (pp. 509-10). And it is these virtues (as we have observed in the case of the Melians and Nicias) that demand precisely foregoing one's self-interest. The Melians' sense of injustice and Nicias' blame of the Athenians' *erōs* are the moral reactions of those who expect others to pursue moral virtue as they themselves believe they have, since moral virtue promises one the best way of life. Palmer (2015) focuses on Brasidas as "the Spartan Alcibiades" one of Thucydides' most preeminent individuals and, possibly, a man who sought to liberate Greece and found a new regime in Sparta. His basis for this is: 1) Brasidas' successes in harming Athens; 2) How well he was received by Athens' subject cities; and 3) The fact that Brasidas had his own army, outfitted with Helots serving under him. This is certainly an intriguing reading of Brasidas and elevates his importance (rightly in my view) in Thucydides' account. An objection to this view, it seems to me, is how difficult it is to imagine a Sparta that is not Sparta. Certainly, we witness regime change in Athens and Corcyra, the latter the result of the larger war and fighting between the few and the many. In Athens, it is also the few and the many that cause *stasis*; that strife is only moderated by Alcibiades. And while Palmer draws useful comparisons between the two figures, it is unclear if the few versus many distinction functions quite the same in Sparta. After all, the many would need to be the Helots and the few the Spartiate citizens including the hereditary kingship. Could regime change occur without devolving into all-out civil war? If Brasidas possesses the long list of qualities Palmer notes Thucydides attributes to him, he surely would recognize the extreme danger of regime change. And since Spartan order rests on its divinely sanctioned laws, we would have to know more about how Brasidas could affect a transition away from their (very) longstanding regime. The precedent, if there is one, would seem to be the re-founding of Amphipolis (5.11.1). Could Brasidas replace Lycurgus?

Both are noted earlier in the war, mentioned seemingly in passing during events of apparently little importance; both receive a eulogy from Thucydides; and both eulogies note each man's "virtue" (*aretē*). The question raised for the reader, then, is whether Brasidas' actions recommend him as a statesman able to overcome the shortcomings of the admirable, yet flawed, Nicias. Those shortcomings cast a shadow over Thucydides' praise. Nicias' virtuous actions were governed by hopes and an attendant blindness both to the good of the city he purported to serve and also to his own continued success and virtue. But unlike Nicias, Brasidas' virtue is not qualified by Thucydides as "law-bred" (7.86.5; cf. 4.81). Even more striking, no other character in his account is accorded the honors of a god by another city for actions in the war: the Amphipolitans replaced their city's founder, Hagnon, with Brasidas (5.11.1). Brasidas thus recommends himself not only as Thucydides' portrait of Sparta's most qualified and admirable statesman, but as *the* most notable statesmen in his account as a whole. And as to the contention that we are lacking evidence to assess Brasidas, this is simply not true.[64]

Given this possibility, along with what we learn of "Spartan" psychology via both the Melians and Nicias, I have refrained from presenting Brasidas in chronological order (Thucydides' presentation placing him closer in time to the events at Pylos and the resulting peace arising from his and Cleon's deaths). Thucydides' statements and narration demonstrating his position as a Spartan commander (and citizen) draw us back toward a deeper consideration of the Spartan individual and the successes of the city as a whole. Observing what we have of Sparta and the Spartans, however, now allows us to properly assess Brasidas' prominence, as both promising and troubling. For Brasidas' qualities are a departure from the slowness and lack of daring the Spartans habitually betray. And by comparing the attribution of virtue to Nicias and Brasidas, Brasidas' virtue, in lacking the qualification of "law-bred" (or "conventional"), cannot be only or even principally the result of Spartan *nomoi*. Thucydides' judgment must be understood as distinguishing his virtue from that of the typical Spartan. Nicias is the traditional, moderate Athenian at the moment the new enlightenment

64 Tigerstedt I (1965) p. 129 astutely observes that Thucydides "reproduces no less than four direct and two indirect speeches by Brasidas, more than anyone else, Pericles not excepted."

thesis, the Athenian thesis, took hold of his city. Is Brasidas perhaps his very opposite?

To understand Brasidas, I will trace the following: First, consider Thucydides' introductory mentions of Brasidas. Second, detail battles Brasidas is involved in, showing his growing abilities set against repeated Spartan flaws. Third, weigh his speeches, where we are allowed to hear *his* vision of Sparta, sharing but departing from that of Sparta itself. Finally, I analyze Thucydides' assessment of Brasidas, offering as it does important conclusions on Spartan psychology and the functioning of the regime.

Thucydides' Introduction of Brasidas

Through seemingly trivial and unimportant events, Thucydides' early narrative of Brasidas presents hints to the reader, a tactic he also employed with Nicias. Thucydides' first mention of Brasidas is during an attack by the Athenians on the vital area of Laconia on the Peloponnesus. Attacking the Peloponnesus was part of Pericles' strategy to combat Sparta and its allies, arguing as he had against fighting on land to protect Attica. By chance, Brasidas is present when the Athenians land in Laconia and he quickly gathers some hoplites to defend the coastal city of Methone, repelling the Athenian attack. This victory wins Spartan praise – in fact, Brasidas was the first to receive such praise during the war (2.25.2). By contrast, the anger and blame by Sparta and Athens, against both Archidamus (for his hesitation in attacking Attica directly) and Pericles (for refusing a full engagement with the Spartans outside of Athens' walls), is mentioned by Thucydides in this context (2.18.1-4, 21.2-3). Brasidas' quickness and initiative, his "daring action" (*tolmēma*), distinguish him from the Spartan king Archidamus' delay at Attica – the first instance of a difference between Brasidas and another Spartan is marked precisely by his quickness or daring or vigor.[65]

Thucydides next mentions Brasidas after the Spartan admiral, Cnemus,

65 Connor (1984) p. 128n45 notes a "surprising number of passages" where Thucydides uses forms of "to run" (*trechō*) or "running" (*dromos*) connected to actions of Brasidas, including the passage I have been discussing above (2.25.2; cf. 2.94.3, 4.112.1, 5.9.6, 10.6). *Tolmēma* at 2.25.2, translated as "exploit" by Jowett (1881), Crawley (1996), and Mynott (2013), is related to "daring" (*tolma*). On the early actions of Brasidas, and Thucydides' language in describing him, see also Palmer (2015) pp. 65-68.

is defeated by the Athenian commander, Phormio, in a naval battle at Naupactus (2.84.3-5). Brasidas is sent, along with two other commissioners, to aid Cnemus in further engagements. Sparta sends the commissioners, as Thucydides notes, out of "anger" (*orgē*) toward Cnemus for the defeat, believing that some "misconduct" (*malakos* – "weakness" or "softness") on his part was responsible. Thucydides instead observes that the inferiority of the Spartan navy and its lack of experience was the true cause of Sparta's defeat (85.2). We are reminded of the blame directed toward Agis after the near battle with Argos, resulting in the Spartans creating a new law sending counselors with the king on campaigns (along with the bribery accusations against Pleistoanax). Perhaps due to his previous victory at Methone, Brasidas here appears to have Spartan trust on his side. Thucydides' own view of the cause of Cnemus' defeat, though, is a reminder of the Spartan tendency to blame their own men, fearing corruption in their intentions, rather than questioning whether they had done what was necessary to gain victory in battle. Sparta was known, after all, for its strength in fighting on land; the sea, as Pericles argued, was the domain of Athens, a Spartan shortcoming Archidamus himself knew well (1.80.4).

With Brasidas and the commissioners arriving, the Spartans and their allies prepare for another battle. Thucydides now presents a speech preceding the battle, a speech delivered by one of the commanders of the Peloponnesians (which commander is left unspecified – 4.86). The speech addresses their previous defeat, while also preparing the men for the upcoming contest. In so doing, it offers us one of the rare accounts of Spartans speaking about themselves. The speech most noticeably appeals to the "daring" (*tolma*) of the Spartans, a daring apparently superior to that of their Athenian opponents (2.87.4-5); it ends by arguing that any misconduct on the part of the men will be deservedly punished, while "honor" (*timē*) will be the reward for the man who conducts himself with "virtue" (*aretē* – 87.9). While Thucydides notes that daring would certainly have aided the Spartans in possibly defeating the Athenians (8.96.3-5; 2.94.1, 3.29.1), their lack of daring is, as we have seen by now, habitual and readily apparent. It is certainly at odds with Archidamus extolling a moderation founded in one's sense of shame.

This speech, then, appears to endorse the Spartans' view of themselves and perhaps also endorses Brasidas' own view of what the Spartan virtues are and those which he himself strives to cultivate and embody. In its anonymity, the speech at least does not distinguish Brasidas from the other commissioners.[66] Besides these remarks, however, the Spartans also partially admit here that experience, i.e., Sparta's lack of naval experience, may have contributed to their loss in the previous naval battle. If this is the more decisive cause of their loss (rather than cowardice), then the Spartan view that their virtue should prove decisive in battle appears problematic. If Spartan virtue, which they laud as courage or daring in battle (considering their continual charge of "misconduct" against their own as well as invocation to daring action) does not compensate for their lack of experience in certain types of warfare, then Sparta must innovate in their arts of war (for example, in their navy) if they hope to achieve victory. But as the Corinthians argued, innovation in laws and arts occur together – seeking improvements in the arts and discovering that innovation does indeed produce superiority, human beings naturally begin to legislate with a view to what appears to be best (1.71.3). Spartan virtue, though, is old, pious, and law-bred, i.e., laws unchanged over a great length of time and sanctioned by the god at Delphi, Apollo. If Sparta was to innovate in their arts of war to confront the contingencies arising from the Peloponnesian War, it appears their regime could also be susceptible to innovation unless the Spartans could improve their laws and still remain fundamentally "Sparta."

With this consideration as background, it is in the context of Thucydides' presentation of Brasidas that we witness the Spartans speaking about their virtue, a rare occurrence (cf. 1.84, 4.17-20). The attribution of daring to the Spartans, in a speech possible given, or at least influenced, by Brasidas raises questions about how the Spartans understand their own qualities as citizens and men, i.e., whether Sparta and Brasidas do indeed agree on how they understand virtue. Possible reforms required by the Spartans for success at war directs our attention to Brasidas. Later, it is Brasidas himself who will employ "art" (*technē* – 5.8.2), in opposition to Spartan virtue and their strict battle order (68), once he realizes the Spartan army is not equal in "worth" (*axiōma*) to the Athenians (5.8.1-4).[67]

---

66 Burns (2011) p. 512n21. Tigerstedt I (1965) p. 129n214 attributes this speech to Brasidas.

67 Wasserman (1966) p. 294 notices that Brasidas extols Sparta's virtues over Athens' experience (here and throughout his account), but does not consider the tension between the needs to innovate in war and the source of the Spartan virtues. Thus, he argues that Brasidas is a "mean" between Archidamus and Gylippus (and Xenophon's

Spartan Failure and Brasidas' Ascent

Brasidas' initial appearances are a reminder of *the* problem facing Sparta even in the early stages of the war, i.e., their prosecution of war. The Spartans act decisively only when they believe no danger is present (3.15.2, 16). When Mytilene is set to revolt from Athens with supposed Spartan support, they again exhibit slowness (27), while Thucydides provides his own judgment suggesting they should have instead made haste (29.1). Alcidas' lack of willingness to proceed to Mytilene to challenge the Athenians' attack on the city (whom the Mytilenians were eventually compelled to come to terms with – 27.1) and his rejection of a proposal by some of Sparta's allies to attempt to affect the revolt of Ionia (which Thucydides notes did in fact have hope for success) does nothing to aid Sparta's interests in the war. And besides Ionia, the Spartans generally were in a position to be successful *if* they capitalized on those cities wanting to liberate themselves from Athens – this would deprive Athens of its sources of revenue, its tributary "allies," a strategy successful later in the war that severely harmed the Athenian empire (6.91.6-7, 7.18.1, 27.3, 28.4). In this denial of aid to Mytilene and further rejecting the proclaimed purpose of Sparta's declaration of war, Thucydides presents Alcidas as affecting nothing, instead slaughtering prisoners of those Athenian allies that Sparta and its allies harassed on their way back to the Peloponnesus (3.32).

After the Athenian debate on the fate of Mytilene and the Spartan debate on the fate of Plataea, Brasidas reappears as counselor to Alcidas, sailing to Corcyra where the revolution there was now unfolding (69). Brasidas' stature in Sparta has been elevated. And again, Thucydides' placement of this reappearance (following as it does on one of the most visible instances of the Spartans' questionable justice) bids us to compare Brasidas as he relates to Alcidas, infamous for his thoughtless killing of Athenian subjects, the very cities Sparta is presumably liberating.

When they arrive at Corcyra, the Spartans and their allies are able to push back the Athenians in a small sea battle. With Corcyra in disorder and expecting Sparta and its allies to attack, Brasidas urges moving on the city but Alcidas again refrains. Corcyra thereby falls into civil war and, despite a faction of the few appealing to Sparta to aid their restoration within the

Lysander) without wondering if this mean can be maintained. Cf. Proietti (1987) pp. 79, 111.

city, Sparta fails to offer support (3.85.3). With the chance to liberate a subject city of Athens, a typical Spartan decides against an opportunity which offered to fulfill both the Spartan pretext for waging war and serve their broader strategic interests. It is Mytilene all over again. The Spartans (including the central Spartan, Alcidas) instead establish a colony in Heraclea, Thucydides noting (as previously discussed) their harsh governance, eventually leading the colony to revolt. Those who joined expected the colony would prosper, given Sparta itself *was* a prosperous city (93.2). But Spartan *nomoi* were unlike those of any other city and failed amongst others.

It is with this background and in this context, with the Spartans now being attacked by the artful Demosthenes and the Athenians on Pylos, that Brasidas reemerges, as it were from behind Alcidas' shadow. He is now a captain ("of a trireme" – *triērarchos*) and "distinguishes" (*phaneros*) himself in this battle (4.11). Despite the difficult position they find themselves in, Brasidas gives an exhortation to the men because he believes they are not forcing their ships through. To the "allies" in particular he urges sacrificing their ships because of the many "good deeds" (*euergesia*) Sparta has done for them (11.4); the allies must now be willing to sacrifice themselves, to aid Sparta in securing the fortification at Pylos. Proceeding forward himself by compelling his ship's pilot to run their vessel aground, Brasidas follows his own exhortation in deed; in the process he is wounded and faints. Thucydides seems to confirm that the landing was in fact difficult, but also reminds us again here (similar to his remarks regarding Cnemus versus Phormio) that the Spartans were not a naval people (12.2-3).

This remark appears starkly out of context, for he had already established each city's strengths in his Archaeology, in the Corinthians' speech, in Pericles' speeches, and in the strategy of Archidamus. Could its repetition serve another purpose here? Brasidas seems not to have accepted Sparta's naval shortcomings or is attempting to alter the Spartan manner by urging them to undertake uncharacteristically daring (and naval) actions. Notably eager himself in all of his actions thus far, this error may have been caused precisely because he was *too* tenacious – Demosthenes knew where to expect the Spartans to attack and *was* correct, while Brasidas failed to account for the difficulty of their position (which Thucydides himself notes – 12.2) and the inexperience of the Spartan navy (2.85.2). Brasidas is harmed by his good intentions; but Thucydides does not blame Brasidas for his un-Spartan daring.

Between Brasidas being wounded and his reappearance at Megara (4.12.1, 4.70-73), the Spartans have been significantly harmed in the war. Even if they had intentions to liberate Greek cities from Athens, that cause has been eclipsed by their desire to end the war and secure the return of their men from Sphacteria. And when the Athenians also attack and hold Cythera, the Spartans are distraught, with Thucydides offering a striking passage adumbrating the numerous problems they now face (55.1-4; cf. 41). Brasidas' ascent occurs, therefore, when Sparta is becoming increasingly disinterested in the overall war – he uses his place in Sparta to pursue the official, yet seemingly abandoned, Spartan war effort. Brasidas pushes forward with a war his city no longer wants, in contradistinction to Nicias' reluctance to pursue an invasion his city fervently desired.

At Megara, Brasidas arrives by "chance" (70.1), his original purpose being to move with his army toward Thrace.[68] While the Megarians refuse him admittance to the city, he is able to gain their confidence by positioning his force before the Athenians, prepared to engage in battle; he is successful here merely by a show of force – the Athenians decide not to engage him and thus the Megarians consider the Athenians defeated simply by avoiding fighting. Both factions within the city await the outcome of the battle (71.2), but the pro-Athenian faction can do nothing after this "victory" (73.4). Brasidas' willingness to place himself in harm's way rather than avoiding risk gains Megara over to Sparta and its allies. Brasidas believed through Spartan willingness to fight the Athenians, they would "justly" (*dikaiōs*) obtain "victory" (*nikēn* – 73.2).

Continuing his expedition toward Thrace (with Thracian cities now in revolt from Athens) Brasidas encounters a difficulty – the Thessalians refuse his army movement across their countryside since Thessaly was sympathetic to the Athenians. In response, Brasidas proclaims he is a "friend" (*philos*) of Thessaly, only at war with the Athenians (78.4). With this, Brasidas is allowed to move through Thracian territory; it also reveals Brasidas' view of the expedition's purpose (i.e., Athenian allies or sympathizers were not his enemy). But Thucydides also hints that the support Brasidas received

68 Connor (1984) p. 129n48 points out Thucydides' repeated references to "chance" (*tychē*) throughout his account of Brasidas (4.70.1, 70.2, 73.3, 86.6, 104.5, 111.2, 112.2, 113.2).

for his expedition was *only* the outcome of Sparta's present difficulties at home. Sparta send out forces to harass the Athenians abroad with the hopes of drawing them away from attacks on the Laconia region of the Peloponnesus (uncomfortably close to the city itself) and Brasidas continues his campaign to Thrace, now with seven hundred Helots as a part of this overall force. In fact, the Spartans agree to send an army with Brasidas precisely because it provided a "pretext" (*prophasis*) to allow Helots in particular to be sent out – the Spartans believed they were in significant danger after the capture of Pylos of another Helot revolt (80.2).

The narrative of Brasidas' campaigns leads Thucydides to now detail the key domestic issue he had previously mentioned in passing: Helots in Sparta (80.1-5. Cf. 4.41.3). Constantly fearing revolution, the Spartans regularly punished a select number of the Helot population to maintain obedience from the whole – they were chosen according to those who distinguished themselves fighting for Sparta in its wars; in their self-selection, Thucydides presents the Helots as believing themselves "most worthy" of distinction (80.3). But the Spartans kill them for precisely this reason, punishing the best Helots for *the* virtue demanded from full Spartan citizens. Indeed, the killing of the Helots who significantly aided Sparta undermines the very principle of justice that animates the entire regime – dedication of the individual to the city, to the common good of Sparta. Protecting the regime, yet while sharing in none of its offices nor its honors, the Helots always present a faction an enemy can exploit. Nonetheless, the cause of the Spartans' execution is also traceable to the distinction they made between those who were their kin and those who were not (3.92.1; cf. 92.4). That the Spartans required a pretext for sending out the Helots signals their inability to admit that the best of the Helots were both a threat and had in fact served Sparta. Could they not have "promoted" the best Helots to citizenship? Alternatively, the pretext allows both a defense against the threat, which they only partially admit to themselves, and allows the Spartans to cover over that admission, an admission which would cause them shame (cf. 1.84).

On the other hand, Brasidas does not hesitate to use the Helots as a portion of his force; he is eager to continue with Sparta's war of liberation. Able to use them as his army, the fear of a Helot revolt in Sparta appears to be alleviated more effectively by Brasidas allowing the Helots to *serve* the city rather than suspecting them of undermining it (even though Spartan fear *was* justified – 1.101.2-102.1). And after Brasidas' death and the continual service of the Helots in the war, the Spartans themselves do eventually recognize Brasidas' Helots' service to the city by granting them their liberty (5.34.1). Thucydides relates this in the context of the loss of liberty (albeit temporarily) of those who were captured at Pylos – the Spartans feared the men who surrendered at Pylos would believe they had suffered a "dishonor" (*atimia*) and thus may themselves attempt to instigate a revolution. The Spartans appear to have recognized, at least by this action, that continued punishment of the Helots without reward was a policy fraught with risks. This liberation is at least more in keeping with their own principles than the policy of killing those who had nobly dedicated themselves to a city to which they did not truly belong.

Thucydides sets Sparta's domestic problems against its commander most successful at combating the Athenians (4.81.1-3). Brasidas successfully conducts his campaigns, gaining allies from previously Athenian cities, while the Spartans stayed at home and trained for war (the Helot population engaging in the labor needed by the city, thus allowing full citizens the leisure for this training).[69] In other words, the war the Spartans were most focused on involved suppressing the Helot population and this kept the regime attentive to domestic politics with less consideration of foreign wars – it was only the undeniable inevitability of Athenian encroachment that stirred Sparta to engage. A regime dedicated to training for war, however, cannot suppress those who seek honors from war, as evinced by the Helots themselves. Brasidas' eagerness for war thus appears to share the desire for private honor that animated Nicias. With Brasidas refraining from any such claim, however, and campaigning vigorously in the attempt to instigate or promote revolts among Athens' subject cities, Brasidas acts on the official cause of Sparta's declaration of the war and presents himself as fighting on behalf of, and for the good of the city, and for the liberation of Athens' subject cities. Rather than limiting Spartan "imperialism" to the Peloponnesus, this foreign policy places Athens in a much more precarious position than any other Spartan was able to affect, while also protecting the city domestically from its dangerous "enemy" within.

69 On Spartan education, see Rahe (2016) pp. 13-29. On the Helots (and Perioikoi, free but limited citizens of Sparta) see Cartledge pp. 138-68, drawing on additional evidence outside of Thucydides.

Brasidas' War of Liberation

The Spartans' focus on their domestic affairs is one of the causes of their hesitation to involve themselves in the larger war. With the scale of the Peloponnesian War, this was simply no longer possible. Some Spartans recognizing this, they "eagerly" (*prothumos*) sent the Helots out on campaign to aid in securing their safety at home, while also aware the Athenians would have to reestablish their colonies, and overall influence abroad, after cities began to revolt, hindering their ability to harass the Peloponnesus as they did with the greatest effect at Pylos. It is clear, therefore, that Brasidas is sent out for this purpose; they also hoped to use those cities he had gained as leverage in later negotiations with the Athenians (4.81.2).

While Sparta thus allowed his campaign to continue, their aim being an end to the war, Brasidas was dedicated to defeating or limiting Athens' imperial activities. This had the effect of encouraging other cities and was thereby, according to Thucydides, "of the greatest worth" to the Spartans (81.1). With this statement, Thucydides makes clear that the openly stated justification for the war, liberation, was *in fact* an advantageous policy for Sparta despite their own failure to execute it. And the cause of this failure is placed in stark relief, Thucydides setting it against Sparta's handling of the Helots. In addition to the Helots, Thucydides now adds that Brasidas proved himself to be "just and measured" (*dikaion kai metrion*) in his conduct, thereby successful in convincing Athens' subject cities to revolt. In proving himself such, those cities had a "firm hope" (or "steady/secure" – *elpida...bebaion*) the other Spartans were like Brasidas.[70] "After the Sicilian war" the "virtue and intelligence" (*aretē kai xynesis*) of Brasidas was known to those who witnessed it (while others heard of it) and was especially responsible for attracting the allies of Athens over to the Spartan side (81.2).

Since "the Sicilian war" must refer to the Athenians' defeat in Sicily, and thus in Thucydides' view their loss (or beginning of their loss) in the overall war, the attraction to Sparta occurred both during Brasidas' campaign of liberation *and* after his death and the near collapse of Athens. That Thucydides was unable to complete his account, or chose to end his account of the Peloponnesian War abruptly in Book Eight, becomes less significant

70 As we have observed with Nicias, Thucydides would not characterize hopes as "secure." He thereby hints that the expectation of Sparta's new allies will be disappointed.

(despite continuing scholarly dispute) – Thucydides implies that other Spartans similar to Brasidas continued to bring over Athens' former allies. These others include especially Lysander (as presented by Xenophon). But as we have also seen within Thucydides, Agis and Gylippus continued Brasidas' campaign and thus continued expanding Sparta's influence, or more clearly, Spartan imperialism.[71] It was only due to Spartans of this kind, those able to carry out campaigns bringing cities over to them which allowed the dismantling of the Athenian empire and rise of Spartan hegemony over Greece. Sparta itself could only win battles, not wars, because their own conduct proves to be at odds with a statesman such as Brasidas and required cultivating virtues not at home in Sparta. Imperialism, a grander imperialism, could only arise with a fundamental change in the regime because it could only be carried out by fundamentally un-Spartan individuals.[72]

Yet it would be an error to overlook Brasidas' Spartan qualities or virtues, and thus too quickly suggest an unbridgeable chasm between him and his city. It is too quick to simply call Brasidas an "Athenian." It is easy to forget Brasidas was born and reared in Sparta, under its laws, among its customs, living its characteristic way of life (as we will detail below). What, then, accounts for the differences between the authorities at home and Brasidas, in his belief in the cause of liberation from the Athenian empire, relieving Sparta of domestic pressure while furthering their stated aim in the war?

His view of Spartan liberation becomes clearer in his speech at Acanthus. Arriving with the Chalcidians, who had a faction inside Acanthus ready to join Brasidas, he delivers his first quoted speech, attempting to persuade those in the city who are hostile to him to hear his proposals.[73] Sparta's "cause" (*aitia*) is liberating Greece from the Athenians; therefore, he argues the Acanthians may harm Sparta's campaign of liberation if they refuse to admit him. Indeed, the only arguments against liberation are

71 Consider Proietti (1987) for its focus on Xenophon's Sparta, notably Lysander.

72 *Ibid.* pp. 109-11. Cf. Finley (1942) p. 198 who refers to Brasidas as "the almost singlehanded savior of the Peloponnesian cause." If Brasidas and the Spartans had the same goals in the war, this would be true. But Finley's conflation of their goals misses this key contrast I am drawing out between this great individual and his city.

73 See 4.11, which may be counted as a reported speech of Brasidas. Whether this is the case or not, I view that exhortation of his men as significant to Thucydides' presentation of Brasidas' character.

that the proposals are unjust or that Brasidas lacks the power necessary to protect those cities that revolt from Athens (4.85.6). Brasidas argues, however, both that the Athenians failed to engage him at Nisaea and that he is bound by oaths to liberate cities such as Acanthus, not to enslave them to Sparta (86.1-2). Sparta will only gain in honor and reputation if they act in a manner that will ensure them gratitude rather than blame. However, if the Acanthians refuse Brasidas' offer, he will be "compelled" (*anankē*) to force their liberation. Such liberation, he argues, is to Sparta's benefit since allowing the Acanthians to remain subjugated means a flow of revenue to Athens that will ultimately harm Sparta in the war *and* set a precedent leading other cities also to refuse Brasidas' offer (87.3). With these remarks, we are reminded of the Spartan practice of uniting justice with Spartan interest. In this instance, Brasidas further justifies compelling Acanthus to revolt from Athens because it serves the "common good" (*koinou agathou*) of Greece – as he admits, without this common good, he would not be justified in compelling the Acanthians (87.4).

Viewing Thucydides' comments introducing and concluding this speech we note that he mentions (twice) the Acanthians' fear for their harvest of grapes (84.2, 88.1). Brasidas' appeals both to oaths and to the justice of Spartan liberation are not as compelling to the Acanthians as fear of acting against Brasidas' wishes (and thus having their crop destroyed). But for Brasidas, his willingness to compel Acanthus' autonomy reveals the seriousness with which he views Sparta's professed cause; however, his seductive arguments (promising autonomy, support, and continuing to live as they have, which had *some* influence over the Acanthians' decision – 86.4-6) are troubling. We are now aware the Spartans do not support the cause of liberation Brasidas is undertaking, and they had only sent him out with the Helots to harass the Athenians, stabilize a potentially volatile domestic situation, and prevent future intrusions on the Peloponnesus itself. This is in direct contrast to Brasidas' opening claim (85.1). Brasidas also reassured the Acanthians by claiming he was victorious at Nisaea despite fighting against a numerically superior Athenian force; but this claim is simply false (85.7; cf. 73.3). These lies are surely intended to gain the Acanthians' confidence that their revolt would be protected by the Spartans. It is all the more striking, therefore, that Brasidas vacillates between repeated uses of the first person throughout this speech (85.3, 6-7, 86.1-3) as well as appeals to "we Spartans" (85.4, 86.5, 87.4).

While delving deeper into Brasidas' increasingly complex motives and character, Thucydides' presentation continues to distinguish city and man by hinting at additional tensions between the two. After Brasidas is able to convince Amphipolis, his next liberation target, to leave their alliance with Athens, Thucydides echoes qualities of Brasidas he mentioned previously. Brasidas acted with "measure" (*metrion*) in his actions at Amphipolis and repeatedly declared his aim as the liberation of Greece (108.2); additionally, both the terms granted to Amphipolis and his "gentleness" (*praotes*) encouraged other cities to revolt (108.3). But Thucydides notes a problem: Athens' power was indeed greater than those cities wishing to revolt were willing to believe. According to Thucydides himself, in a striking remark on the human condition occurring in the context of his Brasidas narrative, by trusting in hope to fulfill their desires, human beings ignore "sovereign reason" (*logismō autokratori* – 108.4).[74]

Is this critique directed also at Brasidas himself? Is *he* flawed in this manner? Did he hope somehow that the Spartans would aid him in the war and thus that his promise of liberation would be fulfilled? That the success of such a liberation would resound to *his* honor? Or that liberation is the worthiest of aims? It is in appealing to the worthiness of his city at Acanthus and to friendship at Thessaly that Brasidas appears to believe in Sparta's professed war cause of liberating Greece from Athens. Brasidas sees himself as liberator. Certainly, Brasidas is in part responsible for the Acanthians' revolt; but the question arises as to whether he could ultimately protect them against Athenian retribution. Thucydides reminds us here that Brasidas' previous promises were "seductive, though untrue" (108.5) confirming he had lied about his forces at Nisaea. And similar to his threats to destroy the Acanthians' crops, Brasidas appears to have at least partially compelled some of the Amphipolitans to revolt by keeping certain citizens' relatives as prisoners (106.1). Has Brasidas admitted, admitted to

74 Hornblower II p. 344 notes the out of place character of this remark, given that it occurs, not in a speech, but in narration. The term *autokratōr* means "ruling for oneself, absolute, autocratic." The Crawley (1996) translation is the one quoted here. Mynott (2013) translates it as "sovereign powers of reason." Thucydides' use of this adjective to modify *logismos* seems to imply that, since desires are strongest in us, hope guides our desires. Yet only reason may determine what is in fact possible, and thus the most prudent course of action requires, and is synonymous with, an education of hope – nothing short of the possible and impossible, the divine and the necessary, the foreseeable and the unknown.

himself, that necessity, and not noble liberation, is motivating other cities, thus securing his own victories but thereby disappointing his own hopes for noble liberation?

Thucydides leads us to wonder what dangers Brasidas has drawn Athens' subject cities into, while also allowing us to notice the attractiveness his policies had for those he sought to liberate; and we must add, perhaps also for himself. Immediately after Amphipolis, Brasidas next arrives in Torone with an offer of similar terms (114.1-2). Proclaiming he does not blame those cities for their friendship with Athens, he nevertheless expects them to join Sparta. Brasidas expects that by acting justly towards the Toronaeans he would prove Sparta to be a better ally than Athens; for Brasidas was acting, as he believed, for the "good and liberty of the city" (*agathō kai eleutheria tēs poleōs* – 114.3), for Torone itself.

But as Brasidas continues this appeal, he reveals his inability to wholly accept the very view he has just stated. He expects the Toronaeans no longer to ally or submit to Athens after their revolt, and will hold them "responsible" (*aitia*), threatening punishment if they "wronged" (*adikeō*) the Spartans. While Diodotus and Hermocrates did not blame the Mytilenians and Athenians in their ambitions, respectively, Brasidas does not accept the necessities Torone must confront, including its own safety or preservation, should they find themselves unprotected by Sparta and compelled to return to the safety of the Athenian empire (3.42.1, 4.61.5; cf. 4.114.5). To expect compliance with Sparta going forward, Brasidas implies that Torone live as an autonomous city apart from Athens, that such autonomy (which is nonetheless alliance with Sparta) is better for the Toronaeans. Brasidas' efforts, however, are not merely because autonomy furthers Torone's interests; rather, Brasidas reveals what we previously suspected. As he now adds, Sparta acts "much more justly" (*hosō dikaiotera*) than Athens and *therefore* the Toronaeans will prefer Sparta to Athens (114.4). Sparta is a just city while Athens is unjust. *This* is the reason Brasidas believes in the Sparta war cause of liberation of Greek cities from Athens.[75]

75 Wylie (1992) p. 81 doubts Brasidas believes his own rhetoric, but does not explain why, only noting its success. I believe this misses both a key hint as to Brasidas' own motives, as well as how, and why, Sparta prosecutes the war as they do.

Brasidas' Spartan Virtue

Only Brasidas is able to forward the cause of liberation, winning honor for this cause. But it reminds us of the support for Sparta at their declaration of the war – most cities inclined to their cause (2.8.4). It is Brasidas, though, who pursues this objective and fulfills the promise of what other cities viewed as Spartan justice in the face of Athenian injustice. Ironically, the Spartans were unaware their broader interests in the war (and thus the policy decisions necessary to secure those interests) were in fact forwarded by their own cause of liberation. But for the city, proclamations of liberation only hid their fear of Athens, and the continued sovereignty of Sparta was their true (if hidden) objective.

Brasidas' gentleness (at odds with what we have seen of Spartan harshness and even Spartan moderation) finds its source in his genuine belief in the aim of liberation. Brasidas' gentleness arises from his initial lack of blame for those compelled to join the Athenian empire. Yet Brasidas does not follow the full implications of his stated claim; he cannot *wholly* exculpate those that do not sacrifice anything for the sake of justice. Justice is being Sparta's ally, not Athens'. In his expectation that cities leave Athens even at potential risk to themselves, he believes sacrificing one's own good is required for deserving the rewards and honors of living justly or virtuously, i.e., living a Spartan way of life.[76]

That Thucydides notes Brasidas' gentleness in the context of Sparta's lack of consideration for those he incited to revolt is telling. The Spartans distinguish between Spartan and foreigner, as Thucydides' presentation of Brasidas and Alcidas together makes clear. Despite the zeal for revolution Brasidas initiates, the Spartans themselves were unwilling to comply with his request for further forces to support these revolutions. In fact, as we now learn, the Spartans did not support Brasidas' actions partially due to the "envy" (*phthonos*) of their first men (and, as we have seen, because they wished to recover their men from Pylos and end the war – 4.108.7).

Spartan envy is rooted in noble actions serving the city; but Brasidas is obtaining honor for himself: striking fear in the Athenians, winning the praises of those he liberates. Spartans at home are unable to distinguish themselves in such a manner, being left only with the honors obtainable within the regime. This envy is an implicit admission by the first men in

76 Burns (2011) p. 520.

Sparta that honor resulting from their offices is not enough. The praise and blame which inculcates obedience to the city naturally directs, at least some, to the desire for honor on a grander scale by those who lead Sparta to victory in war (previously observable in the grand ambitions of Pausanias). Most Spartans could never distinguish themselves since the kingship is a hereditary "office" and even this office finds itself divided into two royal family lines and under the control of other Spartan authorities at home, the ephors.[77] Brasidas' own actions appear, therefore, as a striving to nobly serve his city, while also revealing the limitations to which such service was restricted by Sparta itself.[78]

Despite the tension between Brasidas and Sparta, he does not hold back from what has now clearly become *his* campaign. Startling is the fact that not only did the Athenians desire a truce to stop Brasidas' successful advances against their empire and end the revolts, but also a general peace (4.117). Thanks to Brasidas' "good fortune" (*ēutuchei*) the Spartans are now able to make peace for the sake, not of liberation, but of retrieving their men. Moreover, this Spartan decision results from their belief either that Chalcidice (Brasidas' current target) could not be taken or that further victories would do nothing to return their men. Believing their entire city is at risk after the Athenians captured their men at Pylos and hold Cythera, the Spartans seek to end all hostilities. Brasidas is allowed to continue his campaigns in the north (his march toward Thrace) because he is able to initiate revolts and gain additional cities over to Sparta. But these cities are not liberated (as Brasidas believes) for the sake of autonomy; the Spartans at home were only collecting them as bargaining chips for later negotiations when attempting to end the war (117.2). The entire period of Brasidas' ascendancy and success cannot be understood apart from Sparta's weakened position and resulting irresoluteness. The most successful Spartan in Thucydides' account is only able to serve his city in the war when his service

77 Consider 1.86-87 (Archidamus versus Sthenelaidas), 1.131-134 (Pausanias versus ephors), 4.132 (Sparta send young men to rule the cities Brasidas had liberated), 5.63 (counselors sent by the ephors to oversee Agis).

78 Brasidas' story thus sheds light on the problems raised in Book Five (detailed in Chapter Three). Once the war party in Sparta takes control, they lack a Brasidas to prosecute the war; they return to relying on their king, Agis, and his ability to command, which is deficient until late in the war (Book Eight). And this reliance on their king is a reliance on their laws governing battles; it is directed by their education and training. In keeping with this, the language used by Thucydides echoes the portrait of Sparta delivered by Archidamus (5.69.2; cf. 1.84.2.4).

could result in the peace, or even an end to the Peloponnesian War, that Sparta sought.[79]

Sparta's good fortune in now being in a position to negotiate for the return of their men is entirely a result of Brasidas' victories. And these events, or rather their author, are indeed due to chance – Brasidas possesses virtues that, while perhaps what a Spartan seeks to be, are not wholly inculcated at Sparta. It is these virtues (which Thucydides singles out) – gentleness, justice, and measured conduct – that produce greater success for the city than those of Spartans such as Alcidas or Agis. Brasidas' daring and vigor are also at odds with the rest of the city. While Brasidas' virtue began with his Spartan education, he seems to have contemplated (as revealed in his speeches) what it means to be a virtuous man in a manner that even the best Spartan has not.[80] Alcidas merely adheres to Sparta's habitual hostility to enemies and goodwill to friends. Thucydides' presentation of Brasidas' early career, alongside this harshness and violence of Alcidas, only casts his gentleness and measured conduct in the starkest relief.[81]

Most revealing of Brasidas' awareness is his refusal to blame those compelled to join Athens. Perhaps having reflected on his own virtue, he exculpates those compelled into alliances, but demands virtue of those cities now revolting to whom he offers assistance. Spartan justice seems to reveal its fissures to Brasidas. Blinded to any view of virtue or justice apart from dedication to Sparta, the city cultivated blind obedience to the common good no matter its actions abroad. But obedience to the common good can only be good for the individual if the city itself is noble, just, and good. Did Brasidas' experience, being a subordinate to Alcidas (among others), help him see this issue? Perhaps coming to notice shortcomings of Spartan virtue as practiced, Brasidas' campaign of liberation for Greek cities comes to light as his own pursuit of autonomy from his city and its authorities. Brasidas' desire for success and honor away from Sparta appears as the realization of its possible limitations.

---

79 Strauss (1964) p. 222.

80 Archidamus argued that it might be unlawful for Sparta to declare war when Athens was offering arbitration of their dispute, thereby implying Sparta's cause is not identical with the demands of justice. But Archidamus is still unwilling to doubt that Spartan virtue, shame-induced obedience to the laws of the city, is best and thus that the Spartan educated in these laws is the best citizen and man.

81 This comparison includes not only their moral qualities, but also their awareness of strategy. Consider 3.79 and the lead-up to the Corcyraean revolution.

Returning to the action: With Brasidas successful in aiding Torone's revolt and causing the Athenians to flee, Sparta and Athens now agree to a truce. Yet after the treaty is concluded Scione revolts from Athens and joins Brasidas (4.120.1). Their decision is especially influenced by a speech of Brasidas, which Thucydides reports (121.1). The Scionaeans' elation could hardly be exaggerated, as they crown Brasidas with a golden wreath and proclaim him liberator of Greece.

Thucydides' remark that Brasidas spoke in similar terms here to the speeches at Acanthus and Torone hints at the need to weigh all three, as they bear clear similarities. But what has changed? While we may have believed for a time, along with Brasidas, that the Spartans were in support of his campaign, their recent truce with Athens closes this possibility; thus, we understand Brasidas' strong, emphatic terms at Scione (120.3) to be an attempt to convince not only the Scionaeans of Sparta's cause, but also to convince Brasidas himself. For he must have had doubts at this point about Sparta's support for the war (and the propriety of his own efforts). Nevertheless, Brasidas greatly objects to the failure of the truce to include Scione. Brasidas was deceptive in claiming the Spartans would be the "most trusted and truest friends" (120.3) of Scione – the Spartans had *already* refused to comply with Brasidas' request for reinforcements (108.7) and the revolts from Athens, as Thucydides presents them, were the result of Brasidas' own "seductive but untrue" statements (108.5). In other words, Brasidas' promises to the Scionaeans are known *by him* to be false. The Spartans were preoccupied with the return of their men and with concluding a general peace, as Thucydides repeatedly reminds us during the Brasidas narrative (108.7, 117.2, 5.15.1; cf. 5.14.2, 36.2, 39.2).

As for the violation of the truce (since Scione *did* revolt two days *after* its signing), Brasidas objects as well since he believed the Athenians had themselves committed an injustice (4.123.1). The Spartans offer to place the matter in arbitration, as per the truce, but the Athenians refuse. Brasidas' opinion on arbitration is unclear, but he does immediately aid another city in revolting now. Brasidas appears indifferent to arbitration, along with his own possible breach of the treaty in not submitting to it. The Athenian slaughter of the Scionaeans, led by Cleon, is itself in violation of the truce's clause submitting disputes to arbitration to avoid open war (118.8). But so are the further revolts promoted by Brasidas.[82]

Brasidas' seeming dismissal of arbitration, and the treaty as a whole, sheds light on Thucydides first noting that Brasidas' actions were "just and measured" (*dikaion kai metrion* – 81.2), while later stating only that they were "measured" (*metrion* – 108.2).[83] From a legalistic point of view (i.e., an armistice), Brasidas' actions are unjust, for he could have submitted the matter of Scione's revolt to arbitration. Perhaps aware the Athenians were correct to note the violation of the treaty by a revolt occurring *after* it was signed (as Thucydides confirms *was* the case), Brasidas *himself* instead accuses the Athenians of an injustice, the specific charges being unclear. It is important to note, however, that another city, Mende, daringly revolts *because* of Brasidas' refusal to abandon Scione (123.2). The success of Sparta's professed aim in the war was better served by violating a treaty obligation and therefore committing, from the point of view of the city suffering the treaty breach (here, Athens), an injustice. Sparta would hardly have been the first city to do so (cf. 5.115.1-3).

Brasidas' Own Virtue

Brasidas' refusal to wholly admit to the now obvious antagonism between himself and Sparta is observable in his next speech at Lyncus (4.126.1-6). Having to encourage his small force against a numerically superior hoard of barbarians, Thucydides' Brasidas offers his last explicit remarks on virtue. Brasidas' speech reveals his view of the superiority of Sparta to others and extols the Spartans' "home-grown virtue" (*oikeian aretēn*): the Spartans fight together in "order" (*kosmos*), while the barbarians consider each individual fleeing or attacking as "noble" (*kalōn*). Thus, Brasidas argues, the barbarians do not allow each man to truly test his "courage" (*andreion*) in battle. For Brasidas, Spartan courage is promoted by their battle order, but not wholly determined by it; one must *choose* to act courageously for his city.

82 Connor (1984) p. 137 also notes this problem. One of Thucydides' reminders to readers, in the details of the Brasidas narrative, is that we need to be aware of armistice and treaty terms.

83 For this term, distinguishing it from moderation, see Palmer (2015) p. 83n22. Hornblower II p. 342 does not make this distinction, as Palmer himself observes.

This virtue is rare, as Brasidas admits, akin to the few ruling the many. And as he argues, the few *deserve* to rule the many (126.2), as they do in Sparta, these few who rule having done so by distinguishing themselves on the battlefield.

This portrait of virtue clearly strikes at the heart of who Brasidas is. But this is also a problem for Sparta: It was because of the Spartans' rigid battle order that the hereditary king, Agis, betrayed his inabilities to command, leading Sparta to institute a new law for the sake of improving this order. Indeed, despite praising Spartan order, Brasidas himself immediately departs from it in this very battle (128.1). Brasidas is the rarest of the few, having distinguished himself during his liberation campaign, and yet hindered from leading the Spartans to victory in war. If the few deserve to rule the many by distinguishing themselves in battle (or in other ways), the Spartans would not have encountered problems with all of their "few," kings or commanders – Archidamus and Agis were slow and lacked daring, while Pausanias and Pleistoanax sought private motives (or were accused of such). Only in the case of Brasidas is the Spartan claim of justice or moderation combined with the daring required for victory. While the Spartans first praise Brasidas after he distinguishes himself, they become envious once he takes charge, leading an expedition beyond their control and at odds with their unstated aims.

Not surprisingly, Thucydides informs us in this context that the Spartans sent "certain young men" to Amphipolis and Torone to inspect what was happening and to rule over those cities for the Spartans; they did not want to leave this to those already there, i.e., to Brasidas (132.3).[84] The Spartans even breach one of their own laws (*paranomos*) in sending these young men – it seems they are willing to use any means to combat Brasidas' ascendancy, i.e., one of the necessities of the war that Sparta is unable to deal with. This breach of one of Sparta's laws presages creation of the new law we noted in Book Five. Sparta is unable to deal with either daring or timid statesmen.

The Spartans appear torn – torn between a Sparta both hierarchical and egalitarian. From its founding, Sparta was based on a leveling of the citizens.

84 Thucydides uses *entynchanō* ("fall in with, meet with") a verb that relates to "fortune" (*tychē*) when referring to those already present at these cities. This is a reminder of the relation of Brasidas and Sparta appearing to be one of chance or fortune. As Bury (1909) p. 303 observes, Brasidas "was a Spartan by mistake."

Wealth and luxury were rejected (1.8). But a hereditary office of two kings (drawn from two royal families), first families of Spartiates, and other elected offices excluding some, create tensions within the regime. Pausanias sought recognition, grasped for the kingship, but could never attain it via Spartan institutions. He is, in this way, radically unequal. Brasidas seeks honor and rule based on his worth as an individual. As his remarks here argue, those "regimes" (*politeion*) where the few rule the many are superior (4.126.2); yet we must immediately note that such rule itself does not guarantee the rule of merit, i.e., those best suited to rule. Conventional aristocracy is not natural aristocracy. The rise of Brasidas within Sparta is the rise of *physis* within Sparta. It is the ascendancy of the man naturally suited to rule. Brasidas transforms the notion of the few ruling the many by taking it beyond the limitations of Sparta. Leaving behind the Spartan version, the Spartan *politeia*, Brasidas appears to have envisioned himself apart from, or beyond, Sparta.

Returning to the narrative: After the fall of Torone, in which Cleon enslaves the women and children and the Athenians tear down the city, Brasidas receives information that Cleon is now proceeding to Amphipolis. Thucydides presents, before the speech itself, both Brasidas' intention in his speech and his strategy for the battle (5.8-10).

Brasidas did not want to attack the Athenians with the Spartans' customary battle order because the Athenians present at Amphipolis were "pure" (*katharos*) and their allies had the strongest of their men with them – the "worth" (*axiōma*) of the Athenians was greater than the Spartans despite their numbers being more or less equal; therefore, Brasidas determines that he must employ "art" (*technē*) in combating what we might say is their superior condition. His own men were armed with equipment they were forced (*anankē*) to use, i.e., not the best Spartan arms. Thucydides' presentation of Brasidas' thoughts before the speech thus betrays Brasidas' foremost worries – the Spartans were no longer, in his view, the best men, as worthy of victory as the Athenians (8.2). Nor would Brasidas be able to employ the best weaponry for the battle. Coming to view the Spartans as inferior, not simply technically, but foremost, morally, Brasidas focuses on both material and moral preparations for the battle.

After realizing the weakness of the Spartans, Brasidas' final speech could appear as the speech of a man preparing for his own death (5.9). In exhorting both his men and his fellow commander, Clearidas, Brasidas urges them to sacrifice themselves for the sake of Sparta. Even if they should escape the battle without being captured or dying, they will live a worse life than they would as allies of Sparta and part of a liberated Greece (9.7-9). "Lack of daring" (*atolma*) is not an excuse. Since Brasidas can no longer believe that Sparta's aim is to succeed in initiating revolts of Athens' subject cities from their empire, nor that Sparta will support those liberated cities after their revolt, he appears to seek, as Thucydides later observes, "success and honor" for himself (16.1). For given his realization that complete victory in the war is not, or never was, Sparta's aim, he himself may still die an honorable death. That he is successful on behalf of Sparta may only be the case if Sparta's peace with Athens can be understood as a success. But this success would not be that for which Brasidas, nor Sparta's allies, fought – Sparta was never able to carry out its professed aim because Sparta only ever truly hoped to liberate *itself* from Athens. Brasidas had to lie to the cities he seduced into revolution because he could no longer be wholly honest about the intentions of Spartan authorities at home. And most of all, his lies appear to be in some measure for the sake of himself, hiding his unwillingness to accept being part of a city unable to fulfill its noble goal.

Brasidas' superior nature proves to be at odds with Sparta. But much more than this: Brasidas can never be the savior for Sparta that he is for Amphipolis. Brasidas can never liberate Sparta from the limits, the flaws, of the city itself. As Brasidas comes to see the difficulties within his own city, he is unable to admit that they shirk from liberating other cities from an un-Spartan empire. Thucydides thus allows us to see Brasidas both sacrificing his life at Amphipolis to prove he is an honorable man (5.10.11) and also consecrating land to the goddess Athena as gratitude for what he believes is her overseeing protection and guarantor of his own successes, appearing to him as beyond "human means" (*anthrōpeios* – 4.116.2). The Amphipolitans themselves honor Brasidas as a hero and a liberator, replacing their original founder with this man as their savior (*sōtēra* – 5.11.1). In his dedication to truly fulfilling his city's stated mission, Thucydides' Brasidas highlights human beings' desire for, belief in, and experience of, their political liberty and human freedom. Perhaps Brasidas expected too much from his city, from political life itself. At the same time, Brasidas sacrificing to Athena is a recognition of something beyond himself, beyond politics and beyond human agency, from which he will never be wholly liberated and can only nobly serve.

Conclusion

War will always be of the utmost significance, even cosmic significance, susceptible to interpretations rooted in divine agency, and belonging hand in hand with other phenomena human beings believe to be outside their control. Not surprisingly, we are now in a better position to appreciate Thucydides' mentions of earthquakes, eclipses, droughts, famines, and most devastating, the plague, in his context of disclosing what he viewed as the cause of the Peloponnesian War: Spartan fear and Athenian imperial expansion. Incidents such as these, so-called natural disasters, point decisively to piety, to the human need for causal explanations, and the corresponding attempts to interpret events we are compelled to face. In this way, piety must confront necessity.

What of this confrontation though? Self-destruction, in the case of Nicias and the Melians, is piety rejecting prudence, rejecting what must be done to avoid a particular, and seemingly assured, outcome. Yet these examples are the most extreme, and Thucydides is purposeful in distinguishing superstition and piety. Actions within human control, even when not appearing entirely within human control, afford the chance to reason through the causes operative in nature (1.109.4, 2.4.2, 50.1-2, 102.2, 3.89.2). Nicias need not doubt the will of the gods; but he, or others, may well have doubted the soothsayers' interpretation of the meaning of the eclipse.[1]

But Thucydides, through such reasoning on "the human condition,"

1 Compare Kallet (2013) p. 378n54 and Connor (1984) p. 208n57 (who Kallet cites in this context). Her view is that "[t]here is no suggestion in Thucydides of some deterministic, divine causal schema." Kallet points to Spartan belief in their impiety for declaring war, along with the Athenians' recovery after the Sicilian expedition, as indicative of Thucydides' view of the gods. While we may ultimately conclude with Kallet that this is correct regarding Thucydides' *own* view, his narrative, it seems to me, does suggest possible divine retribution – the Spartans certainly feared this possibility. See also Chapter One note 19.

affected as it is by natural, human tendencies as well as the customs of each regime, has sought to discover both the scope and limitations of human knowledge in directing and comprehending political action. Sparta reveals such limits because human nature is conditioned most noticeably by Spartan *nomoi*, so opposed to the liberty of the Athenian mind. This is beautifully illustrated in Book Three: Thucydides' introduction of the Spartan king, Agis. Set to invade Attica, the Spartans turn back due to an earthquake. In the next sentence, Thucydides notes that earthquakes were also occurring elsewhere at the same time, including some that caused tidal waves affecting the city of Orobiae in Euboea. What was previously land now became sea, the water not receding even after the storm. Indeed, Thucydides goes on to note the "cause" (*aitia*) of such inundations are the earthquakes themselves. Inundations, in Thucydides' own opinion ("I" – *egō*), could not happen in any other way (3.89.1-5).[2] Earthquakes and inundations are necessities; however, Spartan fear of, and reaction to, earthquakes is not a necessity; yet it is perfectly in keeping with their fear of the gods, a fear of doing injustice. Athenian hubris, on the other hand, suppressed such fears. Thucydides, neither simply "Athenian" nor "Spartan," sought to stand back and observe.

Morality and Politics

The Athenian envoys' argument regarding necessity, the Athenian thesis, grounding the actions of human beings in their nature, is met with silence by the Spartans. Sthenelaidas accuses the Athenians of so much talk, i.e., not denying injustice (1.76.2-3, 86), since for the Spartans, Athenian arguments failing to address justice are sophistication deserving of suspicion, to say nothing of the overtly impious tone of statements such as those at Melos. While the Athenian thesis argues all cities will expand should they have the power to do so, we now also notice only the Athenians are so bold as to openly state this view (and even they do not always state it so forcefully – cf. 6.82.3-4). It is the moral desire for honor and greatness, for empire, that leads to expansion, to immoderate courses. Having the power to do so is only half the equation – how the city conceives of itself and its

2 Hornblower I p. 497: "…it is surely significant that earthquakes were popularly thought to be the work of Poseidon, the sea-god."

relation to others drives policies and policy justifications. All other cities during the Peloponnesian War appeal to justice; all other cities argue in moral terms of right and wrong, justice and injustice, honor and shame, nobility and baseness. And these cities, notably Sparta, do so not to disguise pursuit of their own interests or weaknesses, but because they themselves *believe* justice has, or should have, an effect on political conduct. Belief in moral superiority is not simply a means by which to disguise weakness; it is a belief part and parcel of Spartan virtue.

When viewing the actions of the Spartans, we now understand in a deeper way our initial impression (based on the Athenian accusation of hypocrisy) that they merely conflate their advantage with justice. All cities, all human beings, want to believe they are moral in securing their own interests. The Spartans did not believe the Plataeans were justified in their attack on Thebes and the slaughter of their men; the Plataeans may have felt compelled by the Athenians to submit to their empire, but this does not mean the Spartans believed this to be so. One could never imagine the Athenians calling in special judges and engaging in the procedural moves the Spartans did; and when the Athenians put the Mytilenians' revolt before the demos, they vote to kill them as punishment for their transgression, acting as Spartans would act, driven by Cleon's call for revenge. It is Diodotus who convinces the Athenians to reconsider and thereby weigh their true advantage; but even here, he is only able to do so by appealing to justice, the cruelty of their initial decree leading to reconsideration of their initial decision; and even he barely secures the vote for a more moderate course.[3]

The Spartans cannot admit to themselves justice may be dispensed with; the Athenians are too quick to proclaim justice can be dispensed with. If the Spartans conceded they acted out of fear and thus were excused in defense of their city against Athens, they would also be conceding to the weakness of justice and to its only secondary place in political calculations. If the Athenians conceded they acted out of a striving for honor and thus were not compelled by fear, they would be conceding to the primary place for virtue, and even justice, in political calculations. The Spartans do not believe one could secure their interests by acting apart from the dictates of virtue and the demands that it makes. The goodness of virtue proceeds from the virtuous life itself – to be law-abiding, pious, and courageous in

3 For the "anger" (*orgē*) of the Athenians due to perceived injustice, consider 3.36.2, 38.1, 5.42.2, 46.5, 8.1.1; cf. 3.42.1, 43.5, 44.4.

defense of Sparta is a better way of life than that of Athens (and the *nomoi* of other cities). Thus, we understand the Spartan demand that other cities under their authority not be simply allowed to live as they like (in contrast to paying monetary tribute, as Athens demanded); they must model themselves after the Spartan regime, at least to the extent that they are ruled by an oligarchic regime, i.e., the few ruling the many, a superior type of rule, as Brasidas himself extols (4.126.2). Nevertheless, the Spartans disguise their actions, their violations of treatises, and their possible impieties, not merely from others but most especially from themselves. In striking contrast, the Athenians argue no city restrains itself from the supposed strictures of justice; for them, justice has no place in the sober calculations of cities. Cities and men should look to their interests, their own true good; to do otherwise is to forgo advantage for mere hopes and other considerations one cannot know. Yet the Athenian envoys at Sparta, even in their frank statement, justify their own actions by arguing that they do in fact restrain themselves and are not as harsh as their tremendous strength would allow, not due to strictures of piety or possible future retribution, but because they expect (and seek) praise for a gentler, nobler rule that forgoes exercising its ever-increasing strength.

The Spartans' source of restraint is fear, fear of the gods and the punishments for those found to be unjust. But the Athenians believe they need not worry themselves with the gods because gods would understand and exculpate those cities, those human beings, simply guarding their interests. Although we cannot deny the other cities sought a hegemon to lead Greece after the Persian War, as a protector, for understanding and evaluating human action, we notice that even the Athenians need the language of morality, both for others to accept their empire and, as I argue, for themselves as well. The Athenians cannot fully accept their own thesis because that thesis only partially accounts for human nature – it fails to wholly recognize the fundamentally moral element of our nature, affections they deny, but cannot purge, even as they seek to do so.

The Spartans need not balance justice and compulsion because they deny, or only sometimes half-recognize, the compelling character of necessity. Justice has its origins in the gods who will protect and reward Sparta for its just actions. This explains why the Spartans are so cautious and hesitant once they come to admit their own injustice in declaring war and breaching their solemnly sworn treaty with Athens; they feared their defeat at Pylos was the gods punishing them for this injustice (4.20.2, 7.18.2). It seems odd, then, that the Spartans are suspicious of other cities and doubtful of the justice of others. Even when officially allied with Athens, the Spartans grew suspicious of the Athenians aiding them in suppressing the Helot revolt, resulting in the Athenians' expulsion from Sparta. Rather than a belief in the justice of men, Spartan justice places its hopes (and fears) in divine justice; piety and all its customs are not only still relevant, but carefully observed in their decisions during the war (1.102). Piety, not maneuvering around necessity, is required for a good outcome.

As is now clear, the Spartans can only imperfectly act in this manner. They are not Melians – when war's necessities absolutely impinged on them Thucydides quietly mentions nothing about the sacrifices (5.57.1; cf. 54.2, 55.3). Yet this raises the overarching question: When is a "necessity" truly necessary, truly compelling? The apparent necessity of Athens' strength does not dissuade the Melians from resisting, when the most seemingly obvious necessity, safety and self-preservation, is on the line. That this example is the most noticeable in Thucydides requires all the more that it be understood. It is simply not clear what human actions are compelling according to the Athenian thesis, nor how necessity is to be confronted by various cities throughout the war. The envoys present fear *and* the temptations of empire as compelling; Diodotus presents human nature *itself* as compelling; yet this includes hopes, *erōs*, and one's interpretation of chance events. Is this not to say that "necessity" becomes anything human beings can imagine they need or want?

Necessities for one people are not always necessities for others. Not "necessity" strictly speaking, but rather each city's *view* of what constitutes necessity motivates action. The Athenians might believe continued growth and expansion is the only path protecting them against a new Persian offensive or even a renewed Spartan threat; that other cities disagree is irrelevant. The Spartans might believe pious sacrifices and "natural" phenomena are good or ill omens signaling the gods' approval or disapproval of certain actions; that other cities cry hypocrisy is irrelevant. Cities determine policy based on perception of necessity and interests, along with the costs of wholly neglecting justice and conventions or, conversely, their true interests.

What I have referred to as dual motives, which Thucydides presents in a surprising number of instances, cities torn this way and that, highlights that what we mean by "necessity" must be modified based on the city confronting it. Objective necessity (i.e., self-preservation) is not sufficient to ensure all cities will act uniformly; nor is any other interest if the city itself does not recognize it as such. Again, Melos resists Athens. And it is no small part of Thucydides' psychology that human beings are animated by hopes and desires, beliefs and wishes, that lead them away from seeing political realities for what they are. All human beings, everywhere and always, look up to something. All cities therefore unite interests, the good of their city, with moral justifications of that good within a world populated by other cities seeking the same.[4]

This is not to deny that we must recognize the survival of a city, and its flourishing, both foreign and domestic, requires certain objective actions. Melos cannot survive fighting Athens. Sparta cannot ignore its Helot population. But these *become* necessities by the conditions of each polis. Once Athens expands, it faces pressures Sparta does not. Once Sparta takes over the Peloponnesus, it need not expand further to rule its empire. Prudent recognition, however, of what these necessities are, versus the errors arising from hopes and miscalculations, coupled with the limitations presented even to prudence when attempting to secure future goods, circumscribes the degree to which any political community achieves its true interests.

Political life, as Thucydides presents it, is fundamentally guided by morality. Politics is at its root a manifestation of our views of justice and injustice, even though these concerns may distort determinations of advantageous policy and clear-sighted interest. From early in the Archaeology, the moral, political, and social aspects of human nature develop through the origins of Greece, separation of peoples and cities, progressing towards the Peloponnesian War. Human beings are moral before they found political communities; we judge human actions in moral terms, in the honorable actions of the piratical period, before tribes became cities. Thucydides urges his reader, nevertheless, to observe war and human life with caution, to become aware of this source of political errors through a sober investigation of the fears and hopes rendering us most prone to them.

We wonder, though, why Thucydides presents us with an Athenian

4 Those embroiled in the events surrounding Sicily are detailed by Thucydides at 7.57. Although apparently denying motives of justice or kinship, Thucydides in fact reveals that such moral considerations were not at all absent, mentioning specifically hatred, kinship, goodwill, and even friendship. See Chapter Three, note 80.

thesis that seems so compelling and results in his account of the war being viewed entirely through this lens. "Thucydides the realist" did not arise from nothing. Avoiding the issue of Thucydides' "genre" here – whether he is properly classified as a historian or philosopher or theorist (whatever that would mean and whatever result that would have) – we notice that the Athenian thesis sets up a contrast between "Spartans" of the world and "Athenians." One too susceptible to superstition and the other too sure of their own intelligence. Thucydides seeks, not a middle path, but one which elevates our vision such that we may observe the flaws of both, while also sympathetic to both, understanding their place in human life because of the effect they have on how we comprehend the world.

Thucydides must, therefore, allow us to see a strong case *both* for the power of human reason to soberly and prudently guide political decision-making and policy (Periclean Athens, the Athenian thesis), while simultaneously pointing us toward the hold of justice and piety (Sparta, Nicias, the Melians) at the foundations of the city itself. Thucydides presents his account of the Peloponnesian War with a stunning artfulness requiring his reader to explore the political world *as if* an Athenian and *as if* a Spartan. To achieve this, Thucydides must deceive, not allowing his truth to reveal itself before his readers have thoroughly worked through each city's position, each city's views. Evidence of Thucydides' deception is contained in the myriad ways he has been interpreted, categorized, and labelled. Schematization fails, though, because it fails to present the very complexity of human life, a complexity Thucydides seeks to replicate and present.

In the case of each city, we see their numerous internal tensions. Spartan piety is a hindrance to their foreign affairs with other cities: They fail to aid key allies, neglect important engagements, and are above all directed back toward their city, hindering actions abroad which would further their chances for victory in the war. It would therefore be easy to dismiss these beliefs as at odds with political expediency (to say nothing of self-preserving sobriety). The Spartan regime, however, despite some faction during the war, never experiences any of the domestic discord, the *stasis*, present at Athens (and Corcyra). Their city is stable via its long-standing regime, a regime functioning according to laws inculcating the strictest obedience and suppressing the strongest passions of human nature. And these passions are two-fold: The move away from tradition under Pericles, on the one hand, and the resulting *erōs* for empire and conquest, both of which harm Athens, on the other. The former, through Pericles' failure to recognize the moral roots of the city, including tradition, piety, community, and even ties to the land itself; the latter, through the Athenians' confusion of sober policy to solidify the city's interests with noble longing for further conquest, despite manifest risks. In this way, Sparta is closer to ancient times while Athens is thoroughly modern. What does this mean for the war and for political health as such?

Thucydides' Sparta allows us to contemplate the puzzle of reconciling strictures required for stability of the city versus the needs of a city at war. That this appears as obvious hypocrisy to the Athenians does not establish Spartan duplicity. That cities including Sparta certainly reveal motives of fear, interest, and self-preservation does not negate their only partially awareness, or even altogether blindness, to such motivations, nor the manner in which they justify pursuit of such motives in moral terms. Thucydides' statement that Sparta went to war with Athens due to fear (1.23.5-6) does not lead to the conclusion that the Spartans *believed* they went to war due to fear. They believed they went to war to stop Athenian injustice; they hid this fear from themselves because for the Spartans such an admission was impossible. Fear is the truest pretext (*prophasis*) because isolating a cause and thus designating blame (*aitia*) is simply to misunderstand human events as Thucydides presents them. The pretexts are as much causes: Note that Sparta feared not simply Athens the city, but the Athenians themselves, as men, as citizens of another city, as other. In the aftermath of the Persian War, during Sparta's Helot uprising, aid from their fellow Greeks quickly turned to a Spartan indictment of Athenian character (1.102.3). The Spartans feared revolution from the Athenians, a change to their regime that would have affected a change in their way of life itself. The Spartans recognize, and are exceedingly cautious of the fact, that other cities are not Sparta and other peoples (or kin) are not Spartans.

Spartan pious customs, observance of which is so routine the Corinthians are able to manipulate the Spartans based upon it (as the Eleans also attempt to do – 5.30-31), is one of the causes of their caution and fearfulness (and hence moderation) through an education in laws considered immoderate and shameful, for a Spartan, to doubt. Any fear a Spartan admitted to himself was to doubt the goodness or sanctity of Sparta's divinely sanctioned laws. Fear of the gods belongs together with denial of the compelling nature of fear; for while fear exists for those who commit injustice, the denial of it is an attempt to demonstrate one's virtue, one's assuredness of acting as the gods demand. Morality masks and denies aspects of our nature we seek to suppress as weakness. We could even say that it seeks to make us rise above our nature. If there is anything tragic in Thucydides, it is the recognition that nature cannot be conventionally rid of, however much one may wish it so.

Piety and Politics

Differentiating each people, it is precisely Athenian impiety that allows for their extreme and un-Spartan daring. But the Athenians do not know the gods will exculpate them; they merely believe it (5.105.2). The weakness of this belief, and therefore the lesson of Thucydides' Spartan portrait, is visible in the return of piety in Athens late in the war. Athens lost the war at least in part due to the recall of Alcibiades, a political decision originating from accusations of impiety after discovery of the herms' mutilation. The hopes and fears accompanying piety did not leave Athens; they only lay dormant and suppressed, to return in powerful forms that fundamentally damaged domestic stability (during the plague and Sicily). Whether Alcibiades mutilated the statues or whether this mutilation had an effect on the gods' treatment of Athens is irrelevant – the Athenians believed it did. The issue of piety is particularly notable, then, if for no other reason than its striking effect on both cities as they conduct the war. Perhaps even this is not strong enough. The political truth in piety is that Athens cannot expand without considerations of limits given the ill effects such expansion has on life in the city. Athens' continued expansion culminates in the Sicilian expedition, an expedition driven by desires for glory and private profit, by unprecedented daring and exercise of strength, and most notably, by unreasonable hopes (6.24.1-4, 31.2-6). The Athenians are therefore partially blinded to the great risk involved in such an undertaking and only on the eve of the expedition come to realize the gravity of what they have decided upon (31.1). Not surprisingly, it is at this precise moment that they return to their traditional pious prayers and practices (32.1-2). To alleviate any possible injustice, they accuse Alcibiades of impiety, demand his recall, thus removing him and any profane pollution from command of their expedition.

Despite the Athenian statements at Melos, that the gods will exculpate them for doing what humans beings do, the Athenians do not truly believe this when, on the other hand, they do what it seems only Athenians will do. In preparing for Sicily, they resort to pious appeasement to protect their morally suspect mission. In truth, the recall of Alcibiades was of course orchestrated by his political enemies who sought to eliminate his predominance in Athens (28.2). Guided by their own ambitions, rather than what benefited their city, they were able to sway the demos' decision despite the obvious abilities which brought about Alcibiades' command in the first place. Both Athens' statesmen and its demos were driven by private interests, desire for rule and desire for profit, respectively, interests ultimately leading to regime change and near civil war, along with hindering the city's foreign policy. And if Alcibiades' recall allows for their defeat, piety's significance for healthy domestic politics has to be viewed in startling light. Confusion, a moral confusion, takes hold of the Athenians: The old (a traditional, pious, and rural people) and the new (imperial expansion animated by progressive, cosmopolitan notions) confront one another, as exemplified by the assignment of both Nicias and Alcibiades to the expedition.

Athens during the plague, Corcyra's *stasis*, and Athens late in the war are all instances where cities bear a heavy cost for a loss of piety, with political immoderation diverting citizens from active civic virtue grounded in law, a sober balancing of competing interests, and traditional beliefs and practices. Most interesting of all, though, in Thucydides' vivid descriptions of each of these events, is what appears merely as self-interest and survival is instead laden with moral sentiment. The Athenians before Sicily are both driven by interests but also seek divine protection (6.24.3.4); those at Corcyra go out of their way to exact what they believe is justice, in the form of revenge, on their enemies (3.82.7); and the plague at Athens brings a presumably abandoned piety back into the city in a stronger but virulent form (2.54.2-5). Peace, civil concord between the competing parties of any city, suffers when the bonds of that concord – shared beliefs in the founding, customs, and greatness of one's city – are buried through liberation of unrestrained private pursuits.

Aside from such instances, scholars naturally seek to discern Thucydides' own views. In addition to the political expressions of piety, other evidence can be found in his accounts of phenomena with which we began:

Thucydides narrates (and often juxtaposes) naturalistic and pious explanations of earthquakes, storms, the formation of islands, among others.[5] Thucydides certainly presents doubts as to pious explanations of the natural world. Natural (or "scientific") explanations seem compelling, or at least challenge divine agency, once we observe regularity (for example, 2.28.1, 102.3, 3.89.5). But a natural account alone also appears insufficient, since it fails to eliminate the possibility these events are due to divine rule over the cosmos (as the Spartans and others believed) as opposed to natural necessity that is intelligible to human beings.[6] Once alert to the fact that Thucydides ignores neither the natural world nor piety, we notice he guides the reader from preeminently political questions and problems to weighing how possible solutions to these problems involve philosophic questions of the utmost importance. As Thucydides presents it, "Sparta" challenges "Athens" on the possibility of both understanding nature and overcoming the chance events that befall human beings.

Pious beliefs may hold human beings more strongly than their visible experience of the world. Consider the Athenians' reaction to the plague versus Thucydides' analysis of its symptoms and spread (2.47.3-54.5). Justice and its source in gods we cannot see or fully fathom still has an undeniable hold on the human heart. And since politics is ultimately a dispute over justice, piety will always influence how the world is understood. We cannot understate the significance of this for Thucydides. Pericles errs precisely here; so too the Athenians at Melos, claiming the gods act as human beings do. But the Spartans (and Melians) do not share this belief: Neither the gods nor human beings are compelled by nature to act in a particular manner; one *chooses* to act, viciously or virtuously. And even for the Athenians, their thesis does not establish the compulsory character of all human actions – their longing for honor is an act of generosity (on their view) since they are not as harsh toward subject cities as they might be; thus the Athenians are not able to consistently maintain that necessity compels. Evidence of moral confusion abounds: We must weigh the Athenian envoys' arguments at Sparta with the sentiments of most Athenians brought into the city by Pericles' war policy; the Athenians' reaction to the plague after the declaration of war; the numerous purification rituals of the island of Delos set

5 Consider Proietti (1992).

6 Palmer (1982) p. 123; cf. Orwin (1994) pp. 202-3. Consider Xenophon, *Memorabilia* I.4.4-19.

against the Athenians "enlightening" the Melians on the divine; in a word, Thucydides reveals that the Athenian thesis was the preserve of the few; most Athenians, most human beings, view the world through Spartan eyes.

If they understood the Spartan view, they would recognize what Thucydides teaches his readers: What *is* compelling is one's view of what virtuous actions require of us; that our *belief* of what is ultimately good for us, the best way of life, compels human beings to its pursuit.[7] If honor is or becomes compelling for the Athenians, then the war was caused both by Spartan fear and by Athenian exercise of its power. If belief compels human action, only through a change in belief can one change actions, as evidenced in the Spartans' perception of their guilt (7.18). Compulsion, in this sense, can only be understood as a manifestation of both *physis* and *nomos*. But the Athenian thesis does not take *nomoi*, the laws, customs, and defining attributes of the *politeia*, the regime, seriously enough; instead, it treats *anthrōpeia physis*, the natural inclinations and motives of human beings, as sovereign. *Nomoi*, by extension, are thus merely conventions, lacking a compelling power over us. This is a Spartan corrective to the Athenian thesis – the power of laws and customs, the cave, over the human being. This, it appears to me, is why Thucydides speaks of his purpose in presenting "the human [condition]" (1.22.4), and not "human nature." The Athenian thesis, on the other hand, speaks of "human nature"[8] and thereby fails to account adequately for the psychology of a pious people. In this way, it renders the language of hypocrisy all the more problematic, explaining only how Athenians view Spartans, not how the Spartans understood themselves.

The case of Melos is again illustrative. The Melian Dialogue seems to

---

7 Consider Xenophon, *Oeconomicus* 20.29.

8 "Human nature" is used at 1.76, 2.50, 3.45 (3.84), 4.61, 116, 5.68, 89, 103, 105, 7.77, 8.24. (Most commentators regard 3.84 as an interpolation, so I will leave it aside). But it is only used by Thucydides in his own voice at 2.50 and 3.82 – the plague at Athens and Corcyra's *stasis*. Both the nature of the illness, and the nature of human beings, divorces actions from laws. The plague was a natural occurrence too great for human nature, human life, to bear. *Stasis* is an occurrence rooted in human nature's attributes; but it is exacerbated by the moral justifications for actions. Revenge, that is, the desire to see justice done, goes beyond simply the will to survive, since the administration of this "justice" requires one to take risks, risks others will praise (3.82.4). *Stasis*, or civil war, is not simply human nature's rapacity, but the result of human beings seeking revenge on their beliefs, their "values," those arising from *nomoi*. Virtues are redefined and party alignments overtake family and gods. Conventions, in this sense, go beyond nature, natural inclinations or motives.

present a city blind to its manifest good: its safety. But this initial impression is corrected when we consider what Thucydides teaches us through his "Spartans." Believing as just men that they will win the favor of the gods to their side, even the seemingly impossible defense of Melos appears possible. Securing a victory based on their past justice (recognized by either the gods or Spartans or both) is the source of their reliance on hope. And this hope reveals, not that they forego their own safety, but that they believe the *means* to achieving it is inseparable from moral considerations.

The Athenians at Melos are not wrong to direct the Melians to focus on their interests; but reducing interest to safety cannot capture the shame felt by the Melians, the piety by the Spartans, and generally, the psychology undergirding the union of justice and one's own good: acting justly, or in the case of shame, with nobility and honor, as that which makes a people virtuous, ensures a good outcome. Such would be merely "noble words" were it not for the allure even the Athenians never wholly avoid in pursuit of their city's interests. If cities fail to recognize even objective, external necessities, then what precisely qualifies as "necessity" proves problematic.

For Thucydides, most human beings most of the time color their views of the world with hopes, expectations, denials, guilt, that hinder seeing necessity when it is there. Manifesting itself in everything from being free of the Athenian empire to being free of the plague to being free from securing victory in war, even the Athenians, who speak openly about (and have therefore thought about) what drives human beings, are still blind to how their own motives contain hopes and wishes not to be expected nor relied upon. And when they express dual or multiple motives, they vacillate at the moment when sober thinking is required for victory in war; thus they fail to see the Sicilian expedition for what it is and fail to listen to their "conscience," Nicias. On the other hand, Nicias fails to appreciate clear external necessities once present facts impose themselves, because for him the entire expedition is representative of Athens' moral failure, a failure he refuses to accept, a failure clouding his strategic decisions. This leaves Nicias always looking for an escape from either Sicily, or from moral culpability for the expedition, rather than successful prosecution of the mission itself (moral objections and his own reputation at home aside).

That Thucydides' account includes a sustained investigation of piety leads us to wonder where he could be located among contemporary (and fairly recently renewed) debates on religion and politics, or more broadly, morality's effect on politics. His view, I believe, sets him at odds from proponents of atheism today, and apart from current debate on the hoped-for possibility for an enlightenment that will eliminate moral longings. Pious beliefs can certainly lead both to error and violence; self-interest can result in moderate actions if it removes motives of hatred, revenge, and ethnic strife. But the Athenian empire was not a religious imperialism, it was not a holy war, and it was the religious Spartans who stayed at home and were cautious to avoid involving themselves abroad. Piety and fearful restraint belong together for Thucydides. It is not religion per se, as many today argue, but rather certain moral beliefs that may very well manifest themselves in some of humankind's gravest atrocities. Expectations or hopes for what one believes or desires as a future world is an engine for war, be those moral longings religious or secular.[9]

War and the City

For Thucydides, the importance of Sparta is their preservation of domestic stability and, therefore, the possibility of avoiding a war worse than war, civil war, *stasis*. This is not the same as Sparta being a best or perfect regime (howsoever defined). All regimes contain internal tensions and contradictions. War is a violent teacher because it may also destroy a city from within, bringing these internal movements to the surface. Sparta, as a foil, compels us to weigh the harm done to domestic politics through the frankly stated imperial ambitions of the Athenians, as well as the harm done by foreign wars required to sustain it. But the Peloponnesian War forced Sparta to change as well, placing external pressure on *their* regime; or more cautiously, the latent factions witnessed from the beginning, between

9 Thucydides states that the slaughter of those at Mycalessus, including schoolchildren, women, the elderly, and animals, was an act as much to be lamented as any other during the war. Noting that nearly the entire city was put to death (7.29.4), his language here also reminds us of Corcyra (29.5, 30.3; cf. 3.81.5). The kinship of Corcyra and Mycalessus appears to be the loss of moderation, in one case disappearing from within the city, and on the other, disappearing from those at war, acting with the utmost violence because they had nothing to fear. Suffice to add that Thucydides refers to piety and the gods in both contexts, as well as relating that Mycalessus was a small city at peace and possessed a school for boys. On Athens' role (and possible responsibility) for this incident, see Hornblower III p. 597-98 and Price (2001) pp. 215-16.

the hereditary kings and the elected ephors, becomes not simply a tension remaining in balance, but an irreconcilable division within the city exposed and rendered untenable by the pressures of war. Sparta's divinely sanctioned laws structuring the regime required change yet nonetheless failed. It is in combating Athens in such a large-scale war that Sparta is compelled to abandon its isolationist position and, therefore, eventually abandon customs focusing the city on domestic, rather than foreign, affairs.

Yet even assuming Thucydides' account of the war was left unfinished, I nevertheless highly doubt he would have presented the final fall of Athens and the victory of Sparta; for neither would be the apparent resolution to the problem arising from the competing aims of civic health and imperialism. The fall of Athens would not be a celebration of the end of empire, nor the rise of Sparta a celebration of newfound liberation; it would only begin the growth of a Spartan empire that would itself eventually suffer defeat. That Thucydides leaves us with some impression of hope after Book Seven is undermined by the confusion of Book Eight, a characterization of politics as indeterminate and lacking any permanent resolution. Book Eight is, in many ways, focused on Athens saving its city from the Spartans and Persians, the Athenians finally forced to turn from foreign exploits back onto themselves, onto the needs of the city.[10] Thucydides repeatedly refers to an Athens at war with itself, the city coming within a hair's breadth of being marched upon by its own army (8.76, 94). In this way, despite our initial confusion, a certain clarity comes out of Book Eight when we also focus our attention back on the regime, the conditions for a healthy political life.

In so far as peace (or rest) is to be preferred to war (or motion) it is because it appears to allow for the development of more "Athenian" traits – if human nature can develop its better and more fulfilled side, Thucydides, as observer, commentator, and teacher on human nature, must side with "Athens."[11] Yet rest is better preserved by "Sparta," a city ruled by *nomos*. Athens is liberated and thus susceptible to the dangers of liberty, despite Pericles' argument that Athenians need no such strictures. But the limitations of Spartan *nomoi* are precisely that the conditions conducive to

10 On Athens' foreign policy failures in "democratizing" other cities during the war, see Foster (2019).

11 See Strauss (1964) pp. 159-63 for the most detailed discussion of the implication of these terms, motion and rest.

peace can be stifling to human development. Piety and moderation strictly (even brutally) enforced by Spartan laws, along with shaming (or worse) for those who fail to comply, does not develop human beings; it places radical restrictions on them – nurture stifles, or even misdirects, human development. Spartan law was, plainly, cruel and harsh (4.80). There may be no Brasidas without the opportunity afforded by the Peloponnesian War. Nothing would occasion his rise and radical reconsideration of his Spartan upbringing.

In light of these flaws of Sparta *and* Athens, is there something then to the measured and mixed regime of 411? Or a pre-Peloponnesian War Athens, an Athens with a moderate or contained empire and a civic life rooted in, or at least still within reach of, ancestral customs and pious beliefs? Or does Thucydides bid us to go back even further? Thucydides' remarks on the Peisistratus tyranny, brief yet twice mentioned, are highly relevant: it was un-imperial, pious, and law-abiding, cultivating intelligence while adorning the city with beauty and virtue (6.54.5). These remarks are nothing less than a praise of domestic life decidedly un-Athenian when compared with the views expressed by the envoys at Sparta, by Cleon, at Melos, and even by Pericles himself. Believing themselves enlightened beyond the traditional foundations of the city, the health of the regime is neglected by both Pericles and his successors. Athens, or at least Periclean Athens, is not the healthiest city. And even the successes of Periclean Athens disguises the prominence of one individual, Pericles himself. Perhaps the best regime of Thucydides' own time points the way to Thucydides' approximation of the best regime simply, by which we can only mean the parameters of sound domestic politics, a regime that does not suffer (to the degree possible) from the limitations of both Sparta and Athens.

Temptations to empire afforded to Sparta, after Athens finally fell, allowed certain individuals to ascend to prominence, thus shaking one of the foundations of the Spartan regime (as Xenophon's account of Lysander reveals).[12] Or as we noted in Machiavelli's presentation, Sparta's isolation and its strict laws (particularly regarding foreign influence within the regime) would not allow it to flourish as an empire. Imperial expansion and imperial restraint both present problems for the city. Lycurgus' legislation was designed to, and was successful in, thwarting political passions; but these passions came to the fore with Sparta's newfound prominence. As

12 See Proietti (1987) pp. 108-11.

with Athens after the Persian War, those weaker Greek cities which sought a new hegemon under the auspices of guaranteeing their liberty only saw it taken away through the establishment of a new empire, a Spartan empire. Thucydides quietly portends the beginnings of these changes, the fatal flaw Sparta sought to guard against but could never wholly guard against – Pausanias' ambitions and designs *before* the outbreak of the Peloponnesian War, along with Spartan fears of corrupting their best citizens by sending them abroad, presaged Sparta's inability to stifle ambitious men, those who did not find their satisfaction in the rewards and honors offered by the city itself (1.95.7). Even Sparta's king, Agis, eventually acts alone in his attempts to secure Decelea near the end of the war, despite the unprecedented Spartan law established to control the king's independence on campaigns, a law his own failures led the Spartan ephors to create (5.63.4). Having grown ambitious, and possibly looking to fulfill a personal aim in combatting his enemy, Alcibiades, Agis takes hold of Spartan foreign policy, making his city's allies and actions his own (8.3.1, 8.2). The law aimed at limiting the influence of one man (and the faction of the city he represented), as with all laws in Thucydides, was never an assurance for restraining private ambition.

Strict adherence to law did guard against inducements to private honor and rewards, ambition, for a time; however, these laws thereby also hindered cultivation of virtues required to prosecute a large scale, long term foreign war. The Spartan way of life is insufficient to protect them fully from a world ruled by "Athenians" i.e., by any city with such men and such imperial passions and ambitions and daring. And since there will always be such men, the Spartans of the world will be compelled to become like them to fight them. Those familiar with Machiavelli might hear echoes of his thought here. But for Thucydides, the moral longings and psychological effects morality brings with it are not mere appearance. Statesmen seeking to use both the lion and the fox may not wholly understand those animal natures, blinding them to the effectual truth of what needs to be done, fostering hopes for instituting an impossible political reality. As for the Spartans, none are entirely suitable to the task of guiding Sparta during this period – both the Syracusans and the Persians are more able in this regard, especially the former who shared the characteristics not of Spartans, but of Athenians. Perhaps no clearer contrast is drawn by Thucydides than his presentation of Spartan foreign dealings at Plataea (3.68), followed immediately by the beginning of the Corcyraean revolution (3.70). Sparta's foreign policy is plagued by inaction, ineptitude, and strategic shortcomings, while Thucydides' praise of the city of Sparta is its protection against such *stasis* as we witness at Corcyra.

With the singular individual Brasidas, that pious warrior who dedicated to Athena (4.116.2) and was honored as the (new) founder of Amphipolis (5.11.1-2), the Spartans can only find themselves at odds. Their regime, while zealously training for war, was not directed towards offensive wars and conquest, and therefore to the glory that such conquests promise (a glory nearly all Athenian speakers appeal to – 1.76, 2.40, 63.1, 3.45.6, 6.31). Brasidas conducts numerous battles successfully precisely because he approaches the war differently from his unsuccessful colleagues. The troublesome envy he aroused with his military victories reminded the most prominent men in the city of the honors they lacked, and thus the limitations private ambition faced within Sparta. Once the Spartans ceased their Spartan practices, the foundations of the city decayed. Agis and Gylippus both move away from being "Spartan" and become more "Athenian" late in the war (Books Seven and Eight). And although they do not achieve the immense success of Brasidas, both are rather effective against the Athenians, including ironically, Nicias, the Spartan Athenian. Both prove instrumental in aiding Sparta precisely because they learn how to be victorious where previous commanders (including themselves earlier in the war) were not. Thucydides subtly presents the rise of "Athenian" individuals among the Spartans, foreshadowing a rupture in domestic and foreign policy as heretofore practiced, in long-standing, traditional, law-abiding, pious Sparta.

Brasidas' achievements were so envied by other Spartans that his successes only bring out Spartan failures by contrast. The source of his success must be found then in how un-Spartan he was – those observing him became aware of his willingness to sacrifice himself in his campaign against Athens. Brasidas is gentle and thus fosters revolutions within Athens' subject cities; his moderation toward non-Spartans is at odds with Spartan harshness (including, notably, his use of Helots as troops); and while his love of justice is borne in part from his Spartan education, it appears to transform itself into a form of gentleness the Spartans were unable to practice. Brasidas truly aims, and is successful in being, what the Spartans claim to be yet are incapable of. Spartan principles of justice were never applied to those outside of Sparta, despite the Spartan belief in their own justice (in contrast to the rigid adherence to these principles in their refusal to punish Pausanias); thus they act with hesitation to punish one of their own at home (since to do so would be to admit that a Spartan can betray the city) and appear to act hypocritically abroad (since they demand others to abandon completely their own interests); they act inconsistently because they act from competing motives. This is captured in Thucydides' statement that the Spartans acted mostly for the sake of the Thebans in executing the Plataeans; they refused to depart from their interests in this case (siding with Thebes), but also believed these interests coincided with the justice of the verdict they reached. To psychologically mask the interests compelling them, the Spartans hid from themselves behind a denunciation of the injustice of the Plataeans, a denunciation they truly believed.

Brasidas, instead, seeks justice beyond this limited and partial Spartan view. He has come to realize, although tentatively, that the good of Sparta is at odds with another understanding of justice, and hence of their own claim to be fighting for the autonomy of those subject to Athens. Brasidas' vigor in pursuing justice, in pursuing *liberation* evinces his striving for an honor and nobility, for an excellence, beyond the praise and blame administered by adherence simply to Spartan laws. It is Brasidas' hopes, on the one hand, and Spartan fears on the other, that most guide the conduct of each. Hopes and fears, endemic to us as human beings, reveal contradictions and result in inconsistent decisions, which Thucydides' presentation of political life is intended to illuminate and clarify.

Brasidas' seductiveness convinced fearful Athenian subjects to revolt, and this fact is instructive in understanding those cities. Believing Brasidas and Sparta were indeed attempting to secure the autonomy of others (and not only as the result of calculated self-interest), inclination toward Sparta early in the war suggests most cities supported Sparta's moral justification in declaring a war aimed at stopping the Athenian empire's unjust encroachments – the vote for war secured via the charge of Athenian injustice (2.8.4-5). Unable to imagine the Spartans could be overcome by fear, the other cities believed they were genuinely animated by a desire to end Athenian imperialism. Thucydides' view is thus remote from that of either Sparta or Athens, from the city as city. That most cities justify their actions precisely in the midst of pursuing beneficial policy (believing or not in such justifications) is a Spartan corrective to the flawed claim of the Athenian thesis that all cities weigh only their interests, not blinded by any passions rooted in justice – anger, revenge, dishonor, or shame. But the Athenian thesis itself betrays a desire, a felt need, to justify empire at least partially on moral terms: Athens' restraint is, in their view, noble and thus justifies their awareness of infringing on the interests and autonomy of the cities they control. In other words, moral propriety is, for all political actors, a consideration in understanding and acting (part of any calculation) upon their own self-interest.

In the case of Sparta, this works at cross purposes: Spartans want to be just, but do not learn moderation. Spartans are moderate at home, but it is a coerced "virtue." Institutional moderation is bound to fail if conditions arise that allow or compel the loosening of those restraints. Moderation is the political virtue because it recognizes both the need for daring and gentleness when confronted with the necessities of war. Athenian imperialism ignores moderation in the name of nobility; Sparta, in the name of piety. For politics, everywhere and always, moderation is exceedingly rare in both individuals and cities. Chance thus factors in, even though the best cities always aim to build moderation into their regimes, and cultivate it in their citizens, in an effort to stave off the numerous forces always working against its wisdom. Brasidas himself takes advantage of chance opportunities presented to him, opportunities that allow him to aid his city. And Brasidas himself is the product of chance.

If we seek a middle path or a compromised solution to the tension between the Spartan view and the Athenian view, Thucydides does not provide a ready answer. If a solution exists, it appears to reside in those individuals, not cities, who do not figure prominently in the war. Diodotus and Antiphon both are able to guide their city to political sobriety and caution (3.49, 8.68.1-2); Peisistratus and his sons (as tyrants) were able to maintain a law-abiding regime that cultivated virtue and piety among the citizens, respected ancestral laws, and refrained from the dangerous temptations of empire (6.54.5-6); and Demosthenes strikes us as both public-spirited and able, leading Athens prudently and safely in a manner his foil, Nicias, could not. Demosthenes had a rare ability to learn from nature, perhaps also or especially, human nature and thus avoid the pitfalls of other men (4.29-30; cf. 3.112.4). Finally, in Thucydides' own opinion, the regime of 411 was the most well-governed Athens he himself experienced. We, therefore, cannot ignore the tremendous influence of Alcibiades either, while also remaining fully aware of the risks of an Alcibiades to any city (8.86.4).

But none escape the fortunes of war. It is in the example of Thucydides himself where we locate a wisdom – knowledge of politics and human psychology – beyond the view of any single character, beyond those directly involved in the Peloponnesian War, and beyond the narrowness of party and political ideology constraining our own times. Thucydides allows his readers – through his artful narrative presentation, the speeches of his characters, and judgments in his own voice, when properly understood together – to observe the impossible resolution of the partial or flawed views of both Sparta and Athens, and thus to partake of a political education. Sparta's *nomoi* restrain beautiful speeches, ignoring a source of wisdom; Periclean Athens beautifies its city, a beautification hiding tensions in its imperialism; the Athenian thesis rejects noble words at the moment it employs them. Thucydides uses beautiful speeches, not to disguise, but to disclose. In educating how we view the parameters of politics, as observers and students of human life, Thucydides bids us to carefully weigh what is possible and what is best, along with how we may cultivate a deeper awareness of possibilities and problems.

Understanding the less resplendent, but politically fundamental, Spartan qualities deepen this education. Sparta is *the* portrait of a regime least susceptible to faction, infighting, civil war, and ultimately, death. Yet Thucydides' case for what is embodied in "Sparta" is tempered by changes that took hold of the city as it confronted war's necessities when challenging the greatest of empires. Sparta could not preserve its regime in the form that cultivated the strengths Thucydides praises; nor could Sparta consistently produce the type of men required to carry on a war when *their* empire was threatened; and the Spartan education holding the regime together was itself threatened, in the final analysis, by a war of such scale, drawing un-Spartan qualities out of the men forced to face an un-Spartan enemy. It is the peculiar human condition embodied in "Sparta," the shaping of human nature by Spartan *nomoi*, where Thucydides locates political truths for his reader. To say, therefore, that Sparta won the war and Athens lost is both the truth and almost entirely misleading.

Appendix: Thucydides' Account as "History"

Thucydides claims his account is a possession for all times, and this is not a claim one would expect from a contemporary historical account, except in so far as future readers might take some antiquarian interest in the historical event itself. But Thucydides' declaration of permanence is tied to his attempt to present the truth, not merely of the Peloponnesian War, but of war as such. As I have argued, this includes the events leading up to its outbreak, the character of the cities involved, and the individuals leading each city or most involved in the movement of the war. History today, instead, is animated by the importance of accuracy and precision – no one would consider a historical document accurate in which the author admitted to modifying, or even inventing, the speeches of the most important envoys and statesmen. But Thucydides does precisely this (1.22.1).[1] Even Thucydides' sacrifice of chronology (as well as moving suddenly from one incident to another seemingly unrelated one) is at odds with a properly written history of a particular state or war. One should begin at the beginning and include only those details which can be checked, corroborated, and verified. However, even if there were other accounts of the Peloponnesian War, it is not obvious Thucydides would have framed his narrative with any reference to them. Thucydides' account, then, is enigmatic as it continually disappoints and confounds the expectations of the modern reader.[2]

1 Hornblower I p. 59 notes that fabricated speeches were the rule *after* Thucydides. What is unique, he argues, is Thucydides announcing that this is precisely what he is doing. My argument here is not affected – academic scholarship makes a sharp distinction between history and literature (and many other genres). But these genres, in the manner we define them today, were unknown to Thucydides and his contemporaries.

2 Wallace (1964) raises all of the objections noted above. As Orwin (1989) p. 345 observes: "If Thucydides were a modern historian, he would begin by justifying his choice of subject, but also by stating his 'methodology' that is, by distinguishing his approach from other possible approaches to that subject." In tackling the question of

To complicate matters further is "the Thucydidean problem" (*Thukydidesfrage*, as German scholarship designated it): when and how Thucydides composed his account, the presumption being that we are required to understand the "development" in his thinking. Thucydides scholarship has moved, however, from the so-called Separatists – who argue Thucydides wrote different parts of his account at different times and therefore inconsistencies, contradictions, and changes in his views abound throughout the text – to the position that Thucydides' account is indeed a coherent and unified work, the Unitarians, and thus must be understood from a literary perspective.[3] Antony Andrewes exemplifies and doubles down on the Separatist view when he contends that "…indifference to these questions of chronology and revision is possible only for those who believe very devoutly in the homogeneity of his work, but for those who even suspect that he changed and developed it, must be of the first importance to try to distinguish early from late passages, to try to determine how the returned exile of 404 differed from the young man who set out to write the history of the war in the moment it began."[4]

Can we not, however, accept both that Thucydides' views could have matured over the course of the war and that his account *contains* these mature views? No one would reject Andrewes' contention that any author develops their views over time; it is, rather, the assumption that

Thucydides as history or literature, Dover (2009) argues: "however useful the notion of genre may be for the understanding of historiography from the fourth century bc onwards, its utility for the understanding of Thucydides is limited." In fact, Thucydides avoids the word (Hornblower I p. 5). This is noticeable especially since his predecessor, Herodotus, calls his work a "history" (*istoria*). Instead, Thucydides uses the word *xynegrapse* – "he wrote down" (1.1.1). This means, at the very least, that Thucydides is distinguishing his text from that of Herodotus. In his influential *The Idea of History* (1946), R.G. Collingwood compares Thucydides to his predecessor, arguing that if history must proceed according to scientific laws, Thucydides' account (focused instead on "psychological laws") certainly did not qualify (pp. 29-31). Considered also in light of the critiques of Homer appearing early in Book One, Thucydides points us to the question of what type of "writing" his account is.

3 For an overview of scholarship presenting the compositionalist view, as well as a bibliography, see Romilly (1963) pp. 1-10, 380-81. Key debates on particular passages were treated as they arose throughout the text.

4 Andrewes (1959) pp. 223-24. Cf. Ste. Croix (1954) p. 31: "Attempts have been made to sketch that development [of Thucydides' political outlook], in accordance with theories about the dates at which certain parts of the History are held to have been written; but they are all subjective, and agreement has not been reached on any of the major problems involved."

underdeveloped views remain in the text as we have it which is open to objections. The artistry of the text, the more one studies it, is impossible to deny. And most scholars recognize it, especially in sequences such the Sicilian narrative.[5] Instead, it is the Books for which scholars have the most difficulty explaining Thucydides' intention, as it relates to *their* view of the overall text, that they offer up as evidence for their "early" versus "late" determination. It has become increasingly clear, though, that Thucydides employs an artistry, perhaps most notably in these neglected Books – including the Spartan narrative in Book 5 – requiring much closer (and I would add, more sympathetic) consideration.[6]

Initiating this shift in how Thucydides is studied includes W. Robert Connor's influential book *Thucydides*, where he argues persuasively that Thucydides' intention is guided by his aim of educating readers and thus his manner of writing employs puzzles and questions.[7] Following Connor, I have argued and hope to have shown that apparent contradictions, inconsistencies, and seemingly unnecessary details or events actually illuminate our understanding of the war because they allow the reader to work through both political and philosophic puzzles. Hobbes' famous (yet for a time, long forgotten) statement on Thucydides' writing presages Connor and is revealing here:

> Digressions for instruction's cause, and other such open conveyances of precepts, (which is the philosopher's part), he never useth; as having so clearly set before men's eyes the ways and events of good and evil counsels,

---

5 See, for example, Hornblower (1987) pp. 193-97.

6 This artistry is described in various terms. Connor (1984) demonstrates a "ring composition" where arguments are introduced, their parts and subparts move towards a concentrated center, and then ascend again to return to a starting point (a pattern of A-B-C…C-B-A); this is especially apparent in the Archaeology (Hornblower I p. 15). Allison (2013) p. 261n17 refers to "framing" as similar to ring composition, but distinct in picking up the narrative at a different point. Romilly (2012) p. 152 describes Thucydides' piracy proofs in the Archaeology as a "chiasmus," akin to a ring composition. As she goes on to note: "…it cannot be by chance that the words that draw out attention are so often of the same order; and it is clearly Thucydides' interpretation that imposes its presence and weight on every detail of the expression" (164).

7 Consider his "Introduction" (pp. 3-19) as a whole on this issue. See Orwin (1986) for a useful review of Connor's book.

> that the narration itself doth secretly instruct the reader, and more effectually than can possibly be done by precept.[8]

Hobbes' argument is that we need to observe, and weigh, various decisions, various characters themselves, just as we would during any political event. We must ask ourselves: Do they speak as we would speak in the particular situation? If not, why not? What could have been said better or what do they perhaps take for granted in their speech? Based on what they do say, are their actions, their deeds, consistent with their speech? Or do they fail to heed their own advice? If so, why? If not, why not? Do they learn from mistakes that they do make and if so, how does an outcome, good or bad, influence their actions when later confronted with a similar instance? It is questions such as these that I believe Hobbes intends when arguing that Thucydides "secretly instructs" the reader. Thucydides' task, according to Hobbes, is edification. But there is an obstacle to education: Most people have little interest in being told they are wrong; we hold fast to our understanding of the world around us, to our opinions.[9] Coming to notice the errors of others (be they strategic, political, or prudential), instead, with Thucydides as guide, and applying this to one's understanding, will more likely conduce to success, to a political education.[10]

---

8 Hobbes' "Of the Life and History of Thucydides" in *The Peloponnesian War*, p. 577.

9 See Alexander Hamilton's opening arguments in Federalist No. 1 on obstacles to political reform.

10 This approach has also been greatly influenced, if not duly recognized, by the work of Leo Strauss. As Clifford Orwin (1994) argues, Strauss's treatment of Thucydides in his book *The City and Man* (1964) preceded that of Connor; however, I would add, Strauss receives much less attention among classicists and historians, since his work is categorized as political theory or philosophy. Strauss is also not typical scholarship, focusing almost exclusively on the text (he cites only three scholars in his Thucydides chapter). Nevertheless, his attention to Thucydides' details is instructive and his approach starts from the assumption that the text is a coherent one meant to be studied closely. For example, Strauss notices the early mentions of figures such as Nicias and Brasidas as important preludes to their later narratives, while other scholars often dismiss these fragments or events as of little relevance or simply puzzling so-called insertions. In my view (and Orwin's), Strauss' book chapter on Thucydides makes novel and still indispensable observations. Strauss is especially good for focusing on issues many scholars previously neglected, including piety and justice. Strauss also pays more attention to what he calls the "Case of Sparta" than most commentators (that is, why Sparta might be "the good guys" in the Peloponnesian War). Strauss' cryptic writing style and minimal engagement with other scholarship (in part due to few political theorists at that time treating Thucydides and due to Strauss' contention

If the foregoing instances of the literary approach are correct, we begin to find an interpretative path through Thucydides' account. Just as one must interpret speeches and deeds in political life itself, determining how they can be made sense of, so too with the Peloponnesian War. Thucydides has crafted his account to *imitate* politics, allowing his readers to gain an education through the particulars of this war. These particulars, and the universal problems that political communities face, come together. Connor's study thus strengthened the Unitarian view, further supporting Jacqueline de Romilly's argument that it is an error to approach Thucydides with the guiding assumption that his account suffered from problems of composition and incompleteness (as the Separatists claimed) simply because the movement of the text is not always immediately apparent.[11] Thucydides never promises that the truth will be easy, nor apparent, and he himself went through great labors to discover it (1.22.2-5).

The very fact that the status of Thucydides' text, what *kind* of book it is, is continually a subject of debate, is clearly telling. Scholars starting from the Athenian point of view misread Thucydides' intention by ignoring the

---

that Thucydides is a "philosophic historian"), leaves one needing to clarify and supplement his important contribution. This, I believe, has also in part led to a lack of engagement by other scholars with Strauss' work. Interpreting Strauss is further made difficult due to the context of his remarks in *The City and Man* – his own scholarly and philosophic project involved a recovery of classical political philosophy as a challenge to key tenets of modernity (particularly historicism and positivism) and therefore his Thucydides must be placed in this context. Clifford Orwin's own book *The Humanity of Thucydides* (1994) is one of the best book-length treatments of Thucydides by a political theorist. Orwin, following Strauss' suggestions, does not begin from the assumption that Thucydides is a teacher of power politics or a political "scientist." Rather, Orwin delves into the psychology of the actors more than most other accounts and I have profited greatly from both of these outstanding works. As is now clear, however, there are points of disagreement I have with Orwin's interpretation of Sparta. Also see Orwin (1989) pp. 385-86 for observations on political education as it relates to Thucydides' construction of speeches. Discussion of these two influential political theorists include (on Strauss): Benardete (1976), Orwin (2015), Jaffe (2015), Keedus (2016), Kleinhaus (2017). For a discussion of Orwin's Thucydides, consider Balot (2015).

11 In discussing Book Five in Chapter Three, we noticed that Romilly (1963) does not entirely depart from the Separatist view – she argues that Book Five is indeed incomplete and thereby misses many of the interpretive questions Thucydides intends to raise, since that Book does (as she notes) introduce problems when contrasted with Thucydides' presentation of the war during the first ten years. Similarly, Connor (1984) p. 231 acknowledges the work's incompleteness, but denies that this fundamentally detracts from the text. Hornblower III pp. 1-4 rejects the Separatist thesis as well and supports the unity of Books Five and Eight.

literary nature of his account; thus, they fail to understand the Spartan point of view, Thucydides' analysis being both a praise, and critique. This mitigates their interpretation of key issues, especially piety and justice, but most notably, how piety and justice bear on human psychology. The result is a reductionist view of human motives. For example, scholars have long noticed the "Spartan" and "Athenian" dichotomy as a Thucydidean "category," since it is first introduced by the Corinthians (1.70). But then they fail to go beyond it and see how Thucydides offers it to us as a first attempt at categorization, only to abandon this very characterization as definitive. Nicias the "Spartan" and Brasidas the "Athenian" are two striking instances of the need to render this simply dichotomy more subtly. It even leaves us wondering whether we can allow ourselves to rely on such categorizations at all.

Yet why have scholars been so tempted by the Athenian view of the war, and thereby, the Athenian view of politics, their thesis? After all, political stability is an early Thucydidean theme and Sparta clearly bests Athens on this score (at least in Thucydides' initial, and thus most noticeable, remarks – 1.6, 10.2, 18.1). There are two main reasons, one rather superficial and one we must treat further. First, some scholars simply see Athenian bias since Thucydides himself was an Athenian. Being a patriot, Thucydides must have skewed towards preferring his city over Sparta. Thus, for example, he treats Cleon unfairly, does not give Brasidas his proper due, and ultimately sees political life as the Athenians at Melos articulate it. This view is too simplistic to be definitive and simply ignores details of the text itself. Our study of Sparta has provided abundant evidence undermining this view.

More serious, though, is the reading many scholars do come away with: that while Thucydides may not be a simple cheerleader for Athens, he certainly sees the world more through Athenian eyes than Spartan ones. Indeed, on a first reading we do tend to shake our heads, or even laugh, at decisions made by the Spartans.[12] We are also dazzled by Athens, possessing a preeminent navy and dominant as a sea power, both of which indeed figure prominently in the early chapters. But Thucydides also warns us against this overestimation (1.10.2), and certainly he could not present the greatness of the Peloponnesian War were Sparta not a worthy adversary.

And of course, we know Sparta is such an adversary, from the opening sentence (1.1). This problem is due, in my view, largely to misreadings

12 Strauss (1964), for example, notes that the other side of those who see Thucydides' work as tragic, is the often-comic appearance of Sparta (see pp. 222-26 and context).

of Thucydides' text when departing from a literary approach. Thucydides' account is of such wide appeal that various disciplines and their distinct methods of interpretation look to him as an authority. As Neville Morley notes: "Historical readings focus on recovering trustworthy data about the ancient Greek past (which may or may not have a wider significance, but that is secondary), the political theorist or international relations specialist looks for general principles or laws of human and state behaviour (which may or may not have a grounding in historical reality, but that is secondary), while the political philosopher finds timeless wisdom and understanding, reflections on universal problems of human existence."[13] Thucydides' own discussion of his approach lends credence to all of these. But it would be remiss to ignore his most important claim, the hoped-for permanence of his account in offering future readers guidance in interpreting their own times (1.22).

A key controversy highlights an interpretive disagreement hindering Thucydides' aim: the apparent incomplete status of the text itself, which seemingly ends (mid-sentence no less) in Book Eight. Surely this is the mark of an unfinished text. And since the ending signals incompleteness, we are therefore licensed to question the work as whole, wondering if other Books were also left uncompleted and lacking the polish Thucydides may have intended. This would surely detract from its value and the loftiness of Thucydides' claim. Yet since Thucydides states that his account was to reveal the truth, could we not also raise a simple question: Did he not believe that the first twenty-one years of the war served *that* purpose and therefore that we know what *he* wants us to know about Sparta and Athens, the causes for the beginning and end of the war, and when carefully considered, something about the nature of war and politics itself? For it is due to the apparent incompleteness of Thucydides' account, ending where it does in the 21st year of a 27-year war, that leads many scholars to find other themes, questions, and problems as left untreated. It also justifies the attempt to find Thucydides an authority on some issues, but dubious of his account on others. It allows one to treat certain passages as Thucydides'

---

13 Morley (2015). My approach is clearly in line with the expectation that we can find timeless wisdom in Thucydides. See also Strauss (1964) pp. 139-45 and 236-41, the first and final sections of his chapter, where the approach and goals of classical political philosophy as a whole, and Thucydides' place in it, are his theme.

considered view, while disregarding others altogether (often, those that do not fit with the interpreter's overall reading). It allows, in other words, a rudderless reading of the text.

While the final sentence is certainly odd, it is an error to assume Thucydides' account of the war is incomplete (both in ending where it does and in lacking details scholars continue to expect) simply because it ends before the final defeat of Athens and thus the "end" of the war. For besides the fact that he leaves out *other* details some scholars might expect (for example, the Megarian Decree) he also claims his account is a possession for all times. My repeating this statement is not accidental. Intended to be a possession for all times, meaning that it will aid us in understanding war and politics in the future, Thucydides could not simply be concerned with detailing *every* event that occurred during the Peloponnesian War. In failing to cover its final seven years, he may be doing no more than refraining from accounting for those years that had no fundamental effect, in his view, on what the war could reveal about war *as such*, as well as politics and human nature.[14]

Perhaps he had an intention, setting a puzzle before us, in ending with a final, fragmentary sentence. The question of incompleteness will always remain open without a unanimous interpretation of Book Eight; since this is not possible, we must remain open while also not using this Book to decide interpretive questions of the whole work where other internal evidence is available.[15]

---

14 Hobbes' "To the Readers" in *The Peloponnesian War*: "...the principle and proper work of history being to instruct and enable men, by knowledge of actions past, to bear themselves prudently in the present and providently towards the future" (p. xxi). Cf. the first section of Gomme's Introduction to Volume I (1945) pp. 1-25, which is tellingly titled "What Thucydides Takes For Granted," an extended discussion of economic, military, and other matters (including the Greek calendar) that Thucydides fails to detail. Hornblower's *Thucydides* (1987) weighs this question of comprehensiveness versus selectivity in Thucydides' presentation, finding evidence of extremes of both. This, it seems, leaves Thucydides open to critiques based on what we modern scholars would "wish" for (see p. 200: "Nevertheless, I wish..."). On the other hand, Rood (1998) p. 3 argues: "Modern historians have found Thucydides' omissions an obstacle, not an incentive; and increasingly object to the story Thucydides constructs from the events he does include." See also Rahe (1995) pp. 110-12 on Thucydides' use of the ancient art of rhetoric.

15 For other discussions of what Thucydides includes (and excludes) in his account of the war, see Gomme I (1945) pp. 25-29, Hornblower (1987) pp. 34-44 with Hornblower I pp. 59-60. As Connor (1984b) pp. 231-32 argues in his book review of

We cannot ignore, moreover, the fact that we find references to the end of the war at 2.65.12 and 5.26.1 (and, of course, with Thucydides' first sentence). He must, therefore, have written these passages after the war ended. But this is not the invitation to picking apart the text that scholars (such as Andrewes, quoted above) for a long time have taken it to be. Thucydides, like any competent writer, surely edited his book. But why would one edit passages in Book Two and write his "Second Preface" to Book Five, yet not only fail to edit Book Eight, but leave it with an incomplete sentence. Not just a rough draft sentence, but a half-sentence. As Hornblower notes, "a sentence which is itself in need of completion." And as Hornblower goes on to observe, there are references near the end of Thucydides' account to the end of Herodotus' account, as well as repetition or return to the theme of Delos' purification "...that certainly (almost) begins, and (almost) closes, the entire work as we have it."[16] This mirroring of Herodotus (and this is only one such example) seems *awfully* coincidental. There is as much, if not more, evidence that Thucydides' text is complete rather than incomplete.

Is it not merely an assumption that Thucydides' views radically changed? Is it not merely an assumption that Thucydides did not edit his work, removing any of the youthful fancy or misunderstandings of the war before finding its way into his account? The proof lies with the quality of a

---

Gomme V (authored by A. Andrewes): "After 140 years of sustained discussion of the composition problem one would expect that here at least the premises and issues would by now be clearly defined. But once again unspoken assumptions play a crucial role." Such assumptions result in Andrewes' view that Book Eight is "very early and very incomplete." Gribble (1998), as one example, works to undermine this view by focusing on "narrator interventions." Overall, his approach argues not to simply eliminate passages based on the presumption they were added later, particularly given Thucydides' ability to change his "style" throughout his narrative. I concur, and as we observed especially with Book Five, Thucydides' "style" is a function of shifting his presentation to a new phase of the war. Hornblower's *Commentary* offers insight on what we can be certain Thucydides left out, either via comparison to Herodotus or based on archaeological evidence. But he also opines, I believe incorrectly, that Thucydides adds or emphasizes things appearing to be of little importance (similarly, Westlake [1969] pp. 1-38 in his boldly titled essay "Irrelevant Notes and Minor Excurses in Thucydides"). This is a much broader question because it points to the heart of the matter: one's overall interpretation of Thucydides' text.

16 Hornblower III pp. 1053-54. See also Munn (2000) pp. 323-27 and Dobski (2013) for the numerous parallels (and possible significance) of the beginning and end of Thucydides' account.

given interpretation, one which accounts for as much of Thucydides' overall presentation as possible, one which can piece together what all scholars admit is an account of an ancient war unique in human history, offering material for reflections on the human condition even when set beside the most profound authors in any tradition. Is this not enough to recommend our careful consideration?[17]

17 It should be noted, therefore, that the issue is not necessarily one of the differing methodological approaches of various academic disciplines. Rather, it is interpreting Thucydides with the best evidence available to understand his intention, approach, and judgments – namely, his text.

Bibliography

Editions and Translations of Thucydides

Collins, Susan and Stauffer, Devin (Trans.) *Empire and the Ends of Politics: Plato's Menexenus and Pericles' Funeral Oration.* Focus Publishing. 1999.

Hobbes, Thomas (Trans.) *The Peloponnesian War.* (Ed.) David Grene. University of Chicago Press. 1989.

Jones, Henry Stuart and Powell, Johannes Enoch. (Eds.). *Thucydides Historiae.* Oxford Classical Texts. 2 Volumes. 1942 and 1902.

Jowett, Benjamin. (Trans.) *History of the Peloponnesian War.* Prometheus Books. 1998. Originally published by Oxford: Clarendon Press. 1900.

Lattimore, Steven. (Trans.). *The Peloponnesian War.* Hackett Publishing Company. 1998.

Mynott, Jeremy. (Ed. and Trans.) *The War of the Peloponnesians and the Athenians.* Cambridge University Press. 2013.

Strassler, Robert B. (Ed.) *The Landmark Thucydides.* Simon and Schuster Inc. 1996.

Woodruff, Paul (Trans. and Ed.) *Thucydides on Justice, Power, and Human Nature.* Hackett Publishing. 1993.

Primary Sources

Aristotle. *Politics.* (Trans.) Carnes Lord. University of Chicago Press. 1985.

Liddell, Henry George and Robert Scott. *An Intermediate Greek-English Lexicon*: Founded Upon the Seventh Edition of Liddell and Scott's Greek-English Lexicon. Clarendon Press. 1889.

Machiavelli, Niccolo. *Discourses on Livy.* (Trans.) Harvey C. Manfield and Nathan Tarcov. University of Chicago Press. 1996.

—. *Florentine Histories.* (Trans.) Laura F. Banfield and Harvey C. Mansfield. University of Chicago Press. 1988.

—. *The Prince.* (Trans.) Harvey C. Mansfield. 2nd ed. University of Chicago Press. 1998.

Marcellinus. *Life of Thucydides.* (Trans. with introductory essay) Timothy Burns. *Interpretation: A Journal of Political Philosophy.* Vol. 38. No. 1 (2010): 1-26.

Nietzsche, Friedrich. *Daybreak: Thoughts on the Prejudices of Morality.* (Eds.) Maudemarie Clark and Brian Leiter. (Trans.) R.J. Hollingdale. Cambridge University Press. 1997.

Plato. *The Laws.* (Trans.) Thomas L. Pangle. University of Chicago Press. 1988.

——. *Republic.* (Trans.) Allan Bloom. Basic Books. 2nd Edition. 1991.

Rousseau, Jean Jacques. *The Discourses and other early political writings.* (Ed.) Victor Gourevitch. Cambridge University Press. 1997.

——. *Emile or On Education.* (Trans.) Allan Bloom. Basic Books. 1979.

——. *Politics and the Arts: Letter to M. D'Alembert on the Theatre.* (Trans.) Allan Bloom. Cornell University Press. 1968.

——. *The Social Contract and other later political writings.* (Ed.) Victor Gourevitch. Cambridge University Press. 1997.

Xenophon. "Constitution of the Lacedaemonians" in *Scripta Minora.* (Trans.) E.C. Marchant and G.W. Bowersock. Loeb Classical Library. 1925.

——. *Memorabilia, Oeconomicus, Symposium, Apologia.* (Trans.) E.C. Marchant and O.J. Todd. Loeb Classical Library. 1923.

——. *Memorabilia.* (Translated and Annotated). Amy L. Bonnette. Cornell University Press. 1994.

——. *Xenophon: The Shorter Writings.* (Ed.) Gregory A. McBrayer. Cornell University Press. 2018.

Secondary Sources

Adcock, Frank Ezra. "Thucydides in Book I." *The Journal of Hellenic Studies* 71 (1951): 2-12.

Ahrensdorf, Peter. "The Fear of Death and the Longing for Immortality: Hobbes and Thucydides on Human Nature and the Problem of Anarchy." *American Political Science Review* 94, no. 3 (2000): 579-593.

——. "Thucydides' Realistic Critique of Realism." *Polity* 30, no. 2 (1997): 231-265.

Allison, June W. "The Balance of Power and Compositional Balance: Thucydides Book 1" in *Thucydides between History and Literature.* (Eds.) Tsakmakis, Antonis, and Tamiolaki, Mélina. De Gruyter. 2013.

——. "Sthenelaidas' Speech: Thucydides 1.86." *Hermes* 112 (1984): 9-16.

Alker, Hayward R. "The Dialectical Logic of Thucydides' Melian Dialogue." *American Political Science Review* 82, no. 3 (1988): 805-820.

Amit, M. "The Melian Dialogue and History." *Athenaeum* 46 (1968): 216-235.

Andrewes, A. "Thucydides on the Causes of the War." *The Classical Quarterly* 9, nos. 3-4 (1959): 223-239.

——. "The Mytilene Debate: Thucydides 3.36-49." *Phoenix* 16, no. 2 (1962): 64-85.

——. "Eunomia." *The Classical Quarterly* 32, no. 2 (1938): 89-102.

——. "The Melian Dialogue and Perikles' Last Speech." *The Cambridge Classical Journal* 6 (1960): 1-10.

Badian, Ernst. *From Plataea to Potidaea: Studies in the History and Historiography of the Pentecontaetia.* Johns Hopkins University Press. 1993.

——. "Thucydides on rendering speeches." *Athenaeum* 80 (1992): 187-90.

——. “Plataea Between Athens and Sparta” in *Boiotika*: Vortrage vom 5. Internationalen Bootien-Kolloquium zu Ehren von Professor Dr.Siegfried Lauffer: Institut fur Alte Geschichte, Ludwig-Maximilians-Universitat München: 95-111.

Balot, Ryan, K., Forsdyke, Sara, Foster, Edith (Eds.). *The Oxford Handbook of Thucydides*. Oxford University Press. 2017.

——. “Philosophy and ‘Humanity’: Reflections on Thucydidean Piety, Justice, and Necessity” in *In Search of Humanity: Essays in Honor of Clifford Orwin*. (Ed.) Andrea Radasanu. Lexington Books (2015): 17-35.

——. *Greed and Injustice in Classical Athens*. Princeton University Press. 2001.

Bartlett, Robert. *The Idea of Enlightenment: A Post-Mortem Study*. University of Toronto Press. 2001.

Benardete, Seth. “Leo Strauss’ *The City and Man*.” *The Political Science Reviewer* 8 (1978): 1-20.

Bloedow, Edmund F. “The Speeches of Archidamus and Sthenelaidas at Sparta.” *Historia: Zeitschrift für Alte Geschichte* H. 2 (1981): 129-143.

Bolotin, David. “Thucydides” in *History of Political Philosophy*. (Eds.) Leo Strauss and Joseph Cropsey. University of Chicago Press. 3rd Edition. 1987. 7-32.

Bonner, Robert J. “The Book Divisions of Thucydides.” *Classical Philology* 15, no. 1 (1920): 73-82.

Bosworth, Albert Brian. “The Humanitarian Aspect of the Melian Dialogue.” *The Journal of Hellenic Studies* 113 (1993): 30-44.

Bowersock, Glen W. “The Personality of Thucydides.” *The Antioch Review* 25, no. 1 (1965): 135-146.

Bradford, Alfred, S. “The Duplicitous Spartan” in *The Shadow of Sparta*. (Eds.) Anton Powell and Stephen Hodkinson. Routledge. 1994: 59-85.

Bruell, Christopher. “Thucydides’ View of Athenian Imperialism.” *American Political Science Review* 68, no. 1 (Mar. 1974): 11-17.

——. “Reply to Corsi.” *American Political Science Review* 68, no. 4 (Dec. 1974): 1680-81.

——. “Thucydides and Perikles.” *The St. Johns Review* 32 (1981): 24-29.

Brunt, P.A. “Spartan Policy and Strategy in the Archidamian War.” *Phoenix* 19, no. 4 (Winter 1965): 255-280.

Bruzzone, Rachel. “Weather, Luck and the Divine in Thucydides” in *The Religious Aspects of War in the Ancient Near East, Greece, and Rome*. (Ed.) Krzysztof Ulanowski. Brill. 2016: 180-193.

Burckhardt, Jacob. *History of Greek Culture*. (Trans.) Palmer Hilty. Dover Publications. 2002.

Burns, Timothy W. “Nicias in Thucydides and Aristophanes Part I: Nicias and Divine Justice in Thucydides.” *Polis* 29, no. 2 (2012): 217-233.

——. “The Virtue of Thucydides’ Brasidas.” *The Journal of Politics* 73, no. 2 (2011): 508-523.

——. “What War Discloses” in *Recovering Reason: Essays in Honor of Thomas L. Pangle*. (Ed.) Timothy Burns. Lexington Books. 2010.

——. "Anger in Thucydides and Aristophanes: The Case of Cleon" in *The Political Theory of Aristophanes. Explorations in Poetic Wisdom.* State University of New York Press. 2014: 229-258.

Bury, J.B. The Ancient Greek Historians. Macmillan. 1959. Originally published 1909.

Cartledge, Paul. *Sparta and Lakonia: A Regional History 1300-362 BC.* Routledge. 2002.

——. *Spartan Reflections.* University of California Press. 2001.

——. "What Have the Spartans Done for Us?: Sparta's Contribution to Western Civilization." *Greece and Rome* 51, no. 2 (2004): 164-179.

Cartledge, Paul and Debnar, Paula. "Sparta and the Spartans in Thucydides" in *Brill's Companion to Thucydides.* (Eds.) Antonios Rengakos and Antonis Tsakmakis. Brill. 2006: 559-588.

Coby, Patrick. "Enlightened Self-Interest in the Peloponnesian War: Thucydidean Speakers on the Right of the Stronger and Inter-State Peace." *Canadian Journal of Political Science* 24, no. 1 (1991): 67-90.

Cochrane, Charles N. *Thucydides and the Science of History.* Russell and Russell. 1929.

Cogan, Marc. *The Human Thing: The Speeches and Principles of Thucydides' History.* University of Chicago Press. 1981.

——. "Mytilene, Plataea, and Corcyra Ideology and Policy in Thucydides, Book Three." *Phoenix* 35, no. 1 (1981): 1-21.

Collingwood, R.G. *The Idea of History.* Oxford. 1946.

Connor, W. Robert. "A Post Modernist Thucydides?" *The Classical Journal* 72, no. 4 (1977): 289-298.

——. *Thucydides.* Princeton University Press. 1984.

——. *The New Politicians of Fifth-Century Athens.* Hackett Publishing, 1992. Originally published by Princeton University Press. 1971.

——. Review of "A Historical Commentary on Thucydides, Vol. 5: Book 8 by A.W. Gomme, A. Andrewes and K.J. Dover." *Classical Philology* 79, no. 3 (1984): pp. 230-235.

——. "«SACRED» AND «SECULAR»: Ἱερὰ καὶ ὅσια and the Classical Athenian Concept of the State." *Ancient Society* 19 (1988): 161-188.

——. "Thucydides 2.65.12." *Arktouros: Hellenic Studies Presented to BMW Knox* (1979): 269-71.

Cornford, F.M. *Thucydides Mythistoricus.* London. 1907.

Crane, Gregory. *Thucydides and the Ancient Simplicity: The Limits of Political Realism.* University of California Press. 1998.

Diduch, Paul J. and Hadley, Travis S. "The Moral Foundations of Political Trust: Thucydides' Pericles and the Limits of Enlightened Statecraft." *Anamnesis* 5 (2016): 42-67.

Debnar, Paula. *Speaking the Same Language: Speech and Audience in Thucydides' Spartan Debates.* University of Michigan Press. 2001.

——. "Diodotus' Paradox and the Mytilene Debate (Thucydides 3.37-49)." *Rheinisches Museum für Philologie* 143, no. H. 2 (2000): 161-178.

Dobski, Bernard J. "The Incomplete Whole: The Structural Integrity of Thucydides' History." In *Socrates and Dionysus: Philosophy and Art in Dialogue.* (Ed.) Ann Ward. Cambridge Scholars Publishing. 2013: 14-32.

Dodds, E.R. *The Greeks and the Irrational.* University of California Press. 1951.

Dolgert, Stefan. "Thucydides, amended: religion, narrative, and IR theory in the Peloponnesian Crisis." *Review of International Studies* 38, no. 3 (2012): 661-682.

Dover, K. J. "Thucydides on Oracles." *The Greeks and Their Legacy: Collected Papers.* 1988.

——. *Thucydides.* Greece and Rome: New Surveys in the Classics, no. 7. Oxford: Clarendon Press. 1973.

Eatough, Geoffrey. "The Use of ὅσιος and Kindred Words in Thucydides." *The American Journal of Philology* 92, no. 2 (1971): 238-251.

Edmunds, Lowell. *Chance and Intelligence in Thucydides.* Harvard University Press. 1975.

——. "Thucydides' Ethics as Reflected in the Description of Stasis (3.82-83)." *Harvard Studies in Classical Philology* 79 (1975): 73-92.

Erasmus, H. J. "Eunomia." *Acta Classica* 3 (1960): 53-64.

Finley Jr., John H. *Three Essays on Thucydides.* Harvard University Press. 1967.

——. *Thucydides.* Ann Arbor Paperback: University of Michigan Press. 1963 (originally published 1942).

Finley, M.I. *Aspects of Antiquity: Discoveries and Controversies.* 2nd edition. Pelican Books. 1977.

——. *The Use and Abuse of History.* The Hogarth Press. 1986.

Fleiss, J. P. "Political Disorder and Constitutional Form: Thucydides' Critique of Contemporary Politics." *Journal of Politics* 21, no. 4 (1959): 592-623.

Flower, Harriet I. "Thucydides and the Pylos debate (4.27-29)." *Historia: Zeitschrift für Alte Geschichte* H. 1 (1992): 40-57.

Flower, Michael, A. "Spartan Religion" in *A Companion to Sparta.* Vol. II. (Ed.) Anton Powell. John Wiley and Sons. 2017.

——. "Athenian Religion and the Peloponnesian War" in *Art in Athens during the Peloponnesian War.* (Ed.) Olga Palagia. Cambridge University Press. (2009): 1-23.

——. "The Invention of Tradition in Classical and Hellenistic Sparta" in *Sparta: Beyond the Mirage.* (Eds.) Anton Powell and Stephen Hodkinson. Classical Press of Wales (2002): 191-217.

Forde, Steven. *The Ambition to Rule: Alcibiades and the Politics of Imperialism in Thucydides.* Cornell University Press. 1989.

——. "Thucydides on the Causes of Athenian Imperialism." *American Political Science Review* 80, no. 2 (1986): 433-448.

——. "Varieties of Realism: Thucydides and Machiavelli." *The Journal of Politics* 54, no. 2 (May 1992): 372-393.

Foster, Edith. *Thucydides, Pericles, and Periclean Imperialism.* Cambridge University Press. 2010.

——. "Athens' Political Failures in the Central Chapters of Book 4 of Thucydides." *KTÈMA Civilisations de l'Orient, de la Grèce et de Rome antiques* 44 (2019): 163-169.

Fragoulaki, Mara. *Kinship in Thucydides: Intercommunal Ties and Historical Narrative.* Oxford University Press. 2013.

Furley, William D. "Thucydides and Religion" in *Brill's Companion to Thucydides.* (Eds.) Antonios Rengakos and Antonis Tsakmakis. Brill. (2006): 415-438.

Fustel de Coulanges, Numa Denis. *The Ancient City.* The Johns Hopkins University Press. 1980.

Garst, Daniel. "Thucydides and Neorealism." *International Studies Quarterly* 33, no. 1 (1989): 3-27.

Gilpin, Robert G. "The Richness of the Tradition of Political Realism." *International Organization* 38, no. 2 (1984): 287-304.

Gomme, A.W., Andrewes, A., and Dover, K.J. *An Historical Commentary on Thucydides.* 5 volumes. Oxford: Clarendon Press. 1945-81.

——. *Essays in Greek History and Literature.* Oxford: Basil Blackwell. 1937.

——. "The Interpretation of ΚΑΛΟΙ ΚΑΓΑΘΟΙ in Thucydides 4.40.2." *Classical Quarterly* (1953): 65-68.

Gribble, David. "Narrator Interventions in Thucydides." *The Journal of Hellenic Studies* 118 (1998): 41-67.

Griffith, Guy Thompson. "Some Habits of Thucydides When Introducing Persons." *The Cambridge Classical Journal,* no. 7 (1961): 21-33.

Grote, George. *History of Greece.* 12 volumes. 2nd edition. London. 1851.

Gustafson, Lowell S. (Ed.) *Thucydides' Theory of International Relations: A Lasting Possession.* Louisiana State University Press. 2000.

Hammond, N.G.L. "Sparta-François Ollier: Le Mirage spartiate. II e Partie. Étude sur l'idéalisation de Sparte dans l'antiquité grecque du début de l'école cynique jusqu'à lafin de la cité. (Annales de l'Université de Lyon, Troisième Série, Lettres, Fascicule 13.) Pp. 220. Paris: 'Les Belles Lettres', 1943. Paper." *The Classical Review* 61, no. 1 (1947): 26-27.

Harloe, Katherine and Morley, Neville. *Thucydides and the Modern World: Reception, Reinterpretation and Influence from the Renaissance to the Present.* Cambridge University Press. 2012.

Heath, Malcolm. "Justice in Thucydides' Speeches." *Historia* 39 (1990): 385-400.

——. "Thucydides 1.23. 5-6." *Liverpool Classical Monthly* 11 (1986): 104-105.

——. "Thucydides' Political Judgement." *Liverpool Classical Monthly* 15 (1990): 158-160.

Heilke, Thomas. "Realism, Narrative, and Happenstance: Thucydides' Tale of Brasidas." *American Political Science Review* 98, no. 1 (2004): 121-138.

Hodkinson, Stephen. "New Approaches to Classical Sparta." *Journal of Classics Teaching* (2013): 16-25.

——. "The Imaginary Spartan Politeia" in *The Imaginary Polis: Symposium, January 7-10, 2004.* (Ed.). Mogens Herman Hansen. Kgl. Danske Videnskabernes Selskab. (2005): 222-281.

Hornblower, Simon. *A Commentary on Thucydides.* 3 volumes. Oxford University Press. 1991-2010.

——. *Thucydides*. The John Hopkins University Press. 1987.

——. "The Religious Dimension to the Peloponnesian War, or, What Thucydides Does Not Tell Us." *Harvard Studies in Classical Philology* 94 (1992): 169-197.

——. "The Fourth-century and Hellenistic reception of Thucydides." *The Journal of Hellenic Studies* 115 (1995): 47-68.

——. "Sticks, Stones, and Spartans: the sociology of Spartan violence." *War and Violence in Ancient Greece* (2000): 57-82.

Hudson-Williams, H. Ll. "Conventional Forms of Debate and the Melian Dialogue." *American Journal of Philology* (1950): 156-169.

Hunter, Virginia. "The Composition of Thucydides' "History": A New Answer to the Problem." *Historia: Zeitschrift für Alte Geschichte* H. 3 (1977): 269-294.

Hussey, Edward. "Thucydidean history and Democritean theory." *History of Political Thought* 6, no. 1/2 (1985): 118-138.

Jaffe, Seth N. "The Regime (*Politeia*) in Thucydides" in *The Oxford Handbook of Thucydides* (Eds.) Ryan Balot, Sara Forsdyke, Edith Foster. (2017b): 391-408.

——. "The Straussian Thucydides" in *A Handbook to the Reception of Thucydides*. (Eds.) Christine Lee and Neville Morley. Wiley-Blackwell. (2015): 278-295.

——. *Thucydides on the Outbreak of War: Character and Contest*. Oxford University Press, 2017a.

Johnson, Laurie M. *Thucydides, Hobbes, and the Interpretation of Realism*. Northern Illinois University Press. 1993.

——. "Thucydidean Realism: Between Athens and Melos." *Security Studies* 5, no. 2 (1995-96): 169-193.

——. "The Use and Abuse of Thucydides in International Relations Theory." *International Organization* 48, no. 1 (1994): 131-153.

Jordan, Borimir. "Religion in Thucydides." *Transactions of the American Philological Association* 116 (1986): 119-147.

Kagan, Donald. *The Outbreak of the Peloponnesian War*. Ithaca: Cornell University Press. 1969.

——. *The Archidamian War*. Ithaca: Cornell University Press. 1974.

——. *The Peace of Nicias and the Sicilian Expedition*. Ithaca: Cornell University Press. 1981.

——. *The Fall of the Athenian Empire*. Ithaca: Cornell University Press. 1989.

——. "The Speeches in Thucydides and the Mytilene debate." *Yale Classical Studies* 24 (1975): 71-94.

Kallet, Lisa. *Money, Expense, and Naval Power in Thucydides' History 1-5.24*. University of California Press. 1993.

——. "Thucydides, Apollo, The Plague, and The War." *American Journal of Philology* 134 (2013): 355–382.

Keedus, Liisi. "Leo Strauss's Thucydides and the Meaning of Politics" in *Thucydides and Political Order*. Palgrave Macmillan. 2016: 75-93.

Keohane, Robert O. and Joseph S. Nye. *Power and Interdependence*. Little, Brown, and Company. 1977.

Knox, A.D. "A Strange Law at Sparta." *The Classical Review* 43, no. 2 (May 1929): 52-53.

Lebow, Richard Ned. *The Tragic Vision of Politics: Ethics, Visions and Orders*. Cambridge University Press. 2003.

——. "Thucydides the Constructivist." *American Political Science Review* 95, no. 3 (2001): 547-560.

Lee, Christine and Morley, Neville (Eds.). *A Handbook to the Reception of Thucydides*. Wiley Blackwell. 2015.

Liebeschuetz, W. "Thucydides and the Sicilian Expedition." *Historia: Zeitschrift für Alte Geschichte* 17, no. 3 (Jul. 1968): 289-306.

——. "The Structure and Function of the Melian Dialogue." *The Journal of Hellenic Studies* 88 (1968): 73-77.

Lloyd-Jones, Hugh. *The Justice of Zeus*. University of California Press. 1983.

Luraghi, Nino. "Author and Audience in Thucydides' "Archaeology": Some Reflections." *Harvard Studies in Classical Philology* 100 (2000): 227-239.

——. "Thucydides and Spartan Power in the Archaeology and beyond" in *Thucydides–a violent teacher?* (Eds.) Georg Rechenauer and Vassiliki Pothou. (2011): 185-197.

MacDowell, Douglas M. *Spartan Law*. Scottish Academic Press. 1986.

Macleod, Colin. *Collected Essays*. Oxford University Press. USA. 1983.

Mara, Gerald. "Thucydides and Political Thought" in *The Cambridge Companion to Ancient Greek Political Thought*. (Ed.) Stephen Salkaver. Cambridge University Press. (2009): 96-125.

——. "Thucydides and Plato on Democracy and Trust." *The Journal of Politics* 63, no. 3 (2001): 820-845.

Marinatos, Nanno. *Thucydides and Religion*. Königstein/Ts. 1981.

——. "Thucydides and Oracles." *Journal of Hellenic Studies* 101 (1981): 138-140.

Marshall, M.H.B. "Cleon and Pericles: Sphacteria." *Greece and Rome* 31, no. 1 (1984): 19-36.

Millender, Ellen G. "Kingship: The History, Power, and Prerogatives of the Spartans' 'Divine' Dyarchy" in *A Companion to Sparta*. (Ed.) Anton Powell. (2017): 452-479.

Monoson, Sara S. and Loriaux, Michael. "The Illusion of Power and the Disruption of Moral Norms: Thucydides' Critique of Periclean Policy." *American Political Science Review* 92, no. 2 (1998): 285-297.

Morgenthau, Hans. *Politics Among Nations*. 5th ed., rev. New York: Alfred A. Knopf. 1978.

Morrison, James V. "Historical Lessons in the Melian Episode." *Transactions of the American Philological Association (1974-)* 130 (2000): 119-148.

Morley, Neville. Review of Mary Nichols' *Thucydides and the Pursuit of Freedom*. *Bryn Mawr Classical Review*. 2015.06.38.

Nichols, Mary, P. *Thucydides and the Pursuit of Freedom*. Cornell University Press. 2015.

Ollier, François. *Le mirage spartiate*. 2 vols. Paris. 1933-43.

Orwin, Clifford. *The Humanity of Thucydides*. Princeton University Press. 1994.

——. "Justifying Empire: The Speech of the Athenians at Sparta and the Problem of Justice in Thucydides." *The Journal of Politics* 48, no. 1 (Feb. 1986): 72-85.

——. "The Just and the Advantageous in Thucydides: The Case of the Mytilenaian Debate." *American Political Science Review* 78, no. 2 (1984): 485-494.

——. "Stasis and Plague: Thucydides on the Dissolution of Society." *Journal of Politics* 50, no. 4 (1988): 831-847.

——. "Review Essay on Thucydides." *Political Theory* 28, no. 6 (2000): 861-869.

——. "Reading Thucydides with Leo Strauss" in *Brill's Companion to Leo Strauss' Writings on Classical Political Thought.* (Ed.) Timothy W. Burns. Brill. (2015): 50-75.

——. "Thucydides' Contest: Thucydidean 'Methodology' in Context." *Review of Politics* 51, no. 3. (1989): 345-364.

——. "Thucydideses." *The American Scholar* 55, no. 1 (1986): 128-30.

——. "Thucydides on Nature and Human Conduct" in *The Oxford Handbook of Thucydides.* Oxford University Press. (2017): 355-372.

Ostwald, Martin. *Ananke in Thucydides.* The American Philological Association. 1988.

——. "Diodotus." *Greek, Roman, and Byzantine Studies* 20 (1979): 5-13.

Palmer, Michael. *Love of Glory and the Common Good: Aspects of the Political Thought of Thucydides.* Rowman and Littlefield Publishers. 1992.

——. "The Spartan Alcibiades: Brasidas and the Prospect of Regime Change in Sparta in Thucydides' War." *In Search of Humanity: Essays in Honor of Clifford Orwin.* (Ed.) Andrea Radasanu. Lexington Books. (2015): 65-86.

Pangle, Thomas L. and Ahrensdorf, Peter J. (Eds.) *Justice Among Nations: On the Moral Basis of Power and Peace.* University Press of Kansas. 1999.

Parker, Robert. "Spartan Religion" in *Classical Sparta: Techniques Behind Her Success.* (Ed.) Anton Powell. University of Oklahoma Press. (1998): 142-172.

Pouncey, Peter R. *The Necessities of War: A Study of Thucydides' Pessimism.* Columbia University Press. 1980.

Powell, Anton and Hodkinson, Stephen. *A Companion to Sparta.* 2 Volumes. Wiley Blackwell. 2017.

——. *The Shadow of Sparta.* Routledge. 1994.

——. *Sparta: Beyond the Mirage.* Classical Press of Wales. 2002.

——. "Divination, Royalty and Insecurity in Classical Sparta." *Kernos. Revue internationale et pluridisciplinaire de religion grecque antique* 22 (2009): 35-82.

Price, Jonathan. *Thucydides and Internal War.* Cambridge University Press. 2001.

Proietti, Gerald. "The Natural World and the Political World in Thucydides' History" in *Law and Philosophy: The Practice of Theory, Essays in Honor of George Anastaplo.* (Eds.) John A. Murley, Robert L. Stone, and William T. Braithwaite. Ohio University Press. (1992): 184-194.

——. *Xenophon's Sparta: An Introduction.* E.J. Brill. 1987.

Rahe, Paul. *The Grand Strategy of Classical Sparta: The Persian Challenge.* Yale University Press. 2015.

——. *Sparta's First Attic War: The Grand Strategy of Classical Sparta, 478-446 B.C.* Yale University Press. 2019.

——. *Sparta's Second Attic War: The Grand Strategy of Classical Sparta, 446–418 B.C.* Yale University Press. 2020.

——. *The Spartan Regime*. Yale University Press. 2016.

——. "The Selection of Ephors at Sparta." *Historia: Zeitschrift für Alte Geschichte*, Bd. 29, H. 4 (4th Qtr., 1980): 385-401

——. "The Primacy of Politics in Classical Greece." *The American Historical Review* (1984): 265-293.

——. "Thucydides' Critique of Realpolitik." *Security Studies* 5, no. 2 (1995): 105-141.

Raubitschek, Antony E. "The Speech of the Athenians at Sparta" in *The Speeches in Thucydides*. (Ed.) Philip A. Stadter. University of North Carolina Press. (1973): 32-48.

Rawlings III, Hunter R. *The Structure of Thucydides' History*. Princeton University Press. 1981.

——. "The Arche of Thucydides' War" in *Arktouros: Hellenic Studies Presented to Bernard MW Knox on the Occasion of his 65th Birthday*. (Eds.) G.W. Bowersock, Walter Burkert, and M.C.J. Putnam. (1979): 272-79.

Reeve, C.D.C. "Thucydides on Human Nature." *Political Theory* 27, no. 4 (1999): 435-446.

Rengakos, Antonios and Tsakmakis, Antonis. (Eds.) *Brill's Companion to Thucydides*. Brill. 2006.

Roisman, Joseph. "Alkidas in Thucydides." *Historia: Zeitschrift für Alte Geschichte* H. 4 (1987): 385-421.

Romilly, Jacqueline de. *Thucydides and Athenian Imperialism*. (Trans.) Philip Thody. Blackwell. 1963.

——. "Fairness and Kindness in Thucydides." *Phoenix* 28, no. 1 (1974): 95-100.

——. *The Mind of Thucydides*. Translation of *Historie et raison chez Thucydide* by Elizabeth Trapnell Rawlings. (Ed. and intro.) Hunter R. Rawlings III and Jeffrey Rusten. Cornell University Press. 2017.

Rood, Tim. *Thucydides: Narrative and Explanation*. Oxford University Press. 1998.

——. "The Cylon Conspiracy: Thucydides and the Uses of the Past" in *Thucydides Between History and Literature*. Vol. 17. (Eds.) Tsakmakis, Antonis and Tamiolaki, Melina. De Gruyter (2013): 119-138.

——. "The Reception of Thucydides' Archaeology" in *A Handbook to the Reception of Thucydides* (Eds.). Christine Lee and Neville Morley. Wiley-Blackwell (2015): 474-92.

——. "Thucydides' Persian Wars" in *Thucydides*. (Ed.) Jeffrey S. Rusten. Oxford University Press. (2009): 148-175.

Rusten, Jeffrey S. (Ed.) *Thucydides*. Oxford University Press. 2009.

Saxonhouse, Arlene. "Nature and Convention in Thucydides' History." *Polity* 10, no. 4 (1978): 461-487.

Schwartz, Eduard. *Das Geschichtswerk des Thukydides*. F. Cohen. 1919.

Seaman, Michael G. "The Athenian Expedition to Melos in 416 BC." *Historia: Zeitschrift fur Alte Geschichte* (1997): 385-418.

Sears, Matthew A. "Thucydides, Rousseau, and Forced Freedom: Brasidas' Speech at Acanthus." *Phoenix* 69, no. 3/4 (2015): 242-267.

Shorey, Paul. "On the Implicit Ethics and Psychology of Thucydides." *Transactions of the American Philological Association (1869-1896)* 24 (1893): 66-88.

Stadter, Philip A. "Badian on Thucydides – E. Badian: *From Plataea to Potidaea: Studies in the History and Historiography of the Pentecontaetia.* Pp. xiv+ 264. Baltimore, London: Johns Hopkins University Press, 1993." *The Classical Review* 44, no. 2 (1994): 337-338.

—. "The Form and Content of Thucydides' Pentecontaetia (1.89-117)." *Greek, Roman, and Byzantine Studies* 34, no. 1 (1993): 35-72.

Stahl, H.P. *Thucydides: Man's Place in History.* The Classical Press of Wales. 2003 (originally published in German in 1966).

Ste. Croix, G.E.M. de. *The Origins of the Peloponnesian War.* Cornell University Press. 1972.

Strasburger, Hermann. "Thucydides and the Political Self-Portrait of the Athenians" in *Thucydides* (Ed.) Jeffrey Rusten. Oxford University Press. (2009): 191-219.

Strauss, Leo. *The City and Man.* University of Chicago Press. 1964.

—. *Natural Right and History.* University of Chicago Press. 1953.

—. "Preliminary Observations on the Gods in Thucydides' Work" in *Studies in Platonic Political Philosophy.* (Ed.) Thomas L. Pangle. University of Chicago Press. (1983): 89-104.) Originally published in *Interpretation: A Journal of Political Philosophy* 4, no. 1 (1974): 1-16.

—. "The Spirit of Sparta or the Taste of Xenophon." *Social Research* 6, no. 4 (1939): 502-536.

Tigerstedt, E. N. *The Legend of Sparta in Classical Antiquity.* Vol. I-III. Almqvist and Wiksell. 1965.

Wallace, W.P. "Thucydides." *Phoenix* 18, no. 4 (1964): 251-261.

Waltz, Kenneth N. *Man, the State, and War.* Columbia University Press. 1959.

—. *Theory of International Politics.* McGraw-Hill. 1979.

Walzer, Michael. *Just and Unjust Wars.* Basic Books. 1977.

Wasserman, Felix M. "The Voice of Sparta in Thucydides." *The Classical Journal* 59, no. 7 (1964): 289-297.

—. "Post-Periclean Democracy in Action: The Mytilenean Debate (Thuc. III 37-48)." In *Transactions and Proceedings of the American Philological Association* 87. Johns Hopkins University Press. American Philological Association (1956): 27-41.

—. "The Speeches of King Archidamus in Thucydides." *The Classical Journal* 48, no. 6 (1953): 193-200.

Westlake, H.D. "Alcibiades, Agis and Spartan Policy." *The Journal of Hellenic Studies* 58. Part 1 (1938). 31-40.

—. *Essays on the Greek Historians and Greek History.* Manchester University Press. 1969.

—. *Individuals in Thucydides.* Cambridge University Press. 1968.

—. "The Naval Battle at Pylos and its Consequences." *The Classical Quarterly* 24, no. 2 (1974): 211-226.

—. "Nicias in Thucydides." *The Classical Quarterly* 35, no. 1/2 (1941): 58-65.

——. "Thucydides and the Uneasy Peace – A Study in Political Incompetence." *The Classical Quarterly* 21, no. 2 (1971): 315-325.

Wettergreen, John A. "On the End of Thucydides' Narrative." *Interpretation: A Journal of Political Philosophy* 9, no. 1 (1980): 93-110.

White, Mary E. "Some Agiad Dates: Pausanias and His Sons." *The Journal of Hellenic Studies* 84 (1964): 140-152.

Woodhead, Arthur Geoffrey. "Thucydides' portrait of Cleon." *Mnemosyne* 13, no. Fasc. 4 (1960): 289-317.

Woodhouse, W. J. "The Campaign and Battle of Mantineia in 418 BC." *Annual of the British School at Athens* 22 (1918): 51-84.

Woodman, A. J. "Preconceptions and Practicalities: Thucydides." *Rhetoric in Classical Historiography* (1988): 1-69.

Wylie, Graham. "Brasidas: Great Commander or Whiz-Kid?" *Quaderni Urbinati di Cultura Classica* 41, no. 2 (1992): 75-95

Young-Bruehl, Elisabeth. "What Thucydides Saw." History and Theory 25, no. 1 (1986): 1-16.

Acknowledgements

One's first book is always a culmination of all prior research and experience, friendship and conversation. Because of this, I have incurred many unpayable debts in writing it, from my vague, early sketches to the much-expanded version contained herein.

Richard Ruderman, Steven Forde, and Martin Yaffe were my guides during doctoral work at the University of North Texas. It was Professor Ruderman's seminar on Thucydides that first introduced me to this inimitable author and the core problems he poses. Professor Forde's own work on Thucydides offered insights on how to correctly hone in on a single topic from a near inexhaustible text. Graduate study with Martin Yaffe – notably his insights on the Bible, Maimonides, and Spinoza – opened doors for me previously closed.

My political and philosophic study began with undergraduate work in Canada. Robert Burch's Philosophy courses taught me that I knew nothing about it; he also evinced what a true dedication to teaching looked like. Horst Hutter, Maben Poirier, and James Moore at Concordia University in Montreal illuminated the importance of 20th century scholarship and its interpretative debates in understanding fundamental questions the history of political philosophy raises. A now longtime friend, Tobin Craig, introduced me to Professor Burch and to his father, Leon Craig, and therefore to political philosophy.

It was with Leon Craig and Heidi Studer that I first encountered the Greeks and have been spellbound ever since. Despite the enormous workload, Professor Craig took on numerous graduate students, including myself, and allowed me to struggle my way through Plato. His courses on classical political philosophy and science, along with Professor Studer's on Francis Bacon and modernity, were the early foundations of my education. One remembers those times fondly, like Cephalus and his drinking bouts.

Publication of this book would not have come about without the support of Alex Wall and Lewis Slawsky at Political Animal Press. Both offered concrete observations on how to improve the manuscript. As the lead editor, Lewis provided continued support and guidance during final edits and revisions. My gratitude as well to Alex Priou for introducing me to these gentlemen.

This book would be much poorer were it not for colleagues and close friends. From conferences to reading groups to graduate work and early teaching, I have many to thank. At the University of North Texas, fellow graduate students Anna Batta, Timothy Haglund, Nicholas Higgins, Evan Lowe, Stephanie Murphy, and Sara Shiveley. Those who have furnished insights on versions of this project include Andrew Bibby, Murray Bessette, Evan Lowe, John Pascarella, Joshua Parens, John Pidluzny, Matthew Post, Rafe Major, Greg McBrayer, and Michael McShane. A special thank you to an old friend, Natalie Elliot, who was indispensable in my move from Canada to Texas, from student to teacher.

My closest interlocutors have been Paul Diduch, James Guest, and Andrea Kowalchuk. Their thoughtfulness, humor, goodwill, and introspection has spanned our years of study together, from film and art to philosophy and politics. To Paul, in particular – who kindly interrupted his own intense study to read this manuscript in full, as well as conversations along the way that almost certainly placed me back on the proper path – a hearty "I owe you one." Lifelong friendships of this kind are always rare.

Finally, my dedication is to my family. My mother and father were always supportive over the years of study such work requires. My wife, Lisa, has been the model of patience and understanding through these labors of mine. I can only hope sacrifices others have made can be repaid in some small way by this work. Like Thucydides, my purpose has been to present something useful from reflections on the past in the hope it will provide some good for those in the future.

Index

This Index aims to allow the reader to track my discussion of Thucydides' usage of key terms (including their original Greek, where particularly relevant), along with themes arising from my analysis. It does not pretend to be a complete index of Thucydides' text; it only highlights what I believe are the most important words as I treat them in this book, their most prominent usage, as well as variations that may be related to key Thucydidean themes.

Thucydides is a master of language and often different words are used where we in English only have or use one. Variations and related words are therefore indicated where this is the case. Notable terms and phrases are further distinguished by parenthetical citation to Thucydides' text.

Index of Names

Index of Places

Index of Selected Peoples

Index of Authors